Diana Souhami is the author of many highly praised books: *Coconut Chaos*, *Selkirk's Island* (winner of the Whitbread Biography award), *The Trials of Radclyffe Hall* (shortlisted for the James Tait Black Prize for Biography and winner of the US Lambda Literary Award), the best-selling *Mrs Keppel and Her Daughter* (also winner of the Lambda Literary Award and a *New York Times* 'Notable Book of the Year'), *Natalie and Romaine*, *Gertrude and Alice*, *Greta and Cecil* and *Gluck: Her Biography*.

EDITH CAVELL

DIANA SOUHAMI

Quercus

First published in Great Britain in 2010 by Quercus

This paperback edition published in 2015 by
Quercus
Carmelite House
50 Victoria Embankment
London EC4Y 0DZ
An Hachette UK company

A CIP catalogue record for this book is available
from the British Library

ISBN 978 1 78429 132 7
EBOOK ISBN 978 1 84916 680 5

10 9 8 7 6 5 4 3 2 1

Printed and bound in Great Britain
by Clays Ltd St Ives plc

to nurses

The last photograph of Edith Cavell: with her dog Jack in 1915

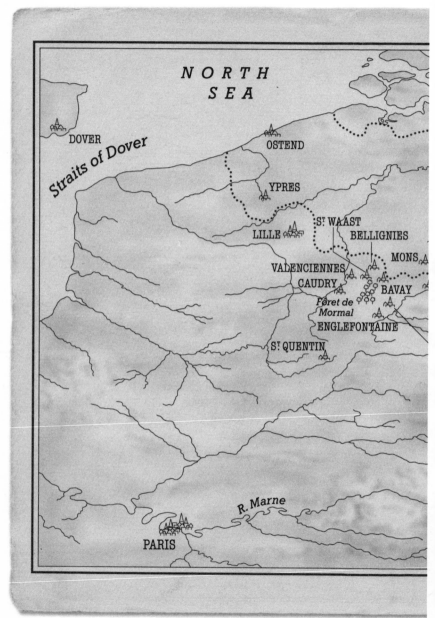

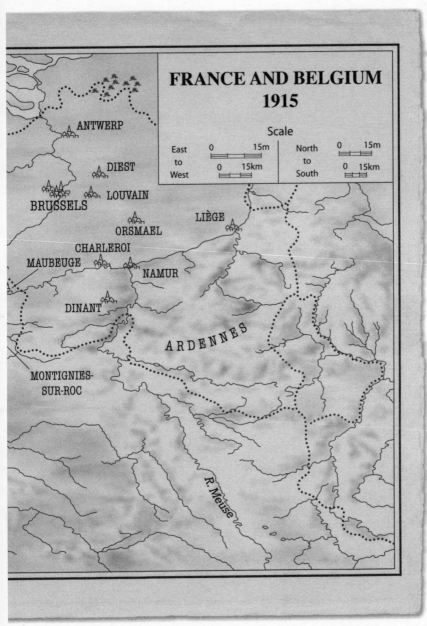

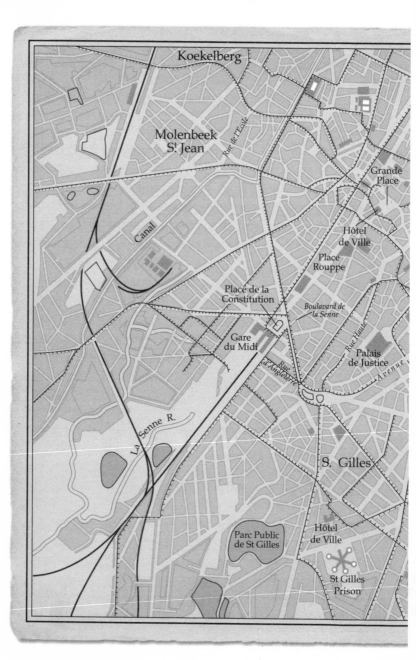

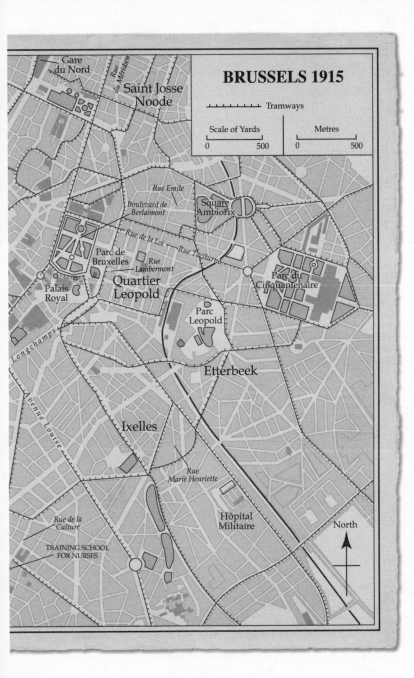

BRUSSELS 1915

Tramways

Scale of Yards

0   500

Metres

0   500

Gare du Nord

Rue du Méridien

Saint Josse Noode

Rue Emile

Boulevard de Berlaimont

Square Ambiorix

Rue de la Loi

Rue Taciturne

Parc de Bruxelles

Rue Lambermont

Quartier Leopold

Parc du Cinquantenaire

Palais Royal

Parc Leopold

Longchamps

Etterbeek

Avenue Louise

Ixelles

Rue Marie Henriette

Rue de la Culture

Hôpital Militaire

TRAINING SCHOOL FOR NURSES

North

CONTENTS

INTRODUCTION
FOR THE CENTENARY EDITION

Twelfth October 2015 marks the centenary of Edith Cavell's execution. One hundred years previously at 7 a.m. on a Tuesday morning, after ten weeks in solitary confinement, she was taken from her cell at St Gilles prison in Brussels to the *Tir National* and shot by the occupying German army. The commanding officer told the firing squad they need have no qualms at shooting her for she was not a mother and her crimes were heinous. A century on her legacy is as a heroine of the First World War, an iconic woman who at a time of evil kept to a focus of hope and goodness. This edition of my biography of her, first published in 2010, is in memory of her death and in commemoration of her work and life.

Her crime had been to conceal Allied soldiers wounded in battle or separated from their regiments, nurse them, then guide them to freedom across the Belgian border into neutral Holland. Her motivation, in accord with her career as a nurse, was to save their lives and alleviate their suffering. If captured, they would have been shot or sent as prisoners to Germany.

Under the rules of a corrupt military regime Edith Cavell was deemed a criminal. Her contempt for the German invasion of Belgium, of the undefended country where she worked, for a 'cruel vindictive foe', turned her, a devout Christian and law-abiding citizen, into a subversive and a resistance worker. 'I am but a looker-on after all,' she wrote to her mother. 'It is not my country whose soul is desecrated and whose sacred places are laid waste. I can only feel the pity of the stranger within the gates, and admire the courage of a people enduring a long and terrible agony . . .'

But it was not her way to be a 'looker-on' when people were suffering. She was a reforming nurse, a public servant, as groundbreaking in her work for revolutionary healthcare as Florence Nightingale. Though opportunities for Victorian women were minimal she championed nursing as a career. She trained at the flagship London Hospital, worked for a decade in England in all branches of nursing, then went to Brussels, seven years prior to the outbreak of war, as head matron of the first ever secular training hospital for nurses in Belgium.

Her pre-war achievements were huge. Her school was described by Antoine Depage, Brussels's chief surgeon, as 'the benchmark for nursing standards in Belgium'. 'Nursing,' Edith Cavell taught her probationers, was 'a great and honourable profession' through which could be found 'the widest social reform, the purest philanthropy, the truest humanity'. In lectures she spoke of her belief in the sanctity of life, the vocation of doing good, and how devotion brought its own reward. The goals of nursing, she taught, were to safeguard life, attend the sick and wounded, allay suffering and help the doctors.

Demand for nurses trained by her was huge. Her ambition was for an army of them to spiral out from Brussels to all Belgium and beyond. Her problem was to find enough recruits. By 1914 under her supervision a new state-of-the-art training school, a centre of excellence, was being built.

War came in like a tide on her hopes and plans. The carnage and catastrophe of 1914–18 was not foreseen. She was not, at the war's outset, a pacifist. Like many, she anticipated the British Expeditionary Force would quickly drive back the invading army and within six weeks restore order and sanity. 'We were full of enthusiasm for the war and full of confidence in the Allies' she wrote in a piece for the *Nursing Mirror.* She did not consider leaving Brussels. This war, she thought, would be a new test of her nursing capability with Brussels the centre of care for wounded soldiers, headed by her under the Red Cross flag and the rules of the Geneva Convention. She supervised the preparation of 18,000 beds and the fitting out of the Royal Palace with wards and an operating theatre. Her expectation was to treat both Allied and German wounded. 'Any wounded soldier,' she told her nurses, 'must be treated, friend or foe. Each man is a father, husband or son.' As nurses they must take no part in the quarrel. Their work was for humanity.

The war was neither swift nor contained. Edith Cavell was one of the estimated thirty-seven million people killed world-wide. The death toll is vague: ten million fighting men, eight million horses. She could not fulfil the role of a war nurse. In Brussels the occupying army staffed their own hospitals and either shot wounded Allied soldiers or sent them to Germany. Edith Cavell's work changed. Each day from her clinic she gave food and clothes to impoverished children. She herself lived on a pittance. When two wounded British soldiers were brought by members of a resistance network to her door she tended them, hid them and arranged false papers, disguises and guides to get them to freedom. Such work escalated and she became part of a large resistance network. In 1915 this network was rounded up by the secret police. She expected this but did not anticipate the death penalty. In court she chose not wear her matron's uniform. She said she was on trial as herself not as a nurse. Out of the seventy accused she was singled out for execution because she was English.

Imprisoned, she was more concerned for the fate of her nurses and the new training school than for herself. 'This time of rest has been a great mercy to me,' she told her priest, Stirling Gahan on the eve of her execution. 'I have no fear or shrinking.

I have seen death so often that it is not strange or fearful to me . . . But this I would say, standing as I do in view of God and Eternity: I realise that patriotism is not enough. I must have no hatred or bitterness towards anyone.' She was a Christian, a vicar's daughter, but it was the essence not the dogma of belief that shaped her thinking.

Her execution provoked public outrage. Calumny was heaped on Germany. The British government exploited her death as propaganda. 'Remember Edith Cavell' became an army recruiting slogan. Recruitment doubled for eight weeks and American neutrality waned. Hospitals, schools and roads were named after her worldwide. A patriotic monument to her was commissioned to stand in Trafalgar Square. Draped in the English and Belgian flags it was unveiled with all pomp at the war's end with 'King and Country' engraved large at its apex.

The National Council of Women of Great Britain and Ireland, which campaigned for women's rights, complained that the essence of her was omitted from this monument. In 1923 they asked for her words questioning patriotism to be added. They hoped these would contribute to world peace. The following year Prime Minister Ramsay MacDonald authorised the adding of 'Patriotism is not enough. I must have no hatred or bitterness for anyone'. So Edith Cavell's statue became a muddled monument of opposing views.

But the legacy that became entrenched was of Edith Cavell the war heroine, the fervent patriot and resistance worker in the man's world of war. Such a view overlooked her belief in the sanctity of life, her visionary ambition for worldwide nursing care, her opposition to slaughter as a means of resolving conflict. It was a legacy that denied her true moral compass and nursing career.

After a flurry of such manipulated posthumous fame she faded from view and became little more than the name of a hospital ward, the landmark of a statue. In 1939 a film about her starring Anna Neagle reinforced the picture of her as the fearless patriot. So did biographies of her in 1965 and 1975 by A. E. Clark-Kennedy and Rowland Ryder. I wanted in my biography, after sixty-five years of peace in Europe but in a selfish society, to give a deeper interpretation of her character, motivation and achievements: to focus on her as a pioneer nurse and a woman whose core values of loving kindness and concern for others might resonate with their universal worth. I do not think I imposed that interpretation on her. As I wrote I was in awe of her goodness. But it was unswervingly there: in her character and nursing career, in her lectures to her probationers, her concern for her patients, her letters to her mother, in the way she treated little children, gave a home to a stray dog and an abused girl, the thoughts she underscored in Thomas à Kempis's *The Imitation of Christ,* her unconcern for her own privilege or safety, the paucity of her possessions, the grace she showed at her shameful trial and in her prison cell and when tied blindfolded to a post at a shooting range. I wanted, when writing about her, to show such qualities but nor did I want to deny or diminish her role as an intrepid resistance worker. In fact her entrenchment in dangerous opposition to the occupying army was far greater than was previously known.

Since first publication of my biography and with the current centenary celebrations there has been a revival of interest in Edith Cavell as a war heroine and as a pioneering nurse with a mission to save lives, but also as a spokeswoman for the antiwar cause, for the belief that violence should not be the way to resolve conflict, a woman committed to the discard of hatred and bitterness, and to a vision of heaven on earth 'when disease shall be unknown' and healthcare universal.

The 2014–18 years of events remembering the First World War are now bleached of jingoism. None the less much of the emphasis is on tours of battlefields, military campaigns, the war from the air, the war from the sea, the trenches, monuments, memorials, medals and generals. Edith Cavell's story sets her beyond the war zones to the territory where the task is to save life, not to take it.

Homage is paid to her in this centenary year: a weekend of events at the Jasper National Park in Canada where a mountain is named after her; a Cavell festival in Swardeston, the village where she was born; commemorative services in Norwich and Peterborough Cathedrals; a 'Cavell fortnight' of exhibitions, concerts, and talks in Norfolk, a sponsored walk and fundraising events for the Cavell Nurses Trust,* a charity, of which I am a patron, that helps nurses, midwives and health-care assistants. In Brussels there is the world premiere of an opera dedicated to her, an exhibition of paintings about her, organised walks that visit places linked to her life, and on the anniversary of her execution a commemoration in her honour at the Belgian Senate attended by the Princess Royal and the Belgian Ambassador.

Her name lives on: an Edith Cavell coin is to be minted, there is an Edith Cavell carpark in Peterborough, an Edith Cavell corona on the planet Jupiter, an Edith Cavell rose. But beyond such tokens, perhaps after a hundred years there is closer attention to the message of her life and work: the obligation to save life, not take it, caution about patriotic fervour, an emphasis on the misery not the glory of war. 'We shall remember you as a heroine and a martyr,' the Reverend Gahan said to her, the night before she died. 'Don't think of me like that,' she replied. 'Think of me as a nurse who tried to do her duty.'

* www.cavellnursestrust.org

PART ONE

I

BIRTH

Edith Cavell[1] was born in the village of Swardeston on a rainy Monday three weeks before Christmas in 1865. The village – sward and town – was four miles from the city of Norwich and had a population of 350. Most of its 900 acres were owned by the lords of Swardeston Manor and Gowthorpe Hall, the Gurneys and the Stewards, who traced their fortunes, their favours from the Crown, back to the sixteenth century. Villagers owned very little – a cottage, perhaps, and a garden. There were six farmers, three gardeners, two blacksmiths, a cooper, a mole catcher, a butcher, a wheelwright, a carpenter, a bricklayer, a schoolmistress, and the keeper of The Dog inn. Their surnames were Skinner, Miller, Till and Piggin; they handed down their trades and skills father to son, married into each other's families and on marriage certificates often 'left their mark' in lieu of signature, for not many had been taught to write. They looked out for each other, knew the vagaries of the weather, how to stack the hay, shoe the horses, make cider.

It was a way of life that seemed immutable, quintessentially English, governed by the seasons, the long nights of winter, the festivals of harvest and Christmas. War was a distant belligerence: the conflicts of empires – French, Russian, Prussian and British ambitions for hegemony – were irrelevant and remote. The preoccupations of Swardeston were with planting and ploughing and the rhythms of village life.

For Edith's father, the Reverend Frederick Cavell – a stern,

[1] Her name rhymes with travel or gravel

bewhiskered man – Christmas was his busiest time. He had been the village's vicar for less than two years. As well as all his pastoral duties he was supervising – and financing – the building of a new vicarage which was to be his family home. He had married the previous year, at the age of forty, and this was only his second Christmas as a family man.

His young bride, Louisa, was twenty-six. She gave birth in the front bedroom of the eighteenth-century farmhouse her husband was renting until the vicarage was finished. The room was quiet and comfortable, aired and clean, with a view over fields of pasture. A fire burned in the grate and all was prepared according to the latest edition of Dr Fleetwood Churchill's *Manual for Midwives*, first published in 1856 and now in its fourteenth edition.

The midwife was a local woman whose only qualification was experience and a willingness to help. It was to be another thirty-seven years before a Midwives Act dictated standards of proficiency. Even so, it was safer to give birth at home and in the country than in hospital or in the city. With home births, whatever the shortcomings of the local helper, five women in every thousand died in childbirth. In hospital it was thirty-four. Florence Nightingale, whose revolutionary nursing methods were to inspire this particular newborn child, in her *Notes on Nursing* advised mothers to avoid hospital 'even at the risk of the infant being born in a cab or a lift'. Childbirth, she said, which was not an illness, in hospitals had an equivalent fatality rate to the major diseases. The cause was cross-infection from other patients and was part of hospital life. Quite why this contagion happened was not known. She blamed 'foul air and putrid miasmas', expectant mothers crowded in together for weeks at a time, students going from a surgical case in an operating theatre to the bedside of a 'lying-in' woman.

She made a plea for cleanliness and improved nursing standards and recommended that childbirth units be separate from hospital wards. She wanted no more than four beds to a unit, each bed with its own window and privacy curtain. She wanted polished oak floors, sinks with unlimited hot and cold water, clean linen, renewable mattresses.

Her plea coincided with breakthrough research in antiseptics, research that crossed national boundaries. In 1864 the French Academy of Sciences accepted the hypothesis of Louis Pasteur, a chemist from the Breton town of Dol, that sepsis happened not spontaneously, as was supposed, but through the spread of destructive micro-organisms invisible to the naked eye. There was 'something in the air' that was harmful and needed to be destroyed and kept away from a wound.

Joseph Lister, a British surgeon, was receptive to Pasteur's experiments and in his own operations set out to block the path of these organisms by using carbolic acid as a barrier. It proved revolutionary. It allowed him to sew up an operation wound without it turning septic. By 1867 he was writing in the *Lancet* on 'the antiseptic principle in the practice of surgery' and was struggling to convince the medical profession that his and Pasteur's findings meant they must change their way of working: they must not go from conducting an autopsy, to a woman in labour, without changing their clothes and washing their hands in carbolic.

But in Swardeston that December 1865 there were the best available conditions for a home birth. The hair mattress was covered with an oiled-silk cloth and sheets folded into four. The midwife had ready scissors, thread, a calico binder. She guided the head of the baby, heard her first cry, made two ligatures in the umbilical cord: one near the navel, the other near the placenta. She twisted out the placenta, wiped the baby's eyes, washed her gently in warm water, dried her in front of the fire, smeared her with oil, rolled her in flannel, then dressed her in soft warm clothes fastened with strings. She removed the soiled sheets from Louisa's bed, washed her, changed her nightdress and cap and made sure everything in the room was in its proper place.

Mother and child survived without mishap. But for the vicar downstairs, though the birth of a healthy daughter was cause for thanksgiving, it would have been more convenient had God deemed that this firstborn be a boy. He had a stipend of £300 a year and had spent all his own money on the new house. Sons were breadwinners. It was they who continued the family name, sat at the head of table, wrote the sermons, were lawmakers, soldiers, politicians, doctors. The monarch was a woman who was to reign for sixty-three years until 1901, but that was an oddity of primogeniture. Queen Victoria had nothing much to do with gender. She was there through divine right, the head of the British Empire. Her crown, orb, sceptre and throne were imperatives of rule. Women were wives, mothers, helpmates, servants. A daughter must find a husband or be a low-paid governess or nurse. 'Thy desire shall be to thy husband and he shall rule over thee,' the Bible said. Women had no vote, no public voice; their place was in the home.

This vicar's daughter, born into Christian piety, English country life and entrenched social values, would make her contribution to new ideas of professionalism in nursing. But for a girl, attempts at professional parity with men were countered by censorious reminders of a woman's place. Most women conformed to the restraints expected of them. A few hit out. In the same year as Edith Cavell's birth a young Londoner, Elizabeth Garrett Anderson, qualified as the country's first woman doctor. When she tried to pursue her training at the Middlesex Hospital the male students issued a complaint to the management: 'The presence of a young female in the operating theatre is an outrage to our natural instincts and is calculated to destroy the

respect and admiration with which the opposite sex is regarded.'
None the less she found a loophole in the discriminatory rules
against women and took and passed the Society of Apothecaries examinations. The Society immediately changed the rules
to prevent other women getting the same idea. Elizabeth Garrett
Anderson's response was to set up her own clinic for women.
And with her suffragist friends Emily Davies, Dorothea Beale
and Frances Mary Buss, she formed the Kensington Society and
petitioned for women's right to vote, go to university, be doctors,
be lawyers . . .

Such feminist campaigning, though, was urban. Swardeston
was shielded from change. Accident of birth defined lifestyle
there. The aristocracy was the ruling class. Socially the vicar was
on a par with the squire, but economically he was not much
better off than the blacksmith. His status came from his connection to God. Ordained as God's servant and spokesman, he was
the pivotal figure of village life and its moral authority. The
60-foot-high tower of the church of St Mary the Virgin rose over
the Reverend Cavell's parish. Its five bells pealed out the command
of devotion. Images of the twelve apostles were cut into the
stained-glass windows. In this church rites of passage for the
villagers were conducted by God's servant: baptism, marriage,
burial.

Edith Cavell was born into the Christian ethic and her father's
insistence on it. From the cradle she was imbued with the duty
to share what she had, help those in pain, alleviate suffering. Life
would take her far from Swardeston, its tranquillity and simple
ways. Chance would take her into evil times. Through these she
would stay true to her roots, her father's orthodoxy and her
mother's kindness. And from the day of her birth as the vicar's
daughter the Christian command of love was her moral standard.

2

THE VICAR'S DAUGHTER

The new vicarage, built to the Reverend Cavell's specification, was Victorian Gothic, sombre and solid with gabled roof and ornate chimneys. He paid for it with £1500 inherited when his father died. It was to be his gift to the parish, for the Old Rectory nearby was now privately owned. It was where he intended to raise his family and be the village's minister for as long as God chose. When he retired or died it would pass to the next vicar.

The architecture of the house reflected his expectations from family life. The church and graveyard were visible from most of its windows, reminders of the omnipresence of the Almighty and the transience of worldly life. He had his initials carved above the front door of the house: FC 1865. In anticipation of a large family there were eight bedrooms. The size and aspect of these defined the status of the occupant: the spacious master bedroom had an adjoining dressing room; the back bedrooms were small with a simple grate. The drawing room had a large marble fireplace and opened to lawns, an orchard, and down to a lake. The kitchen had larders, a stillroom, ceiling hooks for hanging hams, a scullery with a pump. A dark, narrow back staircase for the live-in servants led from it to their cramped attic rooms at the top of the house.

Annexed to, but apart from, the rest of the house, and with French windows that opened to his private path to the church, was the Reverend Cavell's study. It was a room of assumptions about devotion and service. The church loomed and on either

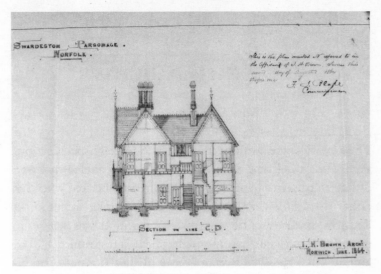

Swardeston Vicarage. Built by the Reverend Frederick Cavell
at his own expense in 1865

side of the fireplace were hand-carved shelves for his theological books.

He was one of five children and had been brought up in London, in Marylebone, in a middle-class home. His father was a law stationer. They were comfortably off and always had a cook and a housemaid. His elder brother John Scott became a professional artist, George was a stockbroker, Edward a solicitor and their sister Ellen, as with most 'respectable' women of the time, drew a blank when it came to 'rank, profession or occupation'. In his teens, with his brother Edward, Frederick studied theology and philosophy in Heidelberg. He then read theology at King's College London and was ordained a priest in 1852 when he was twenty-five.

As a curate at St Mark's Church, Islington, he ministered to orphaned street children and families who could not afford adequate food or medical care. He saw his parishioners ravaged by the contagion of typhoid fever and cholera and he was in

London for the Big Stink of the summer of 1858, when the stench of sewage from the Thames was so overwhelming that sacking soaked in deodorising chemicals was hung at the windows of the Houses of Parliament.

He aspired to the life of a country parson away from the city grime. Settled rural life was possible only with a wife and family. To be unmarried was a barrier to preferment. Single, there would be homes it would be awkward for him to enter. His housekeeper, Anne Warming, was widowed and lived in Philpott Street, Whitechapel, close to the Royal London Hospital. Her husband, a mariner, had left no money. Sophia Louisa, the fourth of her six children, was twenty-five when Frederick Cavell met her in 1861. She was devout, meek and compliant, but uneducated. Her unprivileged childhood was an attraction to him. It suited his thinking to rescue her from near-poverty.

He proposed marriage, but delayed the ceremony until his appointment as vicar of Swardeston. In the interim he worked as a curate at St Mary's church in East Carlton, a village similar to Swardeston and in the same deanery about five miles from Norwich, and paid for Louisa to attend finishing school to learn housewifery and the social skills appropriate to her role as the vicar's wife. When his preferment was secured, he went down to London, married her and took her to the village which would be their home for forty-five years. Her mother then moved to Margate with her eldest and unmarried daughter Christianna, and ran a lodging house there.

In the leafy village of Swardeston the Reverend Cavell presided over a peaceful life of tradition and observance, defined by the Christian calendar, the commands of the Bible, and his own orthodox authority. In the cities in the 1860s there was conflict between science and religion. Charles Darwin had published his *On the Origin of Species* in 1859. Darwin's empirical observations and theory of evolution challenged the claims of the Bible. He and his followers posited that the world was more than six thousand years old and not created in seven days by a communicative God. On 30 June 1860, at the annual meeting of the British Association for the Advancement of Science, the biologist Thomas Henry Huxley clashed with Samuel Wilberforce, Bishop of Oxford. The Bishop scoffed at the idea of evolution by natural selection: rock pigeons were, he said, what rock pigeons had always been. He asked Huxley whether it was through his grandmother or his grandfather that he claimed descent from a monkey. Huxley, tall, thin and quietly spoken, said he was not ashamed to have a monkey for his ancestor but that he would be ashamed to be related to a man who used great gifts to obscure the truth. Science, he maintained, sought justification not by faith but by verification. He said he was willing to accept for

Edith aged five, with her mother Louisa and younger sister Florence

himself as well as for his friends and enemies all actual truths, even the humiliating truth of a pedigree not registered in the Heralds' College. Lady Brewster fainted and had to be carried out. Wilberforce accused Darwin of raising a hypothesis to the 'dignity of a causal theory'. There was no evidence, he said, of any new species developing. Eminent naturalists at the meeting – Professor Richard Owen, President of the Association, and Sir Benjamin Brodie, President of the Royal Society, concurred with Wilberforce.

Darwinism caused a theological stir. A month before Edith Cavell was born a large Church Congress was held in Norwich at St Andrew's Hall: 'Never before was there such a gathering of clergy in the city . . . Bible history was ably vindicated against the objections of geologists and freethinkers,' wrote A. D. Bayne in 1869 in his *Comprehensive History of Norwich*.

The customs and lifestyle of Swardeston were resistant to the objections of geologists, freethinkers and suffragists. Though these customs were formed from a patriarchal spiral down from God to monarch, squire, vicar, bricklayer, woman, ape and rock pigeon, creationist ideas transmuted into the common-sense habits and kindnesses of village life. Such daily life defined Englishness. Change was slow. Things were as they had been, and as they had been, so should they continue.

The Reverend Cavell expected his children to be conformist and devout. Drummed into them was the necessity of salvation through prayer, obligation to the poor and service to others. A second Cavell daughter, born in June 1867, was named Florence, after Florence Nightingale, 'the Lady with the Lamp', the 'ministering angel' whose nursing methods saved thousands of soldiers' lives in the Crimean War. A third daughter, Mary Lilian, followed in September 1870. Their births were further cause for thanksgiving and financial concern. The desired son and heir John Frederick Cavell was born in 1873. Named after his father and grandfather, the expectation for him was that he would carry forward the family name, but he never married and in adult life took to the bottle, suffered bouts of depression and for thirty-two years worked for the Norwich Union Insurance Company.

3

GROWING UP

Edith Cavell described her Swardeston childhood as a time when 'life was fresh and beautiful and the country so desirable and sweet'. Norfolk was a lush county, truly green and pleasant. Its landscape inspired the Norwich School of Painters, with pastoral scenes by John Crome and Joseph Stannard of peasants and horse-drawn ploughs, rain-filled skies, oak trees and thatched cottages. Edith showed a talent for art like her uncle John Scott

Edith Cavell as a teenager

Edith's drawings for greetings cards to raise money for a
Swardeston Sunday School, c. 1885

Cavell, and in her teens did seasonal drawings of girls in bonnets
and short-sleeved dresses gathering grasses on Swardeston
Common or muffled in fur-trimmed coats making footprints in
the snow.

The village was largely self-sufficient. There was much preserv-
ing of fruit and bottling of jam. Crops were rotated, wheat and
barley then turnips and clover. Villagers had smallholdings, kept
a pig for ham, tended a vegetable patch. At the general store
'beefin' apples, baked then pressed flat without breaking the skin,
were sold at sixpence a dozen. There was a bakery, a post office,
cottages where boots were made and mended. Poultry was plen-
tiful, particularly turkeys and geese. Rabbits and pheasants were
trapped and shot, there was an abundance of freshwater fish in
the rivers and streams and huge herring and mackerel fisheries
at Yarmouth twenty-three miles away.

The Cavell children rode ponies on the gated common where horses and cattle grazed, played croquet on the vicarage lawn and in winter skated on the lake by the Old Rectory where their neighbours the Kemp family and then the Blewitts lived.

The life that was fresh and beautiful was seemingly safe. Progress took the shape of better drainage of the turnpike lanes, better suspension for the horse-drawn carriages, more of the railway links that intersected the county. Fast development of the railway companies and laying of tracks meant that by 1880 when Edith Cavell was fifteen, it was possible to go by steam train directly from Norwich to Lowestoft, a journey of thirty miles through a landscape of rivers and water meadows. Lowestoft was a gentrified resort for the Victorian middle class with its promenade, pier and band. For their summer holidays the Cavells rented a house on the seafront with Edith's Great-uncle Edmund's family. He was a country solicitor. Edith was protective of his youngest son, Eddy, who though three years her elder was mentally fragile and too shy to socialise. In adult life he lived alone and managed a smallholding. Some years the two families went to Cromer with its pier, curing houses for fish, cliffs, fine sands and bathing machines.

Despite Swardeston's setting of pastoral tranquillity, it was hard to be a free spirit in the Cavells' large Gothic vicarage. The house was expensive to run – coal and wood for heating and cooking, oil for the lamps, water to be pumped in the scullery, heated and carried to the bedrooms . . . It needed servants. At the time of the 1871 census the family had a live-in cook, a housemaid and a nanny for Mary Lilian, the third child, then three months old. None of the servants was local. All were unmarried women in their twenties who arrived after answering advertisements in the *Church Times*. Their hope was for safe lodgings, their keep and survival pay. They had no security of employment, or prospects, or independence. They inhabited the fireless attic rooms, accessed via the back staircase. In 1876 one of them, a Miss L. Brown, graffitied on to her bedroom wall, 'The pay is small, the food is bad, I wonder why I don't go mad.'[2]

Frederick Cavell held family prayers each morning at eight. Servants in the house attended these too. Sundays were unrelenting in their piety. In her teens Edith told her cousin Eddy, 'I'd love to have you visit, but not on a Sunday. It's too dreadful, Sunday school, church services, family devotions morning and evening. And father's sermons are so dull.' The freshness of childhood was countered by the correction of prayer, indulgence was balanced by a command to share, and freedom was subsumed by the dictates of the Church calendar: Christmas, Epiphany, Easter, Advent, Lent, Pentecost, Communion.

The exhortation to remember the poor, the downhearted and the needy was ever present in the Cavell household. The Reverend Cavell impressed on his children that they must lead by example. Sunday fare might be a well-roasted chicken and vegetables, a marmalade roll pudding and scones for tea, but such privilege must be shared with the poor. The children were sent to give bowls of the food to villagers in need. Their own share, when they ate it, was often cold.

Charity was the civilising force in early Victorian society. The poor depended on it. In every village, town and city there was pervasive need. It served as a prompt to the better-off to give alms and show altruism. Giving was piecemeal and unregulated, haphazard as to place, contingent on creed and conformity and demeaning in its expectation of gratitude. Frederick Cavell was chaplain of the workhouse at Swainsthorpe two miles from Swardeston. Part of his chaplaincy was to conduct marriage and funeral services for the destitute there. In nearby Norwich the

[2] The graffiti has been preserved

rich endowed many charities, all of which held stigma for the beneficiaries and social advantage for the benefactors. The Norfolk and Norwich Magdalen on Life's Green put a roof over the heads of women who 'having deviated from the paths of virtue may be desirous of being restored to their station in society by religious instruction and the formation of moral and industrious habits'.

At the Hospital for the Indigent Blind, women knitted and made nets, and the men made baskets and sacks. There was an endowed lunatic asylum, a female penitentiary, a 'lying-in' charity[3] and an almshouse for the aged poor. There was the Bethel Hospital for 'poor lunatics, and not for natural born fools or idiots', a Mendicity Society for the relief of distressed travellers, a Provident Coal Society for supplying the poor with coal at reduced prices, and a charity for Clergymen's Widows and Children in Norfolk. At the Boys' and Girls' Hospital School for impoverished children, pupils were given a suit of blue clothing every Lady Day – the March festival of the Annunciation of the Virgin Mary. When boys left they were apprenticed; girls were given £3 for clothes so that they could go into service. The Gurneys of Swardeston Manor financed a school in St Stephen's Mews where sixty impoverished girls were taught and given clothes. At the Norfolk and Norwich Hospital, four physicians and four surgeons gave free service to the poor on Saturdays and Tuesdays: 'the operation for the *stone*[4] is performed here in the greatest perfection on these days; the whole number cut for this dreadfull disease since the opening of the hospital is about 700 of whom not more than 100 died.'

Edith Cavell's father was stern and censorious, but her mother was gentle and loving, though her only reading was devotional

[3] Bed rest for women before and after giving birth
[4] Kidney stones

books about Jesus and the gospels. Towards her mother Edith was protective and from her she learned to cook, knit, embroider and sew. The effect on her of her father's exhortations was not as with her brother, to drive her away from religion, but to pursue the practicality of virtue rather than its theory. In adult life her Christian focus came not from the Old Testament but from Thomas à Kempis's spiritual manual, *The Imitation of Christ*.

Like provision for the poor and sick, nineteenth-century education was a haphazard affair. Unregistered teachers gave home tuition or taught in private fee-paying schools. When Edith was five an Elementary Education Act, drafted by Liberal MP William Forster, aimed to provide, through school boards, non-denominational elementary education for children aged five to twelve. Such schooling did not become compulsory until 1880, when Edith was fifteen.

Secular state education met opposition from the Church. Neither vicar nor squire would send their children to the village school. Frederick Cavell's ambition for his daughters was that they should be competent to earn a living in a womanly way in service to the Lord. Service took priority over marriage to the squire's heir – the romantic solution to penury made popular by Jane Austen.

Edith Cavell's home education, until she was sixteen, was a mix of tuition from her father and from a resident governess. Reading, writing with a dip-pen in a clear forward-sloping hand, and arithmetic were standard fare. She had a talent for languages, particularly French, and a love of drawing. From her father she learned of the philanthropy of Thomas Barnardo, who trained as a doctor at the London Hospital and set up homes for street children, and of the nursing achievements of Florence Nightingale. She read Benjamin Disraeli's *Sybil, or The Two Nations* and Charles Dickens's *Hard Times* and *Martin Chuzzlewit*. But the book she was most familiar with was the *Book of Common Prayer*, and when she played the piano it was hymns and devotional songs.

In 1881 when she was fifteen she and her sisters were taught by a live-in governess, Harriet Joyce Baker from Chackmore, a hamlet in Buckinghamshire. Harriet Baker was twenty-seven. Her father, a bailiff for the County Court, had been widowed in his early forties. Six of his children still lived at home. His son Frederick, an organ builder, brought in some money; so did his daughter Anne, a dressmaker, but the other four were under twelve.

In Harriet Baker, Edith Cavell observed the strictures for a governess transplanted into a family house. She received her keep and meagre pay. There was a limbo to her position, for she was not part of the family, though she was a cut above the cook and housemaid. And there was the difficulty of contriving a syllabus for siblings of different ages. When Edith was fifteen her sister Flor, as she called Florence, was thirteen and Lilian was ten. Jack, as John was known, was eight.

Edith Cavell had reason to suppose that to become a governess would be her fate too. It was one of the few occupations open to her of which her father approved. When she was sixteen he caught her smoking a cigarette in his study. It was not an acceptable transgression for a vicar's daughter and soon after it she was sent away to school.

4

SCHOOL

Between 1882 and 1884 Edith Cavell went to three different girls' boarding schools in different parts of the country away from her mother, sisters, brother, home and friends. Her father chose the schools through Church connections and according to the financial concessions they offered to the clergy.

Nineteenth-century private schools for modest fees were institutions of neither comfort nor fun. By the 1880s there was in England a spate of small boarding schools that 'finished' girls from respectable homes. The idea was to equip them with housewifery skills, a smattering of uncontentious information to put to social use, and a genteel femininity. They offered no standardised syllabus and as with most other social provision were subject to no quality control. As early as 1867 the educational reformer Emily Davies was critical of these self-styled schools: 'They are obliged to profess French and music and I do not think they do much besides.'

It was a training designed to prepare Edith Cavell to be the wife of a doctor or clergyman or, if unmarried, a governess with a well-to-do family where she might responsibly look after someone else's children. Academic subjects and all professions were closed to her, whatever her aptitudes, inclinations or dreams.

She spent a few months at a school in Kensington for daughters of the clergy, then was moved to Belgrave House in Clevedon near Bristol for a year. The syllabus was literature, drawing, music, a competency in French and German, and of course the domestic arts. She did not overtly rebel against the limitations of these transient all-female environments. From them she learned self-discipline and application, but a kind of reserve and withdrawal afflicted her, a repression of expression of emotion, an aloneness. She had little choice other than to be serious, devout and inarticulate about personal desire.

At Clevedon when she was eighteen she was confirmed by the Bishop of Bath and Wells in St Andrew's Parish Church. She was five foot three, grey-eyed, had dark wavy hair, and was pretty. She took her vows seriously: affirmation of faith in Christ, the renouncing of sin, rejection of all rebellion against God. Her life was being mapped out in a way that conformed to the traditional values of Victorian England: the authority of God, the superiority of men, the subjugation of women.

When she was nineteen she went as a pupil teacher to Laurel Court School, a large stone house in the precincts of Peterborough Cathedral. The school, owned and run by Miss Margaret Gibson and her partner Miss Annette Van Dissel, had the approval of the Bishop of Peterborough. Miss Gibson advertised in the *Peterborough Advertiser.* Laurel Court offered girls 'a high moral training and the advantages of home life. French and German are the languages of the house. Special attention is paid to the culture of Music.' Drawing was on the syllabus too, and English literature and Italian. Girls were 'to be prepared for the Cambridge and Oxford examinations'. These gave women a qualification to teach simple subjects to young children, as a way of combining low-paid employment with civilising activity. Women were not admitted as Cambridge undergraduates until 1948.

Miss Gibson's school year was divided into three terms. Tuition fees were sixty guineas a year, payable in advance, and a term's notice was required before a pupil left. There were special rates for daughters of the clergy and fees were waived for student teachers like Edith Cavell.

Miss Gibson hated theories of pedagogy and education, liked spicy gossip and had a stern attitude toward right and wrong. Breakfast was at six in the morning, followed by church. School lessons began at seven and the day girls arrived at nine. Miss Van Dissel taught French and German by rote, and girls from France, Holland, Germany and Denmark helped with conversation classes in return, like Edith Cavell, for waived fees.

The family life on offer at Laurel Court was eccentric and entirely segregated from men. Miss Gibson was a lesbian separatist. She referred to men as the Adamses, complained that they never showed chivalry towards Eve, said she detested them, and resisted employing them in her school. There were fifty residents in Laurel Court and one lavatory. Boarders had a weekly bath with little water and no lingering and were in bed with the lights out by nine. There were pianos in many of the rooms and coal fires in winter. The place smelled of cats and there was an evil-smelling wolfskin rug in Miss Gibson's sitting room. All the windows in the school were usually closed. There were no facilities for games or sports.

Miss Gibson, born Margaret Gibson in Mallow, County Cork, in 1837, was the daughter of an Irish clergyman and a French mother. Her family moved to London after the devastation of the Irish potato famine of 1845. She was fluent in French and German so she went as a governess to Holland in the 1860s where she met Annette Van Dissel. They formed an inseparable partnership, travelled to England together and in 1870, after being impressed by a sermon in the Cathedral by Bishop Magee, chose to make Peterborough their home. To earn their living they boarded and taught girls at their house at 2 South View in the London Road then 'within a year' bought out Mrs Freeman, the owner of Laurel Court School in the Minster precincts.

Miss Gibson was small, wore long black dresses with a train, had a muslin bonnet that was always slipping out of place and seldom went outside the Cathedral precincts. She kept her Irish accent, had illegible handwriting, never stopped talking and was an insatiable drinker of tea. Her cats, to which she was devoted, were named Lord Mounteagle and Stumpy. She read omnivorously, remained interested in the fate of her girls after they left her school, and was always ready to help find them a job or a home. She ruled at Laurel Court in an unvarying manner and with the same curriculum year on year. She supervised the kitchen, the maids, the cooks, the girls. Her birthday on 11 November was celebrated each year with a tea party for the whole school. The school food was well cooked and served in silver dishes. Punishment was idiosyncratic. Naughty girls were shut in a cupboard or made to sit cross-legged on the floor with a newspaper over their face.

If it was a family it stretched the definition, as Edith Cavell in her adult life was also to do. She was nineteen when she arrived there and nearly twenty when she left. It was hardly a world of coming-out balls, dances and heterosexual promise. There was scant chance of landing any sort of husband there, let alone one with class.

In the summer of 1886 Edith Cavell went home to Swardeston. She gave her mother an album of drawings and watercolours done at Laurel Court: scenes of flowers and birds and picnicking girls. Miss Gibson carried on with Laurel Court for another forty-three years. After she died in 1928 the school closed.

For Edith Cavell the end of school might have been a time for fun and romantic attachment. But there was little pursuit of romance in the Cavells' social calendar. As ever, there was her father's rule for her to justify her existence and make a contribution. He encouraged her to raise the funding for a Sunday school to be annexed to the vicarage. She wrote to the Bishop of Norwich, John Pelham, and asked for episcopal help. He agreed that if the village raised a certain amount, he would provide the rest. Edith painted greetings cards, her mother and sisters cut them to size and addressed envelopes. These were sold or sent out with a request for money for the enterprise. Sufficient funds were raised and within two years the Sunday school – a long hall attached to the back of the house – was built for the village children.

In January 1887 the Reverend Cavell found a post of governess for her, as ever through Church connections. It was with the family of Charles Mears Powell, vicar of Steeple Bumpstead, a small Essex town.

5

THE ENGLISH GOVERNESS

There were about 25,000 governesses in England in the second half of the nineteenth century. Etiquette manuals advised them and their employers on how to deal with each other. To be a governess meant living in an unfamiliar house with an unknown family in return for a pittance wage and board and lodging. The governess, though herself childless, acted as a quasi-mother. She must not, though, look like a lady or behave with the assertion of a real mother. Her domain was the schoolroom. She was expected to be primly dressed and to ask permission if she wanted to go out. In the evenings she ate with the children, after that she was on her own.

To be a wife and mother was the essential role from which all departure was less. Upper-class girls set the standard with their debutante whirl of coming out, then marriage. 'Spinster' and 'old maid' were ugly words with connotations of being shrivelled and undesirable in a way that 'bachelor' was not. Governesses notoriously ended up as spinsters. Socially they had little opportunity for romance or even close friendship. The preferred age for them was around twenty-five and their careers were short-lived. A woman unmarried at thirty-five was on the shelf.

To be a good governess was a quasi-religious vocation: chaste and self-effacing. The governess must give her energy to her charges but expect little in return. Apart from references, an interview and first impressions, none of the parties knew quite what they were letting themselves in for.

The governess was not a respected figure. 'A private governess has no existence, is not considered as a living and rational being except as connected with the wearisome duties she has to fulfil,' Charlotte Brontë wrote to her sister in 1839. The role was often disparaged in nineteenth-century literature: in Thackeray's *Vanity Fair*, Charlotte Brontë's *Jane Eyre*, Henry James's *The Turn of the Screw*. In Jane Austen's *Emma* Jane Fairfax likened the industry to the slave trade: 'widely different certainly as to the guilt of those who carry it on; but as to the greater misery of the victims, I do not know where it lies'.

Governesses were no more trained, protected or inspected than were midwives, or teachers in private schools. As and when the parents had other plans for their children the governess was dispensed with. None the less there were far more applicants than posts to be filled, such was the paucity of opportunity for women who needed to work.

Edith Cavell was twenty-two when she arrived in the Reverend Powell's household in 1887. Her upbringing had been one of service and compliance, of putting the needs of others before her own. She was conscientious, kind, reliable and had acquired some sort of teaching skills at Laurel Court. But unlike Miss Gibson, as a governess she had no authority to express her personality and views, nor did she have the companionship of girls her own age. It was an isolating occupation. She was transplanted, aged twenty-two, into an unfamiliar household and she was homesick. At home as the eldest daughter she had looked after her siblings; now she was quasi-parent to an unrelated brood. The arrangement was a short-term convenience and the expense to her employers minimal.

Charles Mears Powell was a strict man. Edith Cavell's duties were heavy, for his wife was frail. His four children, three girls and a boy as in her own family, were in her care. She had to accommodate their disparate ages – Kathleen was eleven, Constance eight, Mabel seven and John six – and oblige the vicar and his wife. He employed a cook and housekeeper but Edith Cavell was to feed and clothe the children, set their lessons, mark their copybooks, teach them English, French and music and organise their playtime. She took them for walks and supervised their summer holidays at Clacton-on-Sea. Church duties became her responsibility too, because of Mrs Powell's frailties. She arranged the flowers for services and did whatever the vicar asked.

The Reverend Powell had followed a similar path to Edith's father. He trained for the clergy in London, worked as a curate at All Soul's church in Langham Place, Marylebone, married when he was thirty-five – his wife Margaret was born in Ireland, as was he – then went to Steeple Bumpstead to live the life of a village curate and raise his family there. He had no private money and the vicarage was for his use only for as long as he was curate there.

Steeple Bumpstead, though larger than Swardeston, had the same structure of manor house, church and labourers' cottages. The local inn was called 'The Fox' rather than 'The Dog', the neighbours were cattle dealers rather than agricultural labourers, the landscape was less lush than Norfolk, but the slow tenor of the days was similar. Edith Cavell had a room at the top of the house with a view of the garden and fields. She earned £10 a year but on such a wage could not hope to save. She drew strength from her religion, had a scrupulous honesty, a practised reserve and had long learned not to complain. But it was a dead-end job. To be a governess in a rural vicarage was not an occupation to test her, except in terms of patience. She stuck it for a year then went home to Swardeston in the summer of 1888. Four years after she left Steeple Bumpstead the Reverend Powell died of appendicitis – two weeks before Christmas in 1893. He left £203. 12s. 7d. His widow and children then moved to Twickenham.

6

A GERMAN SUMMER

In the summer when Edith Cavell left the Powells she travelled to Germany. She went in a party with her parents and brother and a girlfriend, Alice Burne, who was chaperoning a widow, Mrs Pigott. It was the year Queen Victoria's eldest grandson Wilhelm became the ninth King of Prussia and the third Emperor of Germany. There was a sense of alliance between the two countries. For the Reverend Cavell it was a chance to show his family the Germany he had known as a theology student. For Edith it was a chance to shake off the dullness of being a governess in a rural vicarage, see different landscapes, use her French and learn some German.

The party travelled by train and ferry. Edith took her watercolours and sketchbook. They went first to the old town of Kreuznach on the River Nahe, a tributary of the Rhine. She sketched the fifteenth-century timber houses built, to save them from flooding, high on the pillars of the river's bridge; beat Alice Burne at tennis, and with her visited the house where Dr Faustus was said to have lived and taught, and St Paul's church where Karl Marx married Jenny von Westphalen in 1843.

On Saturday 28 July she and Alice went on ahead of the rest of the party by train to Frankfurt. She described this display of independence as 'a great lark'. They stayed at the Englische Hof hotel, had tea there and took a tram to the Palmgarten to see its glasshouses, rockery with waterfalls, cactus garden and plants from all over the world. They went to a concert in the Garden, sat at a table on the balcony and 'were nearly overpowered' by the cigar smokers, then left early to avoid the rush and were back at the hotel by ten.

Next day, Sunday, after breakfast Jack Cavell went sightseeing with them while Mrs Cavell attended church. Jack was fifteen. Alice Burne described him as a shrimp. They went to see what was called 'the great boast of Frankfurt', *Ariadne on the Panther,* a neoclassical sculpture by Johann Dannecker. A banker and philanthropist, Moritz von Bethmann, whose family's wealth was on a par with the Rothschilds, had built a special museum for it in the grounds of his villa. The museum did not open until eleven so they had to wander around for a couple of hours, then Jack was refused entry because he was under age. In the afternoon they again walked in the Palmgarten, then Edith and Jack went back to the hotel and Alice went with Mrs Pigott to the Opera House to hear Wagner's *Tannhäuser.* It was 'grand and elevating to the last degree', she told Edith.

The following day she and Edith went together to the Romerberg in Frankfurt's old town and visited the Kaiser Saal where Roman emperors had been crowned, then in the afternoon they all moved on by train to Heidelberg, the Reverend Cavell's old university town. They had reservations at the Hotel Schreider where ten years earlier Mark Twain had stayed.

It poured with rain and they got soaking wet walking to the Heilige Geist Kirche, a fifteenth-century church for both Protestants and Catholics. The Reverend Cavell arrived in a bad mood from Kreuznach. He was particularly intolerant of smoking and had had a horrid journey in a smoky carriage. After supper they played dominoes in the hotel's music room then went to bed early.

On Tuesday 31 July 1888 the party took a carriage up to Heidelberg's romantic ruined castle, eight hundred years old, buried in green woods high above the River Neckar, admired by Goethe and Mark Twain and painted by Turner. They walked among its wooded terraces, ragged towers covered in vines and flowers, and arched and cavernous rooms like 'toothless mouths', as Mark Twain said. They climbed higher to the Molkenkur for views of the castle and the city, then walked down to the hotel for dinner at midday and to relax in the garden. Then the Cavells left for the town of St Goar in the Rhine Gorge and Alice Burne and Mrs Pigott went back to Kreuznach.

For a month the Cavells stayed at St Goar, a month of mountain walks, swimming in the Rhine, tennis and sightseeing. St Goar, a sixth-century saint, had brought Christian teaching to the central Rhine. The town named after him was set between mountains that rose either side of the river. As at Heidelberg there was a medieval castle with ramparts, bastions and casements, painted by Dürer in the sixteenth century and by Turner three hundred years later.

That summer of 1888 was Edith Cavell's introduction to Europe, its time-honoured familial, cultural and religious connections to England, its centuries of civilised living. It made her resolve to find work abroad and a wider horizon for herself. She supposed such work would have to be as a governess, for that seemed the only opportunity and the only training she had. Marriage was not her expectation, nor that of her family. Of the four of them only her younger sister Lilian was to marry and have children.

Back in Swardeston she was reluctant again to append herself to someone else's family as a live-in governess. She was happier at home. To pay her way she worked as a day governess, teaching the small children of John Henry Gurney at Keswick Hall and Hugh Gurney Barclay at Colney Hall. The Gurneys and Barclays were banking families, interrelated and hugely rich. Their manor houses, only a few miles outside Swardeston, already had staff of footmen, a housekeeper, lady's maids, cooks, scullery maids, a nurse and butler. Again she got the work not through an agency or from advertisements in the Norwich library or *The Times*, but because of her father's status as the vicar. The Gurney children, Agatha, Cicely and Margaret, were eight, six and five. At Colney Hall six miles away she looked after two of the Barclay sons, Terence who was seven and Evelyn who was five. She liked children, was a kind, imaginative teacher, and she went home at the end of the day, but she was marking time. The work was not a challenge of the sort she wanted.

In 1889, a year when dockers went on strike in England for better employment conditions, Adolf Hitler was born, and the suicide or murder of Crown Prince Rudolf of Austria and his mistress led to Archduke Franz Ferdinand becoming heir to the Austrian throne, Edith Cavell again took a temporary post as a live-in governess – at Hylands House, near Chelmsford. It was the home of the Pryor family. Arthur Pryor, known as the Squire, owned Truman's Brewery. She was governess briefly to three of his grandchildren: Elizabeth, John and Katherine. The house, a neoclassical villa, was set in 574 acres of parkland landscaped by the eighteenth-century garden designer Humphry Repton, who designed the gardens at Woburn Abbey and Longleat.

Hylands, an extravagance of marble, gold and chandeliers, had a grand staircase, a banqueting room, a gilded drawing room, a library, a 300-foot conservatory, stables, farms, a boathouse, a private church. Not much notice was taken of Edith Cavell. Her domain was the schoolroom. She was only the governess, the spectre at the feast. She was unhappy there and the Pryor family vaguely remembered her as uncommunicative, but nothing more.

The next year her youngest sister Lilian, who was twenty, followed her lead and went to Miss Gibson's school for girls at Laurel Court as a trainee teacher. She stayed a year. Miss Gibson heard how Edith wanted to work abroad. She recommended her as governess to Paul François, a Brussels lawyer whom she knew through the Catholic Church. He had four children. The family lived at 154 avenue Louise, a rich residential part of the city. It was an opportunity for Edith Cavell to live abroad, perfect her French and work in a city that seemed as safe and civilised as Norwich. She left Swardeston in the spring of 1890, though throughout her life it remained the place she viewed as home.

7

THE BELGIAN GOVERNESS

Edith Cavell was twenty-five when she went to Brussels. She stayed with the François family for nearly five years. Affluent and bourgeois, they liked the cachet of having an English governess. They too had three girls and a boy: Marguerite was thirteen, George twelve, Hélène eight and Evelyn three. Neither Paul François nor his wife spoke English. Edith was to converse in French with them and the servants – they employed full staff – but to speak only English to the children.

All was new. Her employers were intelligent, rich and kind. Brussels was a beautiful, historic city; the house was grand. Avenue Louise, Brussels's equivalent to Paris's Champs-Élysées, was wide, straight, two kilometres long and lined each side with double rows of horse chestnut trees. There were paths under these trees for pedestrians and horse riders. Along the middle of the avenue went the horse-drawn carriages. Built in 1847 and named after King Leopold II's eldest daughter Louise-Marie, it led to the city's central park, the Bois de la Cambre – sixty acres of woodland, fields, boating ponds and paths.

It was a grand setting. The family was inclusive and appreciative of her. She ate with them, went on holidays with them and got on well with the François children who in adult life remembered her as a kind, imaginative teacher. But again her domain was the nursery and the schoolroom, and again she was a quasi-parent. She taught the younger children to read and write, walked the elder ones to school in the mornings and collected them in the evenings. She kept them all occupied so that their parents

Edith Cavell as a governess in Brussels in the early 1890s

were free to do other things. She took them on long walks and taught them the English names of flowers and how to draw and paint in watercolours. She taught them to cook simple meals and stage schoolroom plays to which their parents were invited. She got them to read aloud from *Strand* magazine, Frances Hodgson Burnett's *Little Lord Fauntleroy* and from Louisa Alcott's *Little Women*. She introduced them to Dickens, Wordsworth, Tennyson and Longfellow and to a book which impressed her when it was published in 1880, *Robert Elsmere* by Mrs Humphry Ward: a hugely popular virtuous period piece, it was the story of a young clergyman who loses his faith but devotes his life to helping the poor in the slums of London's East End.

Perhaps she wanted to make a point, for there was no imperative of service in the François household, no pre-dinner

The Bois de la Cambre, Brussels central park, in the 1890s

hurrying round with helpings for the poor, as on the Sundays of her childhood. Life's principal domain was social. A menu card decorated by her for one of their family dinner parties detailed an eleven-course affair of oysters, fillet of sole, saddle of lamb, truffles and pâté.

In her teaching, though, she imbued the François children with her strict moral view. 'It was an intelligent way of bringing up children,' Hélène said of her in adult life. The family dogs were in Edith's care and she wrote and illustrated a booklet about their proper care. She took much of the information from a book called *Popular Dog-Keeping* by J. Maxtee. 'A dog,' she wrote, 'soon reciprocates little kindnesses and instinctively takes upon himself the duty of protector.' She described how a kennel could be made from an old 18-gallon beer cask, painted green, set on a stand and lined with sawdust and wood shavings. If the weather was very hot, she wrote, a sack should be put over the kennel's top. Food and water dishes must be cleaned after each meal and uneaten food not allowed to stand from one meal to another. Breakfast should be biscuits, dry and broken small. For the day's main meal the biscuits should be soaked for an hour or two, drained then mixed with pieces of lean cooked meat and covered with broth. The second meal should be boiled oatmeal mixed with milk or gravy. The dog should have green vegetables at least once a week, be brushed regularly, but never just after a meal, and not roughly but 'with the lay of the coat, commencing with the shoulders and fore legs and finishing with the back, loins and hind quarters.'

Edith Cavell spoke French with an unremittingly English accent and there was a family tease about the time when she took the terrier, which had hurt its tail, to the vet, and did not distinguish in pronunciation between *queue* and *coeur* so that the vet thought there was something wrong with the dog's heart.

Edith Cavell on holiday with the François children in the summer of 1894

Refreshing though it was for her to immerse herself in a new culture and a new language, she was biding her time. 'Being a governess is only temporary,' she wrote to her cousin Eddy, 'but someday, somehow, I am going to do something useful. I don't know what it will be. I only know that it will be something for people. They are, most of them, so helpless, so hurt and so

Sketch by Edith Cavell of the François' summer home,
the château de Grenosch-Elderen, 1893

Sketch of roses, 14 August 1893

unhappy.' Helping the hurt and unhappy was more her aspiration than to be quasi-mother to privileged children in a well-off
bourgeois family. Her charges had no expectation of economic
self-reliance or a governess's lot. The Belgian setting was a challenge but there was an innate incongruence in teaching the François girls to be the lady she could not aspire to be because her
father did not have money.

Edith Cavell's aloneness was inevitable. She was a stranger in
a foreign land. Her upbringing and family ethos were a world
away from moneyed Brussels society. She worshipped at the

Anglican Church of the Resurrection, had no particular friends in Brussels, little time to herself and no social calendar of her own. The smart house in the avenue Louise was her temporary residence, not her home. She was trustworthy and well liked, but at heart dispensable. On an occasion when Paul François disparaged Queen Victoria for her prim moral tone Edith Cavell left the room. This was interpreted as her having no sense of humour, but she was homesick and offended by the family's assumption of superiority. Once when Mme François, disinclined to meet with callers, asked her to tell them she was out, she refused, for she would not lightly dissemble.

Though there was scant fulfilment in her work, there was much to enjoy. Paul François had a yacht and stables and owned a summer home: a château near Tongres in Limbourg in the Forêt de Longues near the Dutch border. On holidays and outings Edith Cavell took her watercolours and sketched the racecourse at Boitsfort where all fashionable Brussels went in the racing season, the François family's country château, the river that ran through its grounds, the village of La Plante near Namur where she went rowing on the River Meuse, the château d'Hougoumont where the Duke of Wellington's army defeated Napoleon in June 1815.

Every summer too she went home to Swardeston and took seaside holidays with her family and Eddy. By 1894 both her sisters, Florence and Lilian, had moved away from home. Both had avoided the governess trap and were training as nurses. Lilian was at St Thomas's Hospital in London. Nursing had become a possibility now that it was removed from the stigma of an occupation for women of low character. Social change was breaking through and the instinct of charity was being channelled into a more structured approach to social problems. So-called 'respectable women' could, if determined, step out of a home or quasi-home environment.

Jack Cavell had also left home. The Reverend Cavell's ambition for his only son was for him to go into the Church. He arranged for him to work as an assistant to the Reverend Bartlett, vicar in the nearby parish of Barnham Broom. Jack, unassertive and afraid of his father, failed in his stint as a curate's assistant. He was shy and to hide this developed an abrupt cynical manner. His friends said this was a defence and that he was a kind man. He was widely read and liked the theatre, but his father told him there was no money to spend on higher education and found him a job with the Norwich Union Insurance Company in the Consequential Loss Department.

Jack stayed with the company all his working life. He lived alone, had transient liaisons with women, smoked heavily and drank too much. He dressed as an Edwardian with a watch on a chain and a three-piece suit. He described his work as 'irksome and poorly paid . . . free from either great troubles or real pleasures'. He progressed from being a clerk to editing and writing nihilistic editorials for the in-house magazine. Among articles about clauses in fire policies and the retirement of company personnel he included curious brooding soliloquies about the elusiveness of love and the imminence of death.

Edith Cavell left Brussels and the François family in 1895. Marguerite, the eldest of her charges, was by then eighteen, and the youngest, Evelyn, was eight and going to school. That spring, too, the Reverend Cavell became ill. Though he seldom defaulted on any parish duty, he missed two baptisms on 7 and 17 April. Edith went home to help care for him, give support to her mother and to rethink her life's work.

PART TWO

8

NO HOSPITAL TRAINING

By 1895 Edith Cavell had come to the end of the governess cul-de-sac and marriage was not the solution to the direction of her life. Her two sisters were trained nurses. Given her altruism, her desire to help the hurt and unhappy, to do 'something useful', 'something for people', nursing seemed a profession where she might improve people's lives.

Nursing in England toward the end of the nineteenth century had lost much of its historic stigma as an occupation of last resort for those 'too old, too weak, too drunken, too dirty, too stupid, or too bad to do anything else'. In the early part of the century most so-called nurses were no more than untrained domestic servants. Their wages were pitiful, they were sacked without notice, many were illiterate, and drink was the notorious vice of the profession, as novels like Charles Dickens's *Martin Chuzzle-wit* showed. The well-to-do hired nurses of their choice in their homes to look after their sick. The poor had no money to spend on any kind of medical care. Hospitals were for the down-and-out and most would not take in patients they could not cure. Many districts had no hospital of any sort. The impoverished terminally ill went to the workhouse to die a pauper's death. Their bodies were wrapped in a strip of calico then put in make-shift coffins of unplaned wood. Edith's father held funeral services for the destitute at the Swainsthorpe workhouse.

Florence Nightingale raised the profile of nursing and of hospital care. She overrode her parents' opposition to her becoming a nurse, and campaigned for standards and structured reform.

Her accounts of conditions in military hospitals in the Crimean War and her appeals for proper medical facilities for wounded soldiers were given wide publicity in the newspapers. In 1859 she published her reforming manual *Notes on Nursing*. The following year she founded the 'Nightingale Training School for Nurses' at St Thomas's Hospital, where Lilian Cavell trained. Such schools reformed the whole concept of nursing and hospital provision. In 1851 there were about 8,000 patients in hospitals in England and Wales. Twenty years later there were 20,000.

Florence Nightingale introduced practical apprenticeship under a good ward sister. She began a crusade for hygienic, vigilant nursing: 'sanitary nursing' – fresh air, cleanliness, common sense, good management and loving care: 'If a patient is cold, if a patient is feverish, if a patient is faint, if he is sick after taking food, if he has a bed sore, it is generally the fault,

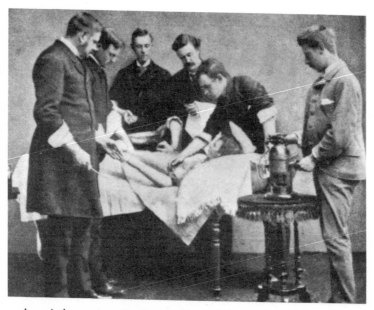

A surgical operation using Joseph Lister's carbolic antiseptic spray, c. 1880

Women in a Salvation Army shelter, 1892. Drawn from life by Paul Renouard
(1845–1924). 'ARE YOU READY TO DIE?' is inscribed above their beds

not of the disease, but of the nursing.' Her nursing methods and
concern for standards of hygiene and total patient care became
the benchmark of good practice.

Her reforms elided with recognition of the need for an integ-
rated approach to social problems. If epidemic disease taught
anything it was that people interdepended. For infection to be
contained, there needed to be isolation hospitals and cohesive
interaction between epidemiologists, bacteriologists, water
companies, plumbers, government and inspectors. No such cohe-
sion existed and progress was piecemeal. In moves to improve
the urban environment, people began to collect and interpret
facts and figures about mortality and morbidity and their connection to district and trades. Questions were asked: What is it about
this place or community which makes for more sickness, a higher
death rate and recurrent epidemics? Surgeons like Lister and
Pasteur applied methodology to their hunches of why infection
took root.

Immediate vacancy

1652

The Metropolitan Asylums Board.

CHIEF OFFICES: NORFOLK HOUSE, NORFOLK STREET, STRAND, LONDON, W.C.

Fountain FEVER HOSPITAL.

APPLICATION FOR THE APPOINTMENT OF ASSISTANT NURSE, CLASS II.

1. Name in full *Edith L. Cavell.*

2. Address *Swardeston Vicarage. Norwich.*

3. Age* *30* 4. Height *5ft 2½* 5. If married, or a widow, number of children *not married*
   * The candidate may be required to produce her birth certificate.

6. Where educated *Kensington.*

7. Present engagement, length of service, annual salary, and other emoluments

   I have had no hospital training, nor any nursing engagement whatsoever.

8. Previous engagements, viz. :—

Name of Hospital or Poor Law Infirmary (beginning with first engagement).	In what Capacity.	Period of Service.		Cause of Leaving.
		From	To	

9. Particulars as to training :—

   (a) Name and address of Hospital } or Poor Law Infirmary† }

   (b) Duration of training :—From _____ 189

   To _____ 189

   † Persons applying for engagement as Assistant Nurses, Class II., must be at least 22 years of age. They will not be required to produce any certificates of training.

   Assistant Nurses, Class II., will be required to serve at least one year before being eligible to become Assistant Nurses, Class I., but they shall not be eligible for promotion as Charge Nurses, until they shall also have satisfactorily passed a period of one year's training in a General Hospital.

10. If appointed, when able to enter on duties *At any time.*

Signature of Candidate *Edith Cavell.*

Date *Dec. 6th 1895.*

This Application must be made in the handwriting of the Candidate, and be forwarded at once to the Matron at the Hospital.

No original Testimonials or Certificates are to be sent, but copies may be made

Edith Cavell's application to be an Assistant Nurse Class II, 6 December 1895

Women were central to the focus for change. Louisa Twining wrote her *Recollections of Workhouse Visiting* and campaigned for trained nurses to treat the workhouse sick; Octavia Hill worked to improve living conditions for slum dwellers; Elizabeth Garrett Anderson broke through as a practising doctor the year Edith Cavell was born; Emily Davies campaigned for women's suffrage and with Florence Nightingale's first cousin – Barbara Bodichon – founded Girton College, Cambridge, for women; Elizabeth Fry pioneered for prison reform. She was a Quaker, born into the wealthy Gurney family for whom Edith Cavell had been a day governess. When she visited Newgate Prison she found neglected women and children crowded in, and sleeping on the floor without bedding. She formed a lobbying group, 'The Association for the Improvement of Female Prisoners in Newgate', and called for female matrons, employment and education for the cooped-up women and children, and their segregation from male prisoners. She also campaigned for soup kitchens for the hungry, and the reform of mental asylums.

Edith Cavell had a strong sense of social justice and she wanted a career. Her years in Belgium had given her independence from her father's repressive rule. She was thirty on 4 December 1895. Two days later she applied to the Metropolitan Asylums Board in the Strand for any vacancy they might have in a London hospital for an Assistant Nurse Class II. Four years earlier the Board had been made responsible for hospital provision for fever and infectious diseases throughout London. On her application form Edith Cavell gave her height as five foot three and a half and her weight as eight stone. She said she had been educated in Kensington. In response to Clause 7 on the form: 'present engagement, length of service, annual salary and other emoluments' she wrote with self-deprecating candour, 'I have had no hospital training nor any nursing engagements whatever.' She added that if appointed she could start at any time.

9

THE FEVER NURSE

Six days after applying to the Metropolitan Asylums Board, Edith Cavell began work at the Fountains Fever Hospital in Tooting in south London. She was the same age as Florence Nightingale had been when she had taken up nursing. It was a stark contrast, to go from the gentility of a grand house in the avenue Louise in Brussels to an environment where people of all ages were gravely ill and often dying.

The Fountains, a hastily constructed makeshift place, had opened two years previously in 1893. The Metropolitan Asylums Board was hard put to provide enough hospitals for the epidemics of infectious disease that swept through London in the 1890s.

Fountain Hospital

The Fountains Fever Hospital, Tooting, 1895

Their aim was to provide one fever bed for every thousand inhabitants. But whatever the target, success was always out of reach, for in London, where four million people lived in proximity and, if poor, in squalor, contagion spread like wildfire.

'Fever' covered typhus – spread by body lice – typhoid fever spread by infected food and untreated sewage, cholera, scarlet fever, smallpox, diphtheria, whooping cough, influenza, tuberculosis and measles. In the hope of isolating sufferers, an Infectious Diseases Act, passed in 1889, made it obligatory for general practitioners to notify local medical health officers about patients suffering from eleven types of infectious disease. Such patients were legally entitled to admission to an Asylums Board hospital irrespective of ability to pay. Early treatment was all-important but the incubation time was often weeks and the diagnosis of the certifying practitioner was too often wrong.

Medical research and its application struggled to catch up with these epidemics. There was a war between 'man and the attacking microbe': 'The infectious diseases replace each other and when one is rooted out it is apt to be replaced by others which ravage the human race indifferently whenever the conditions of healthy life are wanting. They have this in common with weeds and other forms of life – as one species recedes, another advances.'

In 1883 Edwin Klebs, professor of pathology at Zurich University, observed that a bacillus with certain characteristics occurred in the throats of diphtheria patients. The German doctor Robert Koch that same year isolated the cholera bacillus from samples of drinking water, food and clothing, and the bacterium that caused tuberculosis, but there were no antibacterial drugs and only piecemeal understanding of bacteriological spread. Perhaps the biggest contribution to London's health was made by Joseph Bazalgette, chief engineer to the Metropolitan Board of Works. He was a small man, given to attacks of depression and asthma. He had ten children. After the Big Stink of 1858 and a cholera

Sir Joseph Bazalgette (1819–91) the 'sewer king'. He engineered an underground system to carry London's untreated sewage out to sea

epidemic five years earlier that killed 10,738 people, he was given government authority to devise an underground system of pumps and pipes to carry untreated sewage out to sea.

He became known as 'the sewer king'. It took 318 million bricks to build 1300 miles of sewage pipes. His sewers saved countless lives and led to a huge reduction in cases of typhoid and cholera, but then diphtheria increased, followed by measles then whooping cough, and though the principles of immunity and vaccination and the importance of hygiene were understood, and there were vaccines for smallpox and for diphtheria, availability was haphazard.

In 1890 William Halstead, an American surgeon, introduced the idea of wearing rubber gloves during surgery, but there was a huge gap between understanding the need for contagion-free environments and creating them. Nor was it known quite how contagion worked. There was no vaccine for typhoid fever, which felled the privileged as well as the poor. Queen Victoria's consort,

Prince Albert, had died of it in December 1861, supposedly contracted from foul air escaping from the drains at Windsor Castle. Typhoid deaths declined by the end of the nineteenth century, with cleaner water supplies and more effective sewage disposal, but standards varied between districts.

In London in the epidemics of the 1890s care facilities for so-called fever patients were wildly inadequate. To isolate them, hospital ships were hurriedly fitted out on the Thames Estuary. The Asylums Board bought land on the outskirts of the city to build three new hospitals. Residents near the proposed building areas reacted with panic and protest. The ten-acre site at Tooting was bought for £4,395 and the Fountains, a hospital complex of a series of single-storey timber-frame huts with corrugated-iron roofs, was built and fitted out in nine weeks. Hasty building was driven by an outbreak of scarlet fever. There were sixteen wards, each with twenty-four beds, a scullery, a sister's bedroom, a linen room and a bathroom. There were separate huts for nursing accommodation, workshops and for a mortuary.

Staff were urgently required. To be eligible Edith Cavell needed to have had some sort of education and be of satisfactory character – no more than that. On her application form she said she had been vaccinated against smallpox fourteen years previously and had had childhood measles and whooping cough. She had not had rheumatic fever and did not have rheumatism or varicose veins – any of which might have made the long hours of physical hard work and being on her feet difficult. Miss Gibson of Laurel Court and a Norfolk neighbour, Mrs Annette Roberts of Brinton Hall, East Dereham, wrote references for her, and Miss Dickenson, the matron at the Fountains Hospital, interviewed her. On her recommendation Edith Cavell was then appointed by the management committee.

She was issued with her terms of employment as an Assistant Nurse Class II. Rules were strict. She must obey the matron, medical superintendents and charge nurses under whom she worked. They would tell her what to do in the wards and how to care for patients. She must take a bath and change her uniform and stockings before leaving the hospital. She would have twelve free hours weekly, one day off a month, an occasional evening pass from 8.30 to 10 p.m. and three weeks' holiday a year. If after six months her work was satisfactory she would be issued with a testimonial that made her eligible for promotion to Assistant Nurse Class I. To qualify as a charge nurse she needed a year's experience at Class I and a total of two years' service in fever nursing. Her salary would be £20 a year, rising by £1 a year to a maximum of £24. Any promotion or salary increase depended on good reports from the medical superintendent and matron.

So began Edith Cavell's career as a nurse and her immersion into the drama of hospital life. The hazards of fever were many. There was no understanding of dehydration. Scarlet fever led to renal complications, children with measles developed broncho-pneumonia. In her seven months at the Fountains she learned the features of infectious diseases and how to differentiate them. Patients arrived by horse-drawn ambulance. They came from Wandsworth, Clapham, Lambeth and Camberwell. They were brought in suffering with high temperatures, vomiting, diarrhoea and aching limbs. On arrival their own clothes were disinfected, they were dressed in two bed gowns – cotton underneath, flannel on top – and put to bed for twenty-two days. Patients stayed in hospital for a minimum of eight weeks whatever their progress. When allowed up, they were given a warm bath every evening. Those with weak hearts were given port and brandy.

Ward life was regimented. The beds were iron with feather mattresses, a blanket and sheet underneath and three blankets and a counterpane on top. Alternate upper small windows were left open all the time with the ambient temperature kept at sixty degrees. An anti-toxic serum from immunised horses, newly developed by Prussian bacteriologist Emil von Behring, was given to those seriously ill with diphtheria. At first the serum was brought from Paris, but then the Royal College of Medicine stabled and kept ten horses and produced their own. The hospital boards of governors and some patients objected. They did not want biological affinity to monkeys or horses.

Edith Cavell was at the Fountains Hospital for seven months. The annual report of the Hospital for 1896 showed how heavy her workload must have been and how dangerously ill many of the patients were. Of the 3,650 patients treated, 1,335 recovered and were discharged, 1,665 went on to convalescent hospitals, 278 died, a quarter of them within forty-eight hours of admission, and 372 were in the hospital at the year's end. Children were the main casualties. Those choking because of respiratory infection were given immediate tracheotomies. There were no antibiotics, no cure for acute inflammation.

Without informed cures, patient survival depended on good nursing: cold sponging to keep down fever, mustard poultices to alleviate inflammation, enemas of castor oil, repeated turning to prevent bedsores, rest, loving attention, invalid cooking with unlimited milk and eggs and ten ounces of beef tea daily, a calm environment and above all scrupulous hygiene.

Much of Edith Cavell's work was menial: making beds, polishing and dusting, stoking fires, relaying messages, fetching and carrying, distributing meals, emptying bedpans. It was an induction into the procedures of a busy hospital and a test of her stamina and of whether this was the vocation she wanted to pursue. It was hard and dangerous work with chronically sick patients, demanding hours, strict rules and institutional living in an all-female environment with women for the most part younger than herself and from whom she had to take orders. The overriding imperative was that the patient came first. Any lateness or lapses on her part were recorded. The nurses' living quarters were cramped and there was no privacy. In the time she was there, one assistant nurse died from pneumonia, three charge nurses, five assistant nurses and one ward maid caught scarlet fever, and four ward maids got diphtheria.

N.B. *This Paper is to be fully filled in (in the Candidate's own writing) and sent to* "*The Matron, the London Hospital, Whitechapel Road, London, E.*"
Both in the case of *Regular* and of *Paying* Probationers, **every question must be distinctly answered.**
Regular Probationers are required to forward this Form of Application fully filled up, prior to arranging for the personal interview.

1. Name in full, and present address? *Edith Cavell. Fountain Hospital. Lower Tooting S.W.*

...nts living? *1.*

What is your home address, or the name and address of your nearest relative? *Swardeston Vicarge. Norwich.*

...day, date and place of birth? *20. Dec. 4th 1865. Swardeston nr Norwich* [those during to enter on a month's trial, and those ... enter as Paying Probationers, are required ...ee a certificate of Birth.] *Birth certificate returned May 15th*

Where educated? *At home, and at a school in Kensington.*

6. Height and weight? *5 ft. 3 in. 8 stone.*

7. Are you strong, and have you always had good health? *Yes*

8. Have you perfect sight and hearing? *Yes*

9. Have you been re-vaccinated? If so, how long ago? *Yes 14 years ago.*

10. What infectious illnesses have you had? *Measles & whooping Cough.*

Have you had Rheumatism, Rheumatic Fever, or Varicose Veins? *No.*

Edith Cavell's application to be a probationer nurse
at the London Hospital, 17 April 1896

Within a few months of being at the Fountains, Edith Cavell decided to take formal training and make nursing her career. On 17 April 1896 she applied to the London Hospital in Whitechapel in the East End – where her mother had lived as a child – to be a probationer nurse. The pay would be £12 in the first year, £20 in the second – less than at the Fountains. She said she was strong, had always had good health, had perfect sight and hearing and was single. Married women were not accepted unless widowed.

Miss Dickenson gave her a reference. On 25 April she wrote that she had 'known Edith Cavill since December 1895'. Miss Cavill was 'Orderly, Methodical & of kindly & gentle disposition, had an equable temper, a very pleasant manner, was well-educated, intelligent & capable, of good moral character and carried out her work satisfactorily.' She was, said Miss Dickenson, 'a very suitable candidate for training as a hospital nurse'.

The Norfolk neighbour Annette Roberts of Brinton Hall again gave a character reference. She said she had known Edith for fifteen years and was glad of the opportunity to recommend her: she was energetic, adaptable, intelligent, decidedly capable, of high moral character and self-reliant yet willing to follow guidance. She had always had a high opinion of her.

After an interview with Eva Lückes, matron at the London, Edith Cavell was offered a place as a probationer nurse. She accepted it on 18 July. She left the Fountains and went home to Swardeston to spend the summer with her mother. On 3 September 1896 she began, at the London Hospital, to train for what was to be her life's chosen work.

THE PROBATIONER

Eva Lückes had been matron of the London Hospital for sixteen years. Aged forty – only ten years older than Edith Cavell – she was a friend and disciple of Florence Nightingale's and dedicated to making the hospital a centre of excellence for nursing care.

A large, purposeful woman – she looked like Queen Victoria – in group photographs with her nurses she presided at the centre, conspicuous for her size and the dark of her uniform against their rows of starched white. The daughter of a wealthy banker and educated at Cheltenham Ladies' College and a finishing school in France, she exuded the confidence of her class and

The London Hospital, Whitechapel, where Edith Cavell
trained as a general nurse

Eva Lückes c. 1900, Matron of the London Hospital from 1880
until her death in 1919

ruled with the authoritative manner of a headmistress or an army commander.

The demands on the London Hospital were great. The East End was an area of squalid accommodation and bad sanitation, home to immigrants and the urban poor. It was also, because of the development of the docks and England's trade by sea, the commercial centre of the capital. The London was what was called a voluntary hospital, dependent on private funds and charitable donations. Such hospitals had medical schools and were patronised by royalty. They were staffed by the best physicians whose practices for private patients were in the smart West End and who two or three times a week went by carriage to do their hospital ward rounds and to operate. Treatment was for the most part free, but patients were assessed by doctors for admission and turned away if they could afford private care, or were destitute, mentally ill, or incurable.

The London Hospital's seven hundred beds were not enough to cope with demand. Staff nurses were also sent out from the hospital to give private care to paying patients in their homes. For many illnesses there was no reliable treatment: no insulin for diabetes, no knowledge of blood groups, or effective treatment for tuberculosis, no understanding of how to cure meningitis, septicaemia, pernicious anaemia. Purging and bloodletting with leeches were standard, chloroform and ether were used as anaesthetics and post-operative vomiting and confusion were routine.

The suffering of the ill was acute, and nursing care all-important. Following on from Florence Nightingale, Eva Lückes aspired to take nursing from its haphazard, unorganised, untaught, unclean and unrespected status and turn it into a noble profession for women. The day after her appointment as matron in 1879 – at the age of twenty-four – she told the management committee at the London that the nursing staff were grossly inadequate in quality and numbers. Their sleeping quarters, she said, were 'scattered in five directions', they had no proper meals, no terms of employment. She insisted on the provision of decent living accommodation for her nurses, bathrooms for them, a training school.

She set about creating a syllabus of instruction in practical nursing and she persuaded the medical staff to give lectures on anatomy, surgery and physiology. By 1882 she had introduced examinations for probationers with the prompt of prizes and certificates of attainment. There was no centralised state registration. Each hospital awarded its own certificate and set its own standard. State registration, both Eva Lückes and Florence Nightingale believed, would standardise mediocrity.

Nor was there any state funding. Lack of money was a constant curtailment to plans. Windfalls were occasional. In 1884 the East London Railway wanted to extend the line from Whitechapel to Surrey Docks with a tunnel going under the hospital. As compensation for the disruption they paid the hospital £30,000, which was used as core funding for a nursing school and medical college. The Prince of Wales's wife, Alexandra, opened both buildings in 1887.

In the same year as Edith Cavell started at the London as a probationer, Sydney Holland was elected its chairman. He said that despite Eva Lückes's efforts 'there was a blight over everything'.

There was only one operating theatre and only one table, a wooden affair like those in butchers' shops. Aseptic surgery was just coming in but the staff were still doubtful about it. When a surgeon went round he was followed by the beadle who carried a baize-covered tray containing instruments which were used and reused with complete disregard of the principles of asepsis. One tiny room sufficed for bacteriological work. There was no clinical laboratory. Röntgen had discovered his rays but a small shed in the garden was all the accommodation the London could spare for X-ray work. Most of the nurses lived a 'Box and Cox life'[5] and many lodged in the small houses in the district. There was only one Nurses Home. On the financial side the position was depressing. The subscriptions for 1895 had fallen to only £8,750. Nevertheless what I saw impressed me with the ambition to put things right. So I set to work and worked as I had never worked before in all my life.

Between them Sydney Holland – he became Viscount Knutsford – and Eva Lückes transformed the hospital. He was a tireless fundraiser and within a decade had persuaded rich financiers like the Rothschilds to pay for a new isolation ward, an out-patients' unit, new operating theatres, a new nurses' home and a block of new wards.

And so, on 3 September 1896, Edith Cavell began her nursing training at the start of a great movement for reform in the hospital's practice and administration. She was one of an intake of ten. For the first six weeks she lived in at Tredegar House, the probationers' school at 99 Bow Road, a short distance from the main hospital. The house, given to the London by Lord Tredegar, had opened the previous year and was the first preliminary training school in England. Its objective, Miss Lückes said, was 'to soften the ordeal of the first beginning of hospital life for newcomers'.

Edith Cavell had had some experience of hospital life. Not many of the other newcomers knew what to expect. Among them Annie Hogg had worked in a drapery, Ella Robertshaw lived at home, Rebecca Startin had packed cartons for a living,

[5] From a play by John Maddison Morton, 1847, about two lodgers, Box and Cox, who shared a room: one used it by day, the other by night

Probationer nurses at a 'sickroom' cookery class, 1901

Gertrude King was a widow, Marjorie Macfadyen was a masseuse, Gertrude Deighton and Emma Davie had both been teachers.

Probationers were issued with a uniform of mauve check cotton with removable lower sleeves and a white bibbed apron and white cap. They got up at 6.15 a.m., breakfasted at 7.00, then after prayers attended classes on bandaging, practical cooking, splint padding, ambulance work, and the chemistry of food, and lectures on physiology, hygiene and theoretical nursing. They had two hours off duty during the day and finished work at 8.30 in the evening. 'Lights out' was at 10.30. One morning a week was given over to cleaning and housework. A 'monitress', appointed each day, checked there was no talking during class hours.

Miss Lückes kept large ledgers on the qualities, skills and shortcomings of all her nurses. It was a time of leather-bound, gold-embossed ledgers and account books with entries in scripted handwriting. Her manner was tough but personal. She was critical of her nurses and ambitious for them all to do well. She did not challenge the conventional view of 'a woman's place', but in her lectures roused her probationers with vocational zeal and reminded them of their duty of subservience to the doctors and their caring role as women and Christians. Repeatedly she went to the first principles of nursing, to the underpinning concept of care. 'You have chosen a profession,' she told them, 'in which there is simply no limit to the good you can do.'

You must walk worthy of the vocation wherein you are called. The science of medicine and the art of nursing materially assist each other in their ultimate objects; the cure where that is possible and failing that the alleviation of suffering.

Especially when your patients are weak and helpless and irritable you need to be gentle and considerate towards them; they are so completely in your power and they may so easily be made to suffer more than they need to by your having a sharp way of speaking, a rough touch, or a grumbling manner of attending to them. Unless you have been very ill yourself you have no notion how weak patients depend for their own courage on their nurse's strength. The best guide is simply to judge whether you would like to have such offices as you may have to perform for your patients rendered in the same manner that you are adopting towards them.

Truthfulness, obedience, and punctuality, are indispensable qualities. Each of you who wins our certificate of training will have it in your power to make us proud of your connection with us in the future or very sadly the reverse.

Selfishness is pre-eminently a defect which disqualifies a woman from the nursing profession. You must strenuously cultivate a self-controlled manner. A nurse who screams, who flies aimlessly about in all directions . . . Self-control *must* be gained if you are to be thoroughly efficient. A want of self-control is selfish, showing you do not put your patient first.

For Edith Cavell such instruction resonated with what she felt and all she had been brought up to believe. Eva Lückes's exhortations were for her the practical manifestation of the love prescribed in Thomas à Kempis's writings in *The Imitation of Christ*. From her father Edith Cavell had learned the demands and expectations of Christian faith. From Eva Lückes she was to learn that the implementation of charity required goals, high standards, vigilance and management.

After six weeks' induction, probationers moved to the main hospital. Edith Cavell had a room in the nurses' home. There was the same brutal timekeeping. Up at 6.00, breakfast at 6.30, on duty at 7.00. It was a twelve-hour day with half an hour off for lunch, and two hours off during the day when and if pressure of work allowed. On night duty the hours were 9 p.m. until 8.00 in the morning. She had a fortnight's holiday a year.

She worked for an allotted time in all the wards of the hospital. She was moved from a men's surgical to a women's medical ward, from a gynaecological to a children's ward, from admissions to the operating theatre. The objective was to gain experience in all aspects of hospital care. She worked to instruction from the staff nurse and she was overseen by the ward sisters, each of whom had a sitting room and bedroom on the ward where she was in charge. The sisters sent their reports on Edith Cavell to Eva Lückes: her dates of duty, whether she was on days or nights, the range of problems she had faced, an assessment of her performance.

Much of the work of the probationer nurses was skivvying.

Untrained 'scrubbers' were paid to do arduous work like washing the floors and laying and stoking the large open fires, but the probationers dusted the iron bedsteads, polished the brass plaques above the ward beds and the copper tea urns, sorted laundry, gave patients their meals, emptied bedpans, made shrouds for the dead. At 6.00 in the evening they attended lectures. 'Be careful not to get into the habit of leaning up against the tables and chairs and the patients' beds under any circumstances,' their matron taught them. 'It always gives an impression of slovenliness. Of course you will never think of sitting down or of remaining seated while you are speaking or being spoken to by any of the medical staff whether a senior or junior member of it, including the dressers and students. It looks unbusinesslike and unprofessional.' She instructed them in how to warm and oil bedpans, clean splints, give ice baths for typhoid ('brandy is frequently administered to the patient while in the bath'), apply and remove leeches ('a little salt sprinkled on them will cause them speedily to relinquish their hold'). She taught them how to prepare patients for operations ('for amputations or where there is a probability of much bleeding a tray with sawdust should be placed under the operation table ready for use'), how to rouse patients to consciousness after anaesthetic ('water and a towel must be flapped about the patient's face'), how to insert a catheter, clear blocked tracheotomy tubes with a feather, give hypodermic injections ('brandy and other stimulants are sometimes injected hypodermically but this is almost always done by the doctor'). She impressed on them that they must ventilate the wards: 'You have to fight against the proverbial horror of fresh air peculiar to the class of people from which most of your patients come.'

Every detail of care was covered: 'Scarlet blankets form the best sort of coverlets. It is popularly supposed they help to keep away the fleas.'

There was in the hospital a nurses' library and a museum of

Sir Frederick Treves (1853–1923), surgeon and teacher at the London Hospital

specimens and instruments. Physicians gave lectures in pathology and medicine. Frederick Treves, a surgeon, taught anatomy and surgery. It was he who rescued Joseph Merrick, known as 'the elephant man' and who was probably suffering from a disease called neurofibromatosis, from the indignity of being a sideshow exhibit viewed for 2*d*., and gave him shelter at the London Hospital. Treves described Eva Lückes as 'one of the ablest and most remarkable women of the age, an organiser with unequalled genius'. He said she transformed the hospital. 'There breathed through the harsh and dismal building a woman's influence like a breath of Spring. By some magic force the nurses became obedient, efficient and proud of their work.'

Edith Cavell wrote her notes in a black book in the neat forward-sloping handwriting taught her by her father. She wrote of tracheotomies for children with typhoid fever: 'if the tube is coughed out the child must be laid across the nurse's knee with the head thrown back and the wound held open until the tube can be replaced'; of how to stem their bleeding from cut tonsils or from circumcision; of the use of cocaine, morphine and champagne to alleviate pain; of how to give bread and charcoal poultices.

Again and again she recorded the importance of cleanliness and disinfecting. She noted how, when nursing diphtheria patients, she herself should gargle with chloride of potash and carefully cover any cut or abrasion. She wrote of how to read the signs of approaching death and of how to lay out the dead – straighten the dead person's limbs, close their eyes and jaw, wash their body, arrange their hair, attend to their nails, plug their

The nurses' garden created by Eva Lückes.
They called it the Garden of Eden

mouth and rectum with cotton wool and if needs be the uterus too. Throughout her career she was to do this time and again so that no person should lose their dignity in death. She did it out of respect for every human life. The pity was that when she died no one was to do it for her.

As a nurse, hers was an institutionalised life: the terms dictated, every hour accounted for. The work was exacting, the demand for vigilance high. There was no privacy except for hours of sleep, no solitude except what she could find in meditation. When she was ill in December 1896 she was cared for on one of the wards. There was little time for a life outside the hospital. Nurses were forbidden to socialise or go out with doctors or medical students and were dismissed if they did so.

Eva Lückes asked for the provision of a garden for the nurses. They called it the Garden of Eden. It had fountains, hammocks, rose bushes, doves and ducks and deckchairs and a penny-in-the-slot machine for boiling water for tea. Recreation was a walk around it, a ride on a horse-drawn bus, a launch trip down the river to Tilbury.

After three months on the wards Edith Cavell signed a contract agreeing to complete the two-year training course with the hospital and, if she qualified, to stay on for a third year as a staff nurse, or as a private staff nurse in the homes of patients under the hospital's care. The hospital did not want to pay for protracted training of nurses only to have them leave without practising all they had learned.

Edith Cavell curried favour with no one. 'Good' or 'very good' were the usual comments against her written work. She displayed no ego of her own. The ward sisters thought her reserved and unforthcoming and often were cool in their assessment of her. The patients found her kind. When John Bancroft had an operation on his spine without anaesthetic, for three days she sat with him at every available moment. On the black endpaper of his

Entertainment for patients, their families and nurses in the
London Hospital grounds, c. 1900

Bible she painted a spray of apple blossom and wrote one of the
many Thomas à Kempis quotes she had memorised: *If thou canst
hold thy peace and suffer then shalt thou see without doubt the help
of the Lord.* The compassion of her belief was that there was
redemption beyond suffering and that where there was suffering
there was holy ground.

There was no brag or bluster about her, no vanity or indulgence. She asked little for herself. Eva Lückes, who liked a bit of
flamboyance and theatre in her nurses, was critical in her reports
on her: 'Edith Cavell had a self-sufficient manner,' she wrote of
her, 'which was very apt to prejudice people against her.' It was
a curious comment, perceptive yet elusive, for Edith Cavell had
scant reference to self, and paradoxically her self-sufficient
manner came from her detachment from self-regard.

II

MAIDSTONE

In mid-August 1897 a typhoid epidemic began in Maidstone. By 9 October 1,200 cases of the disease had been confirmed and forty-two people had died. On 15 October Edith Cavell, with five other nurses from the London Hospital, was sent by Eva Lückes to help in the emergency.

Maidstone, on the banks of the River Medway, in the 1890s was a thriving market town with a population of about 34,000 and a lower than average death rate. Brewing beer was its main industry and each summer from August to late September hordes of itinerant workers camped in the surrounding fields and picked hops for a pittance wage. Referred to locally as 'strangers', many of them came from London's East End or from Ireland. They were dock labourers, costermongers, woodcutters, hawkers, fish-basket makers . . . On the hop farms they survived in miserable conditions, there was prejudice against them and they were accused of theft and spreading disease.

The town's water was supplied by the Maidstone Water Company. By an Act of 1860 the company was not allowed to take water from the River Medway because this might be 'detrimental to navigation' so the main supply came from a reservoir and four springs. One of these, the Farleigh Springs, flowed into a millpond where the hop pickers washed. In mid-August 1897 this millpond became polluted.

Five years earlier, in 1892, the chief medical officer could not have been ruder about the town's sanitary arrangements. In a report he wrote:

Nearly half the houses in the town have water closets which have no mechanical means of flushing . . . Year by year, for twelve years, I have again and again endeavoured to show the folly that underlies the faith that a system of sewerage such as ours can be made to work satisfactorily without an adequate water-supply properly applied . . .

In Maidstone we have about 6,000 dwellings. Without hesitation I say that at the very least 4,000 of these dwellings have closets attached to imperfectly flushed drains, each of which is nothing better than an elongated cesspool charged with foul, festering filth, that is perpetually producing air-polluting and disease provoking vapours that escape from those drains wherever an outlet presents itself.

Inspection of the water supply was the responsibility of the town council. Mr A. Adams was the officer in charge of the sanitary department. In September 1897 he was on holiday in Switzerland, and his son Percy was standing in for him. On 13 September Percy Adams noted that in the preceding four weeks there had been nineteen deaths from diarrhoea and seven confirmed cases of typhoid fever. A week later this went up to 206 confirmed cases. He checked with the office of the water company and found that all those afflicted lived in an area high in the town with their water supplied by the Farleigh Springs.

He 'communicated his suspicions' to Mr Ware, the manager of the waterworks, and together they went to inspect the area. It was where parties of hop pickers had camped. Earthenware pipes from the springs went to underground catch pits. In one catch pit he found two dead rabbits and human faeces. The Tutsham-in-Orchard spring was fifty yards from the hop pickers' privy which 'was in a disgraceful condition with faeces decomposing and flooding the ground'. The rainfall in August had been heavy, and he found lots of human excrement in the fields and particularly near the hedges.

Mr Adams senior hurried home from Switzerland. The Farleigh water supply was cut off and so were most of the other springs. Water was diverted from the West Kent Company supply. The Maidstone Corporation hired carts and flushed the sewers with river water. They laid a mile and a quarter of new mains drainage in a week, and appointed Dr Sims Woodhead to enquire into the outbreak and advise what to do. He recommended sterilising the reservoirs with chloride of lime. Billboards were posted and printed notices delivered to all houses cautioning them about drinking untreated water.

By the time Edith Cavell arrived the source of the epidemic had been treated, but the disease was still spreading. According to Dr Woodhead this was 'through mischance in nursing, ignorant or careless handling of patients, their soiled clothing, excreta, the pollution of water closets, infected milk . . . house drains . . . the disgusting vapours issuing from the street ventilators and all the filthy pent-up stuff being driven pell-mell along the sewers'.

A special committee was appointed to oversee the treatment of patients. The West Kent hospital could not cope. Seven improvised hospitals were set up in schools and other buildings. Patients were also nursed at home.

Edith Cavell nursed at the Padsole Emergency Hospital and in people's homes. Though she had been seven months at the fever hospital in Tooting, she had not seen a full-blown typhoid epidemic. Patient survival depended on nursing efficiency and the drive to restrict contagion: clean linen, no sharing of towels, much washing with carbolic in clean, well-ventilated rooms, the use of bedpans treated with disinfectants of corrosive acid and hydrochloric acid. The Sanitary Authority washed and disinfected bedding and clothing free of charge. It was all collected, numbered and taken in canvas bags to the laundry. The Inspector of Nuisances superintended the disinfection of every house in which typhoid had occurred. Walls, ceilings and floors of infected rooms were sprayed with water, then fumigated with sulphur. Woodwork was washed with carbolic, ceilings were distempered and wallpaper stripped. Notices were pasted up saying that anyone suffering from typhoid could get food, clothing and relief if sanctioned by any clergyman, doctor or member of the town council.

The incubation period was two to three weeks. The symptoms were fever, diarrhoea and aching limbs. Sufferers were isolated, confined to bed and not allowed to sit up. They were kept quiet, sponged with iced water and allowed no solid food. Beef tea was thought to be good for them, and Brand's Essence and broth jelly. And milk. And brandy. Opium was given to relieve pain and quinine to lower their temperatures. To clean their mouths a piece of linen was dipped in glycerine and lemon juice. A relief committee sent convalescents off for a change of air.

The nurses worked quite literally until they dropped. At the end of a day Edith Cavell was so exhausted she would step out of her clothes and collapse into bed, so her roommate Caroline Bell, another London Hospital probationer, said. The two of them lodged with a large, boisterous lady who ran the town's toyshop, liked vulgar jokes and rum punch and grieved that her guests did not eat enough. Toward Christmas time they all dressed some of the toyshop dolls in nurses' uniforms and these sold well as Christmas presents.

By December the epidemic had died down. Out of a total of 1,847 cases 132 people had died. This was a low mortality rate for a typhoid epidemic. The townspeople were truly grateful. They organised a collection for the 166 nurses who had come to their town and worked so hard and saved so many lives. With the money raised, silver medals were struck with the arms of Maidstone on one side, the name of each nurse on the other and the inscription 'with gratitude for loving services 1897'.

Which was what it was. Loving services. Edith Cavell, like the other nurses, had risked danger and worked all hours to save lives and alleviate suffering. On 8 December a grand reception was held for them in the town's museum and the medals distributed. The Lord Mayor of London officiated in his robes and chains; so did the mayors of Maidstone, Gravesend, Chatham, Colchester, Rochester, Dover and Queensborough and all the local magnates. The speeches went on so long the nurses had to leave to get back to the hospital before the entertainments began: 'music, refreshments and a cinematograph' – films of Queen Victoria's diamond jubilee, pelicans being fed at London Zoo and the *Flying Scotsman* travelling at 60 miles an hour.

12

BACK TO THE LONDON

Edith Cavell returned to the London Hospital in January 1898. Improvements under the chairmanship of Sydney Holland were fast moving. He received £25,000 from the shipping magnate Alfred Yarrow for a new outpatient building, £22,000 from John Fielden for an isolation block, a large annual subscription from James Hora for maternity wards and £10,000 from Edward Raphael for segregated wards for Jewish patients. (Jews were thought to be as different in their ways as women were from men.) Money flowed in. Two storeys were added to the hospital. There were new wards, a separate laundry, an X-ray room 'and the most magnificent operating theatres in the whole of England'.

For another year Edith Cavell gained experience in every aspect of nursing. By the end of it she had nursed children with scurvy and rickets; mothers with mania in pregnancy; patients with concussion, sarcoma of the hip, amputated thighs and arms and with cut throats – a common method of attempting murder or suicide. She knew how to give enemas, bottle-feed a new baby, stem bleeding, apply dressings and distinguish between typhoid and scarlet fever. She had worked on the Charlotte, Cotton and Sophia wards and in the Electrical Department where X-ray apparatus run by batteries had been installed and 'light therapy' was used to treat rheumatism. Such techniques were experimental. The first technicians to work with X-rays at the London, Dr Harnack and Dr Suggers, both suffered X-ray burns and died of cancer. Harnack had both his arms amputated.

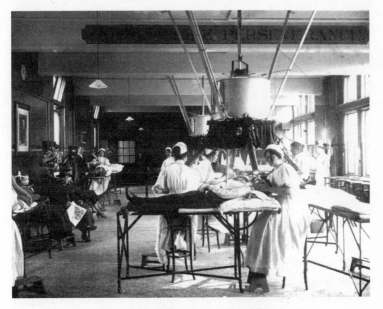

The Finsen Light, used at the London Hospital for the treatment
of tuberculosis of the skin, c. 1900

A close friend of Edith Cavell's, Eveline Dickinson, was chosen
by Sydney Holland to go with another nurse to Copenhagen to
learn the innovative methods used in 'Dr Finsen's Light Treatment for Lupus'. 'She was particularly well-suited for anything
of this kind,' Eva Lückes wrote of Eveline Dickinson in her
register, 'being keenly interested in the intellectual side of the
work and very capable of excelling in any details requiring neat-
ness and finish in execution.' On her return Eveline Dickinson
became Sister of the Light Treatment Ward at the London and
published articles about it in the nursing journals.

In September 1898 Edith Cavell passed the examinations for
her London Hospital certificate, which meant she qualified as a
staff nurse. Eva Lückes gave a starchy evaluation of her in her
register: 'Edith Cavell had plenty of capability for her work when

she chose to exert herself, but she was not very much in earnest, not at all punctual and not a Nurse that could altogether be depended upon. She did good work during the Typhoid Epidemic at Maidstone and had sufficient ability to become a fairly good nurse by the end of her training. Her theoretical work was superior to her practical. She attained an average standard in the latter, giving a general impression that she could have reached a higher standard if she had put her whole heart into the work. I thought her best fitted for the Private Nursing Staff and she was accordingly appointed in that capacity for her third year of service.'

It was a disappointment to Edith Cavell to begin her stint as a staff nurse in the private sector. She would have preferred for her third year to work as a staff nurse within the hospital structure. Private nurses, set apart by a green uniform, were sent to the homes of the doctors' paying patients – the ones they saw in their West End surgeries. The scheme was approved by the Hospital Committee because it brought funds to the hospital. For Edith Cavell it was reminiscent of her time as a governess. Again it was a dislocation. She went where she was sent, to areas where she knew no one, to live as a working guest in the closed confines of a well-off family house.

The matron's view of her sounded damning but was a typical Miss Lückes report. A musing aloud. In her first two years Edith Cavell was marked late forty-six times. It did not mean she was late on the wards. Quite possibly she was giving extra time to patients who needed it. It was simply the time she was marked in for her own meals.

With a constant flow of nurses the matron was too busy to get to know many of them well. She seemed to favour them if they were upper-class, good-looking and extrovert. She held an open evening on Tuesdays in her rooms where nurses could confide their worries, but Edith Cavell was reserved and uncomplaining and made no particular impression on her. Her reserve was often misinterpreted, and being a probationer nurse at the age of thirty-three set her apart from the others.

Eva Lückes seldom gave unequivocal praise or blame in her recorded comments. She viewed her nurses as girls, wanted them all to succeed and helped their careers in every way she could, but often they proved a bar to the excellence she wanted for her hospital. She found them unrelentingly human: Amelia Brandon was 'big and clumsy . . .', Elizabeth Margaretta Rees was 'slovenly and untidy'. Elizabeth Herbert went off with a man and became engaged. Fanny Eastland contracted typhoid fever. Ruth Gow was fetched away abruptly by her parents. 'They collected her and her father shouted at everybody.' Winifred Livingstone was 'an excitable sort of girl, not well-adapted to Hospital work. She did not get on well with her fellow workers and they were under the impression, apparently with some justification, that whenever there was extra work to be done she retired with a headache! She was threatened with flat feet . . .' Eliza Crowe stole another probationer's clothes and left to go to the Metropolitan Hospital. Dora Morris was careless in breaking hospital property. Annie Simpson Sinclair was summoned to nurse her father after two months at the hospital. 'She simply did not return and we heard no more of her.' Gwendoline Harman was 'intensely conceited and not very clever. She expended more time over professing to love the work than in endeavouring to make her individual share of it thorough.' Bertha Waterhouse was vague and self-absorbed, walked in her sleep and had 'a morbid mental condition'. Sophia Jewell was a very capable probationer and had 'the distinction of being the first Jewess holding our certificate. This was not because Jewesses have never entered for training before, but they have lacked either the health or the energy to succeed.' So it went on. A stream of young women who remorselessly fell short of perfection.

As a private staff nurse Edith Cavell went first to Ilford in Essex to nurse a man with terminal cancer and his distraught wife. He died after three weeks. She was then sent to Tottenham for a fortnight to look after a woman with pleurisy and pneumonia; then, for three months, to nurse a fourteen-year-old boy with typhoid in West Norwood. He recovered and she was sent to St Mary's Vicarage in Marlborough where the eight-year-old son of the Bishop had appendicitis. Then it was heart failure in Lewes, cancer at Woburn, an eighty-year-old with gout in Gloucester and, at the end of the year, three weeks at the Royal London Ophthalmic Hospital because the matron there was short of staff. She then took her allotted two weeks' holiday in Swardeston: country air, family, and a short break from obligation. For her fourth year, Miss Lückes needed her to return to the hospital as Staff Nurse on Mellish Ward, a men's surgical and accident ward. Her hours on duty were 7.00 in the morning until 9.30 in the evening with three free hours. The pay was £24 a year. It was to prove a difficult time.

13

MELLISH WARD

The hospital bedspreads at the London were blue-and-white check. Probationers were taught to ensure that precisely nine squares hung over the end of each bed they were making. When the squares did not align, Ethel Hope Beecher, daughter of a colonel, granddaughter of a general, and Sister of Mellish Ward from May 1897 to December 1899, would strip the covers off the beds to humiliate the recalcitrant bed maker. Eva Lückes described Ethel Beecher as 'a smart sister, her nursing instincts beyond question', but she found her excitable temperament, outbreaks of temper and lack of self-control 'much to be deplored'.

Mellish Ward, a men's surgical and accident ward, 1905

In October 1899 the South African government gave an ultimatum for Britain to remove all its troops from the region within forty-eight hours. The Boer War followed Britain's refusal to do so. The British thought the war would be over in two months. It went on for two and a half years. In December 1899, the month when Edith Cavell had her thirty-fourth birthday and started as a staff nurse on Mellish Ward, in one week there were Boer victories at Stormberg, Magersfontein and Colenso, with 2,300 British soldiers killed or wounded. Six nurses were sent from the London to tend the wounded men. Sister Beecher was one of those who sailed from Southampton on the ocean liner *Dunottar Castle* on Christmas Day.

She took with her her favourite staff nurse, Elizabeth Kelso Hamilton, to Eva Lückes's regret: 'I was sorry to lose her from our own nursing staff. E. K. Hamilton was devoted to her work and to her patients. I should always be glad to receive her again should she desire to return to us in the future.' Their going left a vacuum in Mellish Ward. Ethel Mary Jordan was then appointed sister with Edith Cavell as staff nurse. Ethel Jordan was 'one of those women who meant well and are always full of good works', Eva Lückes said. But within weeks of her promotion she had a bicycling accident 'which unfortunately necessitated her having her left arm amputated to the elbow.' She then worked in the matron's office, making convalescent arrangements for patients.

Nurse Jordan's misfortune might have forwarded Edith Cavell's career. Had she then been made Sister of Mellish Ward her whole life would have been different. She wanted preferment at the London Hospital. But because of the year of private nursing, away from hospital work, and Eva Lückes's reservations about her, she was consigned to another year as a staff nurse. The sister's job went to Lilian Gough though she had arrived as a probationer a year after Edith Cavell and was four years her junior. It was hard for Edith Cavell to see younger nurses get the senior jobs. Her friend Fanny Edgecombe had been appointed Sister Victor – the sisters were known by the names of the wards they ruled – three years earlier at the age of twenty-two after two years as a probationer. Eva Lückes liked her punctuality, attention to rules and 'taking manner and prepossessing appearance'. She said she was a 'smart' nurse, her theoretical work good, and she would make an above-average sister, though she was 'very self-opinionated and absolutely certain that she knew best . . . Her manner was partly due to shyness partly to conceit.'

Though meticulous and orderly, Lilian Gough – Sister Mellish – was also lesbian, and her love affairs intruded into her management of her staff. Nurses were not allowed to consort with the doctors nor to continue working if they married, but nothing was prohibited about lesbian love. There was just no mention of it.

Mellish was a men's surgical ward with a heavy intake of emergency cases. The work was worse than dramatic. There were big breweries in the neighbourhood and draymen were often admitted from them after accidents caused by drunkenness. Minor operations were carried out on the ward. Screens were drawn round the bed and as the lighting was poor – gas brackets with burners – light was achieved by a nurse holding a paraffin lamp. Ether was the usual anaesthetic and was usually given through a Clover's inhaler. Patients did not slip lightly into unconsciousness and students would be called to restrain the more muscular of them. The doctors' rounds were occasions of ceremony. The surgeon wore a frock coat; his attendant, in a white coat, had a wooden tray round his neck with forceps, scalpels, catheters and steel dilators.

Sepsis was a huge problem. With deeply infected wounds the necessity for repeated changes of dressings wore down the patient's morale. Severe cases were moved to the two 'septic wards', Rowsell and Blizard. Acute cellulitis was treated by making multiple incisions in the infected skin and applying hot salt poultices. House surgeons and nurses suffered frequently from abscesses and infected fingers.

It was a demanding ward and required good team work from the nurses. This was not achieved under Lilian Gough. Adjoining the ward was her private sitting room with comfortable chairs and a coal fire. Each sister furnished the room according to her own taste, for it was her home for what might be twenty years. She had her meals in it and entertained her female friends.

At first Lilian Gough seemed to favour the night staff nurse, Nora Daly. Eva Lückes noted that Nurse Daly was for a time 'much liked' and 'rather spoilt' by the sister. But then Sister Mellish fell in love with the sister on Davis Ward – Lizzie McLellan. Eva Lückes wrote in her register that they 'struck up one of those morbid friendships'. Lizzie McLellan was thirty-one, widowed, and a good ward manager who taught the probationers well, but, the matron said, 'She was never conscientious or reliable, did not obey the rules and had encouraged a staff nurse to break a rule in a quite unheard of fashion.'

Nora Daly went to Eva Lückes to complain about the working conditions on Mellish Ward and to tell her she had no intention of obeying Sister Gough. Eva Lückes came down on the side of rank and did not investigate what dramas were going on, or what the practical implications were for the other staff of this 'morbid friendship'. She told Nurse Daly that if she did not 'obediently carry out the duties entrusted to her in accordance with the sister's wishes, she would be unable to retain her post'.

Edith Cavell was not given to asking for intervention or help. But the atmosphere was intolerable. Lilian Gough criticised and disliked her, was unfair in the division of work, and allocated tasks to her that should have gone to a probationer.

Edith Cavell put up with it for a year then went to Eva Lückes to tell her she wanted to leave the hospital. 'She is convinced that the ward sister has a prejudice against her,' Eva Lückes wrote in her matron's register, 'and after carefully going into this matter I could not but fear that there was some grounds for this conviction.' But she did not record how this prejudice manifested itself or suggest moving Edith Cavell to another ward. She advised her to resume private nursing, which Edith Cavell did not want to do. She also criticised the quality of her work: 'Edith Cavell is not a success as a staff nurse . . . She is not methodical or observant and she over-estimates her own powers. Her intentions are excellent and she is conscientious but without being quite reliable as a nurse. If she had been happier in her ward I do not think she would have wanted to leave the Hospital. . . . Edith Cavell is steady and nice-minded.'

Eva Lückes found her another job when Miss Moir, Matron of St Pancras Infirmary, asked her to recommend two night superintendents. 'I thought that Nurse Berridge and Edith Cavell would make an excellent combination and work well together. I recommended them accordingly. They obtained the appointment and Edith Cavell left the London Hospital on 3rd January 1901.' Three months later, in April, Nora Daly left the London Hospital too. She went to Liverpool as theatre sister at the women's hospital there. Eva Lückes might have wondered why two good staff nurses left because of their experience on Mellish Ward under Lilian Gough. Had she had time, she might have looked into what was going on.

That same month Sisters Gough and McLellan asked for permission to take their holiday leave together. Eva Lückes allowed this, though it was 'arranged with particular inconvenience'. When they got back Sister Gough, who was extremely nervous about her own health, had a small cyst removed from her groin because she was convinced it was something serious. 'She made a good recovery up to the tenth day when she suddenly became very ill with a curious heart attack. For a few days we were intensely anxious. Her friends were summoned, and her father, who had already had one seizure a few months previously, had another owing to the excitement of the journey and his anxiety about his daughter, so that he had to be warded in a little room in Cotton, while his married daughter and her husband remained here for some time extremely anxious about both patients. Fortunately both made a good recovery.' Neither the physicians nor the surgeons could find anything wrong with Lilian Gough or the reason for her curious heart attack. None the less, during the 'anxious stage' of this seeming illness her lover Lizzie McLellan was allowed to sit with her at nights, and a replacement sister had to cope with Davis Ward. And Eva Lückes promised that, when Lilian Gough recovered, she and Lizzie McLellan could again go on holiday together.

But, she noted in her register, neither of them behaved very nicely during this period of convalescence, which she thought ungrateful, after all the care and consideration bestowed on them both. And then when Lilian Gough recovered she said she must leave the London because her own physician at Clifton had impressed on her the necessity of giving up hospital work entirely. A day after she left, Lizzie McLellan resigned saying she was ill and needed a long rest and 'owed it to her father to spend some months at home'. Dr Warner examined her but could find nothing wrong with her either. Lizzie McLellan and Lilian Gough then ran off together. They stayed first in Bristol, then alone in 'a quiet place' in Devon.

So five months after causing Edith Cavell to leave, Lilian Gough was ensconced in the Devon countryside with her lover, and Mellish Ward was again in need of a sister. A year later Sister Gough visited Eva Lückes who was glad to see her looking remarkably well. She spoke with great regret of having had to leave the London and told her she was doing private nursing, which she did not like, though she had no difficulty in getting work. Dr Samuel Fenwick, who specialised in diseases of the abdomen at the London, had written offering to recommend her for the matronship of a small hospital, but she had not felt it would be wise to apply.

Caught in the fallout of the dramas on Mellish Ward, Edith Cavell had felt compelled to leave the London. It was a disappointment to her not to be made a sister there and to leave in a strained, unpleasant way. She was always to refer to it as 'the dear old hospital'. It was hard for her to achieve promotion for she did not flaunt herself, criticise others, or curry favour. In becoming a night superintendent at the St Pancras Infirmary, a Poor Law institution for the destitute chronically sick, she took on a nursing task of the most demanding sort.

14

THE INFIRMARIES

The infirmaries marked the beginning of state hospitals. They evolved out of concern for the poor, Florence Nightingale's crusade for improved workhouse nursing, and fear that the infections of the destitute sick would spread throughout the population.

The Gathorne Hardy Act of 1867, passed by the Home Secretary, Gathorne Hardy, gave statutory free medical provision to people with no money. After it, boroughs set aside part of their existing workhouse accommodation, or in time built new places, for the sick poor. The St Pancras Infirmary was built in 1885 and

Edith Cavell as Night Superintendent at the St Pancras Infirmary, c. 1901

Florence Nightingale recommended many of its nursing arrangements.

The infirmaries were maintained, with minimal investment, out of the rates. No destitute patient was refused if he or she lived in the borough, and no patient was admitted if he or she could afford to go elsewhere. After the Act, those for whom the voluntary hospitals could or would do nothing went to the infirmaries. Before it they would have gone to the workhouse, along with the 'aged infirm, the blind, the idiotic, the lunatic, the bastard child and the vagrant'.

The infirmaries remained, though, sinks of misfortune. They were staffed by medical superintendents, the less able doctors worked in them, and in a class-conscious society degradation was attached to them. Herded together were the senile; the mentally ill; unmarried mothers; people with venereal disease, inoperable cancer, diabetic gangrene; children with measles, whooping cough, bronchopneumonia.

When Edith Cavell went to work at the St Pancras Infirmary in 1901 the borough had a population of 235,317 of whom 6,307 were listed as paupers. In her first year there were 1,614 admissions of whom one in five died. There were high casualty rates from complications in pregnancy, from epidemics of diarrhoea in summer because of squalid sanitation, and from respiratory disease in winter caused by the city's fog.

As the two night superintendents, Edith Cavell and Emma Berridge were each responsible for 250 beds. The Infirmary, set in parkland, was in north London near Highgate cemetery. Edith had a room at the top of the building up many stairs. She came on duty at 8.30 in the evening before the day staff left. The patients, of all ages, had disparate illnesses, there were only three doctors and there was little specialist care. If a patient's condition became acute, she had to rouse the doctor on call. If a patient was dying the police fetched 'next of kin'. At the London the emphasis was on skilled treatment and cure. Patients were not accepted if medical or nursing treatment held no hope. Few stayed more than a month, they either died or left. The Infirmaries took the elderly, the paralysed, the demented, the inoperable.

An East End London street, c. 1900

That there was nowhere for most of them to go when they left, was a constant problem. Those who left alive went to the workhouse, to friends, to 'outdoor relief', or to a fever hospital if a place could be found.

From the start, Edith Cavell had reservations about working nights – not in shifts but permanently. It meant she was out of kilter with the hours of most people and cut off from the world. She maintained her friendships with nurses from the London, with Fanny Edgecombe and Eveline Dickinson, but it was hard for free time to coincide. She had reservations too about how much she could learn in such an underfinanced, understaffed setting. Within three months she answered an advertisement for a nursing vacancy at Swansea General Hospital, but was not interviewed.

She took such breaks as she could. Her sister Florence was night superintendent at an infirmary in Hendon in north-west London. She met up with her, went home to Swardeston or to the country with Emma Berridge, she spent Easter in Haslemere with friends, walking and sketching. On Sunday 30 June, after a day in the country, she returned rather late to London. It was raining heavily. She was mugged near Liverpool Street and her purse stolen. She was easy prey, a lone woman at dusk in the wet streets of the city. The Infirmary was in north London and it was too far to walk and too wet a night. She walked to the London Hospital and the night staff gave her a bed and money so she could return to the St Pancras in the morning. In her self-effacing way she wrote to Eva Lückes apologising for her own misfortune: 'You will have heard how very unfortunately I was placed on Sunday night . . . If I had had anywhere else to go I would not have returned to the hospital to trespass on the time of the night sisters . . . but it was too wet to walk and there seemed nothing else to do.' And there was nowhere else to go.

She returned to the demands of night superintendent but thereafter scanned the *Nursing Mirror* for vacancies.

For a month in August she stood in as matron of Cheshunt Cottage Hospital in Hertfordshire while the permanent matron was on leave. She was interviewed for the post of matron at Tavistock Hospital, but was unsuccessful. In October she applied for a job that sounded as demanding as the one she had: Assistant Superintendent at the Farmfield Reformatory for Female Inebriates at Charlwood in Surrey. The salary was £50 a year – less than she was getting at the St Pancras, but she was compassionate towards distress, wanted to get as wide experience as she could of all aspects of nursing, and she would not have been working nights. Eva Lückes gave her a bland reference: 'I believe Edith Cavell well fitted in every respect for the position she is seeking . . . She has good health and a gentle nurselike manner . . . She is thoroughly interested in her work.' She did not get the job. All senior nursing posts were heavily contested and she had come to the profession late. It was November 1903 before she had success with an application and she wrote of her hopes from it to Eva Lückes: 'You will I think be pleased to hear that I was elected yesterday to the post of Assistant Matron at Shoreditch Infirmary. I am glad to have obtained day work after my three years on night duty. Also I hope the position will prove a help for the future and the salary is better than the one I am receiving. I shall have the supervision of the wards, under Miss Inglis the Matron and be able to teach the probationers and improve their work; also charge of the linen room, and the laundry. It will be a new experience and I hope to learn much from it.' She was already looking toward the next step. She wanted to be a matron, teach, change people's lives and make a notable contribution.

The main entrance to the Shoreditch Infirmary,[6] which was

---

[6] It is now St Leonard's Hospital

adjacent to the workhouse and had evolved from it, was off Hoxton Street in the heart of London's East End. It was a crowded, insanitary area of slum dwellings, brothels, small workshops and large warehouses, with a population of about 120,000. It was the centre of Jewish immigration and the furniture trade.[7] Charles Booth, in *Life and Labour of the People in London*, in 1902 described it as an area of high poverty, prostitution and thieves. 'The character of the whole locality is working-class. Poverty is everywhere with a considerable admixture of the very poor and vicious.' People eked a living. 'Clobberers' patched clothes, 'dippers' stole handkerchiefs, watches and wallets, hawkers sold whatever anyone would buy, 'crawlers' begged for such food as they could get. There were timber merchants, pawnbrokers, egg merchants, tailors, coffee houses, herbalists, human hair merchants . . . Charles Dickens used to walk the area. He placed Oliver Twist in South Shoreditch and Mr Micawber in City Road.

The matron of the Infirmary, Miss Inglis, had trained under Eva Lückes. No particular affinity developed between her and Edith Cavell. 'I knew her,' Miss Inglis said, 'almost as well after our first meeting as I did at the end of the two years when she left Shoreditch. I liked her, I admired her unswerving sense of duty, but I never felt close to her. Kindliness and a charming personality made her loved by her nurses and patients, but I never knew anyone who felt that she really understood Edith Cavell.' Kindness and an unswerving sense of duty might have been enough in an assistant matron without the need to be really understood.

There were 120 nurses at the Infirmary. As assistant matron, Edith Cavell had her own sitting room as well as bedroom. She taught practical nursing to probationers and she supervised ward

[7] My great-grandfather Abraham Souhami had a veneer import business there

Mothers and babies in London's East End, c. 1902

sisters. She took care over the nurses' careers, arranged seaside holidays for sick children, visited patients after they were discharged, and was a pioneer of 'follow-up' work.

None the less she viewed the job as a stepping stone in her career. On 7 November 1904 she wrote to her London Hospital friend Fanny Edgecombe – no longer Sister Victor, but married to a surgeon, Robert Going, and mother to a newborn baby. She asked about the child and told of her own plans: 'What is she like? Eveline and I have been speculating and hoping she had hair and eyes like you – write to me and give a full description a little later on when you are up again – also what you are going to call her. I am beginning to think of a new appointment and am putting in for the Matronship of the Consumption Hospital at Ventnor – but again with little hope of success – so many are always in for these posts.'

Again Edith Cavell asked Eva Lückes for a 'fresh and more suitable testimonial – all the others I possess having been written under the Poor-Law and so not being so desirable in the view of a Hospital Committee', but she did not get that post, nor others she applied for, and when, after more than two years at the Shoreditch, Eveline Dickinson suggested to her that they take not just a holiday but a real break, and travel together for the summer of 1906, the opportunity seemed too appealing to miss. She wrote to Eva Lückes on 12 January about her hopes and fears: 'Will you forgive me for troubling you about my private concerns, but I am anxious to ask your advice in a difficulty? I have now been nursing for ten consecutive years without a break and feel very much in need of a long rest. The chance of one has just come, through the proposal of a friend that I should accompany her to the south of England and possibly abroad for three months from April or May. I am very anxious to accept, but fear it may be difficult to find another suitable post when I get back. I have been here over two years and feel that I have learned all there is to learn in our branch of the poor law. Would you very kindly help me in August – when I should be ready to return to work – if I wrote to you then? I know well how busy you are, and how little time you have to spare, but I feel I ought not to give up without some prospect of again getting a post.' Eva Lückes gave her an assurance that yes, she would 'certainly help her to get fresh work'. Edith Cavell packed her watercolours and her walking boots and went, not just for the usual allotted two weeks' summer holiday but for a much-needed break.

15

A HOLIDAY

In all, Edith took about six months off work. She left with no real security that she would get a job when she returned, but she was worn out. A photograph of her at the time showed her a stone lighter than in her governess days, her hands swollen from hard work. 'Ten consecutive years without a break', she told the matron she admired. In those ten years she had learned much about almost every aspect of nursing. She had worked as a fever nurse in Tooting; in the typhoid epidemic in Maidstone; in the relative privilege of the London Hospital; as a private nurse in the homes of the well-to-do who could afford to pay; in the Poor Law infirmaries.

Time after time she had assisted recovery and consoled the dying. She had done her best and more. Despite ten years of such service neither her religious faith nor her belief in individual sanctity had diminished. The icon of Christ and the message of love remained the guide to her compassion. She worshipped in church, prayed, read from the *Book of Common Prayer* and Thomas à Kempis, and highlighted in pen such texts as 'he is truly learned that doeth the will of God and forsaketh his own will'. She gave practical application to the Christian message and took to it an aspiration of heaven on earth where disease, poverty and suffering would be overcome. She had seen enough to know such paradise would not be reached soon. In ten years her character had evolved and her ambition hardened. Though as ever she asked little for herself, she wanted a matron's job because she wanted to make a difference to people's lives.

Eveline Dickinson, Sister George at the London Hospital, was the friend who, in the spring of 1906, suggested the holiday. Eva Lückes was put out when, soon after she received Edith Cavell's letter, Sister George handed in her notice. She did not know the two nurses were going away together. Eveline Dickinson was thirty-nine and intended to marry that September. Her husband-to-be, Alastaire McDonnell, was headmaster of Portora Royal School in Enniskillen in northern Ireland where Oscar Wilde had been a pupil from 1864 until 1871. (His name was rubbed off the honours list after his imprisonment in 1895.) She wanted a burst of freedom before settling as the headmaster's wife.

She had already resigned from the London once before in May 1902 'though it was right at the beginning of the holiday season and inconvenient, but Miss Dickinson always thought of herself', Matron wrote in her Register of Nurses. She returned to the London as a 'holiday sister', then went, at Sydney Holland's recommendation, to Osborne, on the Isle of Wight, to nurse the young men at the new naval college. She did not like the job and returned to the London, but had only been back a year as Sister George when she again told Eva Lückes that she wanted to leave, at the end of March 1906. 'She was very apologetic and said if she had known that would happen she would not have taken up a permanent appointment . . . She behaved quite well about it, but of course it is not good for the ward to have such frequent changing.' Eva Lückes described Eveline Dickinson as 'most grasping as to the off duty time'. Though 'emphatically smart', 'very methodical', 'an excellent manager', 'keenly interested in the intellectual side of the work' and with her ward always well kept, she was 'very self-opinionated and her influence on the probationers not good'.

Eveline Dickinson had overseen pioneer treatment of the skin disease lupus at the London. Her fault was to want a life of her own outside the hospital. She might have wanted to balance the two, but hospital rules precluded this. Total commitment was demanded of nurses, on a par with convent life and vows of chastity. Those who married gave up their jobs.

And so, before becoming a headmaster's wife, Eveline Dickinson had a summer with Edith Cavell. The two women were similar in age and independence of spirit and in their regard for 'the great East End Hospital', as Eveline called the London. They spent most of the time in north Cornwall with Eveline's family. Her father, who came from Ireland, had been the vicar of Bodmin, her mother had died when she was three and she was the youngest of six children. They stayed near Rocky Valley between Boscastle and Tintagel. There was woodland and waterfalls, cliff walks, views of Lundy Island. Edith painted watercolours of the coastal landscape: the basalt cliffs and the sea. She did a painting of the corn mill in the valley, Trevillet Mill, painted by Thomas Creswick in 1850.

It was a summer of outdoor living and of time with family and friends. It was restorative after the urban poverty of the East End infirmaries, the demanding hospital routine. She said she 'felt refreshed after a long and pleasant holiday'. She went to see the house where Eveline would live when married – 'in a very beautiful part of Ireland near Enniskillen and just above Loch Erne'. In London they spent 'a busy week' buying clothes for Eveline's trousseau and meeting up with mutual friends from the Hospital: 'What a great bond life together and training in the old hospital is, and what good and lasting friendships result to many of us from them,' Edith Cavell wrote to her matron. At some point Eveline gave her a long gold chain.

In September Edith stayed in Henley in Oxfordshire where her sister Lilian, now married, lived with her husband William Longworth Wainwright. He was a surgeon at St Thomas' Hospital and they had met when she trained as a nurse there. His father was the hospital treasurer. Another surgeon, a Mr Wallace, visited and spoke flatteringly of nurses trained at the London: 'Some from other places suffered much in comparison,' Edith wrote to Eva Lückes: 'I was asked to account for the difference and was very glad to have the opportunity of telling them of your lectures and personal influence and of the tone prevailing at our hospital . . .'

Back in Swardeston after a six-month gap she looked hard for another job as a matron, or superintendent, with a salary of no less than £60 or £70 a year. Her premium for the Royal Nurses Pension was £30 a year. She applied to be matron at the Leeds Workpeople's Convalescent Home, but though her testimonials from Miss Inglis at the St Pancras and Dr Froggett, the medical superintendent of the Shoreditch Infirmary, were paeans of praise, she did not get the job.

In September she was offered a temporary post as a 'Queen's District Nurse in the Sick Poor Nursing Branch of the Manchester and Salford Sick Poor and Private Nursing Institution'. (The Victorians were not given to subtlety when it came to describing provision for those with no money.) There was a great deal of poverty in Manchester. The Institution was financed with public money at the time of Queen Victoria's golden jubilee in 1887, and involved free home visits by nurses. Edith Cavell's appointment was supposed to be for six weeks only, but then the matron, Miss Hall, became seriously ill which meant she would be off work for several months. The Manchester Committee asked Edith Cavell to take charge. 'The Matronship is in my hands for the time being,' she wrote to Eva Lückes on 12 March 1907. 'I feel it rather a heavy responsibility as I know so very little of the Queen's work or the etiquette of this branch of the work. I feel I must try to fill the gap to the best of my ability.' As well as not knowing quite what to do, her branch of the Institution was understaffed. She asked Eva Lückes to send any trained nurses willing to fill a three-month post for a pro rata salary of £30 a year.

She supervised the nurses, assigned cases to them, learned how to deal with mining accidents and illnesses related to mining, sorted the administrative work and the budget for the Home. There was more administration than in her work in the large infirmaries but she was left in no doubt that this was a temporary job. The committee made it clear that Miss Hall would return in July to resume her role as matron.

So Edith Cavell was again on the watch for suitable work. She was forty-one, and though each new appointment widened her experience and was a challenge, it was dispiriting time after time to apply for jobs she did not get. She had experience in most aspects of nursing, but the senior posts were hugely sought after, her reserve and age meant she was often overlooked, and no one spoke up for her in a particularly ebullient way.

But then in May an offer came from Brussels. She was asked by Brussels' leading surgeon, Dr Antoine Depage, if she would become matron of the first training school for nurses to be set up there, to be opened in October. Depage was impressed by the English model of secular trained nurses, as described by Florence Nightingale. He wanted to work with such nurses. They were not to be found in Belgium. He was an innovator and reformer, and wanted, as matron of his pioneering School, an English nurse, with fluent French, familiar with the Belgian way of life, but who had trained at a leading London hospital. Mme Graux, mother-in-law of Marguerite François – to whom Edith Cavell had been governess twelve years previously – was President of the Ladies' Committee which was helping him set up the School. On the recommendation of the François family and with communication facilitated by Mme Graux, Dr Depage asked Edith Cavell to agree to take on the challenge and become the matron.

She hesitated. It would be a huge task. Nursing and medical standards and provision, structures of care, the application of research, had all advanced and were advancing in England in a systematic way. To nurse in Belgium would be like going back in time. 'Until the present they have only had nuns to nurse the sick and they are sometimes dirty and always ignorant,' she wrote. She would be unsupported and separated from friends, colleagues, and family. And yet this was perhaps truly the challenge for which she had been waiting and to which she was ideally suited. It combined her wide nursing expertise, her pioneering zeal, her desire to make a real contribution, her ambition to be a matron, her love of travel, her knowledge of French.

And so she said yes to Dr Depage. 'My work here is over,' she wrote to Eva Lückes in June 1907. 'I am going over to Brussels in August to get everything in readiness.'

PART THREE

16

SETTING UP

École Belge D'Infirmières Diplômées
Bruxelles

19th September 1907

Dear Matron,

Will it weary you very much if I give you a little account of
the new School which is about to be opened here? I arrived
two days ago and found the four houses which have been
made to communicate only partly finished and in much
confusion – the Committee absent on holiday except the
secretary and the president, who returned for a day or
two to welcome me – no servants – only a porteress and
nothing furnished but my sitting room, and we have to
open on October the 1st!

Four probationers are engaged already – all well educated
and full of enthusiasm – I shall see them next week – and
one patient has asked to come! There are many difficulties
in the way – the Committee think night nurses are not
necessary and that if a nurse sleeps on the same floor with
the patients that is sufficient; just now there is no one to
refer to and no money and many necessaries are wanting.
Everyone is very keen but very indefinite, they make notes
on paper of the things needed and there it ends – but I
hope to pull through by and bye and have a model training
school. The nurses sign on for five years, three for training

and two to be passed in private or institution nursing in the service of the School – at the end of that time they will receive their diploma and be able to leave.

There are to be numerous lectures and in the 2nd year the nurses will go to the Surgical Institute opposite for their surgical training (here we shall have only medical work). For this Institute, which belongs to the 1st Surgeon in Belgium, M. Depage, a Matron is wanted and he wishes me to write and ask you if you could send him one. It is a fine new building with two beautiful theatres and eleven rooms for patients thoroughly adapted and designed by him to fit the needs of modern surgery. He wants a nurse who will be able to arrange all his operations and be present to assist him – who will act as Matron, train the nurses and keep certain books. He will give her £50 a year and I think it will be an excellent post – she must speak French fairly well of course. Also he wants three trained nurses to work under him – he offers only £24 the 1st year and they need not have very much knowledge of French. The Institute opens in November. Perhaps from the point of view of money it does not seem worth having but I do think it is work that greatly needs doing and that those who come out should do so with the object of helping on this new movement which if started on the right lines should be of the greatest possible benefit to this country. It is pioneer work here and needs much enthusiasm and courage and intelligence – and as there are many still looking askance at it, it will require great tact also.

M. Depage desires that there should exist a cordial feeling and intercourse between these two Institutions and that I should be regarded as the Head Matron and that other branches should be opened in course of time to which my probationers should go to learn fever work, midwifery etc. Thus we might eventually have a colony of English women here as heads of the branches if we who come first can make a success of it.

I shall be glad to hear from you soon, if possible, as M. Depage is naturally anxious to be settled with a Matron and we feel sure you will know just the woman we want. They were all pleased here to know I had been trained under you as your fame has spread to Belgium and your books are sold in their shops. I have a copy in French and shall use it as the textbook for the 1st year.

Hoping you are very well dear Matron and have enjoyed your annual holiday,

I remain,

Yours affectionately,

Edith Cavell

Edith Cavell had arrived in Brussels with high hopes. The 'difficulties in the way' might have seemed insurmountable to someone less determined. She viewed herself as an ambassador for best English practice and wanted no less than to pioneer a reformation in Belgian nursing.

The premises for the new School were hardly ideal. M. Depage had acquired four domestic terraced houses, numbers 143, 145, 147 and 149, in rue de la Culture[8] in the leafy suburb of Ixelles, 2.5 kilometres south of the city centre. These had been roughly adapted and renovated with interconnecting doors cut through at ground floor and basement levels. Edith Cavell's office, sitting room and bedroom were on the ground floor of 143 with rooms for the probationer nurses on the floors above. Next door at 145 were the nurses' sitting room and dining room on the ground

[8] Renamed rue Franz Merjay after the First World War. Merjay lived at 183 rue de la Culture. He had eight children. He headed a Belgian resistance network and was shot in April 1917

The Training School for Nurses at 143–149 rue de la Culture, Brussels

floor, rooms for patients on the floor above, and at the top of the house an operating theatre and sterilising room. The other two houses were equipped as patients' bedrooms, a waiting room and a consulting room for doctors.

The Berkendael Surgical Institute 'with two beautiful theatres and eleven rooms for patients' was on the opposite side of the street. Antoine Depage was forty-five, energetic, a professor at the University of Brussels, and frustrated by poor standards of hospital provision in the city and the monopoly of nursing care by nuns, notably the Sisters of Charity of St Vincent de Paul. Despite opposition by the Catholic Church to the secularisation of nursing, he campaigned in the universities and hospitals for change. In his own medical units, aided in the enterprise by his wife Marie who was also a nurse, and with Edith Cavell as head matron, he intended to set the new standard.

Depage could not have appointed anyone more dedicated and conscientious than Edith Cavell. Her School was to be a hospital, a private nursing home, a training school for nurses and an agency for finding them employment when they qualified. She intended to bring all her good sense and determination to the challenge. But she arrived to find Depage had no effective support structure or secure funding to offer her. Single-handed she worked to impose the standards of the London Hospital and of Florence Nightingale on what started as a Belgian family concern. She was alone in an unfamiliar setting, far from work colleagues, family and friends. Though her French was fluent she had not spoken it for a decade and she had to learn a medical vocabulary.

She took her old matron Eva Lückes as her role model and guiding light. She turned to her for support, guidance and encouragement. In her first two years in Belgium she wrote frequently to her, voicing anxieties, seeking help and advice, reporting on progress, and mainly asking her to send out qualified nurses to teach at, and staff, the School and Berkendael Surgical Institute. Eva Lückes did all she could. Despite her sharp comments, she was diligent in helping the nurses she had trained and her interest in them lasted throughout their working lives.

The School opened, makeshift though it was, on 1 October: the interconnecting doors were cut between the houses; the furniture arrived; there were four patients with more anticipated, and the four probationers began their lectures in elementary anatomy and physiology, hygiene, internal diseases, the administering of drugs and general nursing.

Each day brought problems. In response to Depage's request for a matron for his Surgical Institute Eva Lückes sent over a Miss Linda Maude. 'I am most grateful to you,' Edith Cavell wrote, 'and feel sure she will be most useful to us.' Miss Maude was to work as Edith Cavell's assistant until the Institute was ready. But from the start her French was most peculiar and 'Monsieur Depage was quite unable to understand what she said. I hoped she would soon become more proficient as she would

Dr Antoine Depage (1862–1925)

hear it spoken but she seems to find it very difficult. Also she does not fall in easily with the manners and customs of the people. Depage thought it would give a bad impression to his clients. She's very disappointed.' He appointed a Belgian matron and Miss Maude was made superintendent to the nurses. As for the three English-trained nurses he had asked Edith Cavell to find, he did not wait for her to achieve this, but hired three Dutch nurses instead 'as they do not expect so much salary'.

He was a difficult man to work for: impulsive and short-tempered. When there were disagreements, his wife Marie tried to conciliate. As for the Ladies' Committee, comprising well-heeled Brussels women, they were, Edith Cavell said, 'on the whole very nice', pleased with her management and keen for the project to succeed, but they were apt to intervene erratically or not be around when decisions needed to be made: 'A few are anxious to limit one's authority and even object to my offering tea to the people who call! I feel this is a little hard under the circumstances.'

Nor did the doctors or patients conform to the English model. 'The doctors are unused to being waited on. They even would help to make beds and draw the sheets if I would let them.' And then there were their liberal views on 'passing the male catheter'. Edith Cavell asked Eva Lückes to give her opinion in writing: 'The doctors here hold that all nurses should do it and that it should be part of their work. It has been brought up continually against the nuns that they are not allowed this work and unfortunately into the doctors' attitude to the question enters a little political feeling. The nuns, for them, represent the Catholic party who form the government by a vast majority and as the School is supported by liberals, the ways of the nuns are anathema. I am very anxious that we should adopt the English idea here and that the nurses should only do it under quite exceptional circumstances. If you would be so very kind as to send me your opinion on the subject (not for myself of course as I know it so well) it would have a good deal of influence. I have also written to Miss Van Eck in Holland and Miss Elston in France to know what is usual in those countries.'

She did not want her nurses to be obliged to handle men's

genitals – only 'under quite exceptional circumstances', presumably like unconsciousness or dementia. It was all too lax and familiar and most unlike the London. And the patients' friends were another problem. 'They go into the kitchen and return with broth or other things to give to the patients or order their meals for them. One woman I found sitting over the kitchen fire in close conference with the cook, having been there the greater part of the afternoon . . . Dear Matron, I hope I do not weary you with all these details.'

Such disregard made it hard for Edith Cavell to assert her authority the way an English matron must. Her main problem was in finding young women whom she considered to be of the right class to sign on as probationers. As a profession, nursing in Belgium was held in even lower esteem than in England in the 1860s. The nuns did it as a supposed service to God, but it was not regarded as a respectable job. Nor were the salaries offered by Depage an incentive. And Edith Cavell had quickly to modify her dream that all her teaching staff and senior nurses should be trained at the London, for even had the pay been good and the work appealing, not many English nurses spoke French.

Recruiting domestic staff was difficult too. They thought it demeaning to take orders from nurses or to serve them their meals. In the psychology of service it mattered that the served should be of superior social standing.

By the end of 1907 Edith Cavell had five probationers: Clara Böhme who like Edith Cavell had worked as a governess, Hélène Stoops, Emilie van de Velde who was thirty-seven and left after a year because she thought she was too old, Noemie Delaunoy and Valentine de Wolf who was a relative of M. Depage but also left within a year. After their three-month trial period all five refused to sign their contracts unless the stints of night duty were altered from a month to a week. 'I had eventually to yield,' Edith Cavell wrote, 'or see them all depart, in which case it would have become known that they left on account of the severity of the regulations. Then I should never have been able to get anyone else.'

None the less by Christmas a fair beginning had been made. There were patients in some of the beds, the probationers had signed their contracts, and the Ladies' Committee provided a tree and presents for all the staff. 'Two of my pupils seem likely to make excellent nurses,' Edith Cavell told Eva Lückes. 'I find them unpunctual and rather noisy but the patients are devoted to them and we already have a reputation for nursing well.'

17

THE SCHOOL GOES ON

'I feel glad to tell you that the School still goes on!' Edith Cavell
wrote to Eva Lückes at the beginning of 1908. 'As it has so many
difficulties to face that single fact alone is quite a consolation
in itself. I never know from day to day what may happen next.'
The School building was hugely inconvenient. The basement
kitchens swarmed with cockroaches and were damp; there were
no lifts; meals had to be carried on trays up steep stairs, and
patients needing operations in Depage's Surgical Institute had
to be carried down these stairs, out into the street and into the
building opposite.

The rooms were cramped and so poorly lit that night nurses
who wanted to study went into the operating theatre at the top
of 145 because it was the only room with enough light. It was an
awkward room for surgery. It was at the top of the house, it got
steamed up and it smelled of chloroform and ether. Nurses who
felt faint had to leave. The patient had to be helped onto the
operating table and water for sterilising was boiled in a kettle.
Edith Cavell in a long white gown would stand at a small table
and hand instruments to Dr Depage or another surgeon. In the
middle of an operation a nurse might be sent out to the Clinic
opposite to get some required piece of equipment.

Edith Cavell took the edelweiss, with its connotations of purity,
as the School's symbol and designed a uniform: dark blue for
herself with a starched white collar and cap, light blue for the
nurses, with white linen aprons, collars, sleeves and caps. She saw
this uniform as symbolic: 'The contrast which they present to

Edith Cavell with her staff nurse and probationers, Brussels c. 1909

the nuns, in their heavy stiff robes, and to the lay nurses in their grimy apparel, is the contrast of the unhygienic past with the enlightened present.' Some probationers felt stupid in it and said workmen threw things at them when they went out. Each new probationer when she arrived was shown into Matron's 'dark little office' then taken down to the sewing room and fitted with two blue dresses with elbow-length taped sleeves with detachable white cotton extensions to make them full-length (for meals and interviews); six white bibbed aprons and six starched 'Sister Dora' caps[9] to be perched on her head 'like Matron wears hers'. The nurses preferred them at an angle. They thought they looked prettier. Looking pretty was discouraged. Each day Edith Cavell sent one or other of them upstairs to 'put her cap on properly'. At times she called them as a group into her office and made them arrange their caps in front of her – the strings tied tight at the back.

The probationer's day began at 5.30 a.m. She filled water jugs,

[9] Named after an Anglican nun, a pioneer nurse, Sister Dorothy Pattison (1832–78)

cleared the locker tops, washed her patients' hands and feet, found out what they must have for breakfast and carried it up from the kitchen on trays. Her own breakfast was at 7.00. Edith Cavell was there at all meals. She sat at the head of the dining table with a watch beside her noting who was late.

Each probationer had patients assigned to her. A later probationer, Nurse Moore, described the challenge of her first patient. She had not seen a naked man before. She had to do everything for him, feed him, wash him all over. She used a large towelling sheet over a waterproof and asked him to wash his genitals himself.

As at the London, practical nursing at probationer level involved a great deal of cleaning: the tops of wardrobes, ledges, lockers, mantelpieces, the iron bedsteads and rails, the floors to be mopped with a bucket and long-handled scrubbing brush, covered first in a wet cloth, then a dry one. On her ward rounds Edith Cavell would run her finger over a surface to check for dust then say, 'The dusting should be done by ten, nurse.' Cleaning the operating theatre was the worst job: the smell of chloroform, bloodstained linen to be removed, everything to be washed and scoured – the tiled floor, shelves, bottles, lockers.

At 10.00 the probationer had a coffee break, made her own bed and put on a clean apron before accompanying the doctor on his rounds.

Each nurse had her own room with a single bed and a stove. Ruth Moore described the delight of two hours' free time a day 'to lie on one's bed with a book, throw off one's uniform, go out, buy a new hat . . .'

Edith Cavell's attention to detail in setting up the School was unremitting. She oversaw care of patients, nurses and probationers; instructed domestic staff; planned and implemented projects with Depage and the committee; interviewed prospective nurses; lectured the nurses and went to the doctors' lectures given to them; did all the administrative work and accounting and sending of bills to patients and their relatives. If there was an operation she assisted the surgeon.

Her main and ongoing problem, on which the success of the enterprise depended, was recruiting probationers and nursing staff. Her dream of 'a colony' of English matrons and sisters, as heads of branches of nursing throughout the city, was elusive. In January 1908 she looked for a teaching sister. Helen Graham, a nurse working in Bruges, and recommended by Eva Lückes, agreed to work for six months at the School. 'I was very glad to take her,' Edith Cavell wrote, 'as I should feel so sure of her teaching and her work and only hope she may feel inclined to stay longer when she has been with us a little while. The air is very good and bracing and the work not so hard, so she will be able to recruit at the same time.' Miss Graham was not inclined to stay. She was 'a great help' but in the summer went back to London and got married.

In April 1908, in the hope of attracting probationers, Edith Cavell published an account of the School in London's *Nursing Mirror*:

One house has been fitted up as a home for twelve nurses. They have a sitting room with a piano. The three adjoining houses provide twenty-four bedrooms for patients each of whom pay 5–8 francs a day. There are gas rings in the bathrooms for boiling water and sterilising instruments. Five pupils have had the courage to come forward and they are already settling down to their new life and seem happy at their work. Each one has five patients to look after. They breakfast at 7 a.m. Then they wash their patients and give them their breakfasts. During the morning they accompany the doctor on his rounds and carry out the treatments which he orders.

Our probationers must be between twenty and thirty-five. They can be of any nationality but French is spoken. Uniform is provided – outdoor uniform is not worn – and they are paid 180 francs their first year, 240 their second, and 300 their third. During their fourth and fifth years they will be paid in proportion to the work they do for the School.

After two months' trial each one is required to sign on for five years. The first three years will be devoted entirely to training; the first in the School, mainly medical nursing; the second in a surgical clinic; the third to the nursing of infectious cases and to midwifery. They will then be required to pass an examination and, if successful, will be granted diplomas after which they will be employed in private nursing homes, as the commitments of the School dictate.

The object of the School is threefold; first to create a profession for women; secondly to forward the cause of science; thirdly to provide the best possible help for the sick and suffering. These first nurses of ours will in the years which lie ahead teach, as no others have ever had the opportunity of doing, the laws of health and the methods of treating disease. They will also prove to their countrymen that education and position do not constitute a bar to an independent life for a woman, as so many seem to suppose over here. Indeed they will show them that education and position are in point of fact good and solid foundations on which to build a career which demands the best and highest qualities that womanhood can offer.

It was hard for Edith Cavell to persuade others to share her view that exacting unremunerative work was worth doing for its own sake. The stigma was ingrained that this was a menial job on a par with cleaning. Probationers served a three-month trial. They paid a fee for this, returnable when they then signed their contracts. Some sacrificed the money and left before their trial time finished. It was particularly hard to find Belgian probationers. Respectable mothers no more wanted their daughters to train as nurses than to go on the stage. The cooks and servants baulked at serving nurses and the doctors treated them as menials. 'I thank you Madame for your letter explaining your daughter's difficulties,' Edith Cavell wrote caustically to a mother whose daughter felt demeaned by the work she was expected to do. 'Such difficulties are unavoidable with all young girls of the wealthier class until they come to recognise that work is not a social stigma . . . Fortunately, in other countries, women of the same class, who have chosen nursing, understand that the only way to elevate the profession to the dignity which it deserves is to put into it all their devotion and their effort. I hope that in time the several excellent foreign students here will encourage the Belgian girls themselves to set an example which will promote and popularise the nursing profession in many ways. We cannot necessarily hope that the girls of the lower classes will progress as swiftly or as well. But we are none the less grateful for the efforts they put forth. I will be pleased to see you during your visit to Brussels. Rest assured that our pupils, far from suffering physically, generally become more robust.'

In September 1908 she went for a few weeks to Swardeston. It was hardly a holiday. She heard that the baby born to Eveline Dickinson, now Mrs McDonnell, had died. 'It is a great grief.'[10] On the School's notepaper she urged Eva Lückes to find her another London Hospital-trained sister now that Sister Graham had left. Her replacement was 'not a good nurse and still less a good teacher. I am afraid I shall never be satisfied with any other

[10] Eveline Dickinson had been Sister of the Light Treatment Ward at the London Hospital and exposed to radiation

than a Londoner to train the probationers. Other methods do not please me and I am anxious to introduce the very best into Belgium. Have you a nurse you could spare? One who would come out soon and would take an interest in the nurses and the work for its own sake? The salary is £40 a year with uniform and washing. . . . The School seems likely to be a success but the difficulties are innumerable and the greatest is the character of the women – unused to liberty they abuse what they have and the most constant supervision is necessary.'

Eva Lückes sent out Sister Eleanor Evans, who proved 'most satisfactory', and a number of staff nurses to work at the School or with private patients. But however many nurses her matron provided, Edith Cavell needed more. She sent a resistible request for a private nurse who spoke no French: 'The patient is a woman of 40 suffering from hysteria. She weeps and is unable to walk and is hypersensitive. The relations however are the worst feature and they are going unfortunately to Cannes with the patient in January for 3 or 4 months. They will want a nurse to stay with them the whole time and I really think it would be just as well if she spoke no French as she would not understand all they have to say.'

Toward the end of 1908 Edith Cavell's hard work began to show results. 'People are beginning to realise the necessity of better nursing and are coming round to English methods,' she wrote. The School became a model of good practice with a reputation for high standards of training and provision. A Dr Pierart asked Edith Cavell to find a matron for the Hospital St Jean in Brussels. Two years earlier lay nurses had been introduced in two wards there. There were five of them looking after fifty beds with no one to supervise them. The work needed courage, firmness and tact to avoid conflict with the nuns. Sister Evans took the challenge, became the matron and proved a great success, 'in every way devoted'. Her starting salary was £80 a year. In time she started a teaching school at that hospital too. Her going left Edith Cavell again without an assistant matron. 'If you could recommend me someone . . .'

Edith Cavell kept her vision, her aspiration for excellence, and by hard graft made the project work. At the end of the year she wrote to tell her mentor that things were going fairly well. Her five probationers 'should make good nurses in the end'. They had been taught anatomy, physiology, hygiene and medicine by Professor Héger, the elderly physician who headed the committee overseeing organisation of the School, and by Dr Le Boeuf, and she herself gave lectures on the art of nursing. She and they had looked after fifty-seven patients according to the principles of nursing set out at the London Hospital.

The following year, 1909, twenty-three probationers signed on for the training course. The number of patients doubled and more doctors sent patients to Edith Cavell for medical and nursing care, and themselves wanted to work at the School. 'Among the things that a nurse must learn,' wrote a doctor on the committee, 'is that there is much that cannot be taught by a professor. Even constant practice at the bedside is not enough. Character has to be shaped. A sense of responsibility has to be inculcated. This is achieved by the intimate evening talks which our Directress has with all her pupils. It is quality rather than quantity in the production of nurses for which we will always aim.' Edith Cavell aimed for both. Two new Brussels schools, modelled on hers, were opened that year at the hospitals of Sainte Camille and St Jean.

Her reputation spread. In the summer she attended the International Congress of Nurses in London as part of the Belgian delegation and gave a lecture on the School's hopes and ambitions. In Brussels, too, she gave public lectures. The city council asked her to provide visiting nurses for all the children in the twelve state schools. She was asked to find nurses for provincial hospitals, private clinics, general practitioners, a tuberculosis hospital in the village of Buyssingham. Her abiding problem remained where to get them. Back home, when seeking work for herself, she had lamented that there were more applicants than posts to be filled. Now it was the reverse. She advertised in the *Nursing Mirror*, sent endless requests to Eva Lückes and even resorted to posters on walls: *Young Girls Wanted*, these read, in large red letters. She took such nurses as she could find, and gave them tuition until her own probationers qualified. An extra house was taken on as an additional nurses' hostel in rue de la Culture.

Within three years the dream of transformation became a reality. In 1910 a new hospital opened in the suburb of St Gilles, half an hour's walk from the School. Financed with government money, and with its upkeep paid for out of the rates, it provided medical care at the point of need. Depage was its leading surgeon and he and the committee asked Edith Cavell to provide its nursing staff and become its head matron. Her nurses took their second- and third-year training at the new hospital, rotating between wards. Dr Pechere lectured them in paediatrics; Dr Godart on diseases of the digestive tract; Dr de Meyer in ophthalmology; Dr Buys on diseases of ear, nose and throat and Dr Weymersch in obstetrics. At the end of their third year these highly trained nurses were sent to the clinics, schools, hospitals and private homes in Edith Cavell's care.

Compared to the School and the Berkendael Surgical Institute in rue de la Culture, the St Gilles hospital was a model of modernity. It was all on one floor, light and airy, with sliding windows, long wide corridors and well-kept gardens. It had 250 beds, a maternity ward, an isolation block, a large outpatients' unit, a children's ward with cots and toys. There was a huge linen room, a kitchen with a gas geyser, a sluice room with a bath. For the nurses who transferred there from the cramped dark rooms and steep stairs of rue de la Culture, it eased their work and raised their morale. Maids polished the floors with mechanical polishers. Edith Cavell appointed a Miss Mann as acting matron, visited every day herself, and gave particular attention to the children's wards which were decorated in bright colours.

That same year she was on the editorial board for the launching of *L'Infirmière,* which became Belgium's professional journal for nurses, equivalent to England's *Nursing Mirror.* She called her introductory article 'Le Devoir d'une Infirmière': the duty of a nurse – toward her patients, their family and friends, toward the doctors, herself and her School. In accord with Florence Nightingale and Eva Lückes was the central idea that no effort was too great for patients in a nurse's care.

After their probationary year, nurses were sent by Edith Cavell to work on the wards at St Gilles and attend lectures there, or to work in the other hospitals she staffed. Jacqueline van Til, a Belgian probationer, joined the School the year the St Gilles hospital opened:

> When I came in 1910 she was already at the head of several
> hospitals in Brussels, together with the Tuberculosis
> Hospital at Buyssingham, a little village in Wallonie,
> Belgium. We nurses were all obliged to be trained in
> different hospitals because the School was too small. For the
> first year we were under Matron's special care and received
> lectures from the physicians. During our second we went
> to the different hospitals which she staffed. There were few
> Belgian girls in the clinic . . . Some came from Germany,
> some from France, some from England. But we all had to
> speak French on duty. In 1910 we numbered sixty . . .
> Miss Cavell never objected to mixed nationalities, but
> she required obedience to her orders. Her remarks were
> often severe and laconic and we never dared to be late for

meals . . . Three times a day she would walk to the various places where she sent nurses, and every night we were required to attend a class in her room. She was indefatigable in her teaching and never spared herself anything that demanded hard work . . . We would often be called to her office to be admonished for laughing too loud or to be warned to be more careful about our manners.

18

FAMILY LIFE

At heart Edith Cavell was not a martinet. She was, though, a Victorian, with a frosty way of enforcing discipline and rules. This came partly from her orthodox upbringing, partly from working and living in a closed female society, but mostly from her determination to train good nurses and make the School succeed. Her probationers were of disparate nationality – Dutch, English, German, Russian, Belgian. They were also of a different generation. Queen Victoria had died in 1901. (Kaiser Wilhelm II, her grandson, had been at her bedside.) Throughout Europe times were more free. The probationer nurses were separated from their families and would have liked some fun. 'The young girls are brought up with no idea of duty and are selfish and too fond of pleasure,' Edith Cavell complained to Eva Lückes.

She imposed the same rules of chastity as at the London Hospital: no married nurses, no going out with the doctors or medical students, lights out and the front door locked by ten. There was no mention of lesbian love: 'morbid relationship' as Eva Lückes called it.

She meted out reprimands for a dusty ward, a badly made bed, talking in corridors, lateness at meals, a cap askew. She wanted every detail of compliant practice observed. Only the best was good enough, and the best meant discipline and constant vigilance. But she was mindful too of the need for love in the School into which she had moved. The poor and hungry called at the door knowing they would be given food and money. Payment terms were arranged for patients who had difficulty with the fees. At Christmas she always arranged a party for the children in her care.

The School was her home and she created an oddball family there. One day in 1910 a dog showed up at the garden door in need of a meal. He was grey on his back with fawn-coloured legs and a foxy tail. He had German shepherd and other species in him. Edith Cavell fed him, so he did not go away. Fiercely protective of her, he was always with her and barked and snapped at anyone who came too near. She called him Jack, walked the streets of Brussels with him, and cared for him according to the principles she had written out some fifteen years back for the François children on how to treat a dog. Mindful of her mugging at King's Cross on a dark wet night in 1901, she felt protected by him. He was top dog and walked ahead, but when he heard approaching footsteps would go to her side until the person had passed by.

The nurses were chary of him. He viewed them as sheep to be rounded up. He sat at Edith Cavell's feet at mealtimes. When the meal was over the nurses bowed to her then filed out. Jack liked to herd them up the stairs and nipped their ankles if they did not hurry or seemed to veer in the wrong direction. They came to dread it, what with the rule about not talking in the hallways.

Jack landed lucky when he chanced on Edith Cavell's care. It was the manner of her care: to find out what a creature needed in order to function well and to provide it if she could. Another dog, Don, came to the door at about the same time as Jack. He was given a welcome and a home, but he disappeared in 1911 amid a rumour he had been stolen.

Edith Cavell's personal rooms at the School were small and sparsely furnished. She had an austere view of what constituted enough, in material terms. An inventory of her things showed that by middle age she had not acquired much: an armchair, a

Edith Cavell with Jack and Don, two strays who arrived at
the School in 1910. Don, left, disappeared in 1911

walnut rocking chair, a tea set, family photographs, a few orna-
ments, a hundred books, a camera, a drawing block and paints,
a silk tablecloth, a rose linen cushion, a muff, a fur, a clock,
a few bits of jewellery, four vases, a few clothes, a bathing
dress . . . Such were her possessions. She ate modestly and seemed
not to concentrate on her food. 'Maybe that was why the food
was always so awful,' Nurse Moore said.

She was abstemious and self-denying and maintained, as religious people do, a dialogue with God: 'Give me instead of all
the comforts of the world, the most sweet unction of Thy Spirit,'
was one of the exhortations highlighted by her in Thomas à

Kempis's *Imitation of Christ*. And yet she created an unorthodox worldly family in Brussels. José, a young Rumanian, the porter and handyman, became a loyal member of her household. He lit the fires, helped carry surgery patients up and down the stairs and willingly did whatever she asked of him.

In 1911 Edith Cavell acquired a god-daughter. The chaplain at the Church of the Resurrection where she worshipped, the Reverend Philip Stocks, contacted her about a thirteen-year-old English girl, Pauline Randall, who had run away from her father – a showman with a travelling circus. She and her younger sister had no memory of their mother. A parishioner of the vicar, a Miss Butcher, had asked him to help. Edith Cavell gave Pauline a room at the School, became her godmother, arranged her education, put money into an account for her, gave her work as her personal maid and took her with her on summer holidays to the seaside in Norfolk. Some of the nurses were resentful and thought Pauline used her closeness to the matron to criticise them.

Grace Jemmett was another of her surrogate daughters. She arrived to live at the School early in 1909, sent out by Edith Cavell's brother-in-law, Dr Longworth Wainwright. The youngest of four children, she had become addicted to morphine after an illness. There was friction with her family, particularly her mother. Dr Wainwright advised a complete break. He knew the School was in constant need of money and thought that, as the Jemmetts were bankers and landed gentry, the monthly fee for Grace's care and lodging would be useful income. Grace's grandfather, George Elwick Jemmett, was lord of the manor in Ashford. In 1856 he had leased a field so the Ashford Cattle Market could be founded. It became the biggest cattle market in England.

Grace took up long-term residency at the School. She had bouts of debilitating depression when she stayed in bed for weeks on end. She called Edith Cavell mother and she too went on

Sister Wilkins, who worked at the School with
Edith Cavell from 1912 to 1915

holidays to England with her. Edith Cavell accepted that her
illness responded to management, not cure, controlled her
morphine intake and cigarette smoking, was patient with her,
and mediated with her unsympathetic family. She felt the
Jemmetts did not care for Grace and that their indifference
contributed to her problems.

It was a relationship that went beyond the boundaries of
ordinary patient care. But, as with Pauline, Grace's place in the
School was problematic. She chain-smoked, had extreme mood

swings and would search for the morphine supply Edith Cavell hid from her.

Sister Wilkins became another abiding member of this family. She replied to one of Edith Cavell's frequently placed advertisements for nurses. It was in the *Nursing Mirror* in the summer of 1912 and asked for a ward sister who could speak French. 'I was a Sister at the Royal Seamen's Hospital Cardiff,' Elisabeth Wilkins wrote in an unpublished memoir. 'There, we naturally got to know a smattering of many languages. I was specially interested in French and was a member of the Anglo-French Society.'

Edith Cavell offered her the job without interview, then wrote to her from West Runton, near Cromer in Norfolk, where she was on holiday with Grace:

My dear Sister,
I am very pleased that you will be able to take up your duties
soon. I shall not be in Brussels myself until Wednesday
August 7th, but the Sister in charge during my absence will
put you in the way of things. The work is good, there is
plenty of variety and we have some of the best doctors for
whom to work. I hope you will be very happy with us and
take a special interest in training the probationers.
Yours very truly
E. Cavell

Sister Wilkins arrived in Brussels on a Sunday and all seemed strange: 'even the thermometers different'. She was twenty-nine. She was put in charge of all the patients in the third house in rue de la Culture, number 147. At that time the house was divided into two wards of five beds, six private rooms, her sitting room and an outpatients' surgery. Her patients were a mix of surgical, medical and maternity cases, works accidents and children. She also had five probationer nurses to teach and a senior nurse to supervise for night duty.

Her first impression of the matron was of a slightly built woman with dark hair turning grey, rather withdrawn, uninterested in superficial friendships but thoughtful, pleasant and sympathetic to all her patients. She became Edith Cavell's deputy in work, her ally and friend, and so devoted to her and the School that she abandoned her plan to travel the world nursing in different countries.

For Edith Cavell nursing was her world; there was no cut-off between work and private life. She was, at centre, reserved and solitary, but to or for someone she wrote lines of doggerel, found among her papers after her death, that suggested a kind of desire:

> Storms may gather, O love, my love,
> But here shall thy shelter be
> And in my arms, my dear, my dear
> The sun shall come back to thee.
> The winter of age, O love, my love,
> For us no shade shall bring
> But in thine eyes divine, my dear, my dear
> For me, 'twill always be spring.

Perhaps it was just the gush in which Victorian maiden ladies expressed loving friendship for each other, but it held a whisper of romance.

If her nurses were ill, she did all she could for them. Jacqueline van Til in a memoir recalled being nursed personally by Edith Cavell who then arranged for her to convalesce at her sister Lilian's home, Upton Lodge in Henley-on-Thames. There, Jacqueline met her mother and her sister Florence, who was matron of Withernsea Convalescent Hospital. Florence Cavell too was fearless and devoted, strict but kind. She was matron there until she was eighty, liked cliff walks and gardening, kept a dog and cats.

Nor was Edith Cavell unremittingly stern. 'Did the patient suffer?' she asked Nurse Buck who complained when a drunk patient lunged at her and forced her to escape through a ground-floor window. 'A nurse's duty is to save life, not to take it,' she told Nurse van de Velde as she restrained her from stamping on a spider on the lecture room floor. If she chanced on a clandestine night-duty party for a birthday or as a leaving tribute, she let it pass, or made some mildly caustic comment about bringing a touch of home to the duty room. She seldom fired a nurse. She was not double-edged like Eva Lückes. She inspired devotion in patients and respect from the doctors. Nurse Moore heard a doctor say that Edith Cavell's nurses were as knowledgeable as his medical students.

At her evening lectures she showed another side of her character from the formidable matron who was a stickler for rules. In them she spoke of her belief in the sanctity of life, of the vocation of doing good, and of how devotion brought its own reward. Devotion, loyalty, steadiness and good management were the qualities she said a good nurse needed. The goals of nursing, she told her probationers, were to safeguard life, attend the wounded, allay suffering, help the doctors.

The content of her lectures ranged wide. She could draw well and illustrated many of them. She taught about the history of nursing, the 'renaissance' in English nursing, the duties of the nurse, the qualities of character needed, the various paths of opportunity: among the sick in the poorest quarters, as a 'missionary' of hygiene, as an academic, as a hospital superintendent.

She taught about the line of communication from patient to doctor; of the need for attention to the smallest detail and for constant vigilance; of crucial points to note in each type of illness. On practical matters she told her students how to administer drugs, give baths and wash patients, give injections, use probes, apply leeches and the cupping glass, how to clean the patient's room, make a bed, ventilate and disinfect a room. Every aspect of care, she taught, should be imbued with compassion. She told of how she tried to get the committee to finance supplies of talcum powder and methylated spirits to prevent bedsores. 'Madame,' one of the committee members told her, 'a bedsore is always a complication of a long illness like typhoid.' Not so, she told her nurses. It was a sign of neglectful nursing. They should rub the backs, heels and elbows of patients enduring long spells in bed.

One of her lectures was '*La Mort*'. She taught of the special needs of the dying and of those close to them and of how a true nurse would help a patient die in a state of grace, in peace and free from pain.

Her own father, the Reverend Cavell, died in June 1910 at the age of eighty-five. He had worked as a minister until a year before his death. His last entry in the Swardeston parish register was for a marriage service on 2 January 1909. When he retired, because of the terms under which he had built the vicarage for the parish, he and his wife Louisa moved to a modest terraced house in Norwich at 24 College Road. They relinquished the vicarage he had built, their family home for forty-five years. Edith went over for his funeral service and burial in Swardeston church-yard. In the summer she took her mother on holiday to the seaside village of West Runton, near Cromer. They stayed at Cumberland Cottage with a Mrs Harrison and her son Freddy. Grace Jemmett made the arrangements.

'We shall be with you on the 6th of next month,' she wrote to Mrs Harrison in late June from rue de la Culture:

and will stay till the 31st. We shall be three as Miss Cavell's mother will be with us – you will find us no trouble and of course for rooms it is alright as we have taken the two bedrooms and sitting room as before – Mrs Cavell will have the front bedroom and Miss Cavell and myself the back one. There is only one thing extra Mrs Cavell will want, and that is a hipbath every morning and one nice can of hot water, otherwise it will be just the same as last year. We shall be out nearly all day. If you cannot get hold of a hipbath we will see about hiring one when we come down. We shall come on the 6th and Mrs Cavell on the 8th or 9th. I know you will be sorry to hear Miss Cavell has lost her father just lately. We think the change at W. Runton will do Mrs Cavell good, after a very trying and sad time, and I know you will help us to make her comfortable. I hope you are well, and Freddy.

Yours sincerely

Grace E. Jemmett

The Harrisons' house was in the village centre and looked out over a duck pond. Next door lived a Mrs Tapscott, a schoolteacher, with whom Edith Cavell became friendly. A neighbour, Jack Thetford, met them from Sheringham Station in a pony and trap. Edith Cavell had bought this for summer holidays, and he made use of it for the rest of the year.

It was similar to Swardeston village life only by the sea: the church, the wheelwright, the publican, shopkeeper and corn miller . . . All that connected her to her tranquil childhood. It was a five-minute walk to the seaside. Cromer, a fashionable bathing town, was a mile away with its long stretch of sandy beach and tremendous cliffs 'much resorted to by sea fowls'. They went there in the pony and trap and to Sheringham with its ravine and wide bay and to the harbour at East Runton where the fishing boats came in. All along the Norfolk coast great quantities of fish were caught and cured or sent by train to London: cod, skate, whiting, crabs and lobsters.

After her father's death Edith worried about her mother living alone and without much money. She sent her a monthly sum and tried to persuade her to move to Brussels and live with her at the School. Mrs Cavell visited in December 1910 but could not feel at home. She did not speak French, and Edith worked intensely hard and could not spend much time with her. Nor was she at ease in the ménage of her daughter's acquired family: the doting Sister Wilkins; Grace Jemmett who seldom got out of her night clothes and searched the cupboards for morphine and tranquillisers; Jack, who bit everybody who tried to get close to Edith. Her daughter was a true Christian – of that she was proud. The sick at heart who came to her door found comfort and a home. But for herself she felt at home in Norwich and Norfolk, not in the middle of Europe. Her son Jack worked close by at the Norwich Union, she felt she could manage in her little house, she had a maid who cleaned and cooked, she stayed often with Lilian and her family in their large house in Henley. After Christmas at the School she went home to Norwich in January 1911. It was arranged that as usual Edith would come over in the summer. She always tried to be home for her mother's birthday on 6 July.

19

FRESH EFFORTS IN THE GOOD CAUSE

In 1912 Antoine Depage gave the opening address to the International Congress of Nurses in Cologne. 'The new Belgian School of Nursing has been an entire success,' he told them:

> Founded in 1907 it now provides nurses for three hospitals, three private nursing homes, twenty-four communal schools and thirteen kindergartens in Brussels. It also sends out private nurses. Our School is the benchmark for nursing standards in Belgium. But we do not have enough nurses. Demand on the School to provide and train them has grown greater and greater.

'The new Belgian School of Nursing has been an entire success.'
Group photograph of Edith Cavell and her nurses in the School garden, 1913

A new, purpose-built nurses' training school was needed. The four terraced houses in rue de la Culture, with their steep stairs and small rooms, had never been fit for purpose. A committee was appointed to advise, fundraise and find a new site. On it were representatives of medicine, the law, science and business from Brussels, Liège and Bruges. Ernest Solvay, a chemist and philanthropist, gave 300,000 francs. The committee worked to double that sum.

The new school had to be near the St Gilles hospital. Its chosen site was the corner of rue de Bruxelles and rue de l'École in the suburb of Uccle. A Monsieur Dewin was commissioned as architect. Antoine and Marie Depage and Edith Cavell advised him. There was to be a central block with lecture halls, treatment rooms and operating theatres, from which two wings would stretch out, with between them a triangular garden. One of the wings would provide rooms for fifty nurses, the other beds for thirty patients. Jacqueline van Til recalled how happy Edith Cavell seemed on the evening when she showed her the plans.

In April 1913 Edith Cavell wrote to Eva Lückes thanking her for sending her – as she did every year – a copy of her annual lecture to nurses at the London Hospital:

> It is pleasant to hear about the dear old hospital and to know oneself not quite forgotten. Your letter braces me to fresh efforts in the good cause. And one needs that bracing here! The work is still very arduous and uphill. The spirit of the people is so opposed to the spirit of nursing . . . But we enlarge our borders and the 'trained nurse' is making progress. All the new nursing homes and hospitals are engaging lay nurses now, and we have more demands than we can supply. The girls of this country come in very slowly and at present the School is cosmopolitan as at least half the pupils are still foreigners.

We have all the board schools under our supervision, with 12 nurses at work in them, and also a staff of 20 private nurses and our hospital, which I am thankful to say has made progress, will, I hope, be a model in point of view of good order, cleanliness and good nursing for the other hospitals in Belgium.

My Committee are very good and kind, and I always feel I have their support in any difficulty. They have the work very much at heart and have raised the necessary funds to build us a new school which will be worthy of the object. We hope to be installed in about 2 years.

With many thanks and most grateful remembrances of happy days under your care.

Yours sincerely,

E. Cavell

It was a letter of confidence and achievement. A far cry from her anxious appeals of 1907 when nothing was in place, not even the furniture, in rue de la Culture. In six years she had set a standard and 'all the new nursing homes and hospitals are engaging lay nurses now'. St Gilles was the model hospital for Belgium, she was honoured by the committee, the new School 'worthy of the object' was under way. She looked back to Eva Lückes, the inspiration of her own training, and forward to all she still needed to do.

That summer, in July, she went to Norfolk on holiday, after a successful and busy year, leaving Sister Wilkins in charge. She took Grace Jemmett with her. They stayed at her mother's house, then all went to West Runton. Sister Wilkins kept her posted about the School and sent her a photo of Jack which she was pleased to receive, though she thought he looked 'sad and mopy thin'.

I don't think he can be eating enough or perhaps he frets poor old chap – I am feeling very rested and quite ready to begin work again. The bathing always does me good. Unfortunately our tent with many others was swept away by a high tide and fierce waves last night and cannot be put up till it is calm again. Last year dozens were lost altogether at the time of the floods. It is still rough and stormy but looks brighter this afternoon. Miss Jemmett who sends you her love is looking very well and brown and amuses herself so well she does not want to return at all. We shall be back on Thursday or Friday week. I will write definitely when I know. My mother who is with us, is very well and does long walks up the beach. We often wish we had Jackie with us.

I suppose all the patients I knew have gone and that you have a number of new people. Is Mrs Stanton in yet?[11] It surely is time. And did not Sister Burt mention another Baby case for us soon now?

Have you any friends who would like to join the private staff? We always need a great many for the winter and I would rather have people we know.

With kindest remembrances my dear Sister,

Matron

All was going so well. The hard work showed rewards. Nothing on the horizon suggested her hopes would be dashed. Her workload was huge: overseeing the new building, supervising at the St Gilles and Buyssingham hospitals and at the Berkendael Institute, assigning nurses to private patients and schools, teaching probationers. She had every reason to suppose she would see her plans through. By the summer of 1914 the new School building was well advanced. She had cause to be proud.

[11] Clara Stanton, née Böhme, had trained at the School as a probationer. Her daughter Annie was the first baby born there

In seven years she had achieved so much. But her dream would not stop with one new nurses' school and one new hospital. From this beginning she wanted an army of well-trained nurses to spiral out from Brussels to the whole of Belgium and beyond.

Nursing, she told her probationers in her evening lectures, was 'a great and honourable profession'. Through it could be found 'the widest social reform, the purest philanthropy, the truest humanity'. Good nurses were 'the handmaids of that science which not only assuages and heals the suffering of today, but reaches on through ever-widening circles to the dawn of perfect manhood when disease shall be unknown, because the laws which scientists discover, and which they help to teach, shall have banished it and taught the world how to live'. She had taken the baton from Florence Nightingale and Eva Lückes. She wanted to hand it on to a dozen matrons like herself in a dozen more towns and cities.

The following July she left Brussels as usual for the same summer holiday in Norfolk. It was her mother's seventy-eighth birthday on the 6th. On 28 June there had been a murder in Bosnia. Archduke Franz Ferdinand, heir to the Austro-Hungarian throne, was inspecting imperial troops in Sarajevo – Bosnia had been annexed by Austria a few years previously. He was with his wife, Countess Sophie Chotek. Fourteen years previously they had married for love to the dismay of Franz Ferdinand's father, the Emperor Franz Joséf, who refused to attend their wedding and made clear their children would not succeed to the throne. The couple were driven from Sarajevo town hall in an open car. Their driver turned by mistake into a narrow street – Franz Joséf Street. As he tried to reverse out, a young man, Gavrilo Princip, a Serb nationalist, a member of *Mlada Bosna* (Young Bosnia), ran out of a café and fired two shots into the car at point-blank range. The bodyguard standing on the running board of the car told afterwards how the Countess slid to the floor, how the

Edith Cavell, Matron, 1914

Archduke appealed to her to stay alive for their children, how he choked on the blood that poured from his mouth . . . Princip swallowed cyanide but it did not kill him. He was arrested and beaten and died of tuberculosis in prison.

The news alarmed the monarchies of Europe. They feared for their thrones. The Austrian Emperor was eighty-four. A Serb nationalist had assassinated his heir. The Archduke's children were barred from succession by the circumstances of their birth. But for most of Europe this was just the Balkans. Their feuds were endless and dynastic and as tiresome and confusing as Irish enmities.

Edith Cavell went to her mother's little terraced house at 24 College Road in Norwich. There was a heatwave and Mrs Cavell found it enervating. She was arthritic and disinclined to travel, though she managed well enough. Her maid helped with her hip bath and prepared her food. Her best present was for Edith to come and stay.

Edith had travelled to England with Pauline Randall that year, leaving Sister Wilkins and Sister White in charge at the School. They had instructions to send a telegram if anything untoward occurred. Grace Jemmett chose to stay in Brussels with friends.

20

WAR DECLARED

On 4 July, there were two paragraphs in the *Eastern Daily Press* about the funeral service in Vienna for the Archduke and Countess, the anti-Serb demonstrations there and the burning of the Serbian flag, but most of the coverage was of the heatwave at home, the strains on the summer train service to coastal resorts and the seemingly endless internecine conflict in Ireland.

Edith spent a week at College Road with her mother, then as usual went to Cumberland Cottage at West Runton, to stay with the Harrisons. She rented the same two bedrooms and sitting room as the previous year. She and Pauline were out all day. They went to Cromer and Yarmouth. Year on year there was change: looser clothes, smaller hats, cyclists in bloomers, cars and motorised buses among the horse-drawn carriages. Twentieth-century freedoms filtered into provincial life, but in essence England stayed the same. It was the hottest of summers. There had been hardly any rain since March.

For three weeks after the murders in Sarajevo Europe remained calm. But the old Emperor of Austria, Franz Joséf, had agreed with Kaiser Wilhelm II of Germany, grandson of Queen Victoria, that there would be no negotiating with Serbia. On 23 July Austria gave a five-point ultimatum to the Serbian government:

1. They must officially condemn anti-Austrian propaganda, publish an apology and a warning to all Serbs that all anti-Austrian machinations would be punished.
2. They must ban all anti-Austrian publications and the

pan-Serb organisation *Narodna Odbrana* – Defence of the People.

3. They must dismiss all officers and functionaries unacceptable to the Austro-Hungarian government and accept the guidance of Austrian agents in these dismissals.

4. They must charge all those involved in the Sarajevo murder plot and any Serbian officials who made anti-Austrian utterances.

5. They must notify the Austro-Hungarian government of the immediate carrying out of these orders.

Serbia was given forty-eight hours to accept these terms. They were told to reply by 6 p.m. on the evening of 25 July and that there could be no extension of the time frame and no mediation from any quarter.

Britain's Liberal Prime Minister, Herbert Asquith, reported to King George, the Kaiser's cousin, that he thought this the gravest event for many years in European politics. Sir Edward Grey, the Foreign Secretary, said the ultimatum was 'harsher in tone and more humiliating in its terms than any, of which he had recollection, addressed by one independent Government to another'. But on the streets there was no particular panic. The *Eastern Daily Press* on 25 July had a paragraph about the shortness of the timescale of Austria's demands. It voiced concern about how Russia would respond, because of its rivalry with Austria for control of the Balkans, but this was viewed as a dispute between Austria and Serbia, not as one that could open the door to a conflagration that would engulf the world.

After two weeks in West Runton Edith Cavell went back to 24 College Road in Norwich and weeded and watered her mother's small garden, parched from the heatwave. She sorted things her mother could not manage. She planned to return again before Christmas; in the meantime she would send money and write often, and Lil and Flor and Jack were there to visit. For Edith Cavell news about hegemony and war was remote from her concerns. She lived in an all-female environment, her ambitions focused on her work as a nurse.

She visited her Swardeston friends Susannah and Mary Blewitt at the Old Rectory – the house they had lived in for over thirty years. After their father died they stayed on there together and gardened, managed the house, and grew vegetables. In seemingly unthreatened rural life they all had tea in the shade of the old wide cedar tree on the lawn by the lake. The scene was a quintessence of peacetime. The mood of late summer and the calm of an English garden. There was no sense of it being a last summer and that Balkan politics might bludgeon into this time-honoured, civilised, courteous life. In view for Edith Cavell was all that had informed her childhood: the church where she had endured her father's dull sermons but found her own piety; the vicarage which it had taken all his money to build and which he could never quite afford to heat or to maintain; the path to the graveyard where he was now buried and where she supposed she too would take her place; the lake where she swam in summer and skated in winter; the orchard where she and her sisters picked fruit for jam making. And all around were the lanes and fields of the England whose seasons she knew, the oak trees and hedgerows, the snowdrops of winter, the primroses of spring, the nettles and cobnuts of autumn; the landscape to which she had to return each year because it was part of her, because it was home, the place to which she would retire when old and her life's hard work done.

On 25 July Serbia responded to Austria's ultimatum by mobilising 200,000 men. Germany urged Austria to declare war on Serbia.

On Monday 27 July Serbia and Austria broke off all diplomatic efforts, five Russian army divisions mobilised in St Petersburg, and General Putnik, Chief of the Serbian General Staff, was arrested in Budapest as he tried to make his way back to Belgrade. He had been in an Austrian health spa because of his heavy smoking. In Berlin there was a run on the banks. In Britain Winston Churchill, First Lord of the Admiralty, ordered the fleet to war stations in the North Sea.

The murder of the Archduke was a catalyst. Austria and Germany were fearful of the threat of the Entente Cordiale, a 1904 alliance between France, Britain and Russia. They were fearful, too, that Russia might intervene to help Serbia. But they were also looking for a *casus belli* to realise a dream of might and power. Since 1905 Germany had had a plan in place to conquer France by marching its army through the neutral countries of Luxembourg, Belgium and Holland, in an encircling web, with Paris at the centre. Called the Schlieffen Plan after Alfred von Schlieffen, the German Army Chief of Staff, it avoided invading France along its heavily defended border with Germany – its 'fortress zone'.

Britain, the richest nation in Europe, hoped diplomacy might succeed. Sir Edward Grey was seen as a peacebroker. He hoped Germany, France, Italy and Britain would work together to reach a settlement. Cooperation was essential if the dispute was to be limited.

On Tuesday 28 July, a month after the Archduke's assassination, the Austro-Hungarian Empire declared war on Serbia. The British fleet took up position at its war stations in the North Sea. Germany rejected Britain's call for a conference and warned Russia to stand aside until Austrian military measures against Serbia were completed. There were huge patriotic displays in Paris as France prepared to mobilise. At last the situation became the lead story in the British newspapers. But still in Britain there were hopes that this was brinkmanship, sabre-rattling, that fears would be appeased and conflict limited.

On Thursday 30 July Russia mobilised its army of six million men and lined up its troops along the Austrian frontier. The Serbs blew up the bridge over the Danube between Semlia and Belgrade. In Vienna market stallholders were beaten up for raising the price of goods like potatoes by 400 per cent.

On Friday 31 July Austria mobilised its army of three million men. Germany demanded an explanation for the deployment of Russian forces and a reply within twenty-four hours. It feared that if Russia attacked Austria and Germany, France, which was an ally of Russia and still humiliated by defeat in the Franco-Prussian War forty years earlier, would attack too. Germany would then be pincered between two hostile powers.

Belgrade was in flames. The London Stock Exchange closed on a business day for the first time in its history. The bank rate doubled. Customers besieged banks to draw out their money. The Tory press demanded war. Academics and prominent men like Thomas Hardy, Josiah Wedgwood and G. M. Trevelyan called for neutrality. And still it was hoped that the world was not slipping out of control, that declarations of alliance were only posturing, that the massive positioning of men and arms was display, that the real issues were local and that resolution would be contained. As they stirred for war all parties spoke of how they wanted peace. Sir Edward Grey wired the governments of France and Germany for assurances that they had no intention of violating the sovereign neutrality of Belgium. France agreed. Germany did not.

On Saturday 1 August Germany mobilised its army of four and a half million men and declared martial law. Holland, Switzerland and Belgium mobilised their small armies, and Sister White sent Edith Cavell a telegram from the School in rue de la Culture about the expectation of war, and expressing concern about how their matron would manage to return. Telephone links and trains between Belgium and Germany were suspended. 'DAY OF GLOOM', declared the *Eastern Daily Press*. In London, the bank rate went from 4 to 8 per cent, the Stock Exchange closed, and the King cancelled his visit to Cowes.

On Sunday 2 August Germany declared war on Russia, invaded Luxembourg and requested the Belgian government to allow German troops to pass through Belgium so they could attack France. They demanded a reply from Belgium by 7.00 a.m. the following day, and said that if Belgium refused it would be treated as an enemy. In haste and alarm Edith Cavell packed to return to Brussels. Everywhere there was a fever of anticipation. It was hard to leave her aged mother at such an anxious time but there was no thought in her mind of abandoning the new School she was shaping, her nurses, her mission. More than ever now it seemed Belgium would need her expertise. This time it would be amputees, the shell-shocked, the wounded. She had been at the London Hospital when nurses sailed to the Boer War. She had read Florence Nightingale's accounts of nursing in a war zone. Whatever was required of her she would give.

It was hard to secure a passage back. Pauline Randall was adamant about accompanying her. Trains and ferry links were being cancelled. Hordes of anxious people were on the move. She managed to get a train to Dover and a late ferry to Ostend crammed with passengers all searching the newspapers for the latest developments. She reached rue de la Culture in the early hours of Monday 3 August.

Throughout the night of 2 August King Albert of Belgium and his Cabinet discussed the crisis. In the morning the King told the Kaiser that his troops were not allowed on Belgian soil, that any invasion was a flagrant attack on the rights of nations, that Belgium was determined to defend her neutrality and would do so by every possible means. He appealed to Britain to safeguard Belgium according to promises made in a treaty of 1839. Sir Edward Grey told the House of Commons the only way for

Britain to keep out of this conflict was by taking a position of unconditional neutrality, which they could not in honour do.

The Chancellor of the Exchequer, David Lloyd George, and Ramsay MacDonald, leader of the Labour opposition, opposed Britain entering the conflict. MacDonald thought war a crime. 'Honour?' he said.

> There has been no crime committed by statesmen of this character without those statesmen appealing to the nation's honour. We fought the Crimean War because of our honour. We rushed to South Africa because of our honour. The Right Hon. Gentleman [Sir Edward Grey] is appealing to us today because of our honour . . . What is the use of talking about coming to the aid of Belgium, when, as a matter of fact, you are engaging in a whole European War which is not going to leave the map of Europe in the position it is in now?

This was not a view that was popular in the country. It was not held by Edith Cavell. In her view Belgium was undefended and threatened and must be protected. Just as England's nurses pioneered good practice, so England's army would put right this wrong.

On 4 August Germany invaded Belgium. That same day Britain declared war on Germany. Mrs Cavell opened the *Eastern Daily Press* that morning to the headline 'GREAT WAR BEGINS'. Her daughter had returned to a war zone. German troops had occupied neutral Luxembourg, which could not resist, and invaded France, without declaring war, at the north-eastern fortress town of Longwy. After a summer of slumbering British people had their eyes opened to the nightmare of what was to ensue. Nineteen million men were under arms in Europe. The central powers – Austria/Hungary and Germany – started with eight million men. The Allied powers – France, Britain, Belgium, Russia,

Serbia, Montenegro – had eleven million men under arms. It was a week when mankind slipped out of control, when fears of subjugation allied with dreams of conquest, when past alliances informed makeshift strategies, and when plans were thrown like paper darts into the killing fields of war. Diplomatically it was a week of haste, miscalculation, humiliating ultimata, reluctance to negotiate and true intent disguised. None of the countries going to war anticipated how long the fighting would last or how terrible the cost would be. It was a war of men in high office, though ordinary men fought it and died for it. In implementing the gamble of the Schlieffen Plan, Germany assumed Russia would take six weeks to arm and that Britain would not go to war to fulfil her treaty obligations of 1839 to defend Belgian neutrality.

Tuesday 4 August had been another hot summer's day in both London and Brussels. Herbert Asquith asked for, and got, credit of £100 million 'for the general purposes of the war'. In Brussels King Albert rode on horseback through the streets past cheering, flag-waving crowds to Parliament House. 'A country that defends its freedom,' he told them, 'can never die.' As evening came in London, Sir Edward Grey looked from a window in the Foreign Office at the man lighting the gas lamps in the street below and said, 'The lamps are going out all over Europe. We shall not see them lit again in our lifetime.'

PART FOUR

21

THE ARRIVAL OF THE ENEMY

On 3 August German troops crossed the Belgian frontier near Liège. 'War was declared by Germany this morning at 9 o'clock,' Edith Cavell wrote home the following day. 'All the ports are blocked and we believe in a state of siege. There is very little reliable news as the telegraph and telephone have been seized by the government . . . There are no soldiers here and Brussels is undefended, only the Civil Guard is keeping order in the town. The treasures and jewels are gone to Antwerp.'

Britain was to send an Expeditionary Force to drive the German army back. 'We were full of enthusiasm for the war and full of confidence in the Allies,' Edith Cavell wrote in a piece for the *Nursing Mirror*.

Flags were hung from end to end and no street, however mean, was without its stripes of yellow, red and black. Crowds assembled everywhere to talk over the prospects of a speedy peace, and the newspapers, published all day long, were sold in hundreds at every street corner. The sun shone out and the glorious warm days of late summer were full of courage and anticipation. In the trams, in the trains, on the telephone one heard nothing but discussions on the situation. People who knew each other slightly, or not at all, waxed quite confidential in relating the latest news. We were preparing 18,000 beds for the wounded; all sorts and conditions of people were offering help, giving mattresses and blankets, rolling bandages and making shirts; our chief thought was how to care for those who were sacrificing so much and facing death so bravely at Liège and elsewhere.

All Germans were ordered to leave the city. The Belgian police checked every house. Edith Cavell took her German probationer nurses to the Gare du Nord and waited all night with them for the special train (the last) that left for Esschen on the Dutch border. 'We saw them off with their hand luggage, all they were allowed to take.' She kept her personal German maid, Marie, who had no one to go to. She tried to send Grace Jemmett back to England. 'I did my best to send Gracie home but she refused to leave me – she is very quiet and brave,' she wrote to her mother. She told Sister Wilkins she would be safer in England, but she too chose to stay.

She anticipated that Brussels would become the centre for the care of wounded soldiers so she prepared beds at the School, at the Institute and at the St Gilles hospital.

> Everyone is volunteering, either for fighting or the Red Cross. Our houses are under the Red Cross flag and we are preparing to take in the wounded who will probably be sent on here from the front – but how to feed them is the mystery. All day long people are coming in for information, offering rooms and beds and personal help and motorcars to transport the wounded. I must have seen 50 persons since the morning.

Her existing patients left, out of fear of the German army. Most went to the coast. Queen Elisabeth offered the Royal Palace for use as a Red Cross hospital. It was quickly converted to the 'Ambulance du Palais'. The great ballroom and the Empire room, with marble pillars and crystal chandeliers, and the state apartments, were divided into wards, and filled with iron bedsteads. The Mirror Room was fitted out as an operating theatre. There was a room for dressing wounds, an X-ray room, a sluice room, a linen room, a mortuary in the grounds. Mme Depage began as the sister-in-charge and staff volunteered to work full time: three surgeons, two chief medical officers, three resident doctors, nine ward sisters, stretcher-bearers, and a team of boy scouts to help with correspondence and organise ambulances. All the staff were Belgian nationals or from Allied or neutral countries. The expectation was that both Allied and German wounded would be treated at the hospital under the Red Cross flag and the rules of the Geneva Convention.

Antoine Depage was President of the Red Cross in Belgium. Queen Elisabeth asked him as chief surgeon to head a field hospital at the coastal town of La Panne. The Océan hotel was converted. Many doctors and nurses from his St Gilles hospital went with him. During the course of the war he and his team were to treat more than 50,000 soldiers suffering wounds, fractures, nitrous gas poisoning, septicaemia and infectious diseases.

Depage wanted Edith Cavell to stay in Brussels, supervise nursing care there, and keep the project of the new Training School moving forward for when this swift war was through. She inspected schools, factories and private houses and supervised their conversion to temporary hospitals.

Yesterday I went to inspect a little factory from which all the plant had been removed. The walls were whitewashed and the air blew through it pleasantly. A gallery runs under the roof, and here and on the ground floor are ranged neat, narrow beds with white linen sheets and blankets neatly tucked in. Small tables are covered with clean towels on which bowls and jugs are ready for use. There is a fresh smell of creosote from the newly scrubbed floor. The cellar has been transformed into a store-room for arms and uniforms, and a little kitchen is invitingly supplied with utensils. All looks clean and bright, and through the good will and generous aid of the working population, the whole installation has only cost 30 francs.

The Red Cross formed a central committee with divisions throughout Belgium to deal with provisions, dressings, ambulances, enrolment of nurses. Doctors, nurses and stretcher-bearers were issued with Red Cross armbands. Edith Cavell flew the Red Cross flag over the School and rapidly trained volunteers to help staff the makeshift hospitals. There was a shortage of money and she posted an appeal in *The Times*.

On 5 August Belgian army officers drove through the streets calling through loudhailers for recruits for the army. The mood was of outrage and determination. There was a rumour the enemy had poisoned the water supply, so people tried to use rainwater to make tea. The windows of German businesses and shops were smashed in the night. Liège was said to be burning in a fierce battle. 'Liège has resisted beyond all our hopes,' Edith Cavell wrote home next day. 'Its defenders are the heroes of the hour.' She was asked to send cars for wounded soldiers who would be arriving on the 6 p.m. train, but most of the wounded were kept on the train and sent on, with doctors, to safer hospitals in Holland.

> Those that are here are for the most part not seriously injured, but are worn out with fatigue, have blistered feet, slight wounds and intestinal problems. They can hardly wait to be patched up before they are off again to join their regiments. One told us he could not lie in a comfortable bed while his comrades were in the midst of a terrible conflict.

She was wrongly informed about the defence of Liège, Belgium's gateway city on the River Meuse, with its citadel, merchant houses and alleyways. The battle to defend it lasted twelve days until 16 August. Outside the city were twelve huge concrete forts, six on either side of the river. But neither those nor the Belgian force of 70,000 men could withstand the German army's onslaught with Zeppelin bombs and Big Bertha guns, which took a thousand men to assemble, had a range of 15 kilometres and fired shells that weighed 820 kilos.

'We have just heard there has been a great battle,' Edith Cavell wrote on 15 August:

> – over 700 wounded. Some have arrived; others will come in during the night or tomorrow . . . Crowds assemble at the railways to see the wounded carried to the waiting ambulances, the men with bared heads and the women with wet eyes. War is terrible in this little country where every one has a relative or friend in the Army and where the fighting furthest from us must still be near at hand. The young men, gone so short a time and so short a distance, and in such brave spirits, are brought back – one dare not think how, even though one has passed twenty years among the sick and suffering.

This was the reality of it: the mutilation of young men. She braced herself to alleviate their suffering – with splints and analgesics, dressings, antiseptics, sustenance, warmth and loving care.

On 17 August the German army began to implement the next stage of the Schlieffen Plan. At Namur, garrisoned with 37,000 Belgian soldiers against 107,000 German troops, morale was low after the fall of Liège. The French and British armies had not arrived. Belgian soldiers had expected their support at Liège. German bombardment with huge shells reduced Namur to rubble in three days. The city was evacuated, thousands of its citizens fled – and from the nearby villages. Ten years previously

Edith Cavell had rowed on the River Meuse and sketched the landscape on holiday with the François family. Now columns of refugees formed, the very old and the very young, with mules, dog carts, pony carts, bicycles and random bundled possessions, and with nowhere to go except out of the path of this marauding army. The town of Louvain was next to be decimated. It had a population of 42,000. It was seized by the German army on 19 August. For a week after that the town was quiet. But on 26 August a Belgian force advancing from Antwerp attacked a German battalion and killed fifty soldiers. And at the *hôtel de ville* the mayor's son shot members of the occupying German staff. The German army then shelled the city, slaughtered citizens and drove out the rest. They then returned with incendiary bombs, set light to them and threw them into houses. Within half an hour the city was ablaze. Next day it was silent. A smoking heap of ruins. The church of St Peter's blackened and caved in, Les Halles destroyed, the library and its treasures gone, the houses in rue du Canal, rue de Diest, rue de la Station and rue Louis Quinze a mangle of ruins, bricks, twisted iron, charred beams and acrid smells. Some affluent houses had been marked not to be torched. They were pillaged instead.

The citizens of Belgium waited for the Allied armies to stop this terror and rescue them. The initial Allied plan had been for the French to hold back the Kaiser's army while the British disposed of his fleet and then, with the seas secured and no danger of invasion of England, the British Expeditionary Force, the elite BEF, would march into Belgium and, in a pincer movement with the French, trap the enemy and send it home.

Within hours and days of delays, misunderstanding and then blunder, it became clear that such plans were over-optimistic. This enemy had been underestimated and misread. To implement the Schlieffen Plan, the paper plan with Paris as its goal, Germany had two million men on the move. Their lines of attack

Louvain was destroyed on 27 August 1914. The *hôtel de ville*

circled from Liège to Mons, from Diest to Antwerp, from Louvain and Charleroi to Brussels, from Ghent to Ypres. The technology of their weaponry was advanced and lethal: trench mortars, poison gas, machine guns, shells, grenades, flame-throwers. And equal to this army's force was its ruthlessness. Allied military intelligence had miscalculated German intentions and strength. General Joffre, in command of the French First Army, had drawn up his Plan XVII but then encountered German forces far greater than his own. And communication was poor between General Lanrezac, in command of the French Fifth Army, and Field Marshal Sir John French, who was in command of the British Expeditionary Force. They could not or did not attack German divisions according to agreed plans. News of carnage filtered through to Brussels. 'After the period of high enthusiasm came the days of anxiety,' Edith Cavell wrote.

It grew keener hour by hour, when we heard Liège had fallen, that Namur followed, and that the enemy was coming on in irresistible force. There were sinister tales, too, of burnt and battered houses, of villages razed to the ground, of women and children murdered, of drunken soldiers and raping and looting and annihilation. And still we hoped against hope. 'We wait for England' was on the lips of everyone, and till the very last we thought the English troops were between us and the invading army.

But the British Expeditionary Force had not arrived, and the German army marched toward Brussels, destroying towns and villages in their path. At the School the nurses could smell burning. They knew fighting was taking place but did not know where. 'We can hear the cannon and from not far away the smoke can be seen with field glasses,' Edith Cavell wrote.

On 18 August King Albert, Queen Elisabeth and the Belgian government moved to Antwerp on the Dutch border. The King decreed that Brussels be an undefended city. He wanted no armed resistance. No bloodshed. Edith Cavell wrote to her mother and told her not to be afraid if she heard the German army had arrived in Brussels. 'They will only walk through. It is not a fortified town. Besides we are living under the Red Cross.' She said how she longed for English newspapers, for she had seen none since she left. 'My dearest love and Grace's. I will write whenever I can.'

At the approaches to the city the *garde civique*, made up of untrained citizens, stood by in postures of defence or crouched night and day in readiness in the trenches they had dug, 'but it did not need a soldier to see that they could pose no possible resistance to the great army of the Kaiser. It was a grateful duty to take these brave men hot coffee and food to fortify them against the nights, already chilly, of late summer.'

Edith Cavell wrote a letter home before the postal service was cut off:

My dearest Mother and my dear Ones

When you open this letter that which we have feared has happened and Brussels will have fallen into the hands of the enemy. The Germans are very close here and it is doubtful that the Allied Armies can stop them. We are prepared for the worst. I offered our dear Gracie and the other nurses to go back home. But none wanted to leave. I appreciate their courage and I would like you to tell the Jemmetts that I have done my best to send Gracie back to them, but she refused to leave me. She is calm and courageous. There is £100 deposited in the Pension Fund which I have never touched and which belongs to me. I beg my mother to take it with my greatest affection. It will replace the little quarterly allowance I made her. If I find means to forward you the few jewels I have, will you divide them among Flo and Lil?. . .

My most affectionate thoughts are for you dear Mother and for you Flo, Lil, Jack and your children and to Eveline McDonnell. God bless you and keep you in His care.

'I shall never forget the evening before the Prussians entered the city,' Nurse Jacqueline van Til wrote. 'We went up to the roof of the School and saw the sky towards the east fiery red, while clouds of thick black smoke rolled in our direction.' The thunder of guns broke the windows of the School. She sat on the landing and wept. Edith Cavell comforted her, told her not to give way to her feelings, to remember her life belonged not just to herself but to her duty as a nurse. 'In the evening came the news that the enemy were at the gates. At midnight bugles were blowing, summoning the Civil Guard to lay down their arms and leave the city.' The 26th Regiment of German Hussars and the 10th Uhlans had arrived at the gates of Brussels. The Burgomaster went out to parley with them. 'Many people were up through

German infantry march into Brussels, watched by civilians.
Place Charles Rogier, 20 August 1914

the dark hours, and all doors and windows were tightly shut. As we went to bed our only consolation was the certainty that in God's good time right and justice must prevail.' At 2 p.m. on 20 August the janitor of the School, 'a stout woman', burst through the door shouting, 'Les Boches sont là!' 'The sun shone in mockery on our fallen hopes as in the afternoon the German troops marched in,' Edith Cavell wrote.

All that day, and the next, columns of troops marched through the city heading south-west toward Paris. Fifty thousand German soldiers with guns, spiked helmets and tired horses passed through Brussels in those two days. The citizens lined the pavements, 'sullen and silent'. They could not cross the roads. The army marched in eight columns with Belgian prisoners between them. From rue de la Culture Edith Cavell and the nurses watched this long procession. When a halt for a meal was called and supplies distributed from carts, some of the soldiers were too exhausted to eat and just slept on the pavement. When they took off their boots their feet were bleeding.

> We were divided between pity for these poor fellows, far from their country and their people, suffering the weariness and fatigue of an arduous campaign, and hate of a cruel and vindictive foe bringing ruin and desolation on hundreds of happy homes and to a prosperous and peaceful land. Some of the Belgians spoke to the invaders in German and found they were very vague as to their whereabouts, and imagined they were already in Paris; they were surprised to be speaking to Belgians, and could not understand what quarrel they had with them. I saw several of the men pick up little children and give them chocolate or seat them on their horses, and some had tears in their eyes at the recollection of the little ones at home.

These were young men from towns and villages and decent living much like her own, conscripted soldiers, forced into a role which in the name of patriotism, or out of pride or fear, they did not or could not resist. In the afternoon armed officers in motor cars drove across the Grande Place to the *hôtel de ville*. They lowered the Belgian tricolour and hoisted the German flag.

That night Edith Cavell talked to her nurses. They were scared. Any wounded soldier, she told them, must be treated, friend or foe. Each man was a father, husband or son. As nurses they must take no part in the quarrel. Their work was for humanity, but they should watch their words and not enter unnecessarily into conversation with patients. The profession of nursing, she said – and not for the first or last time – knew no frontiers.

22

OCCUPATION

'There are two sides to war,' Edith Cavell wrote in an article in the *Nursing Mirror* in August 1914, 'the glory and the misery. We begin to see both. We shall see the latter more clearly as time goes on.'

Later that summer Belgium was torn to pieces and Brussels cut off from the world. The German military rooted in as masters, made and enforced punitive rules, took over all the civic buildings and public services and brutalised a peaceful city.

The supreme authority of this occupation was the Governor General. Appointed by the Kaiser, he was his personal representative. Only the Kaiser, who assumed absolute right over the conquered territories, could overrule him. Neither the German parliament, the Reichstag, its legislative, the Bundesrath, or the Foreign Office in Berlin, had authority over him. He had the power of life and death and his decrees required no countersignature. In peacetime, Belgium was divided into nine provinces each with a Provincial Governor. These were now answerable to the German Governor General in Brussels.

Second in command to him was the Military Governor. He headed the *Kommandantur*, the military police, who were at the heart of German repression of Belgian civilians. They took over two ornate ministerial buildings in rue de la Loi. Every morning from the main doors of the *Kommandantur* building a battalion of armed, helmeted military police emerged: their uniforms grey, their trousers stuffed in their iron-shod boots, rifles with fixed bayonets on their shoulders, black, white and red brassards with the imperial eagle round their jackets, metal discs embossed with POLIZEI on chains round their necks.[12] They patrolled the streets in twos and threes, guarded the *carrefours* and entrances to the city, surveilled and apprehended civilians and returned in the late afternoon bringing people with them, who were charged with any of countless crimes, then taken to the prison at St Gilles.

In nearby boulevard de Berlaimont a block of buildings was occupied by officials of the secret police, the *Geheime Politische Polizei*. Within a year there were thousands of these plain-clothes individuals milling about among the civilian population, spying on them. They kept dossiers on anyone of the slightest importance. Their ambition was to ensnare.

After the German invasion, Belgian officials without authority, in the civil departments of government, kept their jobs though under enemy supervision. Railway and postal workers refused to work for the Germans and were replaced, but the Ministries of Justice, Arts, Sciences and Finance, though constrained and subjugated, continued to function with Belgian bureaucrats. By doing so they helped their nation survive complete catastrophe.

Neutral countries retained a scant diplomatic presence. At the American Legation Brand Whitlock was the minister. He had an assistant, Hugh Gibson, two secretaries, and a Belgian legal adviser, Gaston de Leval. Whitlock, an unhurried individual who wrote novels and memoirs, before the war had served four times as mayor of Toledo in Ohio. In occupied Belgium, food and clothes were sent from America to alleviate the suffering of the civilian population. Its distribution was organised by the Legation. In so far as he could, Brand Whitlock represented the interests of English nationals remaining in the country. The Marquis de Villalobar, a more energetic diplomat who was

[12] The Belgians thought these looked like the labels round liqueur bottles

unafraid to break with protocol, attempted to represent the interests of French nationals there.

The *Politische Abteilung* was the only German office in occupied Brussels which dealt with requests from foreign diplomats.
It was not, in itself, a military department, though it was under
the rule of the Governor General and was headed by a trusted
adviser to him, Baron von der Lancken-Wakenitz.

His Excellency Field-Marshal Baron von der Goltz Pasha was
the first Governor General. He was an old man, big, with a
mottled scarred face and round gleaming spectacles. He wore a
much-decorated blue uniform, a black helmet and an enormous
sword. He liked to travel to the battlefields in order to observe
the bloodshed. While watching fighting at Antwerp, he got
slightly wounded on his face. 'He went to battles as an office-boy
goes to baseball games,' Brand Whitlock said. His first *affiche*,
posted on the city's walls, proclaiming his accession to power,
said that the German armies were advancing victoriously in
France and threatened dire consequences to anyone who committed any act inimical to the German cause. 'It is the hard necessity
of war that punishment for hostile acts falls not only on the
guilty but also on the innocent,' he told the Belgians. With
Louvain, Dinant, Aerschot and hundreds of other towns and
villages smoking and in ruins, such warnings were not taken
lightly. When the much-loved Burgomaster, Adolphe Max,
ventured a defiant *affiche* of his own, he was packed off to prison
at Glatz in Silesia. Thereafter these posters played as large a part
in Brussels life as had newspapers before the war. They did not
provide reliable news, but they made German intentions clear.

The streets were patrolled by sentries, soldiers and spies. Citizens were watched, stopped, asked for identification and had
their houses searched. There was night curfew. Travel by train
was disallowed without a German pass. Cars and bicycles were
forbidden. The post was erratic and all letters had to be left

unsealed to be read by censors. Food became scarce and dear and the sale of alcohol was prohibited. Belgians who defiantly went on flying the national flag from windows and roofs were arrested. It became an offence even to wear little buttons with pictures of the King and Queen. Phone links were cut and Dutch and foreign newspapers banned.

Edith Cavell wrote home that she would 'give anything for an English newspaper'. But in Norwich that August her mother read the *Eastern Daily Press* with horror:

DEADLY STRUGGLE IN FULL SWING * A FRONT
OF 250 MILES * 2,000,000 FIGHTING MEN * FALL
OF NAMUR * WHOLE GERMAN ARMY ENGAGED *
FIERCE CONFLICT ROUND CHARLEROI * BATTLE
FRONT FROM MONS TO LUXEMBOURG

Maps showed shifting battle lines. Photographs showed Belgian towns destroyed and German soldiers marching into Brussels. There were gruesome accounts of peasants beaten to death with rifle butts, the house of a railway watchman torched, of how an old man at the village of Neerhespen had his arm sliced and was burned alive, of corpses being hacked with swords, of young girls raped and little children 'outraged' at Orsmael, of doctors and stretcher-bearers wearing the Red Cross being shot . . .

'My darling Edith,' Mrs Cavell wrote on 21 August,

It is almost against hope that I am writing for news of you
and Gracie – if at all possible do let me have a line or wire –
no news is intolerable, one conjectures all sorts of things – my
anxiety is terrible but I am afraid yours must be much worse.

If you are both safe and well in the midst of all the
horrors of war and invasion I shall be truly thankful –
I pray for you continually, that God will grant you his

loving protection – I go to Sheringham next Monday to
spend a few days or a week with L & L[13] – so if you can
possibly send a line, address to me there
Erpingham House
Cliff Road
Sheringham
   I cannot write on any other topic my heart is full of the
one thing.
My dearest love to you both dear child
Your loving Mother

Her letter arrived at rue de la Culture seven months later, on 11
March 1915.

Edith Cavell was always anxious to reassure her eighty-year-
old widowed mother. She heard of Belgians who knew of ways
to smuggle letters in and out of neutral Holland. She gave her
mother a variety of addresses: a Mme Leon Delhey in Amster-
dam, someone in Mons, someone in Vecht, someone in Ninove.
'Some letters get destroyed,' she told her. 'Some come without
an envelope. Don't send money.' Her 'special' postman called on
Tuesdays. Letters were costly to send and receive and often did
not arrive. She paid nine francs for a letter only to find it was
'from a wearisome person' and of no interest.

'I hope news of the safety of Brussels has been published in
the newspapers,' she wrote on 30 August.

I cannot give you details of things here as this letter might
fall into the wrong hands. We are almost without news
of what is going on . . . We know for certain that there is
fighting near at hand . . . We have a few German wounded
in our hospital but here there are none and the Allies are
not brought to Brussels. There has been terrible loss of

[13] Lilian and Longworth Wainwright

life on both sides and destruction of towns and beautiful buildings that can never be rebuilt. I am keeping a record for more peaceful times which will interest you later. We are still able to get food tho' prices are higher and we have reduced the scale of living a little. We go on quietly with our usual work and hope for the best . . .

The days are very fine & warm & mornings misty – looking over the plains this peaceful Sunday morning, one cannot imagine how near are the terrible dogs of war nor how ruthlessly that peace may be broken. Do not fear for us we are well out of the town as you know. And are not afraid. With my dearest love to you all,
Ever your loving daughter
Edith

Though her letters spoke of danger: the wrong hands, secrecy, the denial of information, battle close by, terrible loss of life, the destruction of towns, expensive food, the 'terrible dogs of war', they spoke also of her optimism. The record she kept for more peaceful times she was later obliged to destroy. Only a fragment of it survived. But she always expected to show it to her mother, to be reunited with her, that, as she put it, 'in God's good time' peace would come and goodness prevail.

Her initial fear had been that there would be too many men to nurse, too many to feed. As news came of carnage in Belgian towns and villages in the German army's push toward Paris, and of battles at Liège, Namur and Louvain, she thought the wounded would arrive in thousands. But only at first were any patients brought to her care. Groups arrived by train of mainly walking-wounded German soldiers. As ever she reminded her nurses that every wounded man deserved their best attention. They complained that she expected them to be like her, and to work until too tired to stand. 'I often saw one or other of my companions lying exhausted in her bed in her off-duty time, sometimes weeping,' Nurse Moore wrote. 'Why did we stay? We were none of us used to that sort of life.'

The German soldiers, she said, at first were 'sulky and undoubtedly apprehensive', but attitudes changed to gratitude and there was even laughter: 'One nurse was struggling to remove the muddy boots from a man near the middle of the ward; he pulled and she pulled until her chair fell backwards and she toppled over with his boot in the air.' But as suddenly as beds filled, they emptied. As the line of fighting moved, field hospitals were set up near the shifting scenes of battle. In Brussels, the German military turned buildings they commandeered into hospitals for their own wounded and supplied their own staff. Captured Allied wounded were sent on by train to prison hospitals in Germany or to prisoner-of-war camps there.

After the first month of the war, the only functioning Red Cross hospital in Brussels was the Ambulance du Palais Royal, run by Belgian doctors and nurses and bound by the Geneva Convention to admit wounded of all the warring nations. The first casualties arrived there on 16 August. Edith Cavell sent eight of her Belgian and Dutch nurses, and Nurse Moore, who though English-born was fluent in German. She wanted them to gain experience in treating the war-wounded. Harrowing though it was, she thought it would make them better nurses. She told them to remember they represented the Training School.

The German authorities were suspicious of the hospital and wanted it closed. They accused the staff of unsatisfactory treatment of German wounded, of interfering with their correspondence, of using the Red Cross flag to send signals. In the middle of the night on 16 September soldiers forcibly removed twenty-three Belgian wounded, several of whom had just been operated on, and sent them to Germany.

Ruth Moore wrote an account of nursing at the Palace and

The Royal Palace. The only Red Cross hospital in Brussels during the war. The Mirror Room became an operating theatre, the state apartments became wards

of the common suffering of wounded men. She was in charge of four German wards. Many patients had terrible wounds, many died. She was summoned whenever a wounded British soldier was brought in. '*Venez, un anglais,*' she would hear at two in the morning. She removed his muddy clothes, dressed his wounds, got him into a clean and comfortable bed and did not tell him that the 5 a.m. ambulance train would take him to Germany. At least, she thought, he might have a few hours' sleep.

A German patient, a sergeant, helped her. He wrote letters for the other men, read to them, went shopping for them. The youngest of her patients she called *Kindchen*. He was grievously wounded. His mother sent him a letter saying his brother had died at sea. Two weeks before that another brother had been killed. One night he asked Ruth Moore to sit with him. He said he too wanted to die. In his locker drawer she found a pistol.

In the evenings from 5.00 to 6.00 the soldiers had a recreation hour and sang and smoked. One night Nurse Moore was on the ward finishing her reports and filling in charts. One of the men started singing '*Das Lied der Deutschen*', the Song of the Germans, and the others joined in. The sergeant told them to stop, asked if they had forgotten where they were and who was in the ward. They changed the song and she left the ward.

The Depages' house was soon closed up. For the first months of the war Marie Depage worked at the Palace Hospital, uncertain of what the nursing requirement would be there. In November she joined her husband at the Océan Hospital at La Panne.

Edith Cavell's frustration was to be denied the opportunity to nurse in the capacity needed. She stayed in a state of readiness, though with fewer nurses and not many civilian patients. At the School, the Berkendael Institute and the St Gilles hospital, beds were waiting and the wards cleaned each day. The cook and housekeeper went to market five times a week to buy supplies as economically as possible. Edith Cavell went on giving daily lectures to her nurses. Every day she walked with Pauline Randall and Jack to check on building progress for the new School. Some work continued, but materials needed were stuck in trucks on the paralysed railway, and workmen could not get in because no movement of traffic was allowed.

Life, she said, reverted to the Middle Ages. There was a shortage of bread. The sort they got was black and heavy. Letters took months to get through, if at all. Poverty became extreme. There were feeding stations for impoverished children, stations to hand out clothes. 'We are engaged in making up all the stuff we can get into garments for the children of the refugees and the other poor,' she wrote in a letter home. Soup kitchens in every *quartier* were organised by the *Comité National de Secours et d'Alimentation*, financed by America. Brand Whitlock, at the American Legation, extracted a guarantee from the Governor General that this food would not be requisitioned. Queues formed of people, each with a number and card, holding bowls and pitchers. They were given soup and bread, coffee with chicory.

As summer turned to misty autumn, Brussels became paralysed. There were 'no gaieties of any sort'. Theatres, cinemas and all places of amusement shut down:

> The once busy and bustling streets are very quiet and silent. So are the people who were so gay and communicative in the summer. No one speaks to his neighbour in the tram, for he may be a spy. Besides, what news is there to tell, and who has the heart to gossip, and what fashions are there to speak of, and who ever goes to a theatre or a concert nowadays, and who would care to tell of their all-absorbing anxiety as to how to make both ends meet and spin out the last of the savings or to keep the little mouths filled, with the stranger close by?
>
> I am but a looker-on after all, for it is not my country whose soil is desecrated and whose sacred places are laid waste. I can only feel the deep and tender pity of the friend within the gates, and observe with sympathy and admiration the high courage and self-control of a people enduring a long and terrible agony . . .
>
> A German officer on a tram politely asked a gentleman for a light; he handed him his cigar without a word, and, on receiving it back, threw it in the gutter. Such incidents happen often and are typical of the conduct of this much-tried nation.

'You would think every day a Sunday,' Edith Cavell told her mother:

so few shops and houses open and so many people walking about with nothing to do. The streets are strangely quiet with no motors, it makes it much easier and pleasanter getting about, you would certainly prefer it. We have the trams as usual, but at night they may not go through certain parts of the town and have to alter their usual course. There are fewer lights too in the evening in the streets, some of which are as dark as in the middle ages, all the houses shuttered and the shops shut. It looks very gloomy and strange.

Survival was the effort of each day. Even when the banks opened there was a restriction on how much of their own money people could draw out. Coal was scarce and Edith Cavell was glad of the blue woollen jacket her mother had knitted for her: 'I wear it every day when I am sitting still over accounts or writing,' she wrote to her. She said it was a great comfort, a reminder of ordinary life. 'I often wish you were here at teatime to pour the tea for me.' She lived on pittance money for herself and gave what she could to those who needed it more. She asked her sister Florence about the possibilities of adoption in England for orphaned Belgian children. She was concerned to feed and care for her Brussels family: her devoted deputy Sister Wilkins, José the Rumanian housekeeper, Pauline Randall, Marie her German maid, Grace Jemmett and the ever-faithful Jack. Grace Jemmett became depressed. The war and an atmosphere of anxiety exacerbated her illness and she took to her bed. Edith Cavell tried to get medical help, but not much was on offer for mental illness. Grace's mother was unconcerned that her daughter was in a war zone. 'She seems to feel no anxiety,' Edith Cavell wrote. The Jemmetts' only involvement with their daughter had been to send a monthly cheque.

Edith Cavell urged her own mother not to tell Grace's parents

A Belgian priest wearing the armband of the Red Cross
passes German soldiers, Brussels 1915

about their daughter's relapse and to keep the money meant for
her board and care, not try to send it on. Before this war Edith
had sent her mother a monthly allowance. The Jemmett money
might serve instead.

She became one of the few English people left in the city.
Most left, and many Belgians too. The Church of the Resurrection, where she used to worship, closed, when there were not
enough worshippers to make the Reverend Philip Stocks's time
in Belgium worth while. He returned to England. He had been
a curate in Hoxton in the late 1880s. Edith Cavell moved to
Christ Church in rue de la Royauté and a new chaplain, the
Reverend Horace Stirling Townsend Gahan, who had been curate
of St Thomas's church in Southborough in Kent.

She was not by nature a looker-on at 'people enduring a long and terrible agony'. It was her grief not to be nursing. Antoine Depage planned to smuggle her out of Brussels to work at his Océan hospital. But by late autumn her war effort had altered. 'The sick have magically disappeared,' she wrote to her sister Lilian on 9 November, 'there is much to do beyond our reach.' Her determination to help had not diminished. She was well known in Brussels, respected and influential, fluent in French and English. In defiance of injustice and hardship people looked out for each other with food, clothing and money. Information was by word of mouth. Resistance to the occupying enemy grew into a network of small deeds and large: the giving of food, carrying a message, the provision of a map, shelter, false papers and disguise, helping an endangered Allied soldier escape to safety.

23

THE LOST CHILDREN

The longed-for British Expeditionary Force, the BEF, had reached Belgium on 21 August, by which time the German army had wreaked destruction on Liège, Namur, Louvain, killed tens of thousands of soldiers and civilians, seized Brussels and was on its way south and west to Paris. The BEF was the best-trained in Europe. Its soldiers had seven years of training against the German conscripts' three. But it was small – 150,000 men, short of officers, ammunition and guns, and in peril because of failures of strategy at top level.

On 22 August the BEF headed down from the Belgian coast to meet up with General Lanrezac's forces at Charleroi. Near Mons Sir John French, Britain's commander-in-chief, was surprised to encounter heavy cavalry patrols from the German First Army. This was contrary to advice he had received from France's headquarters. He decided to take on this army and stop its advance by destroying the bridges over the Mons–Condé canal. The Battle of Mons ensued, the first battle between British and German forces on the Western Front, one of the Battles of the Frontier fought that August at Mulhouse, Lorraine, the Ardennes, Charleroi.

Harry Beaumont was a private with the Queen's Own Royal West Kent Regiment, a unit of the 13th Infantry Brigade of the BEF. He did not know about the Schlieffen Plan and prior to this war had not heard of Mons. He and his unit advanced when told to advance, retreated when told to retreat. They marched down the Belgian lanes: columns of men, horses and wagons dragging munitions and armaments. In the first two weeks of the war 57,000 horses from Britain had been requisitioned: Clydesdale horses from the brewers' drays and railway vans, unused to military harness. During this war a million horses from Britain were killed and 250,000 mules.

Harry Beaumont had been called up sixteen days before from the Army Reserve. He, like all his company, was optimistic that the war would be over by Christmas. 'We had faith in our leaders and confidence in our ability to win through any task that we might be called upon to perform.' He was thirty, not particularly fit and had married the previous year. That August, in ninety degrees of heat, wearing thick khaki and woollen underwear, and carrying a pack and equipment weighing eighty pounds, he and his regiment marched toward Mons. The landscape was hilly and cut by canals and railways. They washed in duck ponds and slept in hay.

On the evening of 22 August they limped exhausted into the mining village of Hornu. Villagers told them they were 10 kilometres west of Mons, gave them beer, cigarettes and food and brought their children to see the British troops who had come to their rescue. Next day was a Sunday. The men were ordered to stay at Hornu for a day of rest then march to Mons on the Monday. There was the sound of church bells, there were cattle grazing. After Mass the German army attacked. There was fire from field guns and the scream of shells and villagers.

Beaumont's regiment was ordered to advance along the nearby canal until they reached the village of St Ghislain where a bridge spanned the canal. They discarded their packs because they were so heavy. Beaumont's platoon took up position in a glass factory outside the village at the canal's edge. They fired at German soldiers with machine guns and rifles and killed many men. When night came they left the factory and took up a new position on the embankment. They again saw the German army advancing and again killed many of them. They felt they were doing well. In a day's fighting only one of their men had been killed and two wounded. But at 1.00 a.m on 24 August they received orders to retreat. They were told that this retreat would be total. They could not believe it or understand why. They blew up the bridge and moved off into the night.

The men doing the fighting did not know of the confusion of their generals – how Sir John French too late realised the superior strength of the German First Army; how he had heard that General Lanrezac had retreated and could offer no support from French troops; how he thought the BEF would be encircled, cut off and decimated; how he had told the British government he feared for the safety of the Channel ports and was going to pull back to Valenciennes, Longueville, Maubeuge – they only knew they were in retreat.

As they moved back along the lanes – long columns of uniformed men, exhausted horses, and guns – they were joined by even longer columns of refugees as the country folk of Belgium fled from their villages, hamlets and farms. Villagers piled themselves and their possessions onto horse-drawn carts, carts drawn by oxen and mules, pony carts, handcarts, landaus, barrows. They rode on bicycles, trudged on foot, carried whatever they could and did not know where they were going. Behind them was the smoke and fire of the enemy drawing nearer.

At dawn on 24 August Beaumont's regiment reached the mining village of Wasmes, 3 kilometres south of St Ghislain and 10 kilometres south-west of Mons. Within hours the German army started to shell this village too. The soldiers of the Royal West Kent were told to make their way to fields where trenches had been dug a few hours before by the Royal Engineers. From these trenches they were to fight a rearguard action, holding back the enemy so that the rest of the Force could retreat. To get to the trenches they had to go through a wood and a cornfield. The corn had been cut and bound in stooks. 'In blissful ignorance we advanced across the stubble.' German soldiers rose from the trenches they were intending to occupy and wiped most of them out in withering close-range fire. Beaumont was hit in the groin. He lay as if dead and watched his fellow soldiers drop dead around him. In a few minutes, four officers and forty-five men were killed. When the gunfire died down he scurried to hide behind a heap of manure. Three other men were there, all wounded. When it was quiet the four of them limped to adjacent woodland. There was a wall close by and Beaumont tried to slide down a bank to it to be shielded from shellfire. A shell hit the base of it and it collapsed on him. When he came to, it was another day and he was alone.

He had become one of those the French called *les enfants perdus*. The Germans called them derelicts. In the bitter fighting of the rearguard action of the retreat from Mons small groups of men got cut off from their regiments. They were wounded by shells, shrapnel and bullets. They had no brandy, morphine, bandages, or splints. They lay in the trenches or in the mud until dark, for only when the fighting stopped could stretcher-bearers search for them. If they were undiscovered, their wounds became a mess of pus and gangrene and they were left to their wits, to luck and the kindness of strangers. They crawled to where they could under cover of night. Even if they got to field hospitals, often they died, for there were no antibiotics. If they surrendered they were sent to prisoner-of-war camps. Some organised themselves into guerrilla groups, or tried to get to Louvain, Brussels or south-west to Liège, Huy, Namur, Dinant.

Like Harry Beaumont, Colonel Dudley Boger was another of the lost children after the retreat to the Dutch border and to freedom. They scattered the land, for the German army's thrust through Belgium was in many directions: north to Antwerp, Furnes, Ostend and Ypres; west to Tirlemont and Mons. He was

Wounded Allied soldiers retreat from Mons, August 1914

forty-nine, Sandhurst-trained, had served in India, Malta and Ireland and was commander of the 1st Cheshires, a battalion of a thousand men. His orders on 24 August were to protect with a rearguard action a mile of the front line near the village of Audregnies. The two regiments in front of him were decimated. Men and horses from the 9th Lancers and the 1st Norfolks were mown down, decapitated by wire, shot at by nine German batteries. Instructions to retreat did not get through to Boger and in the afternoon his battalion fought for three hours against massive infantry attack. Only two hundred of the thousand men were left alive. Most of those surrendered and became prisoners of war. The severely wounded lay where they fell in ditches and cornfields and died.

Boger was shot three times. He was wounded in his side and a spur went through his foot. He lay in a field beside three other wounded men. German soldiers took his revolver and binoculars, broke the men's rifles and left the four of them lying there.

After dark Boger crawled to the nearby village of Wihéries, where the convent hospital was under German guard. About forty other wounded British soldiers were there: Sergeant Fred Meachin, Sergeant Tunmore, Private Lewis, Lance-Corporal Doman . . . Boger's wounds were treated with primitive equipment and makeshift facilities by Dr Valentin van Hassel. When the guards were having breakfast, Colonel Boger and Sergeant Meachin escaped over the convent wall. Van Hassel directed them to the house in the village of his son-in-law, Albert Libiez, a barrister. Libiez and his wife hid them in a barn in the garden and for weeks fed and clothed them. Boger grew a beard, wore a black hat, and tried to look Belgian. Meachin wore labourer's overalls and padded his shoulders to look like a hunchback.

On a day when there was a house-to-house search by 100 German soldiers, the two men fled to the barn in Albert Libiez's mother's garden. At 1.00 in the morning two nuns, Sisters Marie and Madeleine, led them to the Convent of the Daughters of Mary at the nearby village of Wasmes. Libiez sent his friend Herman Capiau, an engineer, to advise them. Capiau had acted as a guide to the British Expeditionary Force and helped to set up a field hospital after the debacle of Mons. He told Boger and Meachin their options were to hide in a coal mine, a forest, or a city. They chose the city. Capiau acquired false identification for the disguised men, took them first to Libiez's town house in Mons and then by train to Brussels. He made several unsuccessful attempts to find lodgings for them, then asked Marie Depage at the Royal Palace hospital if she could help. She suggested he ask Edith Cavell because both men needed medical care as well as refuge.

And so on the afternoon of 1 November 1914 Herman Capiau arrived at the School in rue de la Culture with Colonel Boger bearded and in a black hat, Sergeant Meachin with his shoulders padded to make him look deformed and with a letter to Edith Cavell from Marie Depage telling her that he, Capiau, was to be trusted and asking for her help.

Boger had a temperature and was limping. Edith Cavell took the men in, put them to bed, nursed them, gave them the comfort she could. Dr Gyselinck operated on Boger's injured foot. They stayed with her eighteen days. When they were well, she equipped them with Belgian clothes, found them a safe house in avenue Louise, then helped find guides to take them to Holland and safety. The plan was for Boger to go on a coal barge to Holland. Meachin was to travel with a tradesman who had permission to collect a consignment of fish from the Dutch coast. The idea was that the two men should meet again at the Station Hotel in Flushing. Boger got arrested before he left Brussels and spent the remainder of the war in a German prisoner-of-war camp. Meachin got back to England.

Before attempting to leave Brussels, Boger gave his dispatches about events to Sister Millicent White who nursed at the Royal Palace hospital, but planned to return to England. She bandaged the dispatches to her leg and travelled by barge, on a weekend return ticket and false passport, to Antwerp. At one of the locks passengers were searched. Boger's papers were not found. She reached England after four days and gave his dispatches to the War Office.

Edith Cavell had chosen to stay in Brussels. It was not feasible for her to stand aloof from the suffering and wrongdoing all around her. She was the most law-abiding of women. As a matron and in her ambition to establish a nursing school of excellence she adhered to the need for authority, discipline and even regimentation. But it had to have a moral core, founded in love. Boger and Meachin were the first of the 'lost children', the fugitive soldiers, whom she helped find their way from the battlefields of the Western Front to the Dutch border. She helped with characteristic vigilance, attention to detail and concern for those in need. But previously she conformed. Now she defied. She had been open. Now she was cunning. She had no training for this work. Her life had been institutionalised and maidenly. Now it was as harsh and dark as men could make it. A myriad of ordinary people helped these men. They did not view themselves as heroes. Decent living had been taken from them and they would not acquiesce to this enemy.

The German military countered such resistance by imposing ever-harsher rules and punishments. In Brussels, long proclamations from the Governor General in French and Flemish were posted daily in public places: all men must register at the town hall; no journeys were to be made without military authorisation and a declaration of destination and purpose; citizens must declare every resident and visitor; no movement in the streets after 8.00 at night; anyone who used a private car or bicycle would be shot as a spy; anyone found with arms, munitions, or carrier pigeons would be shot. Markets, bars and cafés were searched and meetings forbidden.

By November 1914 the reality of this war was clear. There was to be not victory by Christmas, but a mayhem of slaughter, destruction and hardship that month on month sucked in half the young men of the world. As swathes of soldiers were killed, they were replaced with the living. On walls all over Britain the face of Lord Kitchener, Minister of War, was posted with his swirling moustache and pointing finger: 'Your Country Needs You'. Recruiting figures reached 30,000 a day. The war spread from the fields of France and Belgium to the deserts of Egypt and Mesopotamia. In its service sixty million men were mobilised worldwide: two million British soldiers were killed or wounded, six million German soldiers, six million French, five million Austro-Hungarian, seven million Russian, one and a half million Italian . . . There would be no definitive list of casualties. The carnage would destroy the records, the men, memories.

Violent threats and punishments did not cow those for whom a sense of freedom and justice remained clear. For many it was a small part to play – to help 'lost children' caught in this madness and get them over the frontier into Holland where they would be safe from reprisal from the occupying power and free to rejoin their regiments if they wished.

Edith Cavell became a principal agent in Brussels of such help, the hub for two escape movements, one from the Belgian Borinage district, the other from the French *Etapés*. She was at pains not to involve her other nurses in any punishable way. Sister White involved herself before returning to England. Sister Elisabeth Wilkins knew some details of what was going on. Edith Cavell's focus was always that normal life must be restored. She and her nurses must move into the new Training School with all its modern facilities. The good cause must continue. War was an evil chapter which later, not sooner, must end.

24

YORC

On the Franco-Belgian frontier, between Valenciennes, Mons and Maubeuge, Prince Reginald and Princess Marie de Croÿ and their English grandmother lived in their family home, the château Bellignies. They were brother and sister, cousins of the Belgian king, and as with many European aristocrats had familial links with Germany, Prussia and France. The Prince had been Secretary of the Belgian Embassy in London for ten years; the Princess was a trained nurse. When Germany invaded Belgium they offered their home as a field hospital. They prepared rooms, stored provisions and flew the Red Cross flag. On 21 August, as the British Expeditionary Force marched to Mons, they gave

BELLIGNIES (Nord) — Le Château

The château at Bellignies

hospitality and maps to a company of the Middlesex Regiment. In the evening sunlight, on the quiet lawn of the château, the de Croÿs ate a meal with the soldiers. They admired the beauty of the horses, the perfection of their harnessing.

On 22 and 23 August they heard the thunder of gunfire. On the 24th neighbours told them of wounded and dying British soldiers lying all along the roadside and in farmhouses. The Prince went out with his driver to find them. Soon the beds in the château were full. He and his sister took those in need of intensive care to the hospital in the nearby small town of Bavay.

Next morning they heard that the British army was marching southward, up the hill instead of down. The Princess went out to speak to the retreating British soldiers. Regiments were mixed up and no one seemed clear about what was happening. She asked an officer if the enemy was coming and told him the château was full of wounded British soldiers. He said the German army would arrive in hours and she must get the wounded men out. All day she and her brother wrapped the men in blankets and lifted them onto the carts of the hordes of refugees moving south. The lanes were filled with traumatised villagers. Some said their houses had been ransacked and food demanded from them at gunpoint. Badly wounded soldiers were left in the hospital at Bavay. Four were too ill to be moved from the château.

From then on, the Prince worked tirelessly in opposition to the German army. He and his sister hid the Allied soldiers' weaponry in a deep unused well, buried the family silver and sent the chauffeur in the family car to help refugees. At 8.00 next morning the Princess heard horses and saw two Uhlans, lances stretched before them, at the château gates. 'Nothing can describe the feeling of revolt, of nausea almost, that the first sight of the enemy in one's country provokes,' she wrote in her memoir. Behind the Uhlans was the German army. They told the de Croÿs they must give lodging to their officers. Long grey cars brought

General von Kluck, his nephew and aide-de-camp Prince Georg of Saxe-Meiningen, the Duke of Schleswig-Holstein and a host of officers. They filled the château. They took the bandages off the English soldiers to check they were not feigning wounds. They feared being poisoned and the Croÿs had to taste their food before they would eat it. They set up an office with telephones and typewriters. Their take on the war was that King George V had instigated it.

All around was the roar of shells, gunfire and aeroplanes as the German army strafed the retreating British and captured towns and villages. The de Croÿs saw prisoners dragged down the lanes. In the gardens of the château, German soldiers set up camp and cooked rabbits and chickens looted from nearby farms. On 26 August they struck camp and left, saying the English army was in full retreat. But then a General von Bauer, the Grand Duke of Mecklenburg-Strelitz, and thirty-five officers arrived. The Duke gave the English soldiers cigarettes and copies of the *Daily Mirror*, and told the Princess he hated this war and that his best friends were English and French.

When that group moved on, other regiments of German soldiers arrived. All seemed confused as to quite what this war was about. They stayed for a while, moved on, were replaced. Wounded German soldiers were brought to the château to be nursed. 'As soon as they are well enough to leave their beds they go into the room where the English are and chat together, one German acting as interpreter,' the Princess de Croÿ wrote.

There was fighting in the nearby towns of Bavay and Maubeuge. Villages that resisted occupation were torched. The whole area was occupied by the enemy and the countryside swarmed with refugees. When, after some weeks, occupation was complete, German soldiers moved out of the château and it became a Red Cross hospital again.

Villagers brought news. A farm worker digging potatoes in a

field had found two English soldiers hiding in a hedgerow. The brewer's sister, Mademoiselle Carpentier, found two more in a lane near her house and hid them. In late September two girls from the village of St Waast, 3 kilometres away, called and asked to speak to Reginald de Croÿ. One was Henriette Moriamé, the brewer's sister and a devout Catholic; the other, Louise Thuliez, was a schoolteacher in Lille, at home on holiday in the village when war broke out. They wanted to know what they should do with seven English soldiers they had originally nursed for slight wounds in August, and kept hidden ever since. There were notices everywhere ordering all inhabitants to declare Allied soldiers or be shot.

The Prince said he would try to find a safe hiding place for them, and in the meantime they should tell other villagers that the men had run away. Near the château was the forest of Mormal – 30,000 acres of woodland. Deep in it were gamekeepers' houses and woodmen's cottages. The Prince thought the soldiers would be safe in one of those. The girls guided them out there one night. The Prince paid their expenses. Word got around and more men arrived at the château. The girls went on long walking tours, looking for stray men in fields and woodland and in all the ravaged villages and towns. The Princess de Croÿ called them the Girl Guides. They asked the mayors, tradespeople, abbots and nuns. They would walk 30 kilometres in a day and a night. At times the Prince joined them. They found men buried half alive in mud, and dead men lying in fields. They took details when they could: pay books, identity discs, letters, prayer books, photos, a rosary. They wanted to notify those close to the dead, tell their regiments, bury them, offer respect. Such details were published in a clandestine newsletter, *Les Petits Mots du Soldat*, which recorded and disseminated news about Allied soldiers.

One day the girls found a large group of English and French soldiers in woodland near the village of Englefontaine. One was an officer. The Princess loaded a donkey cart with provisions, books and rifle cartridges and set off with the girls to take help to the men. The village was no more than a long straggling street surrounded by woods. Hidden deep in the woods was a clog maker's cottage. There, she met Lieutenant Bushell, of the 2nd Dragoon Guards. He asked her to bring him guns. He told of how he had been cut off from his regiment, lain three days and nights in a railway embankment, and crept to a cottage whose owner hid him. He had then gone into the forest and grouped fifty men around him: men from the 11th Hussars, the Sutherland Highlanders, the Gordon Highlanders, the Scots Greys, the Munster Fusiliers, the Royal Irish Rifles, the King's Own Scottish Borderers.

They made a dugout covered in brambles to house themselves. A few villagers knew of them and brought food. The Princess arranged for provisions to be left daily for them at an agreed spot. The men left messages there. A farm girl would arrive at the château, unfurl her hair and deliver these.

And so a network of clandestine help for these lost soldiers grew up, an ever-changing web of provision and communication: of the bringing of bread and clothes, of shelter for a night, of misdirecting the enemy, guiding fugitive soldiers across unfamiliar terrain, forging passports, concealing weapons, sending messages in the braids of hair or the false heel of a shoe, disseminating underground newspapers . . . This was resistance, this was citizenship. There was no way an occupying army as hated as this one could stamp it out.

The château became the headquarters of one cell of this resistance movement. Fugitive French and British soldiers who arrived there, often wounded and traumatised, were given civilian disguise and false identities. The Princess photographed them using an old camera and a stock of large plates she had, which she cut into small pieces with a diamond. The Prince obtained blank identity cards from the Belgian clerk in the Bureau de Population in Mons. The clerk would take these when his German supervisor was at lunch. Georges Derveau, a chemist from Pâturages, contrived an official-looking stamp for the cards, bearing the name of a fictitious commune.

The Red Cross hospital at Bavay was put under German guard. A British officer, Captain Preston of the Royal Artillery, escaped from it one night in October. He came to the château, threw gravel at a window and woke the de Croÿs. They hid him in the old tower, the walls of which were 9 feet thick. They rigged up an alarm system to alert him to danger and conveyed messages to and from him and the men in the forest.

At the beginning of the war it was relatively easy for Belgian civilians to leave the country. The Prince de Croÿ, who had high-level diplomatic connections, managed often to get to Holland and London. He collected money from the British government for resistance work, and gathered and imparted information about the dead, the missing, and the progress of the war. On a twenty-four-hour visit to London in November 1914 he was besieged with pleas for news of missing relatives and friends and requests to pass on messages. He made long coded lists of these and gave them to a spy, with the promise of reward if the list was handed back to him in Brussels. Which it was. One of the requests was from a Mrs Boger who had heard that her husband, a colonel wounded at Mons, had been nursed in an English hospital in Brussels. De Croÿ learned of an English matron at the head of Dr Depage's clinic in rue de la Culture.

Throughout the country, cells of resistance, balancing prudence and risk, interlaced, but so did German surveillance. German patrols divided the Mormal forest into numbered squares and searched these systematically. The men hiding there knew they would be flushed out. Four of the English soldiers were captured. In December the others feared snow would make their footprints visible. One night the Girl Guides brought thirty of them, including their leader, Lieutenant Bushell, in two groups to the château. Henriette Moriamé led one group, Louise Thuliez the other. The men put socks over their boots so as to make no noise as they walked. English army boots had a recognisable imprint. The gardener at the château raked away such signs.

The Princess had difficulty feeding and concealing so many men. She gave them vegetables from the garden, the butcher gave meat, the baker delivered fifteen loaves of bread each night, but it was all too risky. Captain Preston said the men must give themselves up. They could not continually endanger the lives of their helpers. At Lille, citizens had been shot for hiding an English pilot. He and Lieutenant Bushell, because they were officers, would stay in hiding. They moved to the home of a neighbour of the de Croÿs, Baron de Witte, in the Château de Gussignies.

For two days Louise Thuliez and Henriette Moriamé tramped more than 40 kilometres looking for a break in enemy lines to get the other men over the Belgian border into Holland. They failed to find a safe route. The men surrendered from the Red Cross hospital in Bavay. The Germans fined all the forest villages, took the Mayor of Bavay hostage until the fines were paid and sent the soldiers to a prisoner-of-war camp at Wittenberg for the duration of the war.

Too late for those men came news that there was indeed a way of escape across the Dutch border. It came from the Countess Jeanne de Belleville, a friend of the de Croÿs, who lived at the village of Montigny sur Roc. She, her sister, and their nephew Eric de Belleville, had looked after more than 400 English wounded, in the convent at Audregnies, after the retreat from Mons. Her nephew then wanted to get through to join the French army. She found that the Abbot of Longueville led men to the Dutch border from Brussels. 'The Countess was French,'

Louise Thuliez wrote of her: 'she had blue eyes and curly grey hair, an aquiline nose and rapid, energetic walk. She seemed indefatigable. Everything about her breathed simplicity and goodness. Her natural gaiety was such that in the most tragic moments of our adventure she remained smiling and undaunted.' Captain Preston and Lieutenant Bushell decided to try to escape with the Abbot's help. Reginald de Croÿ went to Mons and got false identity cards, passports and papers for them. On 29 December the officers set off to meet him there guided by Louise Thuliez and the de Croÿs' maid, Charlotte Matha, who knew the area well. They met the Prince at the Church of St Waudru in Mons as prearranged. On their new cards the men, who spoke no French, were Belgian hairdressers' assistants. On the tram from Mons to Brussels they got off when the German inspector got on at Enghien, then got on again when he had finished. From Brussels the Abbot of Longueville guided them to the Dutch border. This time they were disguised as carpenters and carrying tools. Both returned to active service: Captain Preston in Mesopotamia and Lieutenant Bushell in France.

With a means of crossing the frontier found, the de Croÿs, Louise Thuliez, Henriette Moriamé, Jeanne de Belleville and others, sought out more *enfants perdus* and helped get them out of Belgium. From the château at Bellignies Reginald de Croÿ directed them to safe houses in Brussels. From these safe houses the men were guided to the frontier and to freedom. One of these safe houses was with Edith Cavell at the Nurses' School in rue de la Culture. When de Croÿ called on Edith Cavell to get news of Colonel Boger, he learned of how she had nursed and sheltered him and helped orchestrate his escape, but that he had been arrested before he left Brussels. He learned that Edith Cavell too was a 'patriot', defying the German authorities despite the risk, and doing all she could to help Allied soldiers cut off from their regiments by the fighting. But whereas he was proactive in espionage and recruitment of soldiers, her role was to help those in peril who arrived at her door: to nurse their wounds, shield them and get them to safety. She told the Prince she would shelter any men he sent to her, either in the School, or in other safe houses known to her. By way of password the men were to say they came from Mr Yorc.

And so from November 1914 until July 1915 a steady stream of men, sent by the Prince, by Jeanne de Belleville, by Louise Thuliez or Henriette Moriamé, arrived at rue de la Culture.

Private Harry Beaumont of the Royal West Kent Regiment came to the door in March 1915 after living as a fugitive for seven months. On the night of 24 August, after the retreat from Mons, when he regained consciousness he had crawled through fields to the village of Wasmes. A villager gave him food and clothes. His wounds were treated in a makeshift hospital in the colliery. Herman Capiau provided him with a false identity card and papers. He survived rough in woodland and was sheltered for four months by an out-of-work family, Émile and Marie Neusy, who denied his existence to Reginald de Croÿ because they were not sure if they could trust him. He then lodged with a prostitute, Marie Godart, and feigned being deaf and mute so as not to reveal he was English. He then again contacted Capiau, who took him to the de Croÿs' château, and from there, with a party of eight Irishmen from the Connaught Rangers, he was escorted to Mons, then Brussels:

> Late in the afternoon our tram arrived at its destination, the Place Rouppe. Here our party alighted and followed our guide by a devious route through the cobblestone streets of Brussels until we were ushered into a hospital clinic in rue de la Culture. Here we were surprised to be welcomed by an Englishwoman who appeared to be in charge. We had not expected that! She showed us a room where the only

light came through a skylight in the roof as it was match-
boarded all round so no prying eyes could peep in through
the windows. It was plainly furnished with scrubbed
wooden tables and benches and heated by a typical Belgian
stove standing in the centre. A dozen or so British soldiers,
waiting for an opportunity to be guided to the frontier,
were there already. Most of the men were from the Munster
Fusiliers.

There were about twenty men to conceal. They were not as
amenable to discipline as her probationer nurses. Edith Cavell
told them they could go out in the evening for walks, singly or
in pairs, but that they must be back by 9.00 when lights were
put out in the wards. She warned there were many German
officers billeted in houses close to the Clinic. On the third night,
by 10.00, only two of them had returned. The others got drunk
in a café, got into a fight and rolled back at midnight singing
'It's a Long Way to Tipperary'.

Next day she broke them into small groups and lodged them
in different safe houses. Beaumont and an Irishman, Michael
Carey, stayed with Louis Séverin, a chemist in Uccle. Carey, with
eleven others from the Munster Fusiliers, had sheltered for
months with a miller at the village of Hiron. One morning when
Carey was out the mill was raided, the other men from his regiment and the miller were shot, the mill and its outhouses were
burned, and the miller's wife and family were sent as prisoners
to Germany.

After seven days with the Séverins, Beaumont and Carey were
led by guides to a monastery at Averbode and eventually crossed
the border disguised as monks.

The network of help interlaced, interacted and expanded,
search parties became more assiduous and determined at finding
lost men, and the number of helpers and safe havens increased.

At the same time, the occupying army became more tenacious at flushing out hiding places, spying on protectors, apprehending guides, wire-fencing the borders, policing the trains and trams, tightening the curfews and increasing punishments. Spies were planted, suspects stalked, death threats posted in public places: house an English or French soldier and you may be shot, send a message by carrier pigeon and you may be shot, publish a clandestine newspaper and you may be shot. Sinister though such threats were, they did not deter Edith Cavell or her friends from giving such help as they could.

25

MY DARLING MOTHER

So Edith Cavell, the most honest and straightforward of citizens, was drawn into deception and danger, alarm at the knock on the door, wariness of footsteps behind her or of apprisal by strangers, the concealment of sealed windows, disguises, false papers and coded exchange.

She was concerned for her mother who lived alone. She was unable to send her money, or freely to write to her. She wanted news of her sisters and brother, birthday wishes conveyed, messages sent to Grace Jemmett's parents, messages relayed to Sister White and Sister Burt when they left the clinic for the relative safety of home.

'We are all well – have no fear for us,' she wrote to her mother on 9 September. 'Brussels is quiet and life goes on the same; don't be afraid if the papers give alarming reports – we are not interfered with at all . . .'

The alarming reports in the papers were of the bloodbath of war. By 1 September 1914 it seemed Germany would achieve its goal of conquering France. Their First and Second Armies got within 40 kilometres of Paris. For ten consecutive days British and French forces had been in retreat. The French government left Paris for Bordeaux, expecting defeat. Instructed by their commander Alexander von Kluck, Germany's First Army began to encircle Paris from the east. But when they reached the River Marne, France's commander-in-chief Joseph Joffre launched a massive counter-offensive, aided by Britain's Sir John French, who agreed to it after being prompted by Lord Kitchener.

It became known as the Battle of the Marne. It lasted from 6 to 9 September. On the morning of 6 September the French Sixth Army of 150,000 men attacked the German First Army. As the First Army turned to meet this attack, a 40-kilometre-wide gap formed between them and their Second Army. French and British soldiers poured into this gap. To add to the force of this assault, on 7 September 6,000 French infantry troops were taxied out from Paris.

On 9 September the German armies began to retreat, pursued by the French and British. In those few days 250,000 French soldiers died, the same number of Germans, and 12,733 British from the Expeditionary Force. Thus the Battle of the Marne: a battle that saved Paris, and turned what might have been a six-week conquest by Germany into a four-year world war. The German army stopped its retreat after 50 kilometres, just north of the River Aisne. Its First and Second Armies then dug in, by preparing trenches. Stalemate and years of trench warfare followed. 'All my thoughts, all my prospective plans, all my possible alternatives of action were concentrated upon a war of movement and manoeuvre,' Field Marshal Sir John French, who led the British Expeditionary Force, had written. He, like the other generals, had expected this war to be over in weeks, or at worst months. None of them had anticipated hundreds of thousands of men spending years slaughtering each other in trenches that became ready-made graves.

Failure at the Marne made the occupying army in Belgium more vicious. Surveillance was stepped up. Edith Cavell was reminded by the Military Governor, General Baron Arthur von Luttwitz, second in command to the Governor General, of her obligations in nursing British soldiers. All must be reported to the authorities. When her nurses went to market in search of food, their baskets were searched to see if they were carrying clothes to help Allied soldiers escape in disguise. Luttwitz, a large, pink, strong-jawed man, wore the black-and-white ribbon of the Iron Cross and the white Maltese Cross of the Order of St John of Jerusalem on his uniform. He had been complicit in the destruction of Louvain. He cancelled payment for requisitioned property and food, tightened censorship, seized ironwork for weaponry – even bronze and copper doorknobs and cooking utensils, and commandeered the park for German officers to exercise their horses – the Bois de la Cambre, at the end of avenue Louise, where all of Brussels liked to go, and where in her governess days Edith Cavell had so often walked with the François children.

Belgians eager for uncensored news paid 15 francs merely to read a smuggled copy of *Le Figaro* or *The Times*. Most information about the war was by word of mouth, but also through clandestine newssheets: *Les Petits Mots du Soldat* for news of and to fugitive soldiers, and *La Libre Belgique,* a four-page 'seditious pamphlet' published weekly 'somewhere in Belgium'. Entirely defiant, it mocked the occupation and incensed the *Kommandantur*, not least by its sardonic tone. Eugene van Doren, in a cupboard-sized room in an outbuilding of his cardboard factory, printed 25,000 copies an issue. It called itself 'a bulletin of patriotic propaganda', contained news censored by the German press and leading articles from other papers, urged readers to pass copies on, and said its objective was to unite Belgian citizens, defy the Germans and tell the truth. 'It will live in spite of persecution and official censure because there is something stronger than might, stronger than Kultur, something stronger than the Germans – the truth! And Belgium is the land of truth and liberty.' On seven occasions, disguised as a German officer, van Doren took documents from the office of the Governor General, and left copies of *La Libre Belgique* in their place. Philippe Baucq, a Brussels architect, was the paper's most intrepid distributor. He was Catholic, a patriot, flamboyant in a long black cloak and

Philippe Baucq (1880–1915)

wide-brimmed hat, and lived with his wife Marie and their two daughters in Schaerbeek, a suburb of Brussels.

Edith Cavell was circumspect in her letters home. 'My darling mother,' she wrote on 15 September:

I have written to you on every possible chance but do not know whether all or any of my letters have arrived. I am most anxious to hear from you and hope soon to be able to send you an address to which you may write. Even now I dare not tell you our news in detail as letters must be left open and are not safe . . . I hope you have not been worrying about me . . . everything is quiet at our end of

the town and except that we have practically no work, life goes on as usual . . . no trains are running to convey letters and the telegraphic communications are cut . . . so do not be anxious because you do not hear. There are a great many wounded in town, but very few Belgians or English – our nurses are busy at work among them. . . . It has turned wet now & chilly & I am very anxious about coal of which our supply is small – none is coming in with no trains – I only hope we may be able to get a good supply before the winter sets in. We are busy making garments for the poor, there will be great need of them this winter – there are so many refugees and so many homeless. . .
My dearest love – don't be anxious.

She was marginally less cautious to her sister Florence. 'Dearest Flor,' she wrote on 18 September:

Your letter was the greatest pleasure to me the first I have had of any sort since Aug. 15th. I have tried to write a great many times or rather to send but I am afraid that the letters – which cost anything up to 3 francs – don't arrive. I am glad that Mother has at last received one as she must have been horribly anxious – indeed she says so – I got a letter from her by the same channel. Of course she urges me to come home & equally of course that is out of the question – we are actually doing no work among the wounded, as everything is out of our hands at present and the enemy have made their own arrangements. I cannot give you any details as our letters may fall into hands not intended for them; this will be carried to Holland & I hope will reach you from there . . . All is quiet just now & life goes on in many ways as usual. At present we have few patients but are affiliated to the Red Cross & may later under different conditions have much work to do.

Little Jack is well and would like to bite certain legs . . .
Thousands and thousands are homeless. The poverty and
misery this winter is likely to be terrible – we spend any
spare time making clothes.

Sending letters became ever more hazardous. She sent those from
a Dutch address, a M. Sturman in Vecht. Her mother wanted her
home. She could not see why, if there was little nursing for her,
her daughter should stay in harm's way. Because she was English,
Edith Cavell was vulnerable. But for as long as she could help she
would remain in Belgium. She was relieved when her mother
went to stay with Lilian in Henley: 'It will shorten the winter for
you.' It also meant her mother was not alone with her fears.

'I am afraid you must have been anxious but I have not been
able to find any means of sending this letter up till the present,'
she wrote ten days later on 19 October. An Englishman, Giles
Hibbard, posted it from London, and offered to deliver a reply
when he returned to Brussels.

The route by which the others went is closed and I can give
you no address to which you can write. I only hope you are
quite well and not worrying about us. Everything goes on
as usual, tho' all around the unusual is happening. We have
very little news, you will know a great deal more than I of
the world in general. We are short of nothing at present
tho' there is scarcity in the poor quarters & there will be
much misery all thro' the winter. We are engaged in making
up the stuff we can get into garments for the children of the
refugees and the other poor. Coal is scarce but we hope that
supplies will soon come in as a means of transit has been
opened. I shall have much to tell you later on but cannot
write it now. Gracie is much better but still not up. She
has had a long spell of illness this time. I hope though it is
nearly over.

Don't write again till I give you an address as no letters reach us now – & keep the envelopes of my letters so that we can see by what means they arrived when I return home. I am glad to think of you all safe & I hope well, with the fleet to keep away all harm from the dear country. The weather is beginning to be cold and dull now but we have had a beautiful autumn. Think of us going steadily on with our work here & at the hospital & living from day to day cheerfully & with good hope for the future.

My dear love to you & the girls & to any of my friends who may write for news.

Gracie sends her love to you & often speaks of you with affection.

As soon as the way is open I will send you an address, but it will probably not be possible for some time yet.
My dearest love to you my darling Mother,
Ever your affectionate daughter
Edith

Building materials for the new clinic were stuck in railway sidings, German hospitals had their own staff, wounded Allied soldiers were taken as prisoners of war . . . What changed was not her dedication, but the kind of work she could do. The divide between nursing, helping the hungry and poor, and shielding vulnerable soldiers was slight. What was new was the need to deceive.

'I seize every opportunity of letting you know that all is well here,' she wrote again to her mother on 22 November,

tho' there is no news that I can give you. It is *bitterly* cold with thick snow and hard frost, but bright sunshine. I suppose you are at Henley and I shall be glad to hear about your journey and arrival and about Lil and the children.

Gracie is staying with some American friends in Brussels

who thought a change after her long illness would do her good; she seems much better but is still very pale and thin.

All English men of a certain age have been taken prisoner and we are very closely surrounded. There is a curious shut in feeling and the atmosphere (moral) presses more and more heavily, tho' if you, as a stranger, walked thro' the city you would see little to indicate a state of war – life goes on just the same and yet with an immense difference. We have had more news lately – people coming from Holland or England think prospects are brighter and are much more hopeful than we are.

We have had some interesting work but are quiet again now. Our people who left last week must have arrived safely as they have not returned – if so you will have had my hastily scribbled letter – and will have sent £2 for me to Miss Millicent White c/o Dr White whose address you know; it is the rest of her salary which I owe her.

We are preparing for our Xmas Tree and the nurses are spending all their spare time in dressing dolls and making war clothes and little odds and ends for our poor children. It is terrible to think of all the misery and suffering, and the cold has begun so unfortunately early.

You said you had heard from several of my friends some time ago – I should be glad to know who has written to you. Did the lady next door to Cumberland Cottage make enquiries?

Several of our nurses and others have been ill with a kind of colic that appears to be due to the black bread, which is not bad, but very heavy to digest. The hospital's half empty. The authorities cannot afford to take in many patients as money is very scarce. A great deal is owing to us which we cannot get and many others are in the same difficulty. Quite rich people are practically penniless and are having to live in the cheapest way possible, some are irretrievably ruined. Numbers and numbers have left the country not to return till conditions are totally changed – servants and employees have been dismissed and great numbers are out of work. You remember how difficult it used to be to get a cook or a housemaid? There is no difficulty now, many men are working for quarter wages. One employer told me some are working for their bread and butter – no wages. Little children are always coming to our door for *tartines* – Marie saves them our bread and butter and when they see her pass the door with the tray there is a rush.

Could you send me 3 or 4 stamps in your next letter as I cannot stamp this and am afraid you may have to pay double postage from London. The house next door is let in flats and the walls are so thin that we can hear a good deal of what goes on – a disadvantage, but compensated by the fact that our house is warmer and drier than in previous winters.

The new School progresses very slowly – some of the glass and the iron work of the doors is stuck on the railways and has been since August – also the workmen are unable to come from any distance on account of the standstill in all traffic. We shall not be in next year now I expect.
My very dear love to you all
Ever your affectionate daughter
Edith

She needed stamps because the letters she sent would be posted by escaping soldiers in England. She needed information about the arrival of these men – needed to know escape routes were safe, for those whom she was yet to help. She worried about her family's safety, about invasion of England and bombardment from the sea. 'We hear the guns at night,' she wrote, and feared the fighting would engulf them too. Lilian returned to hospital nursing again as her part in the war effort; Jack was a special constable and 'doing his share'. 'The lady next door to Cumberland Cottage' was the schoolteacher Mrs Tapscott, who she had hoped would find news about one, or some, of the escaping men. A disadvantage of thin walls between the School and the next-door house was that it was hard to impose rules of silence on young soldiers.

Her life in Brussels was less quiet than she conveyed in letters home. She told her mother about privation: the black bread, the empty hospital, lack of money, the slow progress on the new School. Only by allusion, though, to her mother or anyone, could she confide news about disguised soldiers who knocked at the door with the password Yorc, her contacts for safe houses, the money she raised, the guides she procured, the false papers she acquired.

The 'cruel vindictive foe' tightened its clampdown. In December 1914 the Kaiser sent a new Governor General to Brussels: General Baron Moritz von Bissing. Brand Whitlock at the American Legation described him as 'a man whose name was destined to stand forth to the world as the symbol of one of the darkest, cruellest and most sinister pages of its miserable history'. He was in his seventies, tall, thin, with grey hair plastered back and a wide moustache. He wore a ceremonial sabre, and silver spurs in his boots. He liked shooting deer and hanging their antlers on the commandeered walls. His first act, by a decree of 8 December, was to impose on the Belgian population a war levy of 480 million francs. After that he policed and circumscribed every aspect of their lives. One of his more grisly edicts was that the bodies of dead animals not fit for food be delivered up to the Oelzentrale to be rendered into grease. Word went round that he was using the bodies of dead soldiers – of which there were plenty. *La Libre Belgique* lampooned him mercilessly and incensed him. One issue showed him sitting at his desk reading a copy of it; another showed him bowed down under the weight of arrest warrants for the publishers of the paper; yet another had a cartoon of the Kaiser in hell. Von Bissing offered large rewards for the arrest of those writing, printing and distributing *La Libre Belgique*, declared it espionage to carry a copy across the Belgian frontier, and ruled that to possess it was a crime punishable with a fine of 5,000 to 75,000 francs and imprisonment of up to a year.

Early in the new year he decreed that notices be posted instructing all British, French and Russian nationals to register at the École Militaire on prescribed dates. The decree had previously applied only to men. Now it was extended to women too. Severe punishment was threatened for those who failed to register, or who sheltered anyone required to do so.

Ruth Moore discussed the edict with Edith Cavell who told her she was not going to comply: she belonged to a Belgian training school and was working for the Belgian Red Cross. She advised Ruth Moore not to register and, if questioned by any official, to refer him to her. Ruth Moore felt uneasy at this advice. She thought it might bring trouble to the Red Cross under whose flag she was working, and to herself. As she saw it she was an Englishwoman who had complied fully with the authorities. She had done nothing they might construe as wrong. She had letters from German patients whom she had nursed so well that they had returned to the fighting lines. She sought an interview with the head of the Brussels Red Cross. He said there was no doubt she must register. He told her to get to the École Militaire at rue du Méridien early on the appointed day and wear the Red Cross armband. She had to walk between two rows of German soldiers with fixed bayonets. Some were her old patients. She was given an identity card with her name, nationality and age, and told to check in every fortnight with this card. She wondered why her

NUMÉRO 30 — JUIN 1915

PRIX DU NUMÉRO — élastique, de zéro à l'infini (prière aux revendeurs de ne pas dépasser cette limite)

LA LIBRE BELGIQUE

Acceptons provisoirement les sacrifices qui nous sont imposés......
et attendons patiemment l'heure de la réparation.
Le Bourgmestre ADOLPHE MAX.

FONDÉE
LE 1ᵉʳ FÉVRIER 1915

Envers et personnes qui dominent par la force militaire notre pays, ayons les égards que commande l'intérêt général. Respectons les réglements qu'elles nous imposent aussi longtemps qu'ils ne portent atteinte ni à la liberté de nos consciences chrétienne ni à notre *Dignité patriotique.* Mᵍʳ MERCIER.

BULLETIN DE PROPAGANDE PATRIOTIQUE — RÉGULIÈREMENT IRRÉGULIER
NE SE SOUMETTANT A AUCUNE CENSURE

ADRESSE TÉLÉGRAPHIQUE
KOMMANDANTUR - BRUXELLES

BUREAUX ET ADMINISTRATION
ne pouvant être un emplacement de tout repos, ils sont installés dans une cave automobile

ANNONCES : Les affaires étant nulles sous la domination allemande, nous avons supprimé la page d'annonces et conseillons à nos clients de réserver leur argent pour des temps meilleurs.

AVIS.

On nous fait à nouveau l'honneur de s'occuper de notre modeste bulletin. Nous en sommes flattés, mais nous nous voyons, forcés de répéter ce que nous avons déjà dit pour notre défense. Ce n'est certes pas nous qu'on peut accuser sans manquer à la vérité, de provoquer nos concitoyens à la révolte. Nous ne manquons pas une occasion de prêcher la patience, l'endurance, le calme et le respect des lois de la guerre. Aussi profitons-nous de cette occasion qui nous est offerte pour répéter l'avis que nous avons déjà inséré :

RESTONS CALMES!!!

Le jour viendra (lentement mais sûrement) ou nos ennemis contraints de reculer devant les Alliés, devront abandonner notre capitale.
Souvenons-nous alors des avis nombreux qui ont été donnés aux civils par le Gouvernement et par notre bourgmestre

SON EXCELLENCE LE GOUVERNEUR Bᵒⁿ VON BISSING ET SON AMIE INTIME

NOTRE CHER GOUVERNEUR, ÉCŒURÉ PAR LA LECTURE DES MENSONGES DES JOURNAUX CENSURÉS, CHERCHE LA VÉRITÉ DANS LA « LIBRE BELGIQUE »

M. Max : SOYONS CALMES!!!

Faisons taire les sentiments de légitime colère qui fermentent en nos cœurs.

Soyons, comme nous l'avons été jusqu'ici, respectueux des lois de la guerre. C'est ainsi que nous continuerons à mériter l'estime et l'admiration de tous les peuples civilisés.

Ce serait une INUTILE LACHETÉ, une lâcheté indigne des Belges que de chercher à se venger ailleurs que sur le champ de bataille. Ce serait de plus EXPOSER DES INNOCENTS à des représailles terribles de la part d'ennemis sans pitié et sans justice.

Méfions-nous des agents provocateurs allemands qui, en exaltant notre patriotisme, nous pousseraient à commettre des excès.

RESTONS MAITRES DE NOUS-MÊMES ET PRÊCHONS LE CALME AUTOUR DE NOUS. C'EST LE PLUS GRAND SERVICE QUE NOUS PUISSIONS RENDRE A NOTRE CHÈRE PATRIE.

L'ORDRE SOCIAL TOUT ENTIER DEFENDU PAR LA BELGIQUE.

Le 3 août, le Gouvernement allemand remet à la Belgique une note demandant le libre passage pour ses armées sur son territoire, moyennant quoi l'Allemagne s'engage à maintenir l'intégrité du royaume et de ses possessions, Sinon, la Belgique sera traitée en ennemie. Le roi Albert a douze heures pour répondre. Devant cet ultimatum, il n'hésite pas. Il sait que l'armée allemande est une force terrible. Il connaît l'empe-

reur allemand. Il sait que l'orgueilleux, après une telle démarche, ne reculera plus. Son trône est en jeu, plus que son trône . les sept millions d'âmes — quelle éloquence prennent les vulgaires termes des statistiques dans certaines circonstances! — qui lui sont confiées . il voit en esprit ce beau pays indéfendable ces charbonnages, ces carrières, ces usines, ces filatures, ces ports, cette florissante industrie épanouie dans ces plaines ouvertes qu'il ne pourra pas préserver. Mais il s'agit d'un traité où il y a sa signature. Répondre oui à l'Allemagne, c'est trahir ses consignataires, le

PRIÈRE DE FAIRE CIRCULER CE BULLETIN

La Libre Belgique June 1915. Its faked picture shows the German Governor General Moritz von Bissing 'searching for the truth' in the paper matron chose not to obey this summons to report and thought it a mistake.

Edith Cavell did not lightly disobey an order. Obedience to male command had been impressed on her from the cradle. Her authoritarian father had preached the sermons and made the decisions. His word was law. Eva Lückes had impressed on her that as a nurse hers was a serving role: 'The Doctor prescribes; it is left to the Nurse to carry out that prescription.' But Edith Cavell had travelled far, seen much and grown in independence. Her views were hard won, her courage tested. At the age of forty-nine she was quite sure where virtue lay. This military domain of conquest and suppression was anathema to her. She would not obey the commands of von Bissing and his henchmen. She was too brave a woman to bow to threats of punishment and violence.

'My darling Mother,' she wrote on 8 January 1915 soon after the registration edict was passed:

> I take another opportunity to write to you and hope the letter will arrive. I have heard nothing from you since the two letters of Dec 17 one dated Dec 2nd & the other Nov. 24th. I know you must have written since then but nothing has reached me. I give you again the best address I can.
>
> My name & address here, & then
> c/o Mr d'Aubrie de Bournville
> Bergen op Zoom
> Holland
>
> All is well here still, tho in the country people are in great difficulty for food – bread is scarce & in many places there is none at all, the difficulty of transport is so great with no trains & no petrol & very few horses.

We are more & more shut in and are beginning to feel it a good deal. The frontiers are watched so that no one may leave the country & there is little news & no letters. A vigorous search is still being carried on for all E. men & now all foreign women have to register. The town is quiet & sad, the big shops are partly shut and some threaten to shut down entirely – that means great numbers of people out of work. Numbers of rich Belgians are in England which means that tailors & dressmakers are out of employ. Belgians here are angry about it and say they should have remained to help.

The Avenue Louise is almost entirely shut up and so are other good residential quarters.

The man who takes this letter has just come so I must close. Don't be anxious about us; we are quite well & not in any danger. Gracie is back from her visit & very much better after her 6 weeks change. Will you please send on her letter.

We hear the Gs are getting demoralised & I think they are less & less sure of the victory. The town is full of them.

My dearest love to you all & Best Wishes for a much better & Happier New Year. I hope you are well & enjoying your stay at Henley –
Ever your affectionate daughter
Edith

26

THE MEN WHO DIED IN SWATHES

The men who obeyed Kitchener's pointing finger and were inspired to defend their country, vanquish evil and safeguard freedom, died in swathes. They came from every village, hamlet, town and city, from every class and occupation. 'The British Empire is fighting for its existence,' they were told. 'I shall want more men and still more,' Kitchener said, 'until the enemy is crushed . . . Every fit man owes this duty to himself and to his country.' They were given a uniform and brief training. They were fit when they went to Flanders, in summer, to fields of corn that sparkled with red poppies. In the days and years that followed engulfing horror echoed back: in statistics – 250,000 of them dead in a day; in the poetry and prose of Hermann Hesse, Rudyard Kipling, Guillaume Apollinaire, Erich Maria Remarque, Siegfried Sassoon; in the paintings of Max Beckmann, Otto Dix, George Grosz, Paul Nash, Gino Severini, Wyndham Lewis; in incoherent photographs of craters, men impaled on barbed wire, mutilated horses, donkeys stuck in mud, gleaners raking for morsels of food, the stumps of what was a town, forest, church or leg; fat uniformed leaders covered in medals; dead horses and donkeys, German soldiers goose-stepping down boulevards, dogs pulling gun carriages, corpses in mud, women searching casualty lists, palls of smoke, refugees carrying bundles of bedding; and in the anguish of letters home from battlefields and trenches, censored if they revealed too much pain, but for many the last they heard of the young men they knew. By November 1914, along the border of Belgium and France violent battles for conquest had turned to the stagnation of trench warfare. Two warring lines of trenches stretched 600 kilometres from Switzerland to the Channel coast. Attacks staged by both sides saw advances of no more than 10 kilometres until the spring of 1918.

The entrenched armies were often only yards apart, separated by barbed wire from no man's land between. The British army held a stretch of this Western Front along what was called the

1914

Ypres Salient for 35 kilometres south to the La Bassée Canal. In these fetid ditches between 1914 and 1918 over a million fighting men died. The Allies were determined the cathedral city of Ypres should not fall to German occupation. In the first battle of Ypres, from 19 October to 22 November, British casualties were reported at 58,000.

In December 1914 the weather in Belgium was wet and cold. 'People think it is mud and wet we mind,' Corporal Parr wrote home to a friend. 'That is nothing, absolutely nothing, compared with the nerve-racking hell of bombardment. I can't think that human nature ever had to stand in any kind of warfare in history what the modern infantryman has to stand.' He died a month later, aged twenty-seven.

'Perhaps you don't know the two sorts of shells,' Lieutenant Denis Barnett wrote to his mother: 'There's the big brute, full of lyddite or melinite or some high explosive, which bursts when it hits the ground, and makes a big hole blowing out in every direction, but chiefly upwards, and may kill you some hundreds of yards off . . . The other sort is full of bullets and timed to burst in the air when the bullets carry on forwards and downwards in a fan shape . . . The crescendo effect is rather terrifying.' He had joined the army after leaving school. He was killed on 15 August 1915, aged twenty.

'As for the morals of the war, they are horrible,' Captain John Crombie of the Gordon Highlanders wrote to a friend. 'For instance, listen to this . . . When you come to a dug-out, you throw some smoke bombs down, and then smoke the rest out with a smoke bomb, so that they must either choke or come out. Now when they come out they are half blinded and choked with poisonous smoke, and you station a man at the entrance to receive them, but as you have only got a party of nine, it would be difficult to spare men if you took them prisoners, so the instructions are that these poor half-blinded devils should be bayoneted as they come up. It may be expedient from a military point of view, but if it had been suggested before the war, who would not have held up their hands in horror?' He was killed in France in April 1917, aged twenty.

'I have only had my boots off once in the last 10 days and only washed twice,' Julian Grenfell wrote to his mother from Flanders in October 1914. 'Our poor horses do not get their saddles off when we are in the trenches. The wretched inhabitants here have got practically no food left. It is miserable to see them leaving their houses, and tracking away, with great bundles and children in their hands. And the dogs and cats left in the deserted villages are piteous . . .' He was killed in May 1915, aged twenty-seven.

Eight million horses were to die in this war. They too rotted into the earth like the ten million fighting men. Of the million horses requisitioned by the British Army, 62,000 returned. They came from safe stables, green fields and quiet villages. They had names when they left. They died stabbed in cavalry charges, caught in the path of battle tanks, enmeshed in barbed wire, blasted by shells in battle, or sunk in the mud of shell craters. They gnawed at the wood of gun carriages because they were so starved. They were worked to exhaustion and shot when they could do no more.

'Oh the smell of the cows and the new mown hay, after being in the cage with 22 unburied Germans,' William Grenfell wrote home, two months after his brother Julian died. 'Do you know I had not seen a *corpus vile* since I was fifteen, at the Morgue, and dreamed of it for weeks afterwards. I guess you could not show me much new now in that line . . .' He was killed in Flanders in July 1915. He was twenty-five.

'Do you think that the experience of this War has made the general public realise that there must be other ways of settling points of dispute which are as satisfactory as the way of bloodshed?' Lieutenant Horace Fletcher wrote to his mother in 1916.

A stretcher party carrying wounded men, 1915

Mules and men with the British ammunition corps, 1915

'If man were to make a venture of faith, and believe that there *is* a way (if demanding more patience), such a way would be found.' He had wanted to be a priest. He was killed in March 1917, aged twenty-eight.

'The suffering of men at the Front,' Captain William Mason wrote to his father, 'of the wounded whose flesh and bodies are torn in a way you cannot conceive; the sorrow of those at home who hear of casualties among their dear ones, and the ever present anxiety for those who are not casualties. And all that is being piled up day after day in France, England, Germany, Bulgaria and Turkey! What a cruel and mad diversion of human activity! Food indeed for pessimism if ever there was . . .' He was a lecturer at Bristol University. He was killed aged twenty-seven in July 1916 in France.

'The road thirty yards behind us was a nightmare to me,' Lieutenant Colonel John McCrae wrote to his mother in May 1915. 'I saw all the tragedies of war enacted there. A wagon, or a bunch of horses, or a stray man, or a couple of men, would get there just in time for a shell. One would see the absolute knock-out, and the obviously lightly wounded crawling off on hands and knees; or worse yet, at night, one would hear the tragedy – "that horse scream" – or the man's moan. Seventeen days of Hades . . .' He was a doctor. He was killed in January 1918 in France, aged forty-five.

'Any faith in religion I ever had is most frightfully shaken by things I've seen,' Lieutenant Peter Layard wrote to his parents in March 1916, 'and it's incredible that if God could make a 17-inch shell not explode – it seems incredible that he lets them explode . . . I hate the whole thing, and so do we all, because it shouldn't be.' He was killed in France in August 1918 at the age of twenty-two.

'If I live I mean to spend the rest of my life working for perpetual peace,' Captain Thomas Kettle wrote to his brother a week before he died in France in September 1916. 'I have seen war and faced modern artillery and know what an outrage it is against simple men . . . The bombardment, destruction and bloodshed are beyond all imagination, nor did I ever think the valour of simple men could be quite as beautiful as that of my Dublin Fusiliers.' He was a barrister. He was thirty-two when he died.

'It is VILE that all my time should be devoted to killing Germans whom I don't in the least want to kill,' Brigadier-General Philip Howele wrote to his wife in November 1914. 'If all Germany could be united in one man and he and I could be shut up together just to talk things out, we could settle the war, I feel, in less than one hour. The ideal war would include long and frequent armistices during which both sides could walk across the trenches and discuss their respective points of view. We are really only fighting just because we are all so ignorant and stupid. And if diplomats were really clever such a thing as war could never be.' He was killed in France in October 1916 aged thirty-eight.

A third of Allied casualties were sustained in the trenches. Shells turned them to graves. Snipers' bullets killed those sent out to mend barbed wire, relieve others, bring supplies. There were infestations of rats, brown and black, gorging on dead men, spreading infection and contaminating food. Lice bred in the seams of filthy clothing and spread trench fever. Recovery took twelve weeks. Trench foot was a fungal infection caused by cold, wet and dirt. If the foot turned gangrenous it was amputated.

Antoine Depage's military hospital, the Ambulance de l'Océan at the coastal town of La Panne, was near the trenches. It had begun with 200 beds, had 900 by 1916 and 2,000 by the war's end. Depage organised it into wings and segregated casualties according to their type of wounds. He set up a laboratory alongside it to analyse infected and injured tissue. He also sent mobile units from the hospital to the trenches – four cars to collect the wounded and a trailer fitted as an operating theatre for immediate treatment of grievous wounds.

The trenches of the Western Front were in fertile farmland, cultivated, manured and rich in pathogenic microbes. Seriously wounded men lay in mud until night fell, or a truce allowed them to be taken to medical care. The dead were left to rot in shallow graves: 'mud and dirt pervade everything; and bacteriological investigations of the soil, of the clothing, and of the skin demonstrate the presence of the most dangerous pathogenic organisms in all three.' Alexander Fleming did many bacteriological studies in Depage's research unit. Clothing samples from wounded soldiers contained the bacilli that caused dysentery, tetanus, and streptococcal and staphylococcal infection. Ten per cent of casualties developed gangrene.

Antoine Depage's strategy with mass casualties, extreme injuries and endemic infection, was to treat mortal complications immediately and to keep lesser wounds covered and free from infection until the men could be taken to other hospitals. He thought all war wounds should be viewed as infected, and he used a surgical technique called debridement of cutting away infected and mangled tissue. He would resect the whole area of the wound and not suture it if any bacteria were present: 'The wide debridement of the wound, with resection of contused tissue and removal of particles of clothing and other foreign bodies, must be considered a strict rule . . .' His radical methods, though hugely scarring, at a time when there were no antibiotics saved many wounded men from fatal infection.

27

CHRISTMAS 1914

Christmas Day 1914 in Belgium, France and England was clear, frosty and sunny. The cold hardened the mud in the trenches and made existence more tolerable. In different places along the Western Front a spontaneous truce occurred. In the morning, soldiers put their heads above the trenches and called out 'Merry Christmas' across the barbed wire in their enemy's language. They crawled out to greet each other, met in no man's land, shook hands, exchanged souvenirs, smoked and drank together and played soccer. Many soldiers wrote home about it in wonder. Captain Edward Westrow Hulse sent one such letter to his mother. He had been educated at Eton and Balliol College, Oxford, and was with the Scots Guards:

Flanders 28/12/14

My dearest mother,
Just returned to billets again, after the most extraordinary Christmas in the trenches you could possibly imagine. Words fail me completely in trying to describe it, but here goes!
    On the 23rd we took over the trenches in the ordinary manner, relieving the Grenadiers, and during the 24th the usual firing took place, and sniping was pretty brisk. We stood to arms as usual at 6.30 a.m. on the 25th, and I noticed that there was not much shooting; this gradually died down and by 8 a.m. there was no shooting at all except for a few shots on our left. At 8.30 a.m. I was looking

out, and saw four Germans leave their trenches and come towards us; I told two of my men to go and meet them *unarmed* (as the Germans were unarmed) and to see that they did not pass the half-way line. We were 350–400 yards apart at this point. My fellows were not very keen, not knowing what was up, so I went out alone, and met Barry, one of our ensigns, also coming out from another part of the line. By the time we got to them they were three quarters of the way over, and much too near our barbed wire, so I moved them back. They were three private soldiers and a stretcher-bearer and their spokesman started off by saying that he thought it only right to come over and wish us a happy Christmas, and trusted us implicitly to keep the truce . . .

We then entered on a long discussion on every sort of thing. I was dressed in an old stocking-cap and a man's overcoat, and they took me for a corporal, a thing which I did not discourage, as I had an eye to going as near their lines as possible . . . I asked them what orders they had from their officers as to coming over to us, and they said *none*; they had just come over out of goodwill.

They protested that they had no feeling of enmity towards us at all, but that everything lay with their authorities, and that being soldiers they had to obey. I believe that they were speaking the truth when they said this, and that they never wished to fire a shot again. They said that unless directly ordered, they were not going to shoot again until we did . . . We talked about the ghastly wounds made by rifle bullets, and we both agreed that neither of us used dum-dum bullets, and that the wounds are solely inflicted by the high velocity bullet with the sharp nose, at short range. We both agreed that it would be far better if we used the old South African round-nosed bullet, which makes a clean hole . . .

They think that our Press is to blame in working up feeling against them by publishing false 'atrocity reports'. I told them of various sweet little cases which I have seen for myself, and they told me of English prisoners whom they have seen with soft-nosed bullets, and lead bullets with notches cut in the nose; we had a heated, and at the same time good-natured argument, and ended by hinting to each other that the other was lying!

I kept it up for half an hour, and then escorted them back as far as their barbed wire, having a jolly good look round all the time, and picking up various little bits of information which I had not had an opportunity of doing under fire! I left instructions with them that if any of them came out later they must not come over the half-way line, and appointed a ditch as the meeting place. We parted after an exchange of Albany cigarettes and German cigars and I went straight to H-qrs to report.

On my return at 10 a.m. I was surprised to hear a hell of a din going on, and not a single man left in my trenches; they were completely denuded (against my orders) and nothing lived! I heard strains of 'Tipperary' floating down the breeze, swiftly followed by a tremendous burst of 'Deutschland Über Alles' and as I got to my own Coy H-qrs dug-out, I saw to my amazement not only a crowd of about 150 British and Germans at the half-way house which I had appointed opposite my lines, but six or seven such crowds, all the way down our lines, extending towards the 8th Division on our right. I bustled out and asked if there were any German officers in my crowd, and the noise died down (as this time I was myself in my own cap and badges of rank).

I found two, but had to talk to them through an

interpreter, as they could neither talk English nor French
. . . I explained to them that strict orders must be
maintained as to meeting half-way and everyone unarmed;
and we both agreed not to fire until the other did, thereby
creating a complete deadlock and armistice (if strictly
observed).

Meanwhile Scots and Huns were fraternising in the
most genuine possible manner. Every sort of souvenir
was exchanged, addresses given and received, photos of
families shown, etc. One of our fellows offered a German
a cigarette; the German said, 'Virginian?' Our fellow said
'Aye, straight-cut,' the German said 'No thanks, I only
smoke Turkish!' (sort of 10/- a 100!) It gave us all a good
laugh.

A German NCO with the Iron Cross – gained he told
me for conspicuous skill in sniping – started his fellows off
on some marching tune. When they had done I set the note
for 'The Boys of Bonnie Scotland, Where the heather and
the bluebells grow', and so we went on, singing everything
from 'Good King Wenceslas' down to the ordinary
Tommies' song, and ended up with 'Auld Lang Syne', which
we all, English, Scots, Irish, Prussian, Wurtembergers, etc.,
joined in. It was absolutely astounding, and if I had seen it
on a cinematograph film, I should have sworn that it was
faked! . . .

From foul rain and wet, the weather had cleared up
the night before to a sharp frost, and it was a perfect day,
everything white, and the silence seemed extraordinary after
the usual din. From all sides birds seemed to arrive, and
we hardly ever see a bird generally. Later in the day I fed
about 50 sparrows outside my dug-out which shows how
complete the silence and quiet was.

I must say that I was very much impressed with the

whole scene, and also, as everyone else, astoundingly relieved by the quiet and by being able to walk about freely. It is the first time, day or night, that we have heard no guns, or rifle-firing, since I left Havre . . .

Just after we had finished 'Auld Lang Syne' an old hare started up and seeing so many of us about in an unwonted spot did not know which way to go. I gave one loud 'View Holloa' and one and all, British and Germans, rushed about giving chase, slipping up on the frozen plough, falling about, and after a hot two minutes we killed in the open, a German and one of our fellows falling together heavily upon the completely baffled hare. Shortly afterwards we saw four more hares, and killed one again; both were good heavy weight and had evidently been out between the two rows of trenches for the last two months, well-fed on the cabbage patches many of which are untouched on the 'no-man's land'. The enemy kept one and we kept the other . . .

During the afternoon another coursing meeting took place, with no result and at 4.30 p.m. we agreed to keep in our respective trenches and told them the truce was ended . . .

Ten weeks later Captain Edward Hamilton Westrow Hulse was killed, aged twenty-five.

Along the Western Front British and German front line soldiers, officers and men, sang carols together, took photographs, arranged joint burials of the dead. It was the only unofficial truce of the war. By the following Christmas orders had been given to both sides prohibiting any repeat of it.

These were young men who obeyed orders, who wanted to be heroic, who felt no enmity toward those on whom they inflicted mortal violence. They killed in response to a higher command. Christmas was a day to go beyond military orders to the idea of peace and goodwill to all men. Adolf Hitler, a corporal in the trenches at Ypres, disapproved of this truce: 'There should be no question of something like that during war,' he said. For him, there was no higher law than martial law.

At Christmas Edith Cavell moved her desk to her sitting room and turned her office into a recreation room for the nurses. 'I have a beautiful bunch of chrysanthemums on my table,' she wrote to her mother, 'nearly as big as soup plates and a curious vase which is an unexploded but empty shell that I shall bring for you to see one day.'

She gave an all-day party to which thirty very poor children came, refugees from the villages and towns. Toys, chocolate and candy had been sent by ship from America. For dinner there was roast beef and plum pudding, 'from your receipt', Edith Cavell told her mother. There was a decorated tree and for each child presents of a bundle of clothes, and a doll for the girls, a toy car or train for the boys. Sister Wilkins had a sore finger from so much sewing of dolls and clothes. For tea there were currant buns, jam tarts, and milky coffee. All the Belgian nurses allied to the School came. Many had relatives who were wounded or fighting. Grace Jemmett spent Christmas with her American friends nearby. 'She is still in very poor health and spends a great deal of time in bed,' Edith Cavell told her mother. But Pauline was at the party and José the Rumanian house manager, and Marie, Edith Cavell's German maid, and the cleaners and the cook. The Reverend Stirling Gahan arrived late in the afternoon. He was by then the only English clergyman remaining in Brussels. His wife Muriel was ill, so Edith Cavell sent her present round to their house – a tea service. He was surprised to find half a dozen British soldiers milling among the guests. These soldiers had had their Christmas dinner down in the cellar before coming up to join in the party. Two of them, Sergeant Jesse

Tunmore and Private Lewis, had arrived two days previously. The Reverend Gahan thought there was a 'spice of danger' about their presence, but it did not occur to him that Edith Cavell might be at special risk.

But there was more than a spice of danger in the work she was doing. All involved in resistance were at risk and Christmas was a single day. The Archbishop of Malines, Cardinal Mercier, Primate of Belgium – a Walloon, educated at Louvain – for his Christmas sermon distributed an account of the occupation to be read in churches. The priests who did so were arrested. 'I realise perhaps better than anyone what our poor country has suffered,' the Cardinal wrote:

> and no Belgian should doubt that my citizen's and cardinal's soul has been tortured by all these afflictions. The last four months have seemed like a century.
>
> In their thousands our brave ones have been slaughtered; wives and mothers weep for the husbands and sons they will never see again; homes are broken; misery spreads and anguish is poignant. At Malines, at Antwerp, I have watched the population of two large cities be subjected, one for six hours and the other for thirty-four, to a continuous bombardment and to have been in the throes of death. I have visited the most devastated regions of my diocese – Duffel, Lierre, Berlaer, St Rombaut, Konings-Hoyckt, Mortsel, Waelhem, Muysen, Wavre-Ste-Catherine, Wavre-Notre-Dame, Sempst, Weerde, Eppeghem, Hofstade, Elewyt, Rymenam, Boortmeerbeek, Wespelaer, Haacht, Werchter-Wackerzeel, Rotselaer, Tremeloo, Louvain, Blauwput, Kessel-Loo, Boven-Loo, Linden, Herent, Thildonck, Bueken, Relst, Aerschot, Wesemael, Hersselst, Diest, Schaffen, Moenstede, Rillaer, Gelrode – and what I have seen of ruins and ashes exceeds anything I could have imagined . . .

Churches, schools, asylums, hospitals, convents are almost entirely destroyed or in ruins. Entire villages have practically disappeared. At Werchter-Wackerzeel for instance out of 380 homes 130 remain; at Tremeloo two thirds of the community has been razed; at Bueken out of 100 houses 20 are left; at Schaffen a village of 200 dwellings 189 have disappeared; at Louvain one third of the town has been destroyed and 1074 buildings have disappeared.

In that beloved city of Louvain the superb collegiate of St Peter will never recover its splendour; the old college of St Ives; the Institute of Fine Arts; the commercial and consular school attached to the University; the venerable Halles or market buildings; our Library with its collections, *incunabula*, original manuscripts, archives – all these intellectual, historic and artistic riches, the fruit of five centuries of toil, all has been destroyed.

Many parishes are deprived of their curate . . . Thousands of Belgian citizens have been deported to German prisons – to Münster, to Celle, to Magdeburg. Münster alone holds 3100 civilian prisoners . . .

Thousands of innocents have been shot. I do not possess the sinister necrology but I know that at Aerschot 143 were killed and their fellow citizens compelled to dig the burial trenches. In Louvain 176 people – men and women, old men, women with children, rich and poor, strong and weak, were shot down or burned.

In my diocese alone I know thirteen priests have been executed. We can neither count our dead nor measure the extent of our ruins. What would it be if we were able to visit the regions of Liège, Namur, Andene, Dinant, Tamines, Charleroi, and then toward Virton and the valley of the Semois River, all the provinces of Luxembourg toward Termonde, Dixmude and our two Flanders?

To the German military these were names they could not pronounce of places they did not care about but which, like the Belgian people, were an obstruction to the dream of the Second Reich, the dream of conquest and domination. Nothing and no one was sacrosanct. Any building might conceal armed dissenters; a woodland might house Allied soldiers; a seemingly innocuous letter might be from a spy or to enemy agents; a woman's shopping basket might conceal weapons or clothes for a fugitive; a group of men in a café might be planning to attack the Germans, recruit Belgian soldiers, blow up a train, disseminate subversive views.

For the Belgians in a matter of months all they had known as home, all they had built, worked for, and lived by was destroyed by a war machine that took everything from them, gave nothing to them and denied them the right even to express their opposition. 'What do you think of these brave people?' Edith Cavell wrote in her Christmas letter to her mother of 22 December. 'They have suffered (& are suffering) a martyrdom and in silence. Their attitude is wonderful in reserve and dignity.' Anyone might be shot or imprisoned for an injudicious remark, for being in the wrong street, or for not complying with an ever-increasing plethora of laws and rules. That was war. But Christmas was a time of truce, for after all here were Christian countries, united by a belief in the obligation of charity and love. The Germans cut down the fir trees in the Belgian woods for their Christmas trees. At Liège 700 were cut down.

At the Royal Palace Hospital the German sergeant in Ward 8 asked Sister Ruth Moore to join him, and the soldiers she had nursed, for a glass of punch on Christmas Eve. She declined, but in the morning a night nurse brought to her room a huge bouquet of white chrysanthemums from them all.

In Britain that Christmas there was no particular material hardship. Sons, husbands and brothers did not return, but the bloodshed and pain to which they were consigned, the rats and mud of the trenches of the Western Front, the 'monstrous anger' of guns and shells, were out of sight and sound. There were about 200,000 Belgian refugees in Britain. Technically they were the responsibility of the Metropolitan Asylums Board, but for the most part they were displaced in billets spread over the country. Norfolk turkeys were 10*d.* a pound, there were plenty of Christmas trees, theatres and restaurants were full, the King and Queen went to Sandringham, and the Asquiths went to Walmer Castle. The weather was dreadful and gales and blizzards uprooted trees and sank small ships in east coast harbours. The last horse-drawn tram was withdrawn in London. On Christmas Day a German monoplane flew over Sheerness but dropped no bombs. And so the four months that had seemed like a century to the soldiers and the Belgians extended into another year. The war had not gone the way Schlieffen and the German generals had planned. As it spread into a global battle for hegemony, as German soldiers died in their tens of thousands, and tentacles of enmity gripped the world, the German military authorities in Belgium became ever more oppressive and punishing. Allied soldiers separated from their regiments, if caught, could expect harsh treatment. The few who found their way to Edith Cavell's door saw the light of hope. By November and December 1914 she had helped about twenty men to freedom. In the months that followed she helped hundreds.

28

ORGANISATION

Edith Cavell was a methodical woman. Keeping records was a part of hospital life. Like Eva Lückes she kept ledgers about her nurses – their personal details, work standards, progress and appointments – and about patients' illnesses, operations, treatment and discharge. It was an all-female world of nurture and help. To it she brought stringent discipline, vigilance, and attention to detail. She kept the same standards in her work for Allied soldiers. In nursing she kept to a vision of the conquest of disease and suffering. As a subversive she kept to a vision of freedom and the defeat of tyranny.

The men who came to her were asked to sign a consent form for an operation. Fictitious illnesses were assigned them, and their names, ages, dates of arrival and departure, and photos of them, were all entered in a ledger. She also kept a war diary. 'I am keeping a record for more peaceful times which will interest you later,' she had written to her mother as early as 30 August 1914. In it, in microscopic handwriting, she described the men who lodged with her and the guides who led them to safety. Obliquely, in letters to her mother she would ask for news of their safe arrival in England and say that this news was wanted because the men were relatives of nurses in the School. When the net closed around her and her fellow workers, she burned all evidence that might incriminate or endanger. All that survived of her diary was a fragment for a few days in April 1915. It was sewn into a cushion. Perhaps she hid it there and had left more of it, never recovered, in other secret places. Perhaps it was all that escaped the burning, and a nurse – Sister Wilkins was keen sewing – stitched it into a cushion.

After the war Edith's sister Lilian took the cushion as a keepsake. Thirty years later she gave it to her housekeeper, Mrs Mead, whose husband wondered at its lumpiness. They opened it, and found the diary fragment. It showed what a detailed record Edith Cavell must have kept of her work, and how wide was the network of resistance:

> People are wonderfully generous with their loyal help – I went to a new house & there secured the services of a man who comes up to take our guests to safe houses where they can abide till it is time for departure. A little widow with a big house gives shelter to some & does all the work without a servant, waiting on and cooking for them with the best courage & good will in the world.

For the citizens of Belgium the reasons for fighting were clear. Many resistance workers were women, ordinary people of any age who, like the young men from the hamlets, villages, towns and cities of the world, got sucked into a war which once under way gained momentum from which there seemed no way out except in victory or defeat.

Edith Cavell helped Allied soldiers escape from November 1914 until July 1915. Her network had to be interactive, fluid and informed, yet secret and trusted too. Any error or indiscretion might blow its cover. English and French soldiers came to her from Prince Reginald de Croÿ and his sister and the 'Girl Guide', the schoolteacher Louise Thuliez, who went by different names but usually called herself Mlle Martin. The mining engineer Herman Capiau from Wasmes, and the chemist Georges Derveau of Pâturages-les-Mons, manufactured identities for the escaping men. Capiau had boots with a hollow heel made for the soldiers in which he put messages about German activity for the military

German guards at the Dutch-Belgian border, 1914

attaché in the Hague. The soldiers did not know they were carriers, but in Holland General Dupré and Colonel Oppenheimer knew. Philippe Baucq, the architect, whose *nom de guerre* was M. Fromage, distributed *Petits Mots du Soldat* and *La Libre Belgique*. The barrister Albert Libiez of Mons made a stamp of a non-existent commune, and forged permits and identity cards. The Countess of Belleville shielded men at her home at Montigny sur Roc.

There was also elision between other networks: a Jesuit priest, Father Piersoul, assisted by a boy, Constant Cayron, helped get men to Holland; the Abbé de Longueville and a M. van Samenliet forged papers, a barrister, Armand Heuze, helped Louise Thuliez . . . and a myriad of individuals fed fugitive soldiers, gave them money, disguised them, hid them, or knew of someone who knew someone who would take them to the château at Bellignies, the rue de la Culture, or some other safe place.

Edith Cavell's diary entry for 27 April 1915 began:

Yesterday a letter from Monsieur Capiau who has gone to Germany voluntarily to inquire at Essen! with some other Belgian engineers. The letter came thro a young Frenchman who with 7 others had come from N. France to escape and hopes to get over the Dutch frontier in a day or two. The frontier has been absolutely impassable the last few days. Germany and Holland have been on the verge of war over the sinking of the *Catwyk*. The Dutch refused to allow anyone to cross and had massed their troops & laid mines all along from Maastricht to Antwerp. A sentinel on the Dutch side was posted every 15 metres & all the young men who had left to try & cross were stuck or came back – 5 of ours were heard of at Herrenthall yesterday morning & the guide left to bring them back.

Probably Capiau, who spoke German, had got to Essen 'to inquire' in his capacity as a mining engineer. Information useful to the Allies was communicated by smuggled letter and word of mouth. The *Catwyk,* a Dutch ship with a cargo of grain, was torpedoed on 14 April 1915. The Kaiser sent a personal message to Queen Wilhelmina of the Netherlands saying full compensation would be paid if, as claimed, it had been sunk by a German submarine. His intervention kept Holland out of the war. It also kept a vital escape route open for Allied soldiers.

Within Edith Cavell's resistance group, Reginald de Croÿ and Louise Thuliez focused on helping men escape from the region in the north of France round Engle-Fontaine, Maroilles and Bavay. Libiez and Philippe Baucq focused on men from the Borinage, the mining district near Mons.

When the first two wounded English soldiers arrived at Edith Cavell's door in rue de la Culture, brought to her by Herman Capiau, she had not known what to do with them. She had put them to bed as patients. They stayed with her a fortnight while she found safe houses, roads to the frontier, guides prepared to risk their lives to lead them there. As she became more experienced, more entrenched in subterfuge, wily at disguise, coded exchange, and the art of concealment, and knew – or thought she knew – who to trust, the procedure speeded up and soldiers stayed with her only for a day or at most a week.

Usually she personally took the men to a handover point where a guide waited. The agreed time was often between 5.00 and 7.00 in the morning. Six appointed places in Brussels were: behind St Mary's church; in the waiting room for trams at Place Rogier; opposite the Hôtel de l'Espérance in the Place de la Constitution; under the clock of the École Normale in Place Rouppe; behind the Cinquantenaire at the end of the Chaussée de Tervueren; in the Square Ambiorix.

She became acquainted with the city's side streets and unpatrolled byways. She appeared as a middle-aged woman walking her dog. Jack liked the exercise. The disguised soldiers followed at a discreet distance. She grew adept at circuitous routes, the sudden boarding or getting off a tram, at seeming nonchalant, at watching reflected images of people in plate-glass windows, at taking special note of the road sweeper, postman or builder, who might be a spy. She acquired aspects of the villain's cunning and guile and applied these to her staunch adherence to virtue.

In her surviving fragment of diary she gave a description of one of her guides and carriers of information: a boy, as she called him, of twenty-three, Charles Vanderlinden, one of a family of nine brothers, 'all strong and fighters'.

This fellow is a fine type – about 5ft 6 or 7, slightly made but very strong and muscular. He amused himself when small with boxing a great sack of sand or corn which swung forward and butted him in the face if he failed to hit in the right place. He afterwards got some lessons in boxing & obliged me with a description of the right way to catch a man's head under the arm & 'crack' his neck or to give him a back-handed blow and destroy the trachea or larynx. He is also a poacher in time of peace & sets lassoes in rows so that hares racing to their feeding grounds are bound to be caught in one of them. He & 3 friends will catch from 20 to 30 in 2 or 3 days. The gamekeeper's dogs they hang to the trees when they get the chance. He is nearly always sober but when on the drink will be drunk for 10 days at a stretch. He & his brothers, men equally strong and pugilistic, would fight at times, but when they entered a café together no one dare say a word to any of them. He has one blind eye smashed in a fight with a boxer.

He has travelled far, oftener on foot than otherwise & has many trades to which he can turn his hand – he is extremely intelligent & has a good memory – he has ideas of justice & straight dealing & is very anxious to repay any money given to him. He boasts in the most open manner & enjoys to talk of himself & his prowess. Withal he is, at least here, a gentleman and well-behaved in the house & gives us no trouble, also his conversation is clean and pleasing. He has crossed the line once & taken his news & been back for more which he has started again to deliver. He is very scornful over the young men with no pluck & has a grand contempt for the Gs. He is a *repoussé* – unwillingly on account of his eye, he can swim & walk great distances, also knows how to pass a leisure day sound asleep on our garden grass. He wears grey corduroys, a rough tweed jacket & a striped grey muffler, a cap & had running shoes which he exchanges for sabots when necessary in the country. He wears his trousers tied in at the ankle & under the tie places his letters – or ours. He will be caught one day & if so will be shot but he will make a first class bid for freedom.

Her description of him and admiration of him were not Victorian-maiden-ladyish. She took to this one-eyed binge drinker, boxer and poacher that he was, with his ideas of justice and straight dealing, his fearlessness and contempt for the invaders. He would have been one more to add to her family had he so desired.

Another of her guides, Victor Gilles – that was his *nom de guerre*, a joke about the name of the prison at St Gilles, where he might well end up if caught – was introduced to her by Herman Capiau. He had been 'a simple postman in a little country village', then worked in a field hospital – an *ambulance* – in Mons at the beginning of the war. He was 'a big fellow', she said, powerfully built. 'He dines & sups here occasionally & has quite good table manners learnt from the ladies of the *ambulance* with whom he took meals.'

At the big house of the 'little widow' who shielded fugitive soldiers, Edith Cavell met Nellie Hozier, the younger sister of Winston Churchill's wife. 'She speaks French like a Parisienne and made great friends of the common people.' She had gone to Belgium at the beginning of the war to nurse with the Red Cross. In her diary Edith Cavell wrote of how Nellie Hozier sent Victor Gilles to England with letters asking for money for resistance work, and how, on the evening of his arrival at Admiralty House, Churchill spent 'his one leisure hour with him smoking in the library'.

Raising money was a constant need. Many of the men who came to the School had none at all. Herman Capiau, Prince Reginald, Louise Thuliez, Louis Séverin, Philippe Baucq – all collected and gave money. Edith Cavell gave most of her salary and was always appealing for funds. She made sure each soldier had 25 francs before he went on his journey.

Often there were too many men 'in transit' for her to house at the School. Nor did she want to endanger the nurses. She kept a list of safe houses where she could lodge men at short notice: with Ada Bodart at 7 rue Taciturne then at 19 rue Émile Wittmann; with Marie Mauton at 12 rue d'Angleterre; with Philippe Rasquin at his café at 137 rue Haute; with Madame Sovet at her café at 16 boulevard de la Senne; with Louis Séverin at his house at 138 avenue Longchamp.

'On Monday night over 8000 *blessés* were brought into Brussels all Germans M. Victor tells me,' she wrote in her diary on 27 April 1915. 'The Gare de Schaerbeek was cleared of the public to let them thro. All the Dutch newspapers were burned at the Gare du Midi. None from France or England have come thro for some days. The Gs post a victory on the Yser – but rumour ascribes it to the Belgian and English armies aided by the Hindus.'

She described M. Victor as 'a tradesman of 60 or thereabouts with a pale & puffy face, bald-headed, fat & short. He has a benevolent smile & spends his days in going from place to place to look after our guests. He too holds the Gs in contempt & does his best for the *patrie*.'

The citizens of Brussels were demoralised by being denied access to news, and by constant German bulletins posted on walls claiming victories. But neither side could claim victory in this 'battle of the frontiers'. Vicious attack and counter-attack did not break the deadlock. The River Yser and the flat sodden coastal area around it thwarted the German plan to capture Ypres. The previous October, King Albert, in the first battle of Ypres, had given orders to open the river's sluices and let the sea flood the area. It created an impassable zone 15 kilometres long between Nieuport and Dixmude.

The German army, that April, in the second battle of Ypres, used chlorine gas attacks on the British, French, Canadian, Algerian and African soldiers in the trenches of the Ypres Salient. Six thousand cylinders of it caused agonising death by asphyxiation. They used it after suffering heavy casualties in fighting at Neuve Chapelle: 11,652 British soldiers killed, wounded, missing or prisoners, and 8,600 German soldiers.

As stalemate and carnage continued, in Brussels surveillance was everywhere: 'Today a great airship passed low over the houses & displaying No. 179 – was plainly visible as also the men in the car, crowds rushed out to see it. There are now 2 captive balloons which survey the city from different sides.'

And at ground level Edith Cavell was watched:

Monsieur Fromage brought me word from the town authorities that the house is watched and several attempts I think have been made to catch me in default – several suspicious persons have been to ask for help to leave the country either in the form of money, lodging or guides. People have been taken in this way several times. Today a doctor was had up because a guide who was caught carried a letter on him for post in Holland, he also had one for me, but as yet I have heard nothing of this. A young girl of 22, the Countess d'Ursel,[14] has been taken and is condemned to one year's fortress in Germany. She has been allowed to return home for a week first, perhaps with the idea of allowing her to escape & then making her family pay a heavy fine. Charles is here with plans which he has tried to use but was obliged to return, he tries again in a day or two acting as guide to four young Belgians. People are wonderfully generous with their loyal help . . .

She observed as her own peril grew. With every fugitive soldier,

[14] The Duchess d'Ursel, from a wealthy French family, was charged with giving money to Belgians who wanted to escape Brussels to join the Belgian army

recruit, or guide who came through the door, her complicity in resistance work deepened. Goodness had changed its hue. Just as soldiers showed valour in the face of bombardment, destruction and bloodshed, so Edith Cavell saw generosity and kindness all around her; in the widow who opened her house to fugitive soldiers, in the one-eyed boxer who risked his life getting men and information across the border, in the big postman with his ladylike table manners. All showed the qualities she had tried to apply in her nursing life and to inspire in her students: altruism, courage, attention to detail, working for others without counting the cost. The difference was the context: the civilised structures of peacetime, as opposed to the madness and squalor of war.

29

THE MEN SHE HELPED

Edith Cavell had travelled far, in the company she kept, from Swardeston teas on the lawn with the Blewitt sisters, or from running her finger over the iron bedsteads and telling her nurses the dusting should be finished by ten. The niceties of peacetime were behind her. She could not now be open about her work, easy with the truth, trusting of whoever came to the door. Suspicion was crucial for survival. Her adopted country had been torn apart. The men who shared her house were soldiers paid to kill. Their gamble ahead was to be a prisoner of war, blown up by a land mine at the Dutch border, or to escape. Killing the enemy or avoiding the enemy was the only way out now things had gone this far.

It was not Edith Cavell's prime concern that the soldiers she helped should rejoin their regiments or re-enlist. Every setback to the German military was good news to her, but in getting English and French soldiers to Holland, her objective was for them to reach safety and be out of harm's way. None the less as the months passed the scope of her work widened. In service to Belgian patriots she became the hub in Brussels of an escape network: for British and French soldiers separated from their regiments, for Belgians who wanted to enlist, for men carrying information of use to the Allies.

It took three attempts to get Sergeant Jesse Tunmore and Private Lewis to Holland. They had arrived on 23 December. Lewis had severe shell shock. They had fought at the Battle of Mons the previous August and, like Colonel Boger, been taken to the convent hospital at the village of Wihéries, then escaped the German guard. The miner Auguste Joly, Louise Thuliez's brother-in-law, gave them food and civilian clothes, for months kept them hidden in safe houses, then helped them reach Edith Cavell in Brussels.

Though she found them guides, their first two escape attempts failed. Their papers aroused suspicion with the border guards so they returned to her. At the School only Sister Wilkins and José, her Rumanian house manager, were in her confidence. José suggested Tunmore disguise himself as a Rumanian. It would then be unsurprising if he spoke a bit of English, but no French or German. He helped him into the role. Edith Cavell took identity card photographs of the two disguised soldiers on her box Kodak. In the New Year she set off with them at 5.30 in the morning and guided them to the Louvain road. They got to Holland via Louvain, Diest and the border town of Overpelt.

From Harwich in England on 20 January 1915 Tunmore wrote, as Edith Cavell had requested, to her mother at 24 College Road, Norwich:

> I am writing to you to say that your daughter the Matron of the Nurses' School in Brussels, Belgium, is quite well. I am a soldier of the 1st Norfolk Regiment & she has done a lot for me in helping me to escape over the frontier to Holland. I was a prisoner in the hands of the Germans near Mons. I managed to get away and reached Brussels, where your daughter worked very hard for me as regards to get me money, finding chances for me. One chance was by going off as Roumanian, but I had not got a passport, but got as far as St Nicholas near Antwerp. I cannot express enough thanks for all she done for me, she worked very hard for us indeed, but the 12th of this month all French, Russians, Japanese etc in Brussels had to report themselves to the

Germans, but I left Brussels on the 12th, so I do not know what really happened.

She told to tell you she was quite well. She told me it was some time she received a letter from England. I spent Xmas & the New Year with your daughter.

A month later Jesse Tunmore's father wrote to tell Mrs Cavell his son was suffering from 'acute mania', and was in a straitjacket in the Netley military hospital, near Southampton. When Jesse Tunmore was better he wrote again and Mrs Cavell replied on 29 July:

I was very pleased to hear from you again, and still more to know that you have been restored to health – the best of earthly blessings. I hope you feel thankful to God for His great mercy . . . I have had, as you will know, a very anxious time not knowing what was going on in Brussels but at present all seems quiet, though there is much distress which Miss Cavell and her nurses do their utmost to relieve – May God bless her and bring her home in peace that I may see her again. Life with me is uncertain as I am in my 81st year.

At her great age, she too was caught up, in a way, into resistance work.

At the beginning of the war it had been relatively easy to get across the border to Holland: it took a guide, a bribe to an official, an unguarded bit of moorland. In the first months an estimated 34,000 men got out of Belgium into Holland: young Belgians – as young as seventeen – who wanted to join the army on the Western Front, as well as French and English soldiers.

After the battle of Charleroi in August 1914, French wounded were taken to a hospital at Jumet. One of the surgeons, Dr Marcel Détry, had worked with Depage and Sister White in the St Gilles hospital, and lived near Edith Cavell. At weekly intervals, up to

January 1915, he sent to her French soldiers he had operated on. One by one she got them to the border.

On 27 January the chemist Georges Derveau brought to Edith Cavell, from Mons, Lance-Corporal Doman of the 9th Lancers, and Corporal Chapman of the Cheshires. They lodged with her until 11 February. At Mons, Doman had been wounded in the back by shrapnel. His horse had had one of its legs blown off underneath him. He lay on the battlefield until picked up by German soldiers and taken to the Wihéries hospital. He, Chapman, and a Sergeant Rothwell, escaped and lived rough in the Mormal Forest until scared by German searchers. Rothwell got separated and no more was heard of him. Doman and Chapman with the help of Auguste Joly reached Mons disguised as priests.

At one time eighty fugitive soldiers were hiding in the School, waiting for safe passage. Edith Cavell sent them out in the day, adrift in the city, while she kept the semblance of normal life: lectures to nurses, inspection of the new School, care of civilian patients. At night the soldiers crowded back, into basement rooms, into beds in corridors. When German officials carried out routine inspections the men left the building via the garden, or got into hospital beds. Doman, she told them, was a Belgian agricultural worker with a chronic rheumatic condition. Lives depended on her pretence. She developed an ability to act, to persist with a lie, to be consistent in dissimulation.

A genuine priest helped the onward passage of Doman and Chapman on 11 February. He gave Edith Cavell the torn half of a visiting card and told her of a café where they would rendezvous with their unknown guide. The men must not speak English for that would give them away. She took them there, ordered three beers and put the torn card on the table. A man came in, put down the other half of the card, then guided them to a small village south of Antwerp. Four days later they reached England. Doman wrote at Edith Cavell's request to her mother:

It is with kind permission of your daughter Miss Cavell
of rue de la Culture Brussels that I write to you. I am a
wounded soldier and was taken prisoner in Belgium where
I escaped from. I was passing through Brussels & your
daughter kept us in hiding from the Germans for 15 days &
treated us very kindly. She got us a guide to bring us through
Holland & we arrived in England quite safe. Your daughter
wishes for you to write to her & let her know we arrived here
safe, as you must not let anyone know or they may visit her
home in Brussels. But be careful what you put in. Just say
J. Doman and P. Chapman arrived here safe. Of course full
details cannot be given until after the war. Your daughter is in
good health and quite well. I thought it best to let you know
this in case you have not been able to get a letter from her.

Such letters worried Mrs Cavell. She wrote anxiously to Sergeant
Doman asking how risky the whole business was. He tried to
reassure her:

Referring to it being risky for her well I don't think she has
much to fear as when the Germans are about the English do
not remain in her house, but go out and hide in the town,
& I do not think she will have any more prisoners there as
we were the last two who were left . . . she told me she had
sent a guide with letters to Holland but had an idea that
he had been caught and was taken prisoner and it costs a
considerable amount of money to get these guides to do such
risky work. I think when the war is over she will be highly
praised and well rewarded for the good work she has done.

Such reassurance could not have been total. If the work was so
risky for guides, why was it less so for an Englishwoman, a symbol
of hatred to the enemy? And where was the proof that her
resistance work was done? How did she get the money to pay

these guides? How deeply entrenched was she in war work? Mrs Cavell was eighty. She wanted her daughter home. It disturbed her to have soldiers who had been to hell and back arriving at her door.

By March 1915 an electrified wire perimeter fence had been strung along the whole border. It was patrolled day and night, and scanned by searchlights from watchtowers. None the less Doman was by no means the last of the 'prisoners'. Through March, April, May, June and July, a stream of soldiers booked in as patients or visitors at rue de la Culture. Their decimated regiments were the West Kents, the Munster Fusiliers, the Connaught Rangers, the Cheshires, Norfolks, West Riding and Middlesex, the Royal Irish Rifles, the Royal Scottish Fusiliers, the Royal Field Artillery, the Black Watch, the Royal Scottish Rifles, the 4th Regiment of Zouaves, as well as Belgian and French civilians who wanted to enlist.

In March she dispatched Lance-Corporal Holmes of the Norfolk Regiment who had been gravely wounded at Mons. He lived close to her mother in Norwich. She gave him a Bible and a letter to give to her mother. For Mrs Cavell, the vicar's widow, openly to acknowledge in a letter receipt of a Bible would seem innocent enough. But then Edith Cavell would know of the safe arrival of Corporal Holmes and that the system was still working. Holmes handed it and the letter to the maid at 24 College Road but did not go into the house. Mrs Cavell seemed reluctant to meet him. Perhaps she felt fearful of the implication to herself and others of her daughter's work.

For Edith Cavell, the underpinning steel of endeavour was unchanged. She served and stayed true to her conscience. Her work of reforming Belgian nursing standards was temporarily frustrated. It was a small shift from making clothes for impoverished refugees to making clothes to disguise soldiers who needed to escape, a small step from smuggling letters over the border to smuggling men. But the shift in her citizenship status was total. The German authorities had no moral or legal worth in her view. She would not obey their rule that all foreign nationals should report to them, nor comply with their conception of law. In their terms she was miscreant, criminal, traitor. Her right was their wrong. Her work became ever more dangerous. She put her life on the line for these men who had been through much: Private McGuire, Sergeant Shiells, Captain Motte, Corporal Ribbens, Private Sheldrake, Bandsman Christie, Sergeant Scarrett . . .

Private T. C. Scott of the Norfolk Regiment arrived at the School in April with wounds to his chest and feet. He was very ill. For months the Richez family, relatives of Auguste Joly, had kept him in a boarded-over cellar. After close calls with the military police they brought him to the rue de la Culture. One night when uniformed men with bayonets inspected, Edith Cavell woke him, hid him in a barrel in the garden and covered him in apples.

It became a long, dangerous, expensive journey to the frontier: passwords, disguises, an ever-changing paraphernalia of codes, bribes and cunning. The price of bribes reached a thousand francs. Spies followed close on the heels of resistance workers. Guides were men of courage, men like Charles Vanderlinden. They learned every detail of the terrain, knew of poachers in the woods who would give directions, and how to wrap rubber strips round the electrified wires of the border fence, or push a barrel between them so the fugitives could crawl through. But guides and escapees got caught and shot at the border. Along the River Scheldt were boatmen who might ferry men across at night. Some men swam the river's width despite searchlights that swept the water.

Germany poured more men into the war. Suspicion was everywhere: passenger boats might be loaded with munitions, the postman might be an undercover agent. Citizens coded their patriotism into the colour of their hats or ties. But it was touch and go who could be trusted. Menace was everywhere: the forced entry of uniformed men with pistols and bayonets, apprehension on a tram, in a café, on the street. Survival needed luck and cunning.

Edith Cavell turned away none of the soldiers brought to her. Jack walked with her to the handover points. Behind them followed her 'guests', dressed as agricultural workers or miners. One onward route was by tram to Haacht, 30 miles away. To avoid the guards they would leave the tram before the end of the line. In Haacht they were given information about the movements of the Germans.

In the School it was ever harder for Edith Cavell to discipline these men. They were not, like her student nurses, obliged to do as she said. They were young, had been through hell, and wanted a good time. José took their meals to them and told them when to disperse round the town. Edith Cavell asked them to leave the house singly, keep to the back streets, not to drink, not to speak English, not to return late. But she could not watch them all the time. She was still a working matron.

The men had no capacity for sitting in silence in a walled-off room. They were energetic, unafraid of risk and removed from army discipline. They liked going to the corner café, Chez Jules, and to another café in nearby rue Vanderkindere. They talked in English, for they knew no French. They drank, chatted up Belgian girls, and talked to seemingly friendly workmen. And even when they tried to appear incognito, disguised with felt hats and French moustaches, Edith Cavell told Reginald de Croÿ their singularly English walk and stance gave them away.

Doctors and nurses who lodged in the street spoke of being disturbed by very English noise. The engineer Georges Hostelet, who often visited the School, commented on male laughter and shouting, and urged her to be more cautious. Louise Thuliez heard how a group on a tram told passengers they had come from Miss Cavell's nursing home, were on their way to M. Séverin's house and were then going to cross the Dutch frontier. And there was a problem with Edith Cavell's German maid, Marie, who was divided in her allegiance and antipathetic to this harbouring of wanted men.

A German command post was set up in the same road as the School. Soldiers herded into the School's top rooms could see them in the evenings, playing cards. A field across the road next to Depage's closed Institute, which before the war had been a drill ground for Belgian soldiers, was now used by civilians to grow vegetables. Unknown individuals would question them and watch the School. Unspecific protracted roadworks went on in the street. Danger was near. Edith Cavell grew careless, not with regard to the men she was helping, but in protecting her own skin. Her letters home became incautious. On 11 March she wrote to her cousin:

> My dear Eddy,
> Your letter came from the American Consul yesterday the 10th of March. You apparently sent it on the 1st of Feb! You see our correspondence has gone back to the Middle Ages like so many other things out here at present. It was good of you to remember me and to offer your help. There is so much to do and yet so little actually in Brussels. We have no wounded – the Allies do not come here and most of the Germans are sent back to their country, the few that remain are nursed by their country-women – so we are at present denied the great consolation of being of use in our special way. Of course, there are other things to do and I am helping in ways I may not describe to you now. There are many things I may not write till we are again free.
> As you offer your help do you think you could find

out any news of the soldiers on the enclosed list! They are relations of some of the girls here and are fighting at the front or perhaps wounded or killed. You could write to London or to France but we can't. If you can collect any money for our poor, we should be very grateful, but I don't quite see how you could send it out, as money for the English is confiscated if found.

The last letter from my mother was dated 22nd January. If this reaches you will you send her a line to say all is well here. She is naturally very anxious and I do not know whether she gets my letters. There are not many opportunities of sending.

What do you do these days, are you still farming, or is that given up? I like to look back on the days when we were young and life was fresh and beautiful and the country so desirable and sweet.

Many thanks for your kind letter My dear Cousin from
Yours affectionately
Edith

It was a letter to arouse suspicion if it fell into hostile hands. Who were the soldiers on the list, why did she want money, what were her ways of helping which she could not describe? Three days later, on 14 March, she wrote a similarly incautious letter to her mother:

All is very quiet here still, we are policed by the enemy and people are arrested often without warning otherwise things go on much as usual.

We are very busy in spite of the fact that we have no longer the hospital for any private staff – there has been a great deal to do lately in ways which I must describe to you later. Have you heard from Doman or Chapman?

We go into the new building next month, I will send you

in good time the new address. It is advancing and becoming habitable but will not be finished for May 1st when we should be installed.

An immense Zeppelin passed over the plain and our house yesterday evening seeming just to clear the roof – the first that has visited us for a long while.

Sister Whitelock from the hospital has taken Sister White's place and promises to be a success – I am wondering if Sister Burt is still at Withernsea – Marie has been giving me a good deal of trouble. I expect I shall have to send her away one of these days, but must wait in prudence till after the war. Jackie is well and more attached to me than ever, he won't leave me now even to go for a walk with Gracie – he takes no notice of the Gs but passes them with sublime indifference like all the Belgians.

The *Institut* opposite is still shut up and the owner away at work in Flanders with his wife, who has lately been over to America. I could tell you many things but must save them till later.

My dearest love to you and Lil and the children
Ever your affectionate daughter
Edith
Gracie's love to you all

Coded news from her daughter of sudden arrests, of being policed by the enemy, of a German maid giving trouble, of low-flying Zeppelins, of many things that could be said but weren't, disturbed Mrs Cavell. Zeppelins, huge cigar-shaped dirigibles stuffed with bombs, were already being used to terrorise Paris and London.

In March 1915, with no end to the war in sight and with ever-mounting casualties, Marie Depage had gone to America to raise funds for the Océan hospital and the Red Cross. Queen Elisabeth of Belgium sent her a letter wishing her mission success. Of the

Marie Depage (1872–1915), nurse and resistance worker. She died
when the *Lusitania* was torpedoed, 7 May 1915

Depages' three sons, two had enlisted. They also had plans to
get Edith Cavell across enemy lines to work at the La Panne
hospital.

For two months Marie Depage toured American cities from
Washington to Pittsburgh. 'The big conflict of the present war
is still in the future' she told her audiences.

> We must foresee the coming slaughter and be prepared to
> render instant aid to the thousands of wounded, friends
> and foes, who will fall within our lines. When we follow

the army into our devastated land, we shall find nothing; it is a land stripped bare, and often we shall not find even shelter to house our wounded soldiers. We must, therefore, have in store a number of field hospitals such as the American Red Cross is today sending to Belgium with every supply, including beds, linen, instruments, sterilisers, and ambulances. We shall also need money to be used for fuel and emergencies.

She raised $100,000 in money and $50,000 in supplies. She had planned to return to Europe on the SS *Lapland* but at the last minute changed to Cunard's flagship the *Lusitania*, the 'greyhound of the sea', because it was the fastest ship on the Atlantic. She was in cabin E61. There were 2,150 people on board. It left New York harbour for Liverpool on 1 May. Even on this crossing Marie Depage raised money for the Red Cross from passengers.

On 7 May, 10 miles off the coast of Ireland, a German U-boat surfaced. Its commander Captain Schwieger wanted to recharge its batteries. The *Lusitania* was 700 metres away. He torpedoed its starboard side. There was an explosion and the ship began to sink. Then there was a second larger explosion. The ship keeled over and went down in eighteen minutes. Marie Depage tried to jump from the port side, got tangled in ropes on the deck, struggled free, but drowned.

Fourteen hundred people died including 128 Americans and 95 children. Some of the dead were trapped in the ship's lifts. The sinking of the *Lusitania* shocked the Allied world. It served as a rallying cry for recruitment and for America to join the war. It was viewed as a violation of the rules of engagement, an act of terrorism. Three months previously Germany had overruled an attempted international agreement that non-military vessels suspected of carrying war materials should be abandoned rather than sunk immediately.

Germany denied the accusation that the second catastrophic

explosion was caused by another torpedo. They said it was because the ship was stuffed with munitions. (Recent salvage of the wreck unearthed millions of rounds of .303 bullets. There had been tons of crates in the hold dubiously labelled CHEESE, BUTTER, OYSTERS.) Antoine Depage identified his wife's body. He buried her close to the hospital at La Panne and named his research unit after her: the Institut Marie Depage. There was no time to grieve. There was too much to grieve about. For Edith Cavell it was another blow to all her hopes. The ideal of heaven on earth seemed ever further away. But through the door of Depage's hospital came an unending stream of wounded in need of care. Through the door of the School in rue de la Culture, fugitive soldiers came, desperate for escape.

On Friday 30 April Charles Vanderlinden collected from Edith Cavell three Frenchmen and two young Belgians who wanted to get over the border to enlist. On 5 May the Countess Jeanne de Belleville from Montigny sent a young neighbour, Raoul de Roy, to Edith Cavell. He too wanted to enlist in the Belgian army. She gave him her usual form to sign, saying he had been 'operated on' successfully, and introduced him to a guide called 'Anicet'. With ten others he travelled via Malines, Antwerp and Bergen op Zoom. But helping Belgian civilians enlist was qualitatively different from helping British men escape. The net closed around Edith Cavell, as she knew it would. 'Suspicious people have been to ask for help to leave the country either in the form of money, lodging or guides,' she wrote in her diary. 'People have been taken in this way several times.' She asked Jeanne de Belleville to 'tell all the helpers not to send any more men here for the present, as my situation is becoming more and more strained every day.'

30

WATCHED

At the time General Baron Moritz von Bissing was appointed Governor General of Belgium by the Kaiser, in December 1914, General von Luttwitz had been replaced as Military Governor by General von Kraewel. He was a small man with cropped hair and a little white moustache. He had lived in England and liked to talk about horses and jockeys. Von Bissing found him too lenient.

Each day, whatever the weather, a long bedraggled queue waited outside the *Kommandantur*, the headquarters of the military police – civilians trying to comply with the endless regulations, to register, obtain an identity card or travel pass, to find news of a missing friend or relative. Brand Whitlock said of this constant queue, 'There was something degrading and shameful in the spectacle, as there is in any reckless and irresponsible use of mere brute force.'

In the nearby offices of the secret police, Lieutenant Bergan was head of espionage. He was about forty, tall, red-faced with a large nose, dark eyes and bushy brows. He spoke no French and had worked in the Düsseldorf police force before this war. His senior officer was Sergeant Henri Pinkhoff, a German Jew, thick-set with a black moustache and a large purple naevus between his left ear and nose. He had joined the British army when there was allegiance between the two countries. He then moved to Paris for fifteen years, ostensibly as a travelling salesman for an umbrella firm in rue du Paradis, but at the same time serving as a spy for the German government.

Thousands of casual spies, informers and *agents provocateurs* were in the pay of the secret police – about 6,000 of them in Brussels by the spring of 1915. They were of both sexes and all nationalities. Before the war they had been merchants, gardeners, butchers, prisoners. They rode on trams, hovered in alleyways and side streets, insinuated their way into groups or gatherings, intercepted post, ransacked homes, gave bribes, false gifts and promises, and turned their prey over to the military courts, the prisons and the firing squads. Any perceived crime against German troops or soldiers, any infringement or neglect of decree or edict, was punishable by these courts which rendered 'extraordinary justice', and chose what penalty to apply. Within a year of the occupation 600,000 Belgians had been taken before them, fined, sent to prison, deported or shot. New crimes were defined each day. *Il est défendu . . .* was pasted on the city's walls. Men and women were indicted for housing wounded Allied soldiers, refusing to work for the Germans, assaulting secret agents, preaching patriotic sermons, disseminating or reading foreign newspapers, trying to cross the frontier into Holland, aiding men to join the Belgian army, distributing *La Libre Belgique*, mocking the goose step, whistling 'La Brabançonne', the Belgian national anthem, 'looking insolently at a German woman', providing information for *Les Petits Mots du Soldat*. No household in the land knew, if there was a knock at the door in the morning or at night, that it was not the *Polizei* come to ransack the place and drag away one or other of its residents. A man might leave his home in the morning and not return or be seen again. A woman might return to her home in the evening and be arrested as she tried to go through her front door.

Such trials as followed were a charade, a perverse display of the procedures of justice with its spirit warped, a spectacle that sought by blame to justify its own wrongdoing. 'Important' cases went to the senate chamber before a court of high-ranking German officers.

The prosecutor gave his evidence and whatever penalty he asked was invariably given. The accused were seldom granted counsel, and if they were, the attorneys were not allowed to see their clients before the hearing or receive details of the charges against them. No case for the defence could be prepared. The attorneys could follow proceedings in court and say what they would, which was not of much use because the outcome was prejudged.

Such was the substance of criminal justice in Belgium under German occupation. The rules were these: power is ours because we took it by force. We are the lawmakers now. You must do as we say and go where we tell you or we shall punish you even by taking your life. Dissent is a crime. What you want and believe is irrelevant to us. We have the guns, the bullets, the uniforms, the keys. We will arrest you if we choose, imprison you if we please, kill you if you obstruct us.

Edith Cavell, Herman Capiau and Louise Thuliez discussed the likelihood of arrest. They knew they were watched. By June 1915 their work had become too difficult and dangerous, and the numbers of men who wanted help to escape had increased. Edith Cavell's view, recorded by Louise Thuliez, was, 'If we are arrested we shall be punished in any case, whether we have done much or little. So let us go ahead and save as many as possible of these unfortunate men.'

So they continued, undeterred by consequence to themselves. Messengers still ran from town to town distributing *La Libre Belgique* and *Les Petits Mots du Soldat*. The 'girl guides' Louise Thuliez and Henriette Moriamé continued to search out lost soldiers and take them to the château at Bellignies. Jeanne de Belleville walked 30 kilometres one day, looking for an English officer 'somewhere in Feignies'. (He had left for Brussels with a safe guide.) She got lost in the woods near Montignies when night came, and did not get home until morning. She could not think of what she would say if apprehended.

At the Bellignies château the Princess de Croÿ still sealed fugitive soldiers into the windowless staircase of its tower for three weeks at a time. Guns and ammunition brought in by them were still buried in an arsenal in the garden, then planted over with fir trees. The Germans seldom searched before 7.00 in the morning, so the soldiers washed and shaved early. But the searches became more frequent, random and thorough. Forty soldiers at a time would open books to look for money, purloin wine, sound walls and floors with iron bars to find hollow hide-outs. 'I was thankful that the tower walls were so thick that even near the hiding place they gave out no hollow sound,' the Princess wrote in her memoir.

Unconvincing strangers called at the château and at rue de la Culture. In June, Otto Mayer called, and told the Princess he was an escaped British soldier, and while hiding in Brussels had heard from a priest that she would help get him to England to rejoin his regiment. Mayer worked for the secret police. He was fifty, born in Alsace, had been a waiter in England and India and a guide for the travel agent Thomas Cook. He was fluent in French and English and married to a Belgian woman he met in India. The Princess advised him his wisest course was to give himself up to the German authorities.

Before the fugitive soldiers set off from the château at night for Brussels, the Princess de Croÿ's dog, Sweep, would patrol the grounds and bark if he smelled or heard a stranger. When all was clear the men crossed fields to the first safe house. But by June 1915 such safe houses, convents, and abbeys, increasingly were raided and anyone suspected of complicity arrested. Guides were warned to divulge nothing to the fugitive soldiers that might identify the people with whom they stayed, or the routes they took.

Reginald de Croÿ continued to need money from the British army for guides, food, lodging and bribes for border guards. As suspicion about him from the German military grew, it became increasingly difficult for him to get a pass to travel to Holland.

Routinely and without warning the Nursing School was searched. In June two Frenchmen arrived and gave the password. One of them, Georges Gaston Quien, said he was an officer wounded in the foot at Charleroi and that he needed to get to Holland. He was tall, thin, blue-eyed, soft-spoken, ostensibly charming, but in reality a fantasist, wily and odd, a thief, with a scant hold on the truth. He had an ingrowing toenail which Edith Cavell treated. Next day he said he was not well enough to walk far. Edith Cavell took the other man, a M. Motte, and a group of English soldiers, to the guide Victor Gilles. While she was out, Quien ingratiated himself with the nurses in the School, with the cook's daughter Léonie, with Marie, Edith Cavell's maid, and with Pauline Randall.

Two days later Quien left – Nurse van Til saw three strangers questioning the people gleaning vegetables in the opposite field, a uniformed German officer called at the School to ask for a room for his son who he said was ill, and Victor Gilles called to say M. Motte had disappeared from the group he was guiding to Antwerp and that he suspected he was a spy.

On the day after that Nurse van Til was asked by Edith Cavell to take an unaddressed letter to Philippe Baucq. In Chaussée de Waterloo, Quien approached her and invited her for a drink. She declined. At Porte de Schaerbeek he appeared again. Instead of going to Baucq's house she went to a friend. She was followed by another man. Three hours previously the friend's husband and father had been accused of sheltering French soldiers and arrested.

Quien, when the war began, had been in prison at St Quentin in Picardy for spying against the French. The Germans freed him and he resumed work for them. He incriminated many resistance workers by preying on their kindness and by pretending he was helping Allied soldiers escape. He fed information about the de Croÿs to the secret police. He took two young men to a Mme van Damme and asked her to help them escape. In good faith she and a friend guided them to the frontier. He convinced Mme Bodart, who gave him lodging and a package of road maps, annotated with directions for a safe route to the border, to be delivered to a Mme Machiel. A priest, Father Bonsteels, believed him and gave him a railway map which detailed the latest German modifications. Everyone whom Quien betrayed was subsequently arrested.

Edith Cavell feared turning genuine freedom seekers from her door, so she erred on the side of trust. After Quien's visit a man by the name of Jacobs was brought to her by people who lived at 45 rue de la Culture. He said he had not known the number of her house, that he had escaped from a German prisoner-of-war camp near Maubeuge, and that villagers near Mons had told him of the help she gave men such as himself. He stayed a week, then left with a group who were crossing the border. Sister Wilkins found shredded papers in his room. He was Armand Jeannes, an agent for Bergan.

In mid-June Otto Mayer, in civilian clothes, called at the School. Two Frenchmen and two Belgians were in one of the basements. Sister Wilkins managed to say 'German' to José, who got the men out via the garden. Edith Cavell was in rue Bruxelles, a kilometre away, inspecting the progress of the new Training School. The deadline for moving in May had passed, and she was unsure if all would be ready even by autumn. Mayer showed Sister Wilkins his police badge. She answered his questions and was non-committal. He wanted to see the patients, so she took him to a men's ward with genuine civilian cases. He asked her if she had any more Tommies. She pretended not to know what he was talking about. She was taken to boulevard de Berlaimont and questioned for three hours then released.

When Edith Cavell returned she burned a great many papers:

her diary, addresses, records of the men who had stayed, letters. Next day Mayer came back with four other policemen and searched the place. They found nothing significant. On 14 June, after such scares and warnings, Edith Cavell wrote the last letter to reach her mother, whose birthday was on 6 July. It was careful, measured, and had a tone of valediction:

My darling Mother

Very many happy returns of your birthday & my best love & good wishes – I have always made a point of being at home for July 6, but this year it will not be possible. Even if one could leave the country, to return takes a long while for I heard England expects 2 months notice before giving a passport. It is still a long while to your birthday but I am not sure of having another occasion of sending, & letters probably take a long while to arrive – I still have no more recent news of you than your letter of Jan 24 – except a word from a lady who crosses sometimes & who says you are very well – for this I am grateful.

Do not forget if anything *very* serious should happen you could probably send me a *message* thro' the American Ambassador in London (not a letter). All is quiet here as usual. We are only a small number so many being at the front nursing the Belgian soldiers – but also we have less work for no one can think about being ill at present.

Our new School is still unfinished and I see no prospect of moving in – the little garden in front flourishes but the ground at the back cannot be planted as it is still encumbered with bricks and rubbish . . . If you will reply to the address which will be sent with this letter I shall perhaps hear from you in 3 or 4 weeks time.

We have had some fearfully hot weather followed by severe thunder storm – It is cooler again now & windy.

You will have read of the exploit of Lieut. Warneford. We were awakened by the noise and saw the smoke & flame – I should like to say more but leave all the interesting things till I see you again – all was true and more – the next two days newspapers from Holland were suppressed. I should be glad to know whether Mr Jemmett has sent me the £50 I asked for thro' the Embassy. If not I hope he will do so at once – as we are needing money. We have not heard a word from him or Mrs J. for many months.

I do hope you will get a little holiday at the sea or in the country this year. How does the garden look and have you a good maid? Pauline flourishes but is small – as she is 16½ now I am afraid she won't grow any more.
My dearest love – the post is here.

She was daring to say much less than ever, though she needed to say a great deal more. She was in peril and now expected to be apprehended and imprisoned. She knew she would need help, but she did not want to alarm her mother. The something '*very* serious' was imminent arrest. The only communication possible when that happened would be via the American Ambassador in London, and Brand Whitlock at the American Legation in Brussels.

Reginald Warneford and the newspapers were more thorns to the German military. Warneford was twenty-three and a sub-lieutenant in the Royal Navy. The previous week in a two-seater plane he had chased a Zeppelin from Ostend to Ghent, flown above it, and dropped bombs on it. The Zeppelin crashed to the ground in flames and its crew of twenty-eight were killed. Allied newspapers were full of his heroism. He was given the Victoria Cross and the Légion d'honneur. The German military responded with more intimidation of Belgian citizens and threats of death for anyone found with arms or ammunition.

Many German soldiers had themselves had enough. Levels of desertion were high. The Forêt de Soignes near Brussels was searched for deserters. One day the rue du Commerce was closed, and all houses searched, because six German officers were thought to be hiding there. German soldiers brought back from Russia to fight on the Western Front were said to be 'half mad with terror'. This war was not the joyride the generals had anticipated. In a year of fighting the front had barely moved a few metres.

At the end of June the Princess de Croÿ visited Edith Cavell, travelling with a home-made identity pass, to tell her they must stop their work. Sister Wilkins let her in. Edith Cavell was attending a surgical operation upstairs. The Princess waited:

> I sat in her little sitting room whose sole ornament was two shelves containing books of devotion and works on nursing, until Jack, a big shaggy dog of whom she was fond, but who was anything but friendly to strangers, bounded in, followed by his mistress. Nurse Cavell was slight, but very straight, with large earnest grey eyes which seemed to see through one, and a quiet dignified manner which commanded respect. In her gentle voice she said, 'I wish you hadn't come. I am evidently suspect. Look at those men cleaning the square in front; they have been there several days and are scarcely working at all. They must be set to watch the house.'

The previous day the place had again been searched. When armed police broke in she threw papers in the grate, doused them with alcohol and set fire to them. The men searched her office and took hospital records. She worried how she would explain the School's finances to Dr Depage.

The Princess spoke of how the château was surveilled and searched. She said they must stop. Edith Cavell looked relieved, but then asked if there were more hidden men. The Princess told her Louise Thuliez had found another thirty in Cambrai. Edith Cavell said if that was the case they could not stop: 'If one of those men got caught and shot it would be our fault.' They agreed at least that no more would be sent to lodge with her. The thirty men must be found safe houses. She would supply and direct guides, and communicate information as to how they could get to Holland.

When the Princess left, Edith Cavell told her to go down to the corner where a shop window would reflect the road behind her. Check in this, she said, then turn left where there was a pastry shop by the tram stop. Hesitate, as if about to go into the shop. When the bell sounded for the tram to start, jump on it wherever it was going.

Those were the tactics they were all reduced to. They were tense, unnerved and malevolently stalked. Even in the operating theatre Edith Cavell would pull aside the curtain to look into the street. She started at unfamiliar sounds, was trepidatious of any knock at the door. Sister Wilkins and Sister Whitelock urged their matron to leave this work. But Edith Cavell would not make intimidation by her oppressors her prime concern.

On the last day of June she as usual visited the new building. She was discussing, with Sister Wilkins, a group of nurses and one of the doctors, where taps should be positioned in the various rooms, when a probationer burst in to tell her German police were at rue de la Culture asking for her. She told her to tell them where she was. Sister Wilkins thought she did not expect to be present for the move to the new School. Edith Cavell kept pointing out to her things that must be done and care that must be taken, as if she would not herself be the one to implement and supervise. She confided no thoughts about punishment, no personal fear, no shrinking from a path she knew to be right. She did not doubt that the new School must open, the war must end and Belgium must be restored to its people. As she saw it, God's will would in time shine through these dark days.

As the net closed she destroyed all remaining evidence. She went on working hard, for there was much to be done. Throughout July she and the nurses moved furniture and equipment into the new School. They pushed it there on handcarts to save money. And despite the men outside ostensibly cleaning the road, the probing by strangers of Marie and Pauline and the vegetable growers in the opposite field, the arrival of unconvincing refugees who knew no passwords and were vague about who sent them, the dirigibles that hovered over the streets, the unannounced searches of the School by police, Edith Cavell still managed to take Patrick Bowen, Sergeant Shiells and Private Revelly on the tram to Schaerbeek to hand them over to a trusted guide. She had them all dressed in white as if from a silent order of monks. Their regiment was the Royal Irish Rifles.

31

ARREST

The 21st of July was Independence Day in Belgium and a national holiday. Its celebration dated from 1831 when Leopold I became the country's first king and Belgium declared independence from Holland. As the day approached in 1915, posters were put up in all public places in Brussels, signed by von Bissing, prohibiting celebrations, demonstrations, assemblies or parades. Edicts had already been passed forbidding the display of flags, emblems, or ribbons in the national colours of red, yellow and black. Belgians responded by taking a new symbol for themselves – the ivy leaf with the legend *Je meurs où je m'attache*.[15]

By word of mouth, Brussels decided to make 21 July a day of mourning. Every shop, café and public building would close. Handbills went round telling people not to go to work, and to pull down blinds and close shutters. *La Libre Belgique* published an invitation to everyone, Catholic or not, to assemble at the cathedral of Ste Gudule, near the Grande Place, where instead of the day's customary *Te Deum* of celebration, High Mass would be held to mark the nation's grief.

The *Kommandantur* heard of this plan and posted *affiches* saying the closing of shops would constitute a demonstration, a defiance of the prohibition, and invoke heavy punishment. None the less, on the day, every shop closed and every house drew down its blinds. Only a few German beer houses, and the Palace and Astoria hotels, taken over for German officers, stayed open.

[15] I die where I attach myself

All along the city streets women handed out ivy leaves and little bouquets of red and yellow flowers. Crowds gathered at the Place des Martyrs and threw these flowers round the monument to those who died fighting the 1830 war of independence. The cathedral was packed to capacity and the crowd spilled out into the street. After Mass the organist played 'La Brabançonne', the Belgian national anthem, at first softly then with all stops out. The crowd sang its words, muted, and then with defiance:

> *O Belgique, ô mère chérie,*
> *À toi nos cœurs, à toi nos bras,*
> *À toi notre sang, ô Patrie!*
> *Nous le jurons tous: tu vivras!*
> *Tu vivras toujours grande et belle*
> *Et ton invincible unité*
> *Aura pour devise immortelle:*
> *Le Roi, la Loi, la Liberté!*[16]

The organist played it five times. They sang it five times and cried when they came to the words *Le Roi, La Loi, la Liberté*. They shouted out *'Vive le Roi'*, *'Vive la Belgique'*. Their patriotism was forgivable, for their king was in exile, their law replaced by brutal power, and their freedoms all denied. Repression only provoked their defiance. Throughout the city in all the parishes the churches were filled from early morning.

[16] O Belgium, O dearest mother,
  To you our hearts, to you our arms,
  To you our blood, O Patrie!
  We all vow: you shall live!
  You shall live, ever great and beautiful
  Your unity invincible
  With our eternal pledge to
  The King, the Law, and Liberty!

Von Bissing was more than angered. He criticised von Kraewel for letting it happen and he poured more officials, military and civilian, into the city. They took over the Bois, had all the tables at the smart restaurants, turned Belgians out of their apartments, and punished any Belgian on the slightest complaint from a German.

A week later, on 29 July, the Chief Constable of Norwich delivered a letter to Mrs Cavell from Ruth de Borchgrave, who was staying at Brougham House in Crowthorne, Berkshire. She had been on the Nursing School management committee in Brussels. Her husband Count Camille de Borchgrave had sent a warning message from Brussels. He had been at the School visiting Edith Cavell when two German police officers and a red-faced Englishman with a cockney accent called to question her. The red-faced man told her he could go to England whenever he wanted and get information from her mother and from the Belgian consul in Rotterdam. 'Dear Mrs Cavell' Ruth de Borchgrave wrote:

> I have had a message from Brussels asking me to write and tell you not to speak to *anyone* of your daughter there. Also to warn you against a certain man – reddish face and fair short military moustache, real cockney accent, who says he has a flower shop at Forest Hill, London. I am sending you this letter through the Chief Constable of Norwich whom I have asked to take note of its contents.
>
> Your daughter is an old friend of mine and I would gladly help her in any way.
>
> Please let me know that my letter has reached you.
> Yours sincerely
> Ruth de Borchgrave

Berkshire police passed the warning to MI5 who found no florid man in Forest Hill.

The net of intimidation closed. In Brussels the military police watched, and waited for a time to strike. Bergan and his team had spent months amassing evidence. They did not want to arouse suspicion with single arrests. They intended to trawl in all involved. They named as principal suspects the Prince de Croÿ of Bellignies and, in Brussels, Edith Cavell, head of the Berkendael Institute, and Philippe Baucq, architect. Others in their sights were Louise Thuliez, schoolteacher; Herman Capiau, engineer; Ada Bodart, Louis Séverin, chemist; Albert Libiez, barrister; Georges Hostelet, engineer; Princess Marie de Croÿ, Philippe Rasquin, coffeehouse keeper . . . They had thirty-five suspects. Most were Belgian Walloons. Edith Cavell was the only English national.

On 2 July Bergan had filed a report of his findings to the Governor General: about the actions of all suspects, safe houses, disguises, passwords, guides who led Allied soldiers over the frontier, the distribution of *La Libre Belgique*, the collating of information for *Les Petits Mots du Soldat*.

On the night of Saturday 31 July the military police struck. Louise Thuliez had planned that night to help six Belgian metal-workers from the Maubeuge region cross the border. She had arranged to meet them in a Brussels café near the Gare du Midi then take them to the rooms she had booked for them in a small hotel owned by a resistance worker, a M. Godefroid. In the afternoon she met up with Philippe Baucq to discuss the logistics of this plan. He suggested that, because it would be late after she had seen them into their lodgings, she spend the night at his house at 49 avenue Roodebeek in Schaerbeek. From 8.30 in the evening she waited for the metalworkers in the agreed café near the station. They did not show up. At 10.00 she got a tram to Baucq's house. She half noticed four men in the shadows, hats pulled down, scarves knotted round their necks. They were part of a team who for months had been watching his house, twenty-four hours a day.

Baucq was indoors with his wife, his two daughters aged fourteen and eleven and two nieces aged fifteen and sixteen. They were all folding for distribution the following day the newly printed edition of *La Libre Belgique* – issue No. 37, the issue that prided itself on the success of the 21 July celebrations, and described the day as a slap in the face for von Bissing, von Kraewel and all the 'execrated oppressors'. Louise Thuliez told him the metalworkers had not found the café and that she would have to go to Maubeuge in the morning to collect them. She helped fold the paper and they all talked until about 11.30. Mme Baucq then showed her to her room while Baucq went to take their dog Diane, a German shepherd, for a bedtime walk. As he opened the door, police pushed through. The dog barked furiously. 'Good evening, Monsieur Baucq,' Sergeant Pinkhoff said. 'I know you very well.' He demanded to know where the woman was who had recently entered the house. There were police guarding the street. Baucq shouted to his wife and the girls, who threw bundles of the newspaper from top-floor windows. Pinkhoff told Baucq to shut up or he would hit him. The dog barked hysterically. Louise Thuliez had not stayed in Baucq's house before and did not know its layout. She dashed to the nearest room – the bathroom – and tried to hide her handbag behind the bath. The police seized it. In it was her notebook and a receipt paid only hours before: 'To lodging of six men for four days . . . 66 francs'.

Pinkhoff questioned her. She was not a good liar. She said her name was Mme Lejeune. 'Where is your husband?' he asked. She said she was separated. He asked where she lived. She could not give her family address for then her name would be known, nor the château at Bellignies, nor where she stayed in Mons – at the house of a friend of the Croÿ family, a Mlle Duthilleul, nor the boarding house where she usually stayed when in Brussels because it was in rue de la Culture near Edith Cavell's Nursing

School. So she said she had no fixed abode. Pinkhoff said he would remedy that with St Gilles prison.

Baucq said nothing. He and Louise Thuliez were shut in separate rooms while the police searched the house. They found 4000 copies of *La Libre Belgique* No. 37, other 'seditious' literature and lists of addresses. At 1.00 a.m. Philippe Baucq and Louise Thuliez were taken under armed guard to the police station at rue de la Loi where Lieutenant Bergan was waiting for them. He charged them with sending soldiers to the Belgian front, circulating seditious literature and prohibited newspapers, and with suspected espionage, and declared them under arrest. At 2.30 a.m., escorted by Pinkhoff, they were taken to St Gilles prison. Pinkhoff went into long voluble explanations in German with the police there and kept saying *endlich, endlich* – at last, at last. He was pleased with himself. He had caught his prey. Promotion would follow.

Baucq's house was put under armed guard. His wife, daughters and nieces were allowed to touch nothing. At dawn more police came and ransacked it. They found thirty-two copies of the 'Proclamation du Roi Albert', seven documents stamped *Ligue de la Propagande*, incriminating visiting cards and recruiting addresses, copies of *Petits Mots du Soldat*, papers identifying Baucq as a member of the *garde civique*, a memorandum book and a report on two Belgians who were spying for the German police.

In Louise Thuliez's handbag they found copies of *Petits Mots du Soldat*, her false identity card and a notebook of coded addresses. It took them ten days to break her code. The town of Caudry she'd called Tulle – it was a centre of tulle manufacture; St Quentin was St Ouen. The rue Barrat she called rue Viala because both were named after resistance workers.

At 10.30 on the morning of that Saturday when she and Baucq were arrested, Constant Cayron, the student who helped the priest Father Piersoul get men to Holland, and Philippe Bodart, a schoolboy whose mother lodged fugitive soldiers, had gone to Baucq's house. Next day the police arrested them too. Bodart at first refused to say anything about himself and gave false information. Both were imprisoned at St Gilles.

News of the arrests spread fast. Prince Reginald de Croÿ hurried from Bellignies to Brussels to warn other members of the group to destroy all evidence, lie low, say nothing to anyone. At rue de la Culture Edith Cavell told him she expected arrest at any moment and would not seek to escape. He asked her if she had destroyed all tangible evidence. She said she had: all addresses, letters, newspapers, diaries. Only the fragment of her diary about the occupation, later found sewn into a cushion, existed somewhere. She urged the Prince to leave the country if he could. He said he had never seen her look so tired. The Prince then went to Mme Bodart, who had moved from rue Taciturne to rue Émile Wittmann, and whose son was in prison. She offered to continue to spread the alarm. She was arrested as she crossed the city.

Edith Cavell had not said much to her nurses about her secret work. Sister Wilkins had a fair idea of what was going on, but Sister Whitelock, Nurses van Til, Waschausky, van Bockstaele, Wolf, Court, Hacks, Wegels and Brenez were all busy moving premises, taking handcarts of furniture, equipment and belongings from rue de la Culture to the new Training School at 32 rue de Bruxelles-Uccle. Thanks to Edith Cavell's chivvying and determination the School, her achievement and pride, was finished despite all that was happening around her.

But Bergan and Pinkhoff were hard at work. On Monday 2 August Pauline Randall went for a walk with the daughter of the Flemish cook. A man who had stayed at the School invited them to a café. It was Quien. There were German soldiers in the café. Quien bought the girls drinks, flirted with them, then asked if

Miss Cavell would get his friend to the frontier. He said he had been given her name. It seems Pauline Randall's replies were indiscreet.

Next day Edith Cavell turned away three callers who said they were English. On 4 August a uniformed German officer arrived. He inspected what was left in her office, looked through her books, asked her if she had received any letters from London. He commented that she had neglected the Institute's accounts for the past three months, and said he supposed she had been too busy with other things to pay attention to them.

After he had gone, Edith Cavell told Pauline Randall, Sister Wilkins, Jacqueline van Til and the other nurses to keep cool-headed and calm. The following day, Thursday 5 August, they went on with the task of moving equipment and furniture to the new building. Late in the afternoon, at four, Henri Pinkhoff and Otto Mayer arrived. They ransacked Edith Cavell's office. They could not find much, but anything was incriminating evidence now. They took an innocuous letter from England, sent through the American Legation. On the strength of that, she and Sister Wilkins were arrested. They were marched past the frightened nurses to separate cars. As she passed the nurses, Edith Cavell told them to be strong, that everything would be all right and she would be back soon. She could offer no such consolation to Jack, who whined.

She and Sister Wilkins were taken to Court B in the *Komman-dantur*, in the ironically named rue de la Loi. Bergan was waiting for them. He interrogated them separately. The seized letter was translated and passed to the 'political department' so that 'necessary steps could be taken'. 'From the seal on the back of the envelope, and from the contents of the letter,' Bergan surmised, 'it appears the American Consul in Brussels has taken part in the unlawful transmission of letters.'

Pinkhoff's official account read:

On Aug. 5th 1915 in the afternoon officers of the Secret
Police, Duisberg, Plank II and the undersigned presented
themselves on the order of the chief of the station, Lieut.
Bergan, at the Institute Berkendael, rue de la Culture,
No. 149 and there proceeded to a search in the course of
which was discovered a letter from England which had
been transmitted, in spite of a law forbidding it, through
the agency of the American consul. Miss Cavell and her
head assistant, Miss Wilkins, were arrested at four o'clock
in the afternoon and brought to police station B. After
examination by Lieut. Bergan, Miss Wilkins was released.
Miss Cavell was detained.

Sister Wilkins wrote of her interrogation:

I refused to admit anything and said as I had the first time
they questioned me, that I knew nothing. Otto Mayer
finally said 'You might as well admit these things for we
know that you have harboured men in rue de la Culture
and that Nurse Cavell has furnished them with guides and
money to cross the border. Two of our men have given us
that information – Quien and Jacobs.'

I never knew why I was released but at eight that night I
was told that I might go.

All the way back to the School I kept saying, 'Matron
must be there when I get back.' But I knew that was only
wishful thinking. For if what Mayer had said about Quien
and Jacobs was true, then the police knew the part that
she had played and she was too important a member of
the organisation for them to release her as they had me
. . . I did not see Edith Cavell again until several weeks
later when I was allowed to visit her in her prison cell in
St Gilles. As she walked away from me that afternoon, I

remember how erectly she carried her slight body. Her whole bearing was calm and composed . . .

Sister Wilkins was driven back to the School at 9 p.m. where she and the nurses were kept under armed guard. They could move between the four houses, and go about their nursing business, but they could not go out without permission or unaccompanied. Before midnight they were told by one of these guards that their matron had been detained. Sister Wilkins became hysterical and her cries made neighbours look in through the windows.

Edith Cavell was consigned to a crowded communal women's cell at the *Kommandantur*. On 6 August she managed to get a letter out to Grace Jemmett. As ever her tone was soothing and her concern to reassure. 'My dearest Grace, she wrote,

> I do hope you are not worrying about me; tell everybody that I am quite alright here. I suppose from what I hear that I shall be questioned one of these days and when they have all they desire I shall know what they mean to do with me. We are numerous here and there is no chance of being lonely. We can buy food at the canteen, but I should be glad to have one of your red blankets, a serviette, cup, fork, spoon and plate – not the best ones – also one or two towels and my toothbrush. In a day or two some clean linen. I am afraid you will not be able to come and see me at present. But you can write, only your letters will be read.
>
> Is Sister Wilkins free? I have been thinking of her ever since last night. Tell them to go on with the move as before. If Sister is there, she will know how to arrange everything.
>
> Is Jackie sad? Tell him I will be back soon. The day is rather long; can you send me a book, a little embroidery, my nail scissors and only a very few things as I have no place to put them.

Send me news of Mlle Deves [their laundry woman, who had been ill]. I hope she is going on well. Remember me to the sisters, nurses and household.

There is a little child here of 3 or 4 with her mother. She looks pale and pinched for want of air, though she is allowed out a little every day. I will write again when there is something to tell. Don't worry – we must hope for the best. Tell them all to go on as usual and for you—

The rest of the letter had been torn away.

She was confined in crowded airless quarters with numerous women picked up by the police for whatever reason. There was nothing to do, no amenities, nowhere to put anything, and she was cold at night. But that was not her way of expressing things: 'I should be glad of a cup, fork, spoon and plate – not the best

Louise Thuliez (right) and the Countess Jeanne de Belleville
in prison clothes, 11 November 1918

ones.' The best ones were for better days. Her greater concern was for the child, who should not have been in such a place as that.

Sister Wilkins and other nurses called at the *Kommandantur* to deliver the things Edith Cavell had asked for. They were not allowed to see her. They said the German officers laughed at them and treated them rudely. At the School, police watched their every move. Sister Wilkins seemed at the point of breakdown. Jack lay all day by the door of Edith Cavell's office waiting for her return.

Then the nurses heard of the imprisonment of the Countess of Belleville and Louise Thuliez. 'We felt as though we were engulfed in darkness,' Jacqueline van Til wrote. On Saturday 7 August Edith Cavell was moved from the *Kommandantur* to the prison at St Gilles. She was put in solitary confinement in cell 23.

PART FIVE

32

FIRST INTERROGATION

Edith Cavell was taken from her cell at St Gilles prison on Sunday 8 August to police station B at the *Kommandantur* for interrogation. Lieutenant Bergan, Head of Espionage, Sergeant Pinkhoff, Chief Officer of Criminal Investigation, Sergeant Neuhaus, and the spy Otto Mayer were there. Bergan spoke no French or English. Edith Cavell spoke scant German. Pinkhoff was their translator. Neuhaus was scribe and witness.

Bergan put questions to Edith Cavell in German. Pinkhoff translated these into French. Edith Cavell answered in French, and Pinkhoff translated her replies into German for Bergan's

The prison at St Gilles

279

benefit. Neuhaus wrote in German what Pinkhoff claimed she had said in French. The depositions Edith Cavell then signed were in German. She had no way of knowing whether what she signed was what she had said.

None of the men opposite her had legal training, though like Edith Cavell they had their own interpretation of justice. It was hardly an equitable balance between prosecutor and defendant. She had no legal representation or advice, had spoken to no one since her arrest, been allowed no reading matter, no post, no communication. She did not know that Sister Wilkins was free.

The session began with her being asked to take an oath on the Bible that she would, before God, tell the truth. To refuse would seem to confirm guilt. To take such an oath and then directly to lie would be impossible, given her Christian orthodoxy. And so she became a seeming player in their game, for what else could she be?

After the oath came the standard details that gave a semblance of objectivity. Her name was Edith Cavell. She was head of the Berkendael Medical Institute. Her religion was Protestant. She was born on 4 December 1866 in Swardeston, Norfolk, England (in fact she was born in 1865 and her religion was Anglican). She was British. She lived in Brussels at 149 rue de la Culture. Her father was Frederick Cavell, a clergyman, deceased. Her mother's name was Louise *née* Warming (in fact her mother's name was Louisa, but what did such niceties matter here?). Her languages were English and French. Her financial position was well-off (in fact she had very little money). Against 'Character and Credibility' Pinkhoff put a question mark. Against 'Police Record' he wrote 'apparently none'.

Slips and elisions, from minor to major, punctuated this deposition. The ostensible aim of the interrogation was to obtain facts. In reality it was to incriminate. Pinkhoff was not a disinterested translator. He was a prosecutor, an officer of the secret police, like Bergan. It was his art or guile to seem to record in objective detail the nature of Edith Cavell's complicity, but, by shifts of interpretation and minor additions, enhance her culpability in order to ensure maximum indictment. In order to destroy her, her interrogators must first demonise her. They could not punish her for who she was, for then their own egregiousness would reflect back on themselves. Only by inference could Pinkhoff, face to face with this slightly built grey-eyed woman – the vicar's daughter, with a lifetime's service as a nurse, whose creed was devotion and goodness – put a question mark against her character and credibility, or infer she might have some unrevealed police record.

Edith Cavell had no advice on how to proceed. She knew the cover of her particular unit was blown and their work finished. Reginald de Croÿ had told her Philippe Baucq and Louise Thuliez had been arrested, that the Princess de Croÿ and Mme Bodart were hunted, that he himself would try to escape the country. She had destroyed all evidence of her complicity. Her strategy, in so far as she had one, was to cooperate, give her interrogators the satisfaction of confirming what they already knew, and take responsibility herself where possible. By such seeming cooperation she hoped to spare others in the network and to safeguard the lives of the fugitives. She did not know what these others had said or might say. She was perfectly aware she had broken her prosecutors' laws and knew she would be punished in whatever way they chose.

For the credibility of his deposition Bergan wished her to be precise about numbers, places and amounts of money. He took it as a victory of entrapment when, at the outset, he accused her of receiving 5,000 francs from Reginald de Croÿ to help Allied soldiers escape, and she apparently replied, 'No not 5,000, 1,500.' Such satisfaction had little to do with any mistake on her part. For what did it matter to them or to her if it was five or fifty or five thousand francs? The truth of what mattered was why these men were in this building, in this country, looking out for themselves, while killing and oppressing its citizens and stealing their produce.

Bergan questioned, Pinkhoff translated, Neuhaus transcribed. It suited their purpose by shifts in translation to record that the men whom she helped had not been wounded, that she was at the head of an espionage network, that she guided Allied soldiers to Holland so that they might rejoin their regiments and that she did such work for profit.

These officials were united in their hatred of the English. It surpassed their antipathy to the French or Belgians. It was the English who in their view had prevented the realisation of the Schlieffen Plan and pushed the world into catastrophe. Brand Whitlock described this hatred as 'wild and implacable'. 'We are going to continue this war,' a German official said to him, 'until one can travel around the earth without seeing Englishmen who act as if they owned it.'

Like Jack, who pined for her, Edith Cavell passed by officials like Bergan and Pinkhoff with 'sublime indifference'. She would not report to their offices or take heed of their edicts. She was a stickler for obedience, but obedience had to have its justification in a context of goodness. It was a response to a rule, not a rule in itself. She had spent too much time in the contemplation of good not to have a sense of what it was. She would not do what she believed to be wrong. The law to which she deferred made great demands on her – demands which she met with all grace. She viewed the authority of her accusers and their use of the words law and truth as corrupt. Thus a citizen whose every impulse was law-abiding, became criminalised.

Her manner was anathema to them. 'Edith Cavell had a self-sufficient manner,' Eva Lückes had written of her, as a probationer some twenty years previously, from what now seemed like a different planet, 'which was very apt to prejudice people against her.' This manner seemed to these men to encapsulate all they loathed about the English and the arrogance of Victorian colonialism.

Edith Cavell knew that because she was English they aimed to destroy her. Her conscience was clear. Were she to play by their tricks of wiliness and deceit she would be lost to herself. She would rather be dead than in their shoes.

Bergan's interrogation technique was to switch alarmingly from seeming gentleness to extreme severity and to persuade her that details of her actions were already known. He kept leaving the room as if to corroborate a point with other defendants, whose apparent testimony he then returned to give. His intention was to indict and punish by cunning and guile, according to his ambitions for this prosecution. There was no one to insist, or even to suggest, he play fair.

So, in her deposition, Edith Cavell was recorded as having said:

> I lay particular stress on the fact that of all the soldiers English or French lodged with me two or three only were wounded and in these cases the wounds were slight and already beginning to heal.
>
> I acknowledge that between November 1914 and July 1915 I have received into my house, cared for, and provided with funds to help them to reach the front and join the Allied Army:
>
> 1) French and English soldiers in civilian clothes, separated from the ranks, amongst whom was an English colonel.
>
> 2) French and Belgians eligible for military service who desired to get to the front.

But at least twelve of the British soldiers, including Colonel Boger, and an equal number of French who stayed at the School were severely wounded. The reason they were brought to her was because they were hurt. And Colonel Boger did not reach the front. He was arrested in Brussels and sent to a German prisoner-of-war camp. Nor had she provided the men brought to her with money to help them join the Allied armies. Her intention was to get them over the Dutch border so that they would be free, and not have to live as fugitives or be imprisoned or shot. It was up to them whether or not they rejoined the army.

She was recorded as saying that during those eight months French and English soldiers and Belgian and French men of military age were brought to her by four people: the engineer Capiau of Wasmes; Prince Reginald de Croÿ; Mlle Thuliez who went under the name of Mlle Martin; and the barrister Libiez, from Mons.

Her deposition read that Capiau brought forty English soldiers in civilian clothes to her, including Colonel Boger and an English sergeant, that Reginald de Croÿ visited her six or seven times between January and July 1915, each time bringing men to a total of about fifteen French and English soldiers, and that he gave her 1500 francs so they would have money for their journeys. She said, or they said she said, that Colonel Boger and five others wrote to tell her of their successful arrival in Holland. She apparently confessed that peasants from Mons also brought 'derelict' soldiers to her, that Thuliez brought fifteen French and English soldiers and a hundred French and Belgian men of military age, that Libiez brought six English and ten French and Belgian . . .

She confirmed Bergan's statement that she hid the men brought to her until there was a prearranged time for them to leave. She confirmed the handover points he cited: behind St Mary's church; the tram waiting room at Place Rogier; opposite the Hôtel de l'Espérance in the Place de la Constitution; under the clock of the school at Place Rouppe; behind the Cinquantenaire at the end of the Chaussée de Tervueren; at the Square Ambiorix. Of the score of other safe houses, swap-over points and meeting places she did not speak.

Neuhaus wrote in her deposition that on the day before she took the men to the pick-up point, a guide or messenger would call at her house to check arrangements. Sometimes the guide would leave, then and there, with the men. If she did not have enough space for all those sent to her, or if she supposed the German police might apprehend her, she would take the fugitive men to Mme Ada Bodart at 7 rue Taciturne – who then moved to 19 rue Émile Wittmann; to Marie Mauton at her boarding house at 12 rue d'Angleterre; to Philippe Rasquin at his coffee-house at 137 rue Haute, to Mme Adolphine Sovet at her café at 16 boulevard de la Senne; to Louis Séverin the chemist at 138 avenue Longchamp. She said, or was said to have said, that she handed over about a hundred men in this way.

Thus Edith Cavell was steered into a contrived confession, where the boundaries of what she was supposed to have done were blurred. She had disguised Allied soldiers as monks, assigned false medical papers and passports to them, denied their existence, but that was all to save their lives, not her own. If these officials with bayonets and guns, whose uniform she despised, who to her thinking were complicit in heinous crimes, who told her when to stand or sit, who locked her up – if they wished to parade their cunning in indicting her, so be it. She was not going to try to justify herself to them, nor did she anticipate justice from them. They chose to deprive her of every right, expose her to insult and condemn her to certain punishment, but she was not going to dance to their tune. Had they been her patients she would have attended them with care; had they shown vulnerability she would have tried to help them. But she would not concede to their thinking. If she was afraid, jaded and through with it, it was not for them to know.

Lieutenant Bergan attached a note to the admissions which incriminated her and those in the resistance cell in which she had worked. It read: 'All our suppositions were confirmed by the deposition of the woman Cavell. In order to achieve this we made use of the trick [*Kniff*] of pretending that the information is already in the hands of the law.' What she actually said would never be known. No French transcript of proceedings was made. And they did not need her confirmation in order to indict. Had she said anything quite other, the outcome would have been the same. The hands were Bergan's and Pinkhoff's and the law was of their making. The irony was that while seeming to play into these hands the woman Cavell was quite beyond their reach.

She did not know if this deposition indicted others working in the resistance movement with her, who might have evaded detection. As she saw it, if Bergan and his men thought they had broken the ring they would not look further. And she knew there was much further to look.

The deposition concluded that she acknowledged having worked 'to transmit soldiers into the ranks of the Allies' in collaboration with Prince Reginald de Croÿ, the architect Philippe Baucq, the chemist Louis Séverin, Herman Capiau the engineer, Albert Libiez the barrister, Georges Derveau the chemist, Louise Thuliez the schoolteacher, and Ada Bodart.

The final paragraph of this German document read: 'My statements which have just been read over to me, translated into French, conform to the truth at every point. They are perfectly intelligible to me in every detail, and I will repeat them before the tribunal.'

So much for August 1915. A fragile elision of personal circumstance – Miss Gibson of Laurel Court, Mellish Ward, a recommendation from Marguerite François, an assassination in

Bosnia – had led Edith Cavell to this room and to these men who tricked her into signing a deposition of what they said she had said, as if by doing so they might win a war already lost to all those feeling its pain. She signed where she was told to sign and was then taken back to the prison at St Gilles and again locked in cell 23. Armed guards were posted outside her door, such was the threat she posed to the Axis powers' war effort.

33

BETWEEN INTERROGATIONS

Her cell measured 4 metres long, 2.5 metres wide, 2.75 metres high. It was whitewashed and clean. In it was a folding bed with a wooden headboard that by day served as a table, a metal bucket that served as a toilet, a wooden stool, a crucifix on the wall, a corner shelf to the left of the door, a basin and tap to the right. Two water pipes gave occasional heating. The floor was parqueted oak. Through a spyhole in the wooden door warders looked in, and through a wicket meals were passed. Twice nightly through this wicket a warder shone a torch on her face. Outside, on the door, was a slate on which was chalked her alleged crime.

Cell 23 where Edith Cavell was imprisoned

Near the ceiling a small iron-barred window opened 20 centimetres inward from the top and through it came a shaft of light. A small gas lamp lit the cell at night.

The prison, an early nineteenth-century Gothic fortress, built on a hill, had crenellated battlement towers and daunting walls. Designed as a panoptic, rows of cells radiated out from circular exercise yards. The section in which Edith Cavell was interned had, in peacetime, been for male offenders. Under the occupation it was filled with political prisoners.

The deputy prison governor Xavier Marin and the warders were Belgians, though ruled by the German governor and chief warder and watched by German soldiers. The warders were respectful to political prisoners, though forbidden to speak to them or allow them news of the outside world. On her arrival Edith Cavell was searched and given the prison rules, as drawn up by the German prison governor Lieutenant Behrens:

> Prisoners must obey all laws passed by the Military Authorities of the Prison. Failure to do so will invoke punishment.
>
> When an Officer enters the cell the prisoner must stand to attention face his Superior and stop work of any kind.
>
> When Officers walk through the prison corridors or halls each prisoner must bow his head and, if not manacled, must remove his cap.
>
> Prisoners must rise at 6 a.m. in summer and 7 a.m. in winter. They must wash and clean their cells. They are forbidden to write their names on the walls or to draw thereon. During daytime the window may be opened for change of air but it is strictly forbidden to stand close to an open window.
>
> Prisoners are forbidden to throw pieces of bread or other food through the window or in the toilet, to make a noise,

to talk to other prisoners in loud voices or in sign language, to sing, whistle or tap on the pipes, or to give letters or pieces of paper to each other.

Any attempt to escape will be severely punished. If any prisoner is aware of an attempt to escape and does not inform the Warden he will be severely punished.

Smoking is strictly forbidden.

The condemned prisoner is permitted to write a two-page letter or postcard once a week to his family. He is permitted to receive mail after the Warden has examined it.

The prisoner is permitted to have Twenty Francs on his person. All other money must be handed to the Warden.

All prisoners will be fed by the Prison Administration. Prisoners will be allowed to buy other food occasionally with their own money. They may also receive some clothes and food once a week. Wine and beer and all kinds of alcohol are strictly forbidden.

Signed Bohmer

Chief Warden of the Prison

For half an hour each day Edith Cavell was allowed out of her cell into a circular high-walled yard for air and exercise. For this she walked round and round with other prisoners, without stopping, at a distance that precluded speech, watched by guards and with a hood over her face with holes cut for the eyes. Prison food was cleanly prepared. Breakfast was a bowl of coffee and a piece of bread. Lunch, served on a wooden board and bowl with a knife, fork and spoon, was soup, potatoes and a piece of meat. At five there was more coffee and bread with a piece of cheese. On Sundays a piece of meat was added to this, which prisoners had to eat with their fingers. At 9.00 a bell rang for bedtime.

Bergan and Pinkhoff intended to interrogate her again after they had got what they wanted from others in the network. Until then she was not allowed visitors, or to speak to other prisoners, or to inform anyone what was happening to her, or attend the prison chapel or see the prison chaplain. The one weekly letter she could write was pored over by Bergan and Pinkhoff. Nurses' letters to her were declined or cut until bleached of any but the blandest news. Sister Wilkins came each day to the prison gates. She brought her roses and white chrysanthemums, small amounts of money, clothes, pieces of linen to embroider. Each Sunday she brought a boxed meal and hoped it was given to her. Edith Cavell heard of her freedom and for that was relieved. She asked to see her to discuss practical matters to do with the administration of the School but this request was at first refused.

Her main concern was that she had left her affairs in disarray and that her nurses would find it hard without her to manage the move to the new School. But the move continued, though German soldiers oversaw it. Sister Wilkins said she managed 'the whole caboodle'. Each day José pushed a handcart back and forward from rue de la Culture to 32 rue de Bruxelles. There were seventeen nurses there at the School's start. The German maid Marie vanished, giving strength to rumours that she had aided the military police.

Edith Cavell had known it was a matter of time before she was apprehended. She supposed she would be sent to a German prison for the duration of the war. She found the prison warders kind. She was not a woman who could be demeaned by being made to wear a cagoule to conceal her face or by being obliged to eat scraps of meat with her fingers. Her cell became a place of sanctity, its austerity monastic. Though her demeanour was solitary, throughout the unceasing demands of her working career she had seldom been literally alone. From early childhood she had had the habit of prayer. In times of repose her inner conversation was with what to her was God. Through devotional words she found courage. Her hopes were for her mother, her nurses, the work of the School, Grace Jemmett, Pauline Randall, dear old Jack pining for her return. She submitted to the prison routine and awaited further interrogation, trial and sentence. Each night at eleven she heard the sirens of the German police cars as they brought more prisoners, the sounds of marching feet, shouted orders, doors clanging, keys turning, the cries of newcomers and at times silence.

34

THE OTHERS

Bergan and Pinkhoff rounded up thirty-three others from the resistance network. They knew the organiser was Prince Reginald de Croÿ, but he eluded them.

Philippe Baucq continued to respond to their questions with silence. He was interned in cell 72. He kept a diary on toilet paper and smuggled this out to his wife via one of the Belgian warders. He and his neighbouring prisoner, the barrister Albert Libiez, communicated by laboriously tapping on the water pipes which ran between the cells: one tap for A, two for B and so on. Then they found they could actually talk by whispering into the crack where the pipes were sunk into the wall, and write messages and push them through. The only strategy left to discuss was their own defence. Each day the secret police broke apart a bit more of their resistance network.

Despite repeated questioning Baucq would confirm nothing. After six weeks in prison, and his refusal to corroborate or sign anything, on 15 September at 9.00 in the morning Bergan planted an agent, a *mouton*, Maurice Neels, in his cell. Baucq trusted him, for he had often met him at a café in rue Victor Hugo. Neels told Baucq his house had been ransacked at 7.00 that morning and he had been arrested because the police found copies of *La Libre Belgique*, *The Times* and various French newspapers.

Baucq told him to confess nothing to his interrogators and agree nothing. He boasted that he had held out against them for sixty-seven days, even when confronted by witnesses. Over the course of the day, he told Neels how he controlled distribution of *La Libre Belgique* and recruited for the resistance, and that during the search of his house two reports ready for dispatch to Le Havre had been found. He showed him how to communicate with other prisoners through the pipes in the cell.

Neels was very interested and asked many questions about strategy. Baucq told him how he marked on ordnance maps the best routes for getting to Holland, and how under cover of night he himself often took young men to the border. He said Abbé van Lint was one of his main colleagues in this work, and another was Pastor van Gombergen, who lived at 37 avenue Louis Bertrand. He thought Neels's transgressions would be viewed as mild, and asked him, when he was freed, to warn the Abbé and Pastor and also two Jesuit Fathers, Meus and Piersoul, of the danger they were in because the student Constant Cayron had given away a great deal of information.

Neels was led from cell 72 at 4.00 in the afternoon. Baucq supposed he was going to be interrogated, wished him luck, and hoped the advice he had given him would prove helpful, and that he would continue the work. He felt optimistic when night came, Neels did not return, and his bed was removed from the cell. He supposed he had been released, so the priests would be warned, more lives of fugitive soldiers saved and more Belgians helped to enlist.

Neels reported back to Bergan and Pinkhoff. He told them how Baucq communicated with Libiez in the adjacent cell, and that he saw him push bits of paper into the gaps in the walls where the heating pipes ran through. Baucq was moved to a windowless cell in a different wing on the ground floor. It was damp and cold and there was no one to communicate with on the other side of the wall.

Louise Thuliez was incriminated by the coded addresses found in her handbag, and the bill, paid two hours before her arrest, for lodging six men for four days. But under cross-examination she also stonewalled and did not, like Edith Cavell, corroborate the facts Bergan and Pinkhoff put to her. She was alert to Bergan's *Kniff* – the persuasion that facts were already known in order to trick her into admitting guilt. She insisted she had always acted alone and had never been into the forest villages near Mons. On 20 September her sister tried to visit her at the prison with a friend. They were turned away and followed home.

But Bergan and Pinkhoff did not persevere too much with Louise Thuliez. They wanted a conclusion, sentences passed, personal preferment, an example set to terrorise other civilians, not an endless unravelling of the myriad strands of resistance. That was not achievable. Louise Thuliez made no mention of Henriette Moriamé, the other Girl Guide – the brewer's sister from the village of St Waast, her partner with whom she had trudged through abandoned battlefields, woodland, and razed villages, looking for *enfants perdus* in need of help. She saved, too, from the inquisition of these policemen, other helpers like herself in the north of France who had harboured and risked their lives to protect many men.

'In the circumstances I did not find the Germans very intelligent,' she was to write, some twenty years later, in her memoir *Condemned to Death*.

> Had they questioned a village child in St Waast-la-Vallée, and asked him who I so often went out with, they would certainly have learned the part Mlle Moriamé played in this work for the *Patrie*. As it was, she was not even suspected, and when after my sentence and reprieve my sister came back from Brussels, reassured as to my fate, Mlle Moriamé called to see her. She told her she was going away to become a nun the very next day. She entered the convent

of the Redemptorist nuns at Maffle, took the veil two years later, and died two months before the Armistice.

She was the only friend I had with whom I might have shared the memories of our long night-journeys and all the alarms of forest life. I wrote to her once only from Siegburg[17] on a card from one of my companions, whose name I borrowed so the Germans might suspect nothing. She replied indirectly, as I had written, but I understood that her mother superior preferred that our correspondence should cease. I never wrote again.

Like the other thirty-three defendants, Louise Thuliez was instructed to sign the German deposition, typed up by Neuhaus, of whatever she was supposed to have said. She asked to check certain points. When translated back into French by Pinkhoff she told him, 'I did not say that.' Pinkhoff said it was the fault of the transcription then let the deposition go without changing a word. 'We ought never to have signed those depositions in German,' Louise Thuliez wrote, 'for it was utterly impossible for us to verify the translation.'

Among the accused, only Capiau knew German well. He kept quiet about it, so his captors spoke freely in front of him. He fully understood the ploys they were using to secure convictions and elevate offences.

On 18 September Pinkhoff visited Louise Thuliez in her cell and showed her a list of eight Englishmen she had supposedly helped. 'I denied having had anything to do with them,' she wrote in her autobiography, 'but all the same, on reading the names, I recognised with anguish that it was indeed one of the groups I had guided.'

Disparate evidence was picked up by Quien, Neels, and other agents for the secret police – the men and women whom Brand

<hr />

[17] The German prison to which she was sent

Whitlock called 'the scum and offscouring of the earth'. The story about the eight Englishmen had been published in a Dutch newspaper. It told how the men had been hidden in a château in the north of France, and of their dangerous journey through Belgium. The police collected pieces of the jigsaw until they had enough to make a picture. They intercepted the letters of other men who had escaped and, thankful for their safety and unaware of at quite what risk their freedom had been acquired, wrote incriminating notes of gratitude to Edith Cavell, Madame Bodart and others. One after another in September the group headed by Prince Reginald de Croÿ was rounded up. Albert Libiez the barrister was betrayed by a former employee, Armand Jeannes, who had tried to pass as a fugitive soldier at the rue de la Culture. On Bergan's instruction Jeannes checked out all the coded addresses found in Louise Thuliez's handbag. One morning at the château Bellignies the Princess de Croÿ saw a black car go by with Jeanne de Belleville in the back, flanked by German officers. She went round to try to console her friend's eighty-year-old mother.

The secret police took their time before arresting the Princess de Croÿ. They hoped to use her to snare her brother. She was followed and watched, and on a day in late August two cars arrived filled with German soldiers, and the road to the château was cordoned off. An officer demanded to speak to her brother. The Princess said she did not know where he was. Von Kirchenheim of the Maubeuge military police, who was given to hitting his prisoners' faces with the butt of his gun, urged her to give them his address. This she genuinely could not do.

They arrested the gardener, M. Legat, and interrogated him to try to find the Prince's whereabouts. On 6 September at dawn Pinkhoff and Bergan arrived to arrest the Princess. They told her she was suspected of hiding a French pilot shot down in an aeroplane in the region, that she must make a statement in

Brussels and would be free to return to Bellignies that evening. They took her by train to St Gilles prison and questioned her en route. At the prison, they brought others in the network up from their cells and watched her reaction when she saw them. Bergan told her she would be released as soon as she let them know where her brother was. He said he was in trouble for letting the Prince escape.

35

THE ESCAPE OF THE PRINCE
DE CROŸ

A group of people not known to the secret police helped the Prince de Croÿ escape to Holland. The resistance movement had no fixed centre and was always shifting. As guides were imprisoned or shot, safe houses raided, covers blown, communications cut and documents seized, others took up the cause in another house, convent or café.

But by September 1915 it had become well-nigh impossible to cross into Holland. A Flemish workman, Henri Beyns, who lived on the outskirts of Brussels, was the Prince's main guide to freedom. From the start of the war he had travelled between Holland and Brussels every ten days or so, each time carrying 10 to 15 kilos of letters, to and from the Belgian army. He collected these from, and delivered them to, a nun, who worked under the name of Mlle Josephine, and who also helped repatriate Allied soldiers. Her main postman was an electrician, Michel Richard.

Beyns knew most of the monasteries, convents and safe houses where men were hidden and communications printed. Though aware of it, he did not tell the Prince of his sister's arrest, fearing he would try to go back to rescue her. His first task was to get him a false identity. He acquired the identity card of a Belgian, René Desmet, who had recently died. He then found a witness, 'a brave young lady', who went with the Prince to the Maison Communale to get him a travel pass. The Prince showed the papers of René Desmet. The brave lady affirmed he was Desmet and that she knew him as a neighbour and friend. The Prince was then issued with a pass that allowed him to travel with Beyns by tram to the town of Vilvorde.

From there they continued on foot. They were joined by a M. Van Maldeghem who also wanted to escape from Belgium. A friend of Beyns ferried them across the River Dyle in the dark because all bridges were guarded. They slept in woodland and in farmworkers' cottages. At Baelen they stayed five nights with a truly poor family who shared their potatoes, black bread and chicory with them. At the Abbey of Tongerlo they were hidden by monks. The guides who were supposed to take them to the crossing point did not show up. Seven kilometres from the Dutch frontier a guide known to Beyns agreed to get them and four other fugitives across the guarded canal at night. Only the Prince and Van Maldeghem could swim. Beyns was carrying packets of letters and military documents. He had a length of rope, and a canvas bag for the papers and all their clothes. The Prince swam the canal with one end of the rope and tied it high to a tree so that Beyns and the other non-swimmers could pull themselves across and keep the clothes and letters dry. Beyns got across with the clothes and papers, but the cord broke under the weight of the next man. The splash as he fell into the water alerted guards who turned a searchlight toward the noise. The two who had crossed the water hid in rushes until the light averted. There were four men without clothes on the other side of the bank and one in the canal who could not swim. The two safely across left the clothes of the others, with the hope they would find them, then made their own way through the marshes to safety. At the Hague, the de Croÿs' cousin Prince Albert de Ligne was Minister Plenipotentiary and Envoy Extraordinary. Treatment was first-class from there on.

36

THE SECOND INTERROGATION

On 18 August, after ten days alone in her cell seeing no one except the warders who passed food through the wicket in the door and escorted her to the exercise yard, and who were themselves victims of this occupation, Edith Cavell was interrogated again. It was the same trio – Bergan, Pinkhoff and Neuhaus, with Otto Mayer as witness, the same procedure and technique, the same scramble of languages and manipulation of evidence to support conclusions already reached. This time they sought to fit all the information they had acquired into seeming incrimination by Edith Cavell of others in the network. They wrote admissions as if she had made them, though in reality they put words into her mouth. She did not give them information but neither did she deny the evidence they said they already had. As before, she stayed quiet about the wider network, and made no mention of guides like Charles Vanderlinden or 'Girl Guides' like Henriette Moriamé. Far more effectively than the others she had destroyed evidence. She was too meticulous over detail and concerned for the safety of nurses in the School and the guides and soldiers still in the enemy's reach, to risk divulgence. The German police did not find letters or address books of hers, or copies of *La Libre Belgique*. All they could produce was a letter addressed to her which made reference to a soldier who reached England.

In this second deposition it was written that she confirmed in every detail all she had previously signed. She was recorded as having said that men 'seeking to cross the border to rejoin their regiments or enlist' were brought to her from Louise

Thuliez, Herman Capiau, Georges Derveau, the chemist Maurice Crabbé, Georges Hostelet and Louis Séverin; that Capiau supplied all false papers for the soldiers; that Louise Thuliez knew her well, had stayed at her house and brought about twenty fugitive English soldiers to her at the instigation of Libiez, Capiau and the rest. 'I recollect clearly that often the accused Thuliez said to me, "I come with the men from the lawyer Libiez," ' she was reported to have said. She was supposed to have admitted that on one occasion Louise Thuliez visited with her brother-in-law Auguste Joly, that Georges Hostelet, who lived in Uccle, introduced the chemist Séverin to her and gave her 500 francs to finance the journeys of Allied soldiers seeking to re-enlist.

Thus the document of indictment that was prepared. But after the war's end, in 1919 when the spy Georges Gaston Quien was tried for war crimes in Paris, Otto Mayer, giving witness, stated that Edith Cavell, apart from her initial response about the amount of money given by de Croÿ, when she apparently corrected Bergan and said it was not 5,000 francs but 1,500, had evaded answering any question directly. Her deposition was according to Bergan and Pinkhoff.

During this interrogation the barrister Albert Libiez was brought in. She was asked if he had visited her house. She apparently said she was not sure, she could not remember, she did not think she knew him but it was quite possible he had been to her house in her absence. She said – she was said to have said – that she used guides known to her as Louis and Victor Gilles; she did not think they were related; she had no idea where they lived; she supposed those were not their real names; yes, one of them was sent by Séverin, the other by Capiau; yes, one was about twenty-eight, tall and thin, powerfully built with a brown moustache turned up at the ends and bushy hair parted in the middle.

This second deposition was again read to her in Pinkhoff's French. She again signed the German version. As before, she had no idea what she had signed. Her signature was witnessed by the document's author, Sergeant Henri Pinkhoff.

Edith Cavell was taken back to her cell. Three days later on 21 August she was again taken before Bergan and Pinkhoff. They had now arrested Countess Jeanne de Belleville and wanted an indictment of her. Yes, Edith Cavell was supposed to have said, the Countess had brought eight or ten men to her, English and Belgian, who wanted to cross into Holland. She did not know where the Countess lived, she received no money from her, knew nothing about the men brought to her; yes, she concurred, the countess was from forty-five to fifty years old, grey-haired, wrinkled, unmarried. It would not have been Edith Cavell's way to describe a friend and a woman whom she respected in quite such words. Louise Thuliez said of Jeanne de Belleville: 'She had blue eyes and curly grey hair, an aquiline nose and rapid, energetic walk. She seemed indefatigable. Everything about her breathed simplicity and goodness. Her natural gaiety was such that in the most tragic moments of our adventure she remained smiling and undaunted.'

Quite what Edith Cavell said or did not say was lost in perverse translation. Her signed statements were shown to the other prisoners. Georges Hostelet later said that when he read the apparent depositions by her and Louis Séverin he just did not believe they had made them. He could not believe Edith Cavell would have said things that were so compromising, above all to herself. He told Bergan he was distorting the truth and intent on false conclusions. 'By insinuation and false translation, they altered the sense of confessions and obtained what they wanted,' Georges Hostelet was to write in his account of this trial. Thus the law, at this particular time, in this particular place: an edifice of dishonour that compounded the wrongdoing of those who created and exercised it. Aeschylus wrote in *Agamemnon* in 458 BC that the first casualty of war is the truth. Bergan and Pinkhoff ignored evidence that failed to support what they intended to prove. Helping men to the Dutch border slipped into recruitment of troops for the enemy. Resistance to occupation slipped into espionage and treason.

Edith Cavell did not bend or demur to the criminal investigation techniques of the *Kommandantur*, to the uniformed authority of Pinkhoff and Bergan. Her uniform was put away. She was not before them as a nurse. She dissimulated and was vague over the numbers of men she had helped, their whereabouts after they moved from her care, the identity of the guides. She knew her unit was finished, but that the work would go on elsewhere.

And so the prosecution prepared its case. The German military had commandeered all civic buildings in Brussels. The scene would shift to trial by military tribunal at the Brussels Senate, the building where the nation's founding principles were enshrined. The military courts, under the command of the Governor General, exercised criminal jurisdiction in cases of 'treason in time of war'. Of all the accused due to appear before this tribunal Edith Cavell was at greatest risk. She was English, and therefore viewed by her prosecutors as a small but vital and tangible incarnation of the enemy.

37

SOLITARY CONFINEMENT

She expected a cursory trial and imprisonment. As a nurse she had counselled many people, uncertain about the time left to them, on the need to leave their affairs in order, settle debts and make their wishes known. She knew events might now move fast and that she had to relinquish control.

The day after her second interrogation she wrote a letter about her affairs to Sister Wilkins:

My dear Sister,

I am sorry you have had to wait so long for an answer. I have asked to see you but it may not be till after sentence so do not try any more – just write all you want to know and I will reply on the first occasion.

1. Miss Jemmett owes the School about 420 francs. I send her 25 francs to be kept by you for immediate needs. Tell M. Héger all about her professionally and ask him to do what he can for her – explain that it is since last year only she has been so ill and tell him I have done all in my power, as we cannot communicate with her father. I have been obliged to go on as you know – he will pay all expenses on the first opportunity. I do hope he will allow her to stay as a patient – otherwise I cannot see what will become of her.

2. Pauline's money is in the bank and she shall have it when I am again free. I send 25 frs also for her wants. Will

you explain her case to M. Héger and tell him that she has been with us over 2 years and is only 16, and that she is my godchild. Perhaps he will let her stay as she works well and I am afraid greatly for her if she left.

3. You will find 2 cheques in my room, of last summer (not signed) which should go in the School cash box. Also there is owing to the School 30 francs for little Edith Marguaty. I paid her pension on August 1st and have not been repaid. M. Héger knows all about that.

4. I think you had better state the case of old Mme de Blanc. Perhaps as she cannot pay it would be well for the Committee to decide about her at once. Explain that we took her when we had practically no patients – and out of pity when the Hospital was closed.

5. Many thanks for all your kind thoughts for me. I should like some blue and white striped combinations from my drawer, a little notepaper and some handkerchiefs – also my *Imitation of Christ* – a little red book in my shelves and my prayer book.

I am sorry about the maids but not surprised. Tell Pauline to be a good girl. I hope José and his family go on well. My dear old Jack! Please brush him sometimes and look after him. I am quite well – more worried about the School than my own fate. Tell the girls to be good and work well and be tidy. I am sure you have many worries. Are all my things put away safely? With camphor? Don't buy anything for me, I do very well with what I have. My love to you and Sister and Nurse Horn *et mes bons amitiés à toutes mes jeunes filles – Mlle Maturin et Nurse Progloff, dites des bonnes choses de ma part aux domestiques dans la maison et la cuisine, que je pense toujours à tout le monde.*
Affectionately yours
E. Cavell

Please see the nurses going for their exam for the 2nd time in October *study regularly*.
23rd August

Thus her concerns. 'I am quite well – more worried about the School than my own fate.' As she awaited her 'own fate' she tried to do what was right by all she had loved and worked for. And so she worried that Grace Jemmett would not be housed or her depression treated, that Pauline might be homeless, Jack not brushed and pining, that the School's finances would not be in order, the student nurses might fail their exams, that old Mme de Blanc might go uncared for.

For herself she turned to the little book Sister Wilkins delivered to her: Thomas à Kempis's *Imitation of Christ*. She scored lines against many of its texts: *Vanity it is, to wish to live long, and to be careless to live well.* She would have liked to live long. She had paid into her pension fund. She and her sister Florence talked of founding a retirement home for nurses, with a garden like the Garden of Eden at the London Hospital, with hammocks, flowers and fountains and a machine for making tea. England was her home and she thought to go back there when her working days were done. She would have liked a tranquil old age, in the company of nurses, with the ordinary pleasures of peacetime. But to be careful to live well was of more importance to her. It was a clear path. It meant being unselfish and doing her best and what was right, wherever she found herself and however demanding that might be.

O God who art the truth make me one with Thee in everlasting charity. Charity was love and in her religious belief, truth and love elided. Love guided her work as a nurse. In the shocking times in which she found herself she kept allegiance to it, beyond the frenzied carnage outside her locked cell door.

He is truly great that is great in charity. He is truly great that is little in himself and that maketh no account of any height of honour. He is truly learned that doeth the will of God and forsaketh his own will. It was a demanding aspiration but one impressed on her since childhood, and one from which she did not swerve. Her imitation of Christ was truly how she had chosen to live, truly how she dreamed the world might be.

Neither is it any such great thing if a man be devout and fervent when he feeleth no affliction; but if in time of adversity he bear himself patiently there is hope then of great proficiency in grace. She had so often, to those she nursed, at their time of great affliction offered hope, and urged patience. She was in a time of adversity now. Her world was taken from her: the old Nurses' School and the new, her family, her mother, Swardeston, Norfolk. She would 'bear herself patiently', for she knew the importance of a state of grace.

It was not that she had her eye on the reward of heavenly pastures, pleasant living conditions beyond the grave; it was rather that love, goodness, devotion, grace, God, by cast of mind and upbringing defined her. So, alone in her cell, she took courage from the thoughts of a fifteenth-century mystic who went deep into the human heart to find what it meant to be good: *Man looketh on the countenance, but God on the heart. Man considereth the deeds, but God weigheth the intentions.*

Days of solitary confinement turned to weeks and months. On 14 September she sent her permitted one letter a week to all her nurses, a careful prison letter, in French, composed with an awareness that it must pass her gaolers:

> Your charming letter gave me great pleasure and your lovely flowers have brought life and colour to my cell, the roses are still fresh, but the chrysanthemums did not like prison life any more than I do, and did not last long.
>
> I'm glad to hear you're working hard and are devoted to your patients and that the patients are well pleased. I

hope you get on with your studies just as if I was there. Examination time is near and I very much want you to succeed. The new term begins very soon; try to learn from past experience and be on time for lectures and don't keep your tutors waiting.

At every point in life we learn something new. If you were in my place you would realise how precious freedom is, and how grateful we should be for it.

It seems the new School is coming along nicely. I hope to see it again one day soon and all my nurses too.
Au revoir. Be wise, be good.
Your devoted Matron
Edith Cavell

It was a stilted letter, directed at Bergan and Pinkhoff to let them know all she needed to do, but written to give hope to her nurses. She did not sound subdued. Philosophical and demanding, yes, but that was familiar to them and reassuring. It was not her way to generate anxiety. Professor Héger told the nurses he expected she would be sent to a German prison. That was bad enough news. 'We could not believe it to be possible,' said Jacqueline van Til.

The following week Edith Cavell wrote to Professor Héger:

Saint Gilles Prison, Sep. 22, 1915

Monsieur Héger,
Miss Wilkins has told me that you would like me to write to you. I am glad to respond to your request. Unfortunately I have not been able to send any letters.

I deeply regret having been forced to leave the School at the time of our moving and to have left all my affairs in disarray. I hope that by now everything is well organised and as you would wish it.

I very much hope to see you a little later on; there will be things to arrange and discuss and I hope to have the opportunity to speak with you.

Please give my regards to all the members of the Committee.

Edith Cavell

Two days later she received a letter from a Mme Francis, with news that Pauline had left the School and was working as a maid for a woman in another part of the city. For her next weekly letter Edith Cavell wrote to Pauline on 27 September:

My Dear Pauline,

Will you thank Madame Francis for so kindly writing to me and for being kind enough to take an interest in you? I was very glad to hear you were with a kind lady and hope you will try to please her and stay with her, for as I told you it is no good to keep changing. I was very sorry to hear you had left the School, but I hope now all is for the best.

Do not worry about your money. If I am free soon I will come and see you, if not, I will leave it in the hands of Miss Butcher for you. I hope you will try not to spend it as it will be very useful for your little sister perhaps one day. You had 235 francs on July 1st but spent some of it on linen and I sent you 25 francs by Sister, so now you should have 200 francs which I will arrange for you alone. If you can still continue saving give the money to Miss Butcher to put with the rest. Be a good girl and don't forget all I have tried to teach you. Say your prayers and go to church when you can and remember not to make friends with people you don't know and that you must never repeat the things you hear which are not your business.

Goodbye my child. If I want a little maid you must come back to me. Write me a line now and then. Let Miss Butcher always have your address so that I may know where to find you.

Your affectionate godmother

E. Cavell

27th Sep 1915

It was a goodbye letter, an acknowledgement she could do no more and must relinquish guidance and financial help. She offered only a mild rebuke for the gossip to Quien that had cost her dear.

By the end of September, though the Prince de Croÿ had eluded them, Bergan and Pinkhoff had what they needed, including Baucq's admission to Neels. Edith Cavell was allowed to see Sisters Wilkins and Whitelock in the presence of a German guard. 'We talked,' Sister Wilkins wrote, 'of the nurses and the nursing, the domestic staff, the patients and her beloved Jackie, who was terribly lonely without his mistress.'

'She appeared so frail,' Sister Whitelock wrote, 'walking down the long corridor between two German soldiers, and as soon as she had received us she was recalled to be questioned again, but happily was allowed to come back and stayed with us a whole hour. She talked of the School and her nurses and begged us to look after them until she came back.'

On 4 October, Edith Cavell's permitted letter was to Sister Wilkins:

My dear Sister,

The bill 115 frs per month must go into the rue du Fort on Oct 1st for 6 months i.e 69 frs. We pay it monthly to Mlle de Camp.

The money from MJ, 800 frs, please keep in hand till I tell you how to place it. I hope you will get it soon, as I want to arrange all before I go.

Bring me the cheques to sign which you will find in a box in my room. If the sisters or trained nurses want testimonials from me please bring Christian names and dates – also when S. Whitelock entered and left St Gilles hospital. Servants characters also.

Will you please send me at once:
My blue coat and skirt
white muslin blouse
thick grey reindeer gloves
grey fur stole
6 stamps

So sorry not to have seen those who came Sunday, many thanks for everything. Love to you all. I hope to see you again soon as time may be short.

Matron

Time indeed was short. The date of the trial was set for 7 October. She wanted her blue coat and skirt, her white muslin blouse and her grey fur stole for her appearance in court.

38

THE EFFORTS OF OTHERS

Bergan and Pinkhoff put together evidence for the military tribunal. The accused stayed isolated in St Gilles prison. A lawyer on the governing committee for the Nursing School, a M. Van Alteren, attempted intercession on Edith Cavell's behalf. He was arrested by the military police. The committee then engaged Thomas Braun, a Belgian lawyer who spoke German and French and had appeared at many of these tribunals. He would not be allowed prior communication with her, but he could speak for her in court.

On 23 August, three weeks after Edith Cavell's arrest and six weeks before her trial, news of her plight reached England. Her brother-in-law Longworth Wainwright wrote to the Foreign Secretary Sir Edward Grey next day: 'I have news through Dutch sources that my wife's sister, a Miss Edith Cavell, has been arrested in Brussels and I can get no news as to what has happened to her since August 5.'

He received an immediate reply:

The Under-Secretary of State for Foreign Affairs presents his compliments to Mr Longworth Wainwright and with reference to his letter of the 24th instant is directed by Secretary Sir E. Grey to state that he has requested the United States Ambassador to make enquiries by telegram as to the arrest of Miss Cavell at Brussels.
Foreign Office
August 26th 1915

Edith Cavell at the time of her trial, 1915

The American Ambassador in London, Mr Page, duly sent a telegram on 27 August to Brand Whitlock, minister at the American Legation in Brussels. Whitlock wrote memoirs and novels in flowery prose and took his time to respond to letters. 'One day in August,' he wrote in his memoir, 'it was learned at the Legation that an English nurse named Edith Cavell had been arrested by the Germans. I wrote a letter to the Baron von der Lancken to ask if it was true that Miss Cavell had been arrested.'

The 'one day in August' was the 27th when he received the telegram from London. Four days later, on 31 August, he wrote to Baron von der Lancken-Wakenitz, head of the *Politische Abteilung*, the office which dealt with requests from foreign diplomats. It was not, in itself, a military department, though it was under the rule of the notorious General von Bissing to whom von der Lancken was a trusted adviser.

'Your Excellency,' Whitlock wrote:

My Legation has just been informed that Miss Edith Cavell, a British subject residing in rue de la Culture, is said to have been arrested. I should be greatly obliged if Your Excellency would be good enough to let me know whether this report is true, and, if so, the reasons for her arrest. I should also be grateful in that case if Your Excellency would furnish this Legation with the necessary authorization from the German judicial authorities so that M. de Leval may consult with Miss Cavell, and eventually entrust someone with her defence.
I avail etc.
Brand Whitlock

Gaston de Leval was the Belgian legal adviser to the American Legation.

Ten days passed without a reply from Baron von der Lancken. Whitlock knew him well, viewed him as 'one of the ablest of the young men in German diplomacy', had negotiated many times with him on diplomatic matters, and toured the front line battle-fields with him. He could have called on him within half an hour. Von der Lancken, tall, well-groomed, about fifty, with black hair, a short-cropped moustache and blue eyes, spoke many languages fluently, owned landed estates in Silesia, and before the war had for ten years worked for the German Embassy in Paris.

Whitlock had not heard of this English nurse, Miss Edith Cavell. He did not see anything more significant in her case than in any of the numerous others brought to his notice. He heard

Brand Whitlock (1869–1934), Minister at the
American Legation in Brussels

that her offence was aiding young men to cross the Dutch frontier. Such charges were common and the sentences meted out not severe according to the standard of the occupation. Deportation to some German prison and internment for two or ten or twenty years – it all amounted to the same thing, because prisoners would be freed when peace came, if ever the war ended.

He did not hurry or dwell on her case. He was far more agitated at the news of the arrest of the Princess de Croÿ and the Countess de Belleville. These were Belgium's nobility, close to the monarchy, personal friends of Queen Elisabeth, 'old' families, owners of châteaux and vast tracts of land, to whom deference and service were *de rigueur*.

After further prompting from London, on 10 September Whitlock again wrote to von der Lancken:

The American Minister presents his compliments to the
Baron von der Lancken and has the honour to draw His
Excellency's attention to his letter of August 31 respecting
the arrest of Miss Cavell, to which no reply has yet been
received. As the Minister has been requested by telegraph
to take charge of Miss Cavell's defence without delay, he
would be greatly obliged if Baron von der Lancken would
enable him to take forthwith such steps as may be necessary
for this defence, and to answer by telegraph the dispatch he
has received.

Brussels, September 10, 1915

Baron von der Lancken consulted with Bergan and Pinkhoff
then two days later sent a speedy if acerbic reply to Whitlock:

Sir,

In reply to Your Excellency's note of the 31st ultimo, I
have the honour to inform you that Miss Edith Cavell
was arrested on August 5 and that she is at present in the
military prison at St Gilles. She has herself admitted that
she concealed in her house French and English soldiers, as
well as Belgians of military age, all desirous of proceeding
to the front. She has also admitted having furnished these
soldiers with the money necessary for their journey to
France, and having facilitated their departure from Belgium
by providing them with guides who enabled them secretly
to cross the Dutch frontier. Miss Cavell's defence is in the
hands of the advocate Braun, who, I may add, is already
in touch with the competent German authorities. In
view of the fact that the General Government as a matter
of principle does not allow accused persons to have any
interviews whatever, I much regret my inability to procure

for M. de Leval permission to visit Miss Cavell as long as she is in solitary confinement.

I avail etc.

Von der Lancken

The damaging phrase was 'all desirous of proceeding to the front'. Edith Cavell had not admitted any such thing. Nor had the advocate Braun seen her or had permission to defend her confirmed.

Whitlock moved in an all-male world of exchanged memoranda, meetings in ornate buildings, deference to status and procedure. He was a diplomat who valued peace and justice, but he kept to the bureaucratic procedures of civilised society, even when these procedures were to no avail. Edith Cavell needed high-level intervention of a vigorous sort, not the passing of letters from one bureau to another.

Though Whitlock had not met her, he described her as 'a frail and delicate little woman about forty years of age . . . with the *naïveté* of the pure in heart she assumed that the Germans were charging her with the deeds she had committed . . . a tortured little woman'. But she was not that little, naive, or tortured. Naivety was a long time gone. She knew only too well what the German military were up to. She hoped, by taking focus on herself, to divert interest away from others. She had nursed through a typhoid epidemic and in workhouse hospitals among the slum-dwellers of Victorian London, assisted at operations where blood dripped into a bowl under the table, sat at the bedside of the dying, broken unwanted news to relatives, founded an innovative nursing school in a foreign land in a foreign language. Hers was not the work of a frail and delicate little woman. She was tougher than most, sustained not by the belief that she was right, but that doing good was right and that the opposite was the opposite.

So Brand Whitlock penned news to the American Embassy in England of the admission of culpability of this frail little woman, to whom justice of an unjust sort would be meted out, by a corrupt court, at a faster pace and with more guile than he would show. A month had passed from when Longworth Wainwright asked the British Foreign Secretary to intervene over his sister-in-law's arrest:

American Legation, Brussels
September 21, 1915

Sir,
Referring to your telegram of August 27 in regard to the case of Miss Edith Cavell, who was arrested on August 5 and is now in the military prison at St-Gilles, I beg to enclose herewith for your information a copy of a communication which I have just received from Baron von der Lancken in regard to the matter. The legal adviser appointed to defend Miss Cavell has informed the Legation that she has indeed admitted having hidden in her house English and French soldiers and has facilitated the departure of Belgian subjects to the front, furnishing them money and guides to enable them to cross the Dutch frontier. The Legation will of course keep this case in view and endeavour to see that a fair trial is given to Miss Cavell and will not fail to let you know of any developments.
I have etc.,
Brand Whitlock

Even allowing for diplomatic courtesies, it was not a letter of urgent intervention and concern: 'for your information . . . endeavour to see . . . will not fail to let you know'. Edith Cavell had no legal adviser. No one was allowed to see her. The words purporting to come from this notional legal adviser were Pinkhoff's. What was her defence? How was a fair trial to be achieved?

Six weeks had passed since her arrest. Pinkhoff and Bergan had stored up evidence, real and contrived. And she was in solitary confinement, not knowing if anything was being done on her behalf, dwelling on her primary concern: the fate of the Nursing School.

Brand Whitlock's endeavours at intervention went no further than a promise to the American Ambassador in London to 'keep closely in touch with the matter'. In-house governmental memos at the Foreign Office made clear their policy was to do nothing. 'I am afraid it is likely to go hard with Miss Cavell. I am afraid we are powerless,' the British Undersecretary of State for Foreign Affairs, Sir Horace Rowland, wrote on 1 October. Lord Robert Cecil concurred: 'Any representation by us will do her more harm than good.'

Then came a defining blow. The Military Governor, General von Kraewel, was replaced by General von Sauberzweig. Von Bissing, the Governor General, had not found von Kraewel severe enough. German soldiers were deserting. 'Brussels was nearer black despair than it had ever been,' Brand Whitlock wrote. Sauberzweig belonged to the Cavalry Corps and was an apostle of *Kriegsbrauch* – 'requirements of war' which postulated that violent and extreme procedures were more humane because then resistance would be over quickly. His brief reign in Brussels was one where all and any tactics were used to defeat opposition. Each day *affiches* posted on walls reported the activities of the firing squad. He compelled unemployed Belgians to work for the Germans, requisitioned cattle and the country's centuries-old walnut trees to make stocks for rifles – not one was spared – took tram rails, metal from houses, rubber, wool, and the machinery from factories and shipped it all to Germany. He wanted foreign diplomats to leave the country and, ominously, he replaced the military prosecutor with a German lawyer, Dr Stoeber, who was as vicious and high-handed as himself.

The trial was fixed for Thursday 7 October. A few days before it Thomas Braun was told by the German prosecutors that he could not attend on behalf of Edith Cavell. They had been angered by his criticism in court, in a different case, of a Belgian witness who gave evidence against his own countrymen. Any whim could sway the decision-making of this court. The committee for the Nursing School hastily engaged Sadi Kirschen, a Belgian lawyer, to defend her. He would not be allowed to see her in advance of her court appearance or receive prior details of the charges against her. His German was not fluent.

On 5 October, Gaston de Leval wrote to Sadi Kirschen and asked him to keep the American Legation informed of the progress of the trial and, as it proceeded, to send details of the charges against Edith Cavell. Kirschen did not respond to this letter.

Seventeen nurses from the School delivered an appeal, signed by them, to the Governor General's office. It was written in German on their behalf by Nurse Aerschodt's Swiss father. It was worse than ponderous in style:

> To his Excellency Baron von Bissing, Governor-General in Belgium
> Excellency,
> We the undersigned nurses of the Clinic situated at 32 rue de Bruxelles, Uccle, Brussels (formerly at 149 rue de la Culture), take the liberty of approaching your Excellency, in consideration of your benevolent intentions towards the whole population, in the hope of shortening the term of imprisonment of our former matron, Miss Cavell, who was arrested on 5.8.15 and, if it were in any way practicable, of procuring the suspension thereof.

We should like your Excellency to know that Miss Cavell has been the Superintendent of our Clinic for eight years and, by her self-sacrificing work in the service of charity, has won lasting recognition from all her patients as well as her staff.

Confident of the benevolent reception which your Excellency will accord to our petition, we have complete faith that your Excellency will recognise our sad position and graciously set our minds at rest concerning the fate of our esteemed Matron. In this hope we beg to assure your Excellency of our lasting gratitude.

Marguerite Genonceaux
A. Court
Margarehte Oppliger
E. Hacks
P. Van Bockstael
E. Wolf
N. Andry
G. van Aerschodt
E. Balty
A. Steckmann
C. Aulrebs
J. Brenez
R. Schurmann
E. Docht
M. Bonnie
E. Wegels
M. Waschausky
Nurses of the Belgian School for Trained Nurses
32 rue de Bruxelles-Uccle
Brussels
3.10.15

His Excellency did not recognise their sad position, set their minds at rest, or have any particular concern about the fate of their esteemed matron. He was in Germany on sick leave and would not be in Brussels at the time of Edith Cavell's trial.

39

THE TRIAL: THURSDAY 7 OCTOBER

On the morning of 7 October a prison bell rang at 5.30. Edith Cavell put on her dark-blue skirt and coat, white muslin blouse, grey fur stole and straw hat with a feather. The Princess de Croÿ and Louise Thuliez both later said they wished she had worn her nurse's uniform, to impress the military tribunal as an 'emblem of charity and mercy'. But Edith Cavell was not representing her profession at this court. She stood accused as herself. She did not wear her uniform outside of work and would not seek to impress the tribunal or risk incriminating other nurses from the School.

At 7.00 she was led by armed German soldiers along the prison corridors to a police van in the yard. The Belgian warders saluted as she passed. In the van were the chemist Louis Séverin, the student Constant Cayron, the barrister Albert Libiez, the Countess Jeanne de Belleville, the engineers Herman Capiau and Georges Hostelet, and two armed soldiers. The prisoners tried to talk to each other but were ordered to be silent. The rest of the accused followed in the prison bus.

They were driven to Parliament House, the Belgian National Palace, an ornate eighteenth-century monument to monarchic opulence and civic pride in the rule of law. They were herded up the Grand Staircase to the Senate. Edith Cavell came from two months of solitary confinement in a whitewashed cell to every emblem of grandeur in this place where justice was supposed to prevail: a high cupola worked with gold leaf; oak panelling inlaid with the crowns, wreaths and swords of monarchy, justice and nationhood; marble columns; life-size paintings of Belgian rulers 'from Pipin von Heristal down to Charles of Lorraine'; murals painted in 1895 of Waterloo battles; coats of arms of the Belgian provinces; a wide raised – and empty – public gallery; crimson chairs embroidered with gold lions rampant; a raised rostrum with high chairs where the judges would sit.

The Princess de Croÿ was given special treatment because of her rank and aristocratic German relations – the Duke and Duchess de Croÿ-Dülmen. She had not been imprisoned at St Gilles like the others, but had rooms at the *Kommandantur* with views over the courtyard, and was allowed a personal maid. Gottfried Benn, senior doctor to the Brussels military, gave special attention to her. Alexandre Braun was to defend her and Countess Jeanne de Belleville. He was the father of Thomas Braun who had been dismissed from defending Edith Cavell. While in custody the Princess had been allowed back to her château to visit her sick mother, accompanied by Braun and in his car. They discussed her defence. None of the others had been allowed any contact with their defence lawyers. Braun told her to say she was acting solely under the influence of her brother. They knew he was safe in England. Her maid and a soldier accompanied her to the tribunal. As she entered the Senate, Gottfried Benn bowed and asked her to call him if she felt unwell.

There were thirty-five accused: twenty-two men and thirteen women. They were variously charged with having conveyed soldiers to the enemy, or assisting with such conveyance, circulating seditious pamphlets, assisting in the illegal transmission of letters, concealing arms, or evading compulsory registration. The six main defendants: Edith Cavell, Marie de Croÿ, Jeanne de Belleville, Louise Thuliez, Herman Capiau and Philippe Baucq, were given senators' seats, facing the judges. They could not see their counsel or the witnesses. Soldiers with fixed bayonets stood either side of each seat. Other prisoners sat on benches with their backs to the rostrum.

The defence lawyers entered, four Belgians and one German: M. A. Dorff represented seven of the accused, Sadi Kirschen nine, Monsieur Braffort six, Alexandre Braun two, and Lieutenant Thielmann of the Battalion of Landsturm, Flensburg, represented eleven. The lawyers sat behind their clients and had no communication with them.

The court stood for the entrance of the judges. All were uniformed, bemedalled, from the Landsturm Battalion and adorned with the Iron Cross. There were five of them: Werthmann, von Cornberg, Eck, Stenger and Paul. Last, came the military prosecutor, Sauberzweig's henchman, Dr Eduard Stoeber. Sadi Kirschen said he looked dressed and coiffeured as if for a military ball. He was tall, thin, had a waxed moustache and a monocle and modulated his voice like an actor. He carried a fat dossier and a copy of the German military code. He put these and his helmet on the table in front of him. A German officer, Herr Brueck, was interpreter for the prosecutors and defendants. The key witnesses – the police officers Lieutenant Bergan and Sergeant Pinkhoff – were well known to all the accused. Madame Bodart's young son had been tricked into testifying against Philippe Baucq.

Stoeber opened proceedings by reading the charges in German, then Bergan made a long deposition, also in German. The core of the prosecution was paragraph 90 of the German military penal code which defined as treason crimes against the Fatherland such as 'conducting soldiers to the enemy'.[18]

The accused were then sent out and brought in singly to be tried. Edith Cavell was first. She was told to stand in front of Stoeber. He put his questions in German. Brueck translated these

[18] '*dem Feinde Mannschaften zuführt*'

into French. She replied in French. Brueck translated her replies into German. No written statement of her charge had been given to her attorney Sadi Kirschen, whom she had never met, whose German was not good, who had had no communication with the American Legation and who at this same hearing, all of which was to be got through in one day, was also defending Ada Bodart, the chemists Louis Séverin and Georges Derveau, a Michel Cavenaile and his wife Celine who was a primary school teacher, a coffeehouse keeper Maurice Pansaers, and two barristers Adolphe Demonstier and Armand Heuze.

Sadi Kirschen later wrote that Edith Cavell's French was fluent, though her English accent was strong. She spoke in a low voice and appeared proud, calm and unafraid. Stoeber put it to her that from November 1914 to July 1915 she harboured French and English soldiers, including a colonel, all in civilian clothes. That she helped give Belgian, French and English of military age the means to get to the front by taking them into her Clinic and by giving them money.

'Yes,' Edith Cavell replied.

'With whom did you collaborate in doing this?'

'With M. Capiau, Mlle Thuliez, M. Derveau and M. Libiez.'

'Who was the head of this organisation?'

'There was no head.'

'Was it not the Prince de Croÿ?'

'No. The Prince only sent men to us and gave some of them a little money.'

'Why have you committed the acts of which you are accused?'

'At the start I was confronted by two English soldiers whose lives were in danger. One was wounded.'

Stoeber told her martial law did not carry the death penalty in the event of them being captured. Edith Cavell replied that it was her belief and theirs that if she did not help them they would be shot.

'Once they were across the frontier did you get news of these men?'

'Only of four or five of them.'

'Baucq and Fromage: are they the same person?'

'Yes.'

'What was Baucq's role?'

'I know little about him. I met him only once. I did not ask what he did.'

'Do you stand by all you have said at your interrogations concerning the people with whom you have worked, in trying to obtain recruits? That is, with Prince Reginald de Croÿ, Baucq, Séverin, Capiau, Libiez, Derveau, Mlle Thuliez and Mme Ada Bodart?'

'Yes.'

'Do you realise that by recruiting men it has been to the disadvantage of Germany and to the advantage of the enemy?'

'My aim was not to help your enemy but to help those men who asked for my help to reach the frontier. Once across the frontier they were free.'

'How many men have you helped get to the frontier?'

'About two hundred.'

She was asked if some of the men she helped were French and Belgian. She said they were. 'That made a serious difference,' one of the judges said. Another judge asked her if she had been foolish to help English soldiers because the English were so ungrateful.

'The English are not ungrateful.'

'How do you know?'

'Because a few of them have written from England to thank me.'

That was all. No more than ten minutes of questioning, for there were thirty-four other men and women to dispose of in the day.

Stoeber and the others were keen to incriminate Edith Cavell as the head of a structured recruiting organisation for the Allied armies. Her key statement, which her prosecutors chose to ignore, was that she was working not to recruit soldiers but to help trapped men get out of a war zone. Any defence lawyer, given proper process, would not have allowed their elision. Nor would a charge of treason hold against someone who was neither a German national, nor living in Germany.

She remained in the Senate room after her questioning. One by one the others were called in. She saw the charade unfold. Louise Thuliez was next. Unlike Edith Cavell she faced material evidence against her: the receipt in her bag for lodging six men, the book of coded addresses, a faked identity certificate, copies of *Petits Mots du Soldat*. She told Stoeber she had helped 'about 126' men reach the frontier. He asked her if she had received any subsequent news from them. She said she had not.

Stoeber then asked her about the structure of the 'organisation'. Who was the chief? Who gave the orders? She said it was not like that. They were not divided into chiefs and subalterns. She told him each of them did the best they could and that they were all motivated by the desire to save lives.

Baucq was questioned next. In reply to the questions was he Belgian and Catholic he said '*Oui, et bon patriote.*' This angered Stoeber who repeated it time after time, with scathing theatricality, as he asked his accusatory questions. Baucq admitted distributing *La Libre Belgique* and working with Reginald de Croÿ, Louise Thuliez, Ada Bodart and Edith Cavell to get men to the frontier, but he denied the rest, said he had never guided the men himself and did not know who did what.

Ada Bodart, who was Irish, admitted sheltering French and English soldiers until Louise Thuliez or another guide came to fetch them. She admitted too that she received a card from one of these men saying he had arrived safely in Holland. She said she did not know the Prince of Croÿ and did not know who organised the guides. She said she took one English soldier to St Mary's church in Schaerbeek and handed him over to Baucq.

So it went on throughout the morning. Little was added to the confessions obtained by Bergan and Pinkhoff. Libiez admitted telling fugitive soldiers, stranded at Wihéries, that they would get help from Edith Cavell at the rue de la Culture. He confessed to making a stamp, with the name of a fictitious commune, to forge identity cards. Capiau said he only wanted to get Allied soldiers out of his district because local people feared German reprisal. He admitted faking passports but denied there was any structured resistance organisation with leaders and plans.

The day was Stoeber's marathon. He intended to get through all thirty-five cross-examinations by its end. Séverin the chemist stood before him with the same story as the others. He had given refuge to Allied soldiers. He spoke of a day when Edith Cavell brought two wounded English soldiers to him.

> I took them in. But after a while I went to her and asked her to find alternative accommodation for them. She said she did not know where to house all the men who came to her for help. I thought of my old employee Louis Gille. I thought he would make a good guide and get these men to the frontier. He agreed to do it for a payment of 20 or 30 francs per man. I suggested to Miss Cavell that she use him. I loaned her 400 francs.

Was this to pay for the men's transport? Stoeber asked.

'No, it was just a loan. I knew thirteen Frenchmen had asked for her help to get to the border and that she was short of money.'

Did he hear from them after they had crossed the border? Stoeber asked. Yes, sometimes, Séverin said. Some of them signed their letters with women's names.

The Princess de Croÿ, in court, was allowed a chair in front of the judges. Briefed by Braun, knowing her brother had safely escaped, she put the blame on him. In her memoir she wrote she had hoped all the accused might have exculpated themselves by accusing him – but it was hard to see how they could have managed that.

I am asked if it is true that I am the sister of the Prince of Croÿ. I answer that I am the sister of two Princes of Croÿ, one a Belgian officer at the Front the other of whose whereabouts I am unaware. I am asked if it is true I have housed French and English soldiers who had been hiding in the countryside. Knowing this can be proved I answered Yes.

Do I own to having photographed these men when they were with me? Yes. Why? Here I had to be careful because to Bergan and Pinkhoff I had denied all knowledge of false papers. I answered that the men required photos to obtain their identity cards to travel to Brussels.

Did I not know that it was to enable them to leave the occupied territory as I had said in my deposition to the police? I answered 'Ainsi qu'on m'a fait dire.' ('As I was made to say.') This angered Bergan and Pinkhoff for it showed, what was a fact, that they had turned our words and changed their significance in their interpretation. I said my aim in helping these men was to get them out of the *Étapes*, their lives were in danger, we were continually hearing of men being taken and shot, like at Hiron where eleven soldiers as well as the miller who was hiding them had been shot together.

Where did these soldiers go?

To Brussels.

Who took care of them?

I don't know.

Who escorted them there?

My brother and Mademoiselle Thuliez.

Why did you do this?

Because my brother asked it of me.

Did you know what danger you ran by acting so?

One must do one's duty without thinking of the consequences.

The session was suspended for lunch at noon. The judges, lawyers and police officers went out to eat. The prisoners stayed under guard in the Senate room. Some had bits of food in their pockets. Libiez offered pieces of chocolate and bread and butter to Edith Cavell and Louise Thuliez. The two women whispered to each other about the progress of the trial. Edith Cavell said, 'I think Baucq, Capiau, you and I have a bad chance. But that's all right as long as we don't get shot.'

A tureen of soup was brought for the soldiers. What they left in their bowls they offered to the prisoners. 'Most of us refused,' Libiez said. Hot weak coffee was brought in but there was nothing to drink it out of. One of the women offered the heel of her shoe, which caused laughter. The interpreter Herr Brueck returned and shouted at them to be silent. He then shouted at them to stand as the judges entered. Stoeber declared the session reopened.

The afternoon passed. Prisoner after prisoner was brought in and questioned. A story unfurled: the man who for no money let two Englishmen stay in his garden shed for a few weeks before Louise Thuliez guided them to Brussels. The lawyer who hid a fugitive English soldier for a night. The student, Constant Cayron, who confessed he had given Father Piersoul the address of fifty Belgians of military age who wanted to join the Allied armies, including his own brother who was now fighting in France.

For most of the prisoners their main consideration was not to recruit for the army they hoped would defeat these German invaders, but to give aid to the traumatised men who came as beggars to their door. Many of the prisoners called, undefended, before the prosecutor that Thursday afternoon, lived in what once was the tranquillity of the countryside. They spoke the patois of the Borinage, the coal-mining area around Mons. Only in one or two cases was their motivation financial gain. More often they had risked their lives out of simple humanity. That was the common theme. They had no chiefs of staff, no generals or foot soldiers. None of them carried arms, planted bombs, destroyed property, attacked German soldiers. They were citizens conditioned to peacetime who found themselves surrounded by carnage, injustice and wrongdoing on an unprecedented scale.

Toward the day's end Lieutenant Bergan was called as a witness. Under oath he swore that his interrogation of the prisoners had been conducted with scrupulous fairness in the presence of two witnesses, Pinkhoff and Neuhaus; that the prisoners' statements had been read back to them phrase by phrase; that no confession had been obtained under pressure as some of the accused sought to imply. He was convinced, he said, that this was a highly organised ring. All the accused knowingly assisted in sending soldiers and men of military age to join the Allied armies, particularly for Joffre's recent offensive.[19]

Bergan said there were two groups organising this recruitment drive: one in northern France under the Prince and Princess de Croÿ, Capiau, Derveau, de Belleville and Thuliez, the other in the Mons district headed by Libiez. 'The Cavell woman managed the headquarters of the whole thing in Brussels.'

[19] In the third week of September, in the Battle of Loos, General Joffre had ordered a two-pronged British/French attack on German lines. Chlorine gas and 250,000 shells were thrown at the German army. About 25,000 German soldiers died

The only civilian witness, Philippe Bodart, was then called. He was fourteen with black curly hair. His mother Ada was sitting among the prisoners. He was warned if he made a false statement he would get ten years' hard labour. He was asked if Baucq had taken packages of *La Libre Belgique* to his mother's house. Yes, he replied. He was asked if he had heard Baucq say he had mapped a route for escaping soldiers to take to reach the frontier. Yes, the boy said again. Baucq called out that he had said he intended mapping a route, not that he had actually done so. The boy was too young to understand, he called, French was not his usual language, he spoke English at home. Baucq was told to be quiet. The Princess de Croÿ said he put his head in his hands. 'His shaking shoulders betrayed his emotion. It was terrible, helplessly to look on at the despair of this brave father of a family, young and with a bright future before him and to realise his life was in jeopardy.' But despair was the currency of this war that destroyed brave fathers and bright futures. Stoeber told the boy to say goodbye to his mother Ada Bodart who faced imprisonment. The boy kissed her. Some of the prisoners cried.

At 7.00 in the evening the court adjourned. It was to convene again in the morning. Braun conversed with his other titled client, the Countess Jeanne de Belleville. The other lawyers had no words with the prisoners who went out to the waiting black vans and back to their cells at St Gilles. Hostelet was pleased to find a new gas lamp in his, so that he could see to write to his family. Louise Thuliez ate her evening ration then slept, worn out with fatigue. Baucq wrote in his diary of the Bodart boy, 'He has certainly brought me the *coup de grâce*.'

And Edith Cavell? She went back to the cell in which she had been for two months alone. She was far now from any consolation of home, the comforting presence of Jack, the attentive respect of her nurses. 'The terrible dogs of war', as she had called them, had bayed her into a trap. She knew she would lose her freedom. She did not know she would lose her life. As ever she prayed: *Grant me patience O Lord even now in this emergency. Help me my God and then I will not fear how grievously so ever I be afflicted.*

She laid out her clothes for the morning, then turned the table into her bed. The prison bell would ring at 5.30 for Stoeber and Bergan's judgement day.

40

THE TRIAL: FRIDAY 8 OCTOBER

Next morning, Friday 8 October, the court convened at 8.00. This second session was held in the equally ornate Chamber of Deputies. There was the same pomp and ceremony as on the previous day. The uniformed soldiers, the jaded prisoners. As before, the chief accused sat apart from the others, facing their judges, their backs to their so-called counsel.

For two hours Stoeber gave a theatrical peroration in German. He congratulated the police for apprehending these recruiting agents. The prisoners, he said, had conveyed numberless soldiers and men of military age to Holland via Brussels to join the Allied armies. They had acted in a manner prejudicial to the military power of the German Empire. The soldiers they recruited were at this moment fighting in France against the Fatherland. Each time he alluded to the brave German soldiers who fell as a consequence of this plot, Stoeber turned to the judges to receive an approving nod.

He said that all admissions by the accused of involvement and culpability had been drawn up by Lieutenant Bergan with meticulous accuracy, carefully translated by Sergeant Pinkhoff, and only signed in each case after being read and accepted. The depositions of the prisoners corresponded exactly with their own statements. There was no truth in the assertion that their words had been distorted. The intention to transmit men to the enemy was clear, though culpability and division of work varied. Most of the accused had disclosed the particular way they worked.

Where this was not the case, other prisoners had done so. Stoeber then went through the prisoners' crimes:

EDITH CAVELL was among the chief organisers. Between November 1914 and July 1915 at the Nursing School at 147 rue de la Culture she received fugitive soldiers in civilian clothes, including an English colonel, and Belgian and French men of military age who wished to join the Allied army. She looked after them and gave them funds to facilitate their journey to the frontier and to the ranks of the Allies. She escorted the men brought to her in Brussels to prearranged places, to hand them over to waiting guides who were known to her. She had confessed that she received news of the safe arrival in Holland of several of these men.

LOUISE THULIEZ between March and July 1915 took to Brussels, or arranged to be taken by special guides, fugitive French and English soldiers and French and Belgian men of military age, from parts of northern France occupied by the Germans. She collaborated with the Prince de Croÿ to seek out such men. She had been seriously incriminated by Miss Cavell as one of the people with whom arrangements were made to convey soldiers to the Allied army. She had further infringed decrees of the Governor General, dated 4 November and 15 December 1914, paragraph 9b, on the law on the state of siege, by circulating *La Libre Belgique* on a large scale and distributing contraband letters by means of *Les Petits Mots du Soldat*.

PHILIPPE BAUCQ between June and August 1915 had assisted Cavell, Thuliez, Bodart and the Prince de Croÿ in conveying soldiers to the Allied armies. He set on their way soldiers of military age after nominating a leader among them. Miss Cavell had admitted that under the name of Fromage he procured guides for the journey to the frontier. He had revealed his strategies to a secret agent interned with him in his cell. Prisoner Bodart had named him as a member of the *Comité pour l'Éloignement des Mobilisables*. Mme Bodart's son had heard him telling his mother about routes to the frontier for soldiers setting out to rejoin the ranks.

THE COUNTESS OF BELLEVILLE took English and French soldiers and Belgians of military age from Montigny sur Roc to Miss Cavell's house for transport to the frontier. She was in close communication with the Prince de Croÿ who brought English soldiers to her. After she handed them over to Miss Cavell she told the Abbé de Longueville what had been done. The Abbé himself transported soldiers but had escaped. The Countess gave Miss Cavell's address to Belgians and French of military age and told them to go to Brussels. She acted as a guide and obtained false papers for these men. She was one of the prisoners chiefly implicated in this business of conveying soldiers and recruits to the enemy ranks.

LOUIS SÉVERIN was one of the most zealous assistants in this work. He sheltered the men, provided them with guides and gave Miss Cavell money to facilitate their journey to the front.

MME BODART sheltered men eligible for service, and enemy soldiers, until Thuliez or some other guide came to collect them. She herself took an English soldier from her own house to St Mary's church where she handed him over to Baucq. She had admitted receiving news from one of these fighting men of his arrival in Holland.

HERMAN CAPIAU supplied false papers to English and French soldiers and French recruits. He received photographs for these forged documents from Mlle Thuliez and the Prince de Croÿ. Miss Cavell had confessed that he brought men to her of military age.

ALBERT LIBIEZ provided lodgings for English fugitive soldiers, made out false papers for them, and induced poor people in the region where he lived to provide accommodation for them.

GEORGES DERVEAU escorted English fugitive soldiers in civilian clothes from the Mons district to Brussels and handed them over to Miss Cavell to be taken to the frontier. He was the mediator between Capiau and a M. van Samenliet who forged identity documents. He knew all the plans and aims of the organisation.

PRINCESS MARIE DE CROŸ, at the instigation of Thuliez, had taken photographs of French and English soldiers at the château of Bellignies for use in forged documents. She gave money to Thuliez to defray expenses for the conveyance of these soldiers. Her château was a meeting place for these soldiers. She was a link in the chain of those who intended injury to Germany by reinforcing the Allied army with the influx of these men. Her actions could not be ascribed to motives of charity as she claimed. But as she was influenced by her brother, the court should admit her case to be less serious.

GEORGES HOSTELET had assisted Miss Cavell in conveying soldiers to the Allied army and spent some thousand francs to this end. His agreement with Miss Cavell was that each month she should send the guides they used to him so he could pay them. In mitigation, at the outset of the war he had given protection to a German journalist.

CONSTANT CAYRON gave Father Piersoul the addresses of fifty men who wished to join the Allied ranks, and ten men with technical qualifications who wished to reach England or France. He was under eighteen when he did this. He knew Father Piersoul was engaged in the transport of such men. Among them was his own brother and one of his brother's friends. Both were today bearing arms against Germany in Allied ranks . . .

'He went on talking and talking,' Libiez wrote. The room got hotter. There was no drinking water. All that most of the prisoners understood was when their names punctuated Stoeber's monologue. Toward the end of it they heard the word *Todesstrafe* – death penalty. They were impassive until Brueck, the interpreter, translated into French the sentences called for by Stoeber.

That was the only part of his oration that was translated. The German army, Stoeber said, had been put in great danger through the activities of these wretched people. They were guilty of treason, which the German military code punished with death, according to paragraph 68: 'Whosoever with the intention of helping the hostile power or of injuring German troops is guilty of one of the crimes listed in para. 90 will be sentenced to death for treason.' That included 'conducting soldiers to the enemy'. He called for the court to pass the death sentence on Cavell, Baucq, Thuliez, Capiau, de Belleville, Bodart, Séverin and Libiez and to sentence the others to long terms of imprisonment with hard labour.

Libiez, in his memoir, wrote that Baucq seemed crushed, Louise Thuliez seemed not to understand the reality of it, Séverin screwed up his eyes as if he were already facing the firing squad, and Mme Crabbé fainted. 'Only Edith Cavell,' he said, 'kept her imperturbable calm.'

Then the defending lawyers were called. Except for Alexandre Braun, who represented the two aristocrats, they had not corresponded with or seen their clients prior to these two days. They had not received written or verbal account of the charges against them or been allowed time to prepare any kind of defence. Each lawyer was speaking for between nine and eleven people with disparate degrees of involvement in a fluid organisation. Thus the court tried and indicted thirty-five people for capital crimes in two days.

The barrister M. Dorff spoke first. He was defending Capiau, Libiez, Baucq, Hostelet, Cayron, and Maurice Crabbé. He told the court there was no structured organisation. Assembled was an ad hoc collection of individuals each of whom had acted out of circumstance and humanity. Each had done his or her best to help for different motives. If they were to be punished it should be proportionate to their individual actions. The student

Constant Cayron should be acquitted because he was under eighteen at the time of the alleged offences.

The prisoners were then called singly. Each was asked if they had anything to say in their own defence. Most tried to mitigate the sentence that hung over them. Capiau said the charges against him were overstated. There was no organisation. He had not given Miss Cavell a thousand francs as it was claimed she stated. He had never given her any money.

Stoeber turned to Edith Cavell. He ordered her to stand. She stood by her chair, as ever controlled and calm – '*toujours maîtresse d'elle même*', her lawyer Sadi Kirschen said. Stoeber asked her if she had lied.

Capiau was right, she told him. He had not given her money. Why had she lied?

'My memory was confused,' she said, for as ever she would disadvantage herself to help another. 'Afterwards I remembered it was not from him.'

'The rudeness, the brutality even,' the Princess de Croÿ was to write in her memoir, 'used towards this brave lady were unworthy of any civilised nation.'

The other prisoners represented by Dorff were called. They tried briefly to defend themselves. Libiez reiterated he only helped English soldiers escape from Wihéries because he feared they brought the region into danger. Hostelet, too, claimed that fear of endangering the lives of others had prompted him to give money to help these fugitives. Baucq denied Philippe Bodart's claim that he had mapped a route for escaping soldiers, or that he had ever had anything to do with the Prince de Croÿ.

The Belgian barrister Sadi Kirschen then stood to defend Edith Cavell, Mme Bodart, Séverin and four others. He too denied that they were part of an organisation. Miss Cavell, he said, had devoted her whole life to nursing the sick. Extreme circumstances had led her to where she now was. She could not have refused these men who asked for her help. A psychologist would be better suited to try this woman than trained judges. A psychologist would understand how impossible it was for her, whose nature it was to help others, not to do what she could for the British, French, and Belgian soldiers she hid and protected. The first Englishmen who came to her were wounded. The lives of all these men were in danger.

Stoeber intervened. This was not the case under German military law, he claimed. Kirschen protested that she, like the other accused, had not known that. All believed the lives of the men they helped to be threatened. The only way to help them had been to get them over the frontier. Her objective had not been to damage the German cause. Her accusers must prove whether these men again enlisted because of the help of Nurse Cavell. Only that would make her actions liable to the death penalty.

Perhaps, he suggested, she had exaggerated the number of men she had helped reach Holland. If he had seen her notes and spoken to her before the trial he might have ascertained the truth, but he had become her lawyer without any means of defending her. This tribunal, he said, did not have the moral right to condemn to death a trained nurse. He implored the judges to recognise that her life was dedicated to the sick and wounded, that German soldiers owed their lives to her care. If she was to be condemned then at least let her sentence be mitigated to attempted treason, not treason itself. The most that was needed or merited by the prosecutors was a sentence to curtail her until the end of the war.

Stoeber turned to Edith Cavell. Again she stood. What had she to say for herself? he asked. He looked at her and saw an ageing spinster, an enemy agent. What might she say to him? *'Je n'ai rien à ajouter,'* she said, I have nothing to add.

Kirschen moved to a cursory defence of the other five prisoners.

Mme Bodart and Séverin had helped when Edith Cavell had no room for these men. Did that merit their death? Neither of them had guided men to the frontier. Stoeber saw this assertion as a challenge to the integrity of the court. He flew into a rage. He accused Kirschen of insulting him. Kirschen became defensive. He said he had been a barrister for sixteen years. He knew that to offend the judges was not a good way to defend a client. He was speaking in German which was a foreign language for him. He might have used an expression unwisely. He was in an emotional state because a woman he was defending was sentenced to death.

Damage accrued. This was a court where decisions were made out of personal antipathy and on nasty whims. It counted against Kirschen that French was his first language. It counted so much more against Edith Cavell that she was English, a woman, unmarried, unrepentant. It counted against Baucq that he distributed *La Libre Belgique* which poked fun at generals and self-styled Governors.

Then it was the turn of the respected German lawyer Thomas Braun to defend the Princess de Croÿ and the Countess de Belleville. To their advantage both women were aristocrats. Both had benefited from counsel prior to the hearing. No matter that the de Croÿs' involvement spanned escape, recruitment and espionage. Breeding and wealth put the Princess in a superior league, in this court's view, to nurses, teachers and engineers.

The Princess, Braun said, had acted under the influence of her brother. Her sole aim had been to save life. At the outset of the war both women had cared for the German wounded. How could they be expected not to care for their own kind? They were caught between helping their own people or denouncing them. They chose to help them. All Germans to whom he had spoken about the case said they would have acted the same way.

The Princess stood. She said she took full responsibility for what she had done but that she must speak out for Miss Cavell. What had been said about her was not true. She was not at the head of an escape organisation.

'She was brought into danger by my brother and me. We sent the men to her.' It was, the Princess said, at first she herself who sheltered and hid these men. 'And even when Miss Cavell told us she could not lodge any more, that her School would be in danger if more men were sent to her, we still sent others to her and so did our confederates. The responsibility should fall on my brother and me. I am ready to take her place. *Pour moi je le répète, je suis prête à prendre la place qui m'incombe.*'

Libiez in his diary wrote of her intervention:

The Princess looked frail. Usually there was nothing remarkable in her appearance, but at that moment, standing in the half light of the Chamber, her shoulders drawn back, her right hand raised, she appeared beautiful. And as she said these words I could have applauded her. I said to myself I must make the same declaration as this Princess, but my courage failed, I let the moment pass. Five minutes later it was too late and I bitterly regretted my own cowardice.

It was too late for Edith Cavell. It was a declaration that needed to be made. The rest of the hearing was hurried on. Thirty-five people must be dealt with in two days. For eight of them the death penalty had been demanded. This second session lasted from 9.00 in the morning until 5.00 in the evening without a break. There was continuing confusion over language, the single interpreter, a muddle over names and who was charged with what. Treason became an ever more loosely used word. The accused were told their sentences would be communicated to them in prison. The court rose. Sadi Kirschen tried to approach Edith Cavell as she was led from the court but a soldier stopped him.

Edith Cavell and Jeanne de Belleville were driven back to St Gilles. They asked the German guard in the prison van if the rumour they had heard was true – that following the execution of a woman prisoner at Liège no more women were to be condemned to death. The guard said he thought that was now the case. In the prison hall the two women were left alone together for ten minutes. They did not discuss the trial. With a revision downward of what constitutes good fortune, they hoped to meet each other again in the prison camp at Siegburg. Edith Cavell was allowed brief exercise in the prison yard. She was then led back to her cell to await sentence.

41

SATURDAY 9 OCTOBER

Then it was the weekend. At the American Legation the minister Brand Whitlock was ill in bed. Quite what was wrong with him was unclear, but he was depressed and homesick for America. Injections from his doctor had not helped. Edith Cavell was not on his mind. But the Legation was the only place from where, at this point in time, appeal on her behalf might be made or diplomacy galvanised.

Edith Cavell's defence lawyer Sadi Kirschen had endured a tiring and frustrating two days. After the fiasco of the trial he went straight to his country house at Quatre Bras, a small woodland village outside Brussels. He did not communicate the trial's outcome to Brand Whitlock. He did not feel obliged to do so. He was under instruction from the Nursing School, not the Legation. Anyway he supposed there would be ample time for appeal. It had taken ten weeks from when charges were made against Edith Cavell for her case to come to trial. He assumed the process of law would continue to move slowly.

The nurses at the School were sleepless with anxiety. Elisabeth Wilkins went to the prison for news, hoping for permission to speak to her matron. She was turned away.

The German prosecutors worked over the weekend. That Saturday the court of five judges, for a third and final time, sat in secret session to formulate the sentences according to the Imperial Military Decree Concerning Extraordinary Criminal Proceedings in Time of War Against Aliens.

Based on the prosecution document drawn up by Bergan and

Pinkhoff, and embellished by the prosecutor Herr Stoeber, they summarised their findings:

> From their own statements and the assertions of their fellow prisoners the Court concludes that de Croÿ, Baucq, Thuliez, Cavell, Belleville and Séverin were the main organisers of two seditious groups one based in northern France the other in the Borinage, which helped English and French fugitive soldiers and French and Belgians of military age, escape to Holland in order to join the Allied armies.
>
> The château at Bellignies was put at the disposal of the organisation by the Prince de Croÿ. It was the main grouping place for the soldiers on their way to Holland via Brussels. The Prince's sister gave hospitality to the men and took photographs of them to enable Capiau and Derveau to fake identity papers stating that British and French soldiers were Belgian nationals.
>
> The men were then taken to Brussels and hidden in different places by Cavell until they could be taken over the frontier by guides hired for this work. In this way Cavell has made it possible for some two hundred and fifty men to reach Holland. Baucq was her chief assistant. Six of these men notified those who helped them of their arrival in England or France.
>
> It is the opinion of this Court that most of the prisoners were aware they were conveying fugitive soldiers and men of military age to the enemy. It was their deliberate intention to send reinforcements to the hostile powers to the detriment of our own German troops.

The judges then ruled on the punishments to be meted out: death for Philippe Baucq, Louise Thuliez, Edith Cavell, Louis Séverin and Jeanne de Belleville; fifteen years' hard labour for Herman Capiau, Ada Bodart, Albert Libiez and Georges

Derveau; ten years' hard labour for Marie de Croÿ; from two to eight years' hard labour or imprisonment for seventeen of those on minor charges; the acquittal of eight others.

The court was closed. A process had been followed, a verdict reached. The court clerk, Neuhaus, wrote up the court's findings for approval by the Military Governor, and in her cell Edith Cavell waited. She drafted letters to her mother, to Sister Wilkins, to Grace, to the nurses.

In England that day Edith Cavell's brother-in-law Longworth Wainwright, who had received no news, again wrote to Britain's Foreign Secretary. The family, he said, would be 'very grateful for any further information that may be obtained and also for instruction as to whether it is possible to communicate with or send comforts to Miss Cavell.' No such information was to be obtained, communication made or comforts given. Mrs Cavell endured an unbearable silence.

Her daughter looked to prayer, for hope and comforts beyond injustice and harm. Among the texts she highlighted were:

> *Thou that rulest the power of the sea and stillest the violent motion of its waves, arise and help me.*

> *Scatter the nations that desire war.*

> *There is no other hope or refuge for me, save in Thee, O Lord my God.*

42

SUNDAY 10 OCTOBER

God did not intervene. Neither did the diplomats or defence lawyers who seemed to be doing the minimum their professions required. Whitlock had known of Edith Cavell's arrest since 26 August. He had told Britain's Foreign Secretary he would try to ensure she had a fair trial and would keep him informed as to what was happening. Those assurances were as far as his involvement had gone. Her defence lawyer Sadi Kirschen had gone off to his country house without communicating the outcome of the trial to the Legation.

On the morning of Sunday 10 October, Herr Stoeber submitted the judges' report and sentences to the new and brutal Military Governor, Brigadier-General von Sauberzweig, who viewed even von Bissing the Governor General as not severe enough – he thought he compromised military security. Sauberzweig's reply was brief and immediate: 'I confirm the judgement,' he wrote back.

Elisabeth Wilkins again visited the prison and again was turned away. Nurse Aerschodt asked her father, who had penned the nurses' luckless petition for clemency to the Governor General, to find out what he could from the prison guards about Edith Cavell's fate. Aerschodt heard from a Belgian warder that the prosecution had asked for the death sentence for the nurses' matron, the Princess de Croÿ, the Countess de Belleville and others. He gave this news to Sister Wilkins. She went straight to the American Legation. She was told that Brand Whitlock was too ill to see her. She spoke to Gaston de Leval. He relayed the information to Whitlock.

'That's only the usual exaggeration of the prosecutor; they all ask for the extreme penalty, everywhere, when they sum up their cases,' Whitlock said.

'Yes,' Gaston de Leval replied. 'And in German courts they always get it.'

De Leval sent a note to Sadi Kirschen's Brussels house asking him to come on Monday morning at 8.30 to the Legation or to send information regarding Miss Cavell. He received no acknowledgement so he went to the house of one of the other lawyers[20] to clarify what had taken place at the trial. This lawyer said no judgement had been pronounced, the judges did not seem to be in agreement, and that he did not think Edith Cavell would be condemned to death.

So much for the effort of the day. It was Sunday. It was wily of Stoeber and Sauberzweig to finalise their plan on what was for the defendants' representatives a day of rest. News of confirmation of the judgement was not given to anyone who might move to help the accused.

That night Edith Cavell had an intimation of the gravity of her plight. When she put out her gas lamp, her Belgian warder opened the wicket, passed matches to her and told her to relight it. This, he said, was an order from the prison governor, Lieutenant Behrens. The previous night Maurice Pansaers, a Brussels coffeehouse keeper convicted for lodging Allied soldiers, had hanged himself in his cell. The military authorities did not want such self-determination from its prisoners. So, at fifteen-minute intervals on the night after Sauberzweig confirmed her death sentence, the wicket in Edith Cavell's cell door creaked open and torchlight was shone over her.

[20] This is from Whitlock's account. He does not say which lawyer

43

MONDAY 11 OCTOBER: DAY

At 8.30 in the morning on Monday 11 October Gaston de Leval went to the *Politische Abteilung* in rue Lambermont to get news of Edith Cavell. He spoke to Herr Conrad, the Secretary, who was 'always and unfailingly kind', according to Brand Whitlock. He asked if, now the trial was over, he – Leval – and the Reverend Stirling Gahan, the British chaplain in Brussels and rector of the English church where Edith Cavell worshipped, might be allowed to see her in prison.

Conrad said he would make inquiries and send news to Leval by one of the Legation's messengers who would be bringing papers to the *Politische Abteilung* later in the morning.

Leval went back to his desk. The messenger duly returned with news that neither Leval nor Gahan would be allowed to see Edith Cavell until after judgement was officially pronounced. At 11.30 Leval phoned Conrad who repeated what the messenger had already told him. Conrad assured Leval he would inform him as soon as judgement was confirmed. He thought this would probably be on Tuesday or the day after. But even then, he said, to be ratified it would have to be signed by the Military Governor. All this would take some days. Leval, but not the Reverend Gahan, would then be permitted to see Miss Cavell. For security reasons she could not see anyone English. There were German pastors at the prison, and if she needed spiritual counselling she could call on one of them to minister to her.

After this conversation Leval went to Sadi Kirschen's house. There was no sign of him so he left his card, then went on to another of the defending lawyers who said he had been told no judgement would be pronounced until the following day. Leval went back to the Legation and recounted to the Secretary, Hugh Gibson, who was in charge while Whitlock was ill in bed, all he had ascertained. At around 4.00 in the afternoon he left for home. Before leaving, he asked Gibson to phone Conrad again before he himself went home. At 6.20 a clerk, Mr Topping, phoned Conrad on Gibson's behalf and heard the same story: judgement had not been pronounced; the *Politische Abteilung* would inform the Legation as soon as they had news. And so all the lawyers, secretaries, clerks and messengers left their desks and went home for the night.

But those in German military uniform had been busy throughout the day. At three o'clock a warder opened Edith Cavell's cell door and told her to come and receive her sentence. She was taken to the central hall of the prison. The other prisoners were standing in a semicircle. Stoeber arrived flanked by two officers, the German Catholic prison chaplain Father Leyendecker, the interpreter Herr Brueck and the German prison governor Lieutenant Behrens. In German he read the sentences conferred by the judges and confirmed and signed by von Sauberzweig the previous day, 'as if he was reading a list of honours'. Five times the prisoners heard the word *Todesstrafe*: for Philippe Baucq, Louise Thuliez, Edith Cavell, Louis Séverin, Jeanne de Belleville. Then Brueck translated: la mort . . .

Baucq, according to Georges Hostelet, cried out in despair, 'his cheeks flushed and knees bent'. Séverin handed in a plea for mercy which he had already written. Edith Cavell leaned against a wall, seemingly impassive, though Jeanne de Belleville said her face had flushed almost violet. Hostelet went over to her and urged her to make an appeal for mercy. 'It is useless,' she answered. 'They want my life.' Jeanne de Belleville asked the prison chaplain Father Leyendecker what they could do. He told them they could still appeal to the Governor General. Louise Thuliez asked Edith Cavell if she would do so. 'No,' she replied. 'It is useless. I am English.'

They were ushered out of the hall. Baucq turned and shouted his innocence. He was dragged out. The others were taken to their cells. As they walked through the corridor the prison chaplains, the prison governor and the warders bowed. Louise Thuliez asked the officer escorting them if she and Jeanne de Belleville might share the same cell. 'If we are to die together may we please pass our last hours together?' He did not answer. She repeated the request to Father Leyendecker. He agreed. She moved her mattress from her cell, number 32, and carried it to Jeanne de Belleville's – 22, adjacent to Edith Cavell's. She asked him if Edith Cavell might join them too. No, he said, that could not be. There could not be three prisoners in a cell. He then helped them write their appeals for mercy.

After he left, the two women hugged each other, 'forgetting for a moment our mutual distress'. The Belgian warder instructed them to position their mattresses in the middle of the cell so he could see them through the wicket. As on the previous night they were to keep the gas lamp alight. At about 7.00 in the evening he opened the wicket, whispered 'There is hope,' then closed it. The two women talked until 2.00 in the morning. 'We had so much to say to one another and so many messages to leave for our respective families because we hoped against hope that one or other of us might be spared.' Next door Edith Cavell was alone. Several times during the night they heard her cell door open and shut.

The chaplain passed their appeals to Stoeber. Stoeber passed these to von Sauberzweig and updated him on proceedings: 'The sentence together with its confirmation was made known to the prisoners through the interpreter Brueck.' Sauberzweig's reply was immediate:

Court of the German Imperial Government
Brussels
11.10.15
Brussels 11b 3301/15
I deem that the interests of the State demand that the
sentence against Philippe Baucq and Edith Cavell be carried
out <u>immediately</u> [underlined in red] and I hereby order
this.

I adjourn the death sentence on the other prisoners until
a decision has been reached concerning the appeals for
clemency now pending.
Brigadier General von Sauberzweig

Lieutenant Behrens replied with equal speed: 'The death penalty
against Baucq and Cavell will be carried out on 12.10.15 at seven
a.m.' Late in the afternoon Edith Cavell was taken from her cell,
to a side room of the prison, to be told this news by the German
prison chaplain, Pastor Le Seur:

It was intolerably difficult for me to carry out my task but
she came to my aid.

'How much time will they give me?' she asked.

I replied 'Unfortunately only until tomorrow morning.'

For a moment her cheeks flushed and a film passed over
her eyes, but it was only for a few seconds and I offered her
my services as a pastor saying I was at her service any hour
of the day or night. She politely declined.

'Can I not show you some kindness?' I said. 'Please do
not see in me now the German but only the servant of our
Lord who places himself entirely at your disposal.'

She asked if it would be possible to tell her mother in
England. I promised to do all I could to ensure this and
I kept my promise. But it was a burden on my heart that

I could not serve her in her bitter need. I knew that from
me, as a German, in the uniform she must have hated,
she could not receive spiritual help. Also, according to
the principles of her Church it was not possible for her to
receive the sacrament from a Pastor who did not subscribe
to them, but I knew the Anglican chaplain in Brussels, the
Reverend Stirling Gahan, a pious Irishman who had been
allowed to continue his religious duties throughout the
Occupation. So I asked Miss Cavell if she wanted him to
come to her to take the Holy Sacrament.

Her eyes lit up and she accepted gratefully. Finally I told
her it was my duty to stand by her side at the end and I
asked if she would prefer the Reverend Gahan to be there
instead.

She declined and said it would be too much for him.
He was not used to such things. 'Miss Cavell,' I said, 'I too
am not used to such things but I would be rendering you a
service if, instead of meeting you outside the Tir National
rifle range I came here to the prison to collect you.' She
accepted this offer. I said a few words of comfort from a
deeply moved heart and we parted.

Le Seur went straight to the Reverend Stirling Gahan's house. He
and his wife were out. He left a pencilled note, 'An Englishwoman
is about to die.' He asked him to visit him at once.

Elisabeth Wilkins and another Sister, Beatrice Smith, desperate for news, went to the St Gilles prison in the late afternoon.
The Belgian deputy governor Xavier Marin saw them. He told
them that the death sentences had already been made known to
the prisoners and that Edith Cavell and Philippe Baucq were to
be shot at 7.00 in the morning. He advised the two nurses to go
at once to the American Legation's lawyer, Gaston de Leval, at
his house in the avenue de la Toison d'Or.

44

MONDAY 11 OCTOBER: EVENING

The Reverend Gahan got home at about 6.30 on the evening of Monday 11 October with his wife Muriel. He found Le Seur's note. He had met the German military chaplain once before, in July, when he had asked him for a prayer book for a wounded English soldier. 'Found him Christian and courteous,' he wrote in his diary.

He did not know to whom this current note referred. 'I went at once to his lodgings at 18 rue de Berlaimont.' He was shown into the sitting room. It was 7.00 p.m.

The Pastor arrived. I thought he was looking rather pale and distressed. To my surprise he opened the conversation by asking me if I knew Nurse Cavell. This was a necessary formality he was bound to observe. I answered 'Yes, I know her very well, she attends my church and I have often visited her in the Nursing School.'

Then he said quietly 'I am sorry to have to tell you that she has been condemned to death and is to be shot tomorrow morning.'

My feelings at this intelligence I will not attempt to describe.

I asked a few questions, and then he proceeded to say 'I asked her if she would like to receive the Sacrament at your hands and she said "Yes". I also asked her if she would like you to be with her at the time of her execution tomorrow morning, but she answered "No, Mr Gahan is not used to such things."'

Then I said I should be quite willing, but Pastor le Seur answered 'I am very sorry but it is now too late to obtain that permission.'

Then he continued 'I have here the permit which will give you admission to St Gilles prison this evening.'

Gahan took the permit, went home and told his wife, then set off for the prison with his Communion set. Muriel Gahan left to plead with Whitlock at the American Legation.

Sisters Wilkins and Smith arrived at Gaston de Leval's house at about 8 p.m. He was at his desk writing an appeal for Edith Cavell's pardon, in Brand Whitlock's name, to be given to both the Governor General von Bissing and to von der Lancken, Head of the *Politische Abteilung*. Elisabeth Wilkins was in tears (*toute en larmes*). Beatrice Smith was calmer. Sister Wilkins told de Leval how she had just learned the court had condemned Edith Cavell to death, that the judgement had been read to her at 4.30 that afternoon, that she was to be shot at 2.00 in the morning.

De Leval was disbelieving. He had feared swift judgement, but not so swift as this. An hour previously he had heard from the Secretary's office at the *Politische Abteilung* that judgement had not been pronounced and would not be, until the following day. The nurses impressed on him that they had been given the news directly by the deputy governor of the prison and that it was he who had told them to come straight to him.

De Leval added the information they gave him to the clemency appeal he was drafting in Brand Whitlock's name, then went with them to the Legation. He, more than any other of the bureaucrats, had absorbed how serious this situation was.

The two nursing Sisters waited downstairs with Whitlock's wife, the Legation Second Secretary Caroline Larner, and Muriel Gahan. De Leval went up to Whitlock's bedroom. 'And there he stood pale and shaken,' Whitlock was later to write. From his sickbed Whitlock signed the documents de Leval had prepared:

Mr Whitlock, American Minister in Brussels to Baron von Bissing, Governor General in Belgium.

Your Excellency,

I have just heard that Miss Cavell, a British subject and consequently under the protection of my Legation, was this morning condemned to death by court martial.

If my information is correct, the judgement in the present case is more severe than all others passed in similar cases tried by the same Court. Without going into the reasons for such a drastic sentence, I appeal to your Excellency's humanity and generosity and ask that the death penalty passed on Miss Cavell be commuted, and that this unfortunate woman should not be executed.

Miss Cavell is the head nurse of the Brussels Surgical Institute. She has spent her life in alleviating the suffering of others, and her School has sent out nurses who have watched at the bedside of the sick the world over – in Germany as in Belgium. At the outset of the war Miss Cavell gave her care as freely to German soldiers as to others. Even without going into other reasons, her career as a servant of humanity is such as to inspire the greatest sympathy and to call for pardon.

If the information I have is correct Miss Cavell, far from shielding herself has, with commendable straightforwardness, admitted the truth of all the charges against her, and it is the very information which she herself has furnished and which she alone was in a position to furnish that has aggravated the severity of the sentence passed against her.

Therefore with confidence, and in the hope of its
favourable reception, I have the honour to present to Your
Excellency my request for pardon on Miss Cavell's behalf.
I avail etc.
Brand Whitlock

De Leval had drafted the same letter for von der Lancken. The
only amendment was in the final paragraph where he wrote, 'I
beg your Excellency to submit to the Governor-General my
request for pardon on Miss Cavell's behalf.'

As he signed, Whitlock 'at the last minute' wrote on the
bottom of von der Lancken's copy,

My dear Baron,
I am too ill to present my request to you in person, but I
appeal to your generosity of heart to support it and save
this unfortunate woman from death. Have pity on her!
Votre bien dévoué
Brand Whitlock

Whitlock told de Leval to send a messenger to find the Legation
First Secretary, Hugh Gibson, and get him personally to present
the pleas. If possible Gibson should also find the Marquis de
Villalobar, the Spanish Minister in Brussels, and ask him, too,
to plead with von der Lancken. Whitlock then sent a telegram
to London: 'Miss Cavell's trial has been completed and the
German prosecutor has asked for sentence of death penalty
against her. I have some hope that the court martial may decline
to pass the rigorous sentence proposed.'

The women downstairs were joined by Pauline Randall and
Grace Jemmett and other nurses from the School who had heard
the news. All were disbelieving. No court, not even a German
court martial, would condemn a woman to death at half past

four in the afternoon then shoot her before dawn. It was cold and raining outside. Quite what was wrong with Whitlock was unspecified.

45

MONDAY 11 OCTOBER: NIGHT

The messenger found Hugh Gibson. Together Gibson and de Leval then went in search of the Spanish Minister, the Marquis de Villalobar. He was dining at the house of Baron Lambert of the Rothschild dynasty and Émile Francqui, a Belgian banker who chaired the committee for relief work. They were on their coffee. Gibson, Leval and Villalobar then went to the offices of the *Politische Abteilung* in rue Lambermont.

The offices were in darkness. They rang until the concierge showed up. Everyone was gone, he said. The Governor General was in Berlin. Baron von der Lancken was at the theatre. Which theatre? they asked. He did not know. They told him to find out. He went up and down stairs a few times then came back with an official. Von der Lancken was at a variety theatre, he told them, Le Bois Sacré in the rue d'Arenberg. They said they must see him, told the man to fetch him, gave him use of their car and waited in the salon on the Louis XVI white-lacquered chairs upholstered in yellow satin.

Von der Lancken was irritated at being disturbed. He would come when the show was finished, he said. At about ten o'clock he reached rue Lambermont. He was joined soon after by two of his assistants: Count Harrach and Baron von Falkenhausen. Harrach, from a rich German family, had been a sculptor at the outbreak of the war. He spoke several languages and was head of the *Press-Zentrale*. His job was to make news disappear. Falkenhausen had been educated at Cambridge, was polite and had no clout.

The Marquis de Villalobar (1864–1926), Spanish Minister in Brussels. He pleaded with the German military to try to save Edith Cavell's life

'What is it, gentlemen?' von der Lancken asked. 'Has something serious happened?' Gibson told him. Von der Lancken raised his hands, said it was impossible, he had heard something that afternoon of a sentence for spying, but he did not think it had anything to do with Edith Cavell and anyway they would not put a woman to death that night. He was scornful that credence was being given to an unofficial report. What was the source of the information? he asked. 'Really, to come and disturb me at such an hour you must have information from a serious source [*Car, enfin, pour venir me déranger à pareille heure il faut que vous ayez des renseignements sérieux*].' He insisted he be told the precise source. Gibson did not want to divulge this. He did not want further to implicate any of the nurses. Von der Lancken insisted it was improbable such a sentence had been pronounced, that even if it had, it would not be carried out in such a short space of time and anyway it would be quite impossible to do anything until the morning. 'Come and see me tomorrow,' he said.

'It was of course pointed out to him that if the facts were as we believed them to be, action would be useless unless taken at once,' Gibson wrote in his report of the meeting.

Villalobar urged von der Lancken to ascertain the facts immediately. Reluctantly von der Lancken then telephoned Herr Werthmann, the presiding judge at the court martial. He came back to say yes, it was as they said, and it was intended that the sentence be carried out before morning.

De Leval gave him Whitlock's sickbed plea. Von der Lancken read it 'with a little sarcastic smile' according to de Leval, then said it was necessary to have a plea for mercy too. Leval produced this. Gibson and de Leval, in their plea for delay, forcibly went through the case for the defence: they spoke of the horror of executing a woman, of how the death sentence had only been imposed for actual cases of espionage and Edith Cavell had not even been accused of that. Gibson pointed out how Secretary Conrad at the *Politische Abteilung* had failed to inform the Legation of the sentence, that Edith Cavell had been in prison for many weeks now; delay could not endanger the German cause. Villalobar warned that such summary execution would have a profound effect on public opinion in Brussels and abroad and would encourage reprisals. He urged clemency, delay, appeal to the Governor General.

But they had left it all so late. Midnight horse-trading by a junior American diplomat was no match for Sauberzweig and his team. It needed sovereign intervention, a cutting-through of all the twine of bureacracy, protocol and rank, to save Edith Cavell's life.

Von der Lancken argued that the Military Governor was the supreme authority (*Gerichtsherr*) in these matters. He had discretionary power to accept or refuse any appeal for clemency. Only the Emperor could overrule him. The Governor General had no authority to intervene and anyway he was in Berlin.

Eventually von der Lancken agreed to phone General von Sauberzweig, the Military Governor, to see if it was true that he had ratified the sentence and to ask if there was any chance of clemency. There was no reply, so he called on him. Sauberzweig was playing skat – a German card game of tricks and trumps – and angry at being disturbed. Von der Lancken put Whitlock's letter of appeal on the table. Sauberzweig swept it to the floor. He said Cavell's immediate execution was necessary to ensure the safety of German troops. Von der Lancken retrieved the letter, asked how Cavell's execution, when she was in prison, could protect German troops and suggested it would cause a stir and be used as propaganda by the Allies. Sauberzweig got angrier, said he took responsibility for the decision and would not change his mind.

Von der Lancken returned to the diplomats. He had been gone half an hour. Sauberzweig, he told them, had acted only after 'mature deliberation'; he considered the death penalty imperative and declined to accept their appeal for clemency or any representation on the matter. Von der Lancken then handed Brand Whitlock's note back to Gibson. Gibson demurred about taking it. Von der Lancken insisted.

'Von der Lancken was deaf alike to pity, and to considerations of international opinion,' Gibson was to write. Villalobar became impassioned. He took von der Lancken by the shoulder and 'literally dragged' him into a nearby room. They talked for about a quarter of an hour. 'It is madness, what you are doing,' the others heard him say. 'You'll have another Louvain.' He urged von der Lancken to telephone to General Headquarters at Charleville, and have the matter laid before the Emperor. This von der Lancken refused to do: it was not possible at such an hour of the night. 'I am not a personal friend of my Sovereign like you,' he sarcastically told Villalobar. 'What a grand opportunity for becoming a personal friend of your Sovereign you are missing,' Villalobar is supposed to have said.

Villalobar then asked von der Lancken for permission to phone the Kaiser himself. This would be invidious, von der Lancken argued. It was late at night. Ultimate authority lay with the military Governor. The Kaiser would not be able to get the advice of his ministers at this hour. If the Kaiser refused to override Sauberzweig, this would transfer opprobrium to himself, von der Lancken, with dire results.

So nothing was done, the Kaiser was left to sleep, and Edith Cavell's chance of life slipped away.

While Villalobar and von der Lancken argued, de Leval and Gibson pleaded with the younger German officers. In such a power-based structure such pleading was no better than chat. Von Falkenhausen was young and sympathetic to England. Harrach said the life of one German soldier was more important to him than any number of these old English nurses. Gibson and de Leval reminded them that the American Ministry had worked for German subjects at the outset of the war and during the siege of Antwerp. 'We persevered until it was only too clear that there was no hope of securing any consideration for the case.'

It was all too little, too late. After a catalogue of inactivity, this flurry of junior diplomats talking among themselves and appealing only to the man most complicit in this killing, a man known to favour harshness and to use the law to fit ruthless intention, was the last stage in unforceful diplomacy. Whitlock never met Edith Cavell or Sauberzweig. Von der Lancken in his memoirs said the Legation had not been much concerned about Edith Cavell's trial.

Villalobar returned. They all left the *Politische Abteilung* shortly after midnight. De Leval was as white as a sheet, Gibson said. He took him home then went back to the Legation. 'It was a bitter business leaving the place feeling that we had failed and that the little woman was to be led out before a firing squad within a few hours,' he wrote in his diary.

But it was worse to go back to the Legation to the little group of English women who were waiting in my office to learn the result of our visit. They had been there for nearly four hours while Mrs Whitlock and Miss Larner sat with them and tried to sustain them through the hours of waiting. There were Mrs Gahan, wife of the English chaplain, and several nurses from Miss Cavell's School. One was a little wisp of a thing who had been mothered by Miss Cavell, and was nearly beside herself with grief. There was no way of breaking the news to them gently, for they could read the answer in our faces when we came in. All we could do was to give them each a stiff drink of sherry and send them home.

From his bed Whitlock heard the street door open as the nurses went out into the rain.

46

WHAT WAS LEFT OF THE NIGHT

The little woman was in a locked cell. Next door Louise Thuliez and Jeanne de Belleville had the comfort of each other, and whispered reassurance of hope from a Belgian warder. Edith Cavell was alone. Ada Bodart managed to see her for a couple of minutes at about six o'clock. She gave a German guard ten francs to be taken to her cell to say goodbye. He had worked for years in Birmingham. Edith Cavell kissed her and told her she would rather give her life than have 'her soldiers' fall into the hands of the Germans. 'She was wonderfully brave but a little nervous.'

Edith Cavell then finalised the letters she had drafted the previous day: to her mother, her nurses, to Sister Wilkins. To her nurses she wrote in French in her clear forward-sloping script:

My dear nurses,
It is a very sad moment for me because I write to say my goodbyes. I recall that the 17th of September – a few weeks ago – marked eight years of my directorship of the School. I was so happy to have been called on to help organise the project our Committee had founded.

On the 1st of October 1907 there were only four young probationers. Now there are many of you – about fifty or sixty in all I think, counting those who have gained their certificates and left the School.

At various times I have told you about those early days and the difficulties we encountered – even down to the

Edith Cavell's farewell letter to her nurses, two days before she was shot

choice of words like 'heures de service' and 'hors de service' etc. Everything about the profession was new for Belgium.

Little by little we built up one service after another: certificated nurses for home nursing, school nurses, nurses for the St Gilles Hospital, for Dr Depage's Institute, for the Sanatorium at Buyssingham, for Dr Mayer's clinic and now many are called (as perhaps you will be later on) to tend the brave men wounded in the war.

If during the last year our work has diminished, the cause is to be found in the sad times we are going through. When better days come our work will again grow and resume all its power for doing good.

If I speak to you of the past it is because it is good sometimes to stop and consider the path we have travelled and to take account of our progress and mistakes.

In your new beautiful Institute you will have more patients and all that is necessary for their comfort and your own.

To my sorrow I have not always been able to talk to each of you privately. You know I have always had much to do, but I hope you will not forget our evening conversations. In them I told you devotion would bring you true happiness and the thought that before God and in your own eyes you have done your duty well and with a good heart will sustain you in the hard moments of life and in the face of death.

There are two or three of you who will recall the little talks we had together. Do not forget them. As I had already gone far along life's road I was perhaps able to see more clearly than you and show you the right path.

One word more. Beware of slander. I must tell you, I who love your country with all my heart, that this has been a great fault here. During these last eight years I have seen many misfortunes which would have been avoided or lessened if a little word had not been whispered here and there, perhaps without evil intention, but which destroyed the happiness or even the life of someone. Nurses all need to think of this and to cultivate loyalty and team spirit among themselves.

If any of you has a grievance against me I beg you to forgive me; I have perhaps sometimes been too strict but never knowingly unjust, and I have loved you all much more than you can know.

My good wishes for the happiness of all my girls, as much for those who have left the School as for those who are still there and thank you for the kindness you have always shown me.

Your devoted Matron

Edith Cavell

10 Oct. 1915

She then wrote a letter to her mother. A letter of love and reassurance no doubt, but it was never passed to her, or its contents revealed.

Through the eternity of this war Edith Cavell had kept to her agenda of good. Now she wanted to die in a state of grace and without her affairs in disarray, rancour in her heart or love left undeclared. She turned to the faith that was an indivisible part of the rituals of her childhood, that taught the obligation of goodness and love, and led her to believe that mercy and justice might one day prevail. It had always been her way to direct her thoughts to God. To be not just a servant of life but a servant of the source of life, whatever that might be. She scored lines against the devotional words that gave her courage to get through this ordeal: *Occasions of adversity best discover how great virtue or strength each one hath. For occasions do not make a man frail, but they shew what he is.* She could not change the circumstances in which she found herself. The door was locked from the outside. She strived for the acceptance world: *If it be Thy will I should be in darkness be Thou blessed; and if it be Thy will I should be in light be Thou again blessed. If Thou vouchsafe to comfort me, be Thou blessed; and if Thou wilt have me afflicted be Thou ever equally blessed.* Such was her devotion. It had in itself to be its own reward. To love for gain seemed to her a diminishing of the idea of love.

She had not sought martyrdom or thought it would be imposed on her. At this point of affliction she had either to question the faith by which she lived or surrender to it. The sentence of death imposed on her took her to the ultimate test of her faith: to the Crucifixion. *Cast thy heart firmly on the Lord and fear not the judgement of men when conscience testifieth of thy dutifulness and innocency*. These and others were the texts she highlighted. In a condemned cell she stayed true to her conscience and to the idea of heaven, as much on earth as beyond. And so her cell became not a prison but a sanctuary, away from the slaughter in the nearby fields. The texts urged her to stay true, have courage. Her enemies had judged and despised her. Against the words: *It were more just that thou should accuse thyself and excuse thy brother* she scored two lines and wrote 'St Gilles Oct 1915'. It was her way of saying she forgave them. She chose to ignore hate's territory.

Stirling Gahan arrived at the prison at 9.30 p.m. He rang at the gate. A German guard let him in when he showed he had dispensation to see Edith Cavell. The guard said of her that she was a fine woman. 'Like this,' he said, and stiffened his back.

Edith Cavell had given up hope of his coming and was in her dressing gown. Gahan had with him a silver Communion set: chalice, cruet, pyx and paten. He had been apprehensive as to her state of mind. Seeing her, he was reassured. She told him it was good of him to come and gestured to him to sit on the one wooden chair. He noticed that her cell was clean and adequate, but the flowers her nurses had sent her were dead.

She did not complain about her trial. She did not know that the others who stood trial with her and whose involvement in resistance work had been greater would be reprieved. She said she willingly gave her life for her country. She perhaps did not know that the aid she had given to Allied soldiers was not sufficient, even under the maverick laws by which she was indicted, to justify the sentence passed on her. She told Gahan that the German pastor, Le Seur, had been kind, and she accepted that he be with her at the end. She was thankful for the imposed silence of her ten weeks' imprisonment. It had been, she said, 'like a solemn fast from earthly distractions and diversions'. She told him:

> I have no fear or shrinking. I have seen death so often that it is not strange or fearful to me. Life has always been hurried and full of difficulty. This time of rest has been a great mercy. Everyone here has been very kind.
>
> But this I would say, standing as I do in view of God and Eternity: I realise that patriotism is not enough. I must have no hatred or bitterness towards anyone.

They sat on the narrow bed, used the chair as the Communion table and shared the wine and wafer, the belief in connection to truth and love, of goodness incarnate, that a sip of wine might represent divine blood, a wafer divine flesh. That Communion might be to the best in a human, away from the impiety of war. They observed the ritual of two thousand years, said the consoling well-worn words: *Come unto Me all ye that labour and are heavy laden and I will bring you rest.* Edith Cavell asked Gahan in his uniform of a priest for the forgiveness of her sins. They whispered the idea of everlasting love: 'I draw near unto Thee with hope and reverence and I do truly believe that Thou art here present in this Sacrament both God and Man.'

The ritual of Communion linked her to her childhood in Swardeston, to the always visible church, to her stern father and devoted mother, to the career decisions she had made, to her country which she looked to as a liberator from the injustice of this brutal occupation.

She spoke to Gahan of her unworthiness and her uncertainty about heaven. She asked him to send farewell messages to friends and relations. He said, 'We shall remember you as a heroine and a martyr.' She replied, 'Don't think of me like that. Think of me as a nurse who tried to do her duty.'

'At the close of the little service,' Gahan wrote, 'I began to repeat the words "Abide With Me" and she joined softly in the end:

> Swift to its close ebbs out life's little day;
> Earth's joys grow dim, its glories pass away;
> Change and decay in all around I see;
> O Thou who changest not, abide with me.

> I fear no foe, with Thee at hand to bless;
> Ills have no weight, and tears no bitterness.
> Where is death's sting? Where, grave, thy victory?
> I triumph still, if Thou abide with me.

He had stayed with her an hour. He said, 'Perhaps I had better go. You will want to rest.' She replied with her dry humour, 'Yes, I have to be up at five.' She gave him her watch to give to Grace Jemmett, and twenty francs for Sister Wilkins to settle such debts as she had. She asked him to give Xavier Marin the assistant governor the letters she had written to her mother, to the nurses, to Grace Jemmett. By the cell door they shook hands. She smiled and said, 'We shall meet again.' He replied, 'Yes, we shall. God be with you.'

The two German gaolers guarding her cell let him out. After he left the lock was turned.

She wrote a final letter to Elisabeth Wilkins:

My dear Sister,

Mr Gahan will give you twenty francs from me to pay my little debts. Miss J. owes me (she will remember) a hundred francs. Take it to buy a clock for the entrance hall. At the end of the daily account book you will see the Red Cross accounts; money spent out from the School funds but not entered, which should have been covered by the two cheques I told you of and which is not entered either.

I am asking you to take charge of my will and a few things for me. You have been very kind my dear, and I thank you and the nurses for all you have done for me in the last ten weeks.

My love to you all, I am not afraid but quite happy.

Yours

E. Cavell

October 11th 1915

She had settled her accounts, written her letters, bequeathed a clock, prepared her soul. She had been taught that the reward for virtue was eternal life. 'By the grace of God' was the caveat for what might not be so, for the landscape of heaven was less coherently mapped and charted than the fields and lanes of rural Norfolk. But in her mind the terrain of each was familiar.

From her earliest years the concept of God was as everyday as blackberrying and Sunday dinner. In her demanding life as a nurse she had gone beyond church dogma to the meaning of quiescence. She had loved without consideration for profit or preferment. Devotion truly had been its own reward. She now could do no more than hope for Jack to be brushed and fed, her nurses to be conscientious, the new School to triumph, her mother to be consoled and for this malign war to end. For her cousin Eddy whom she had told in 1895, 'I am going to do something useful . . . It will be something for people,' and to whom seven months previously she had written, 'I like to look back on the days when we were young and life was fresh and beautiful and the country so desirable and sweet,' she now inscribed the flyleaf of her copy of *The Imitation of Christ*:

> Arrested 5 August 1915
> Brussels Prison de St Gilles 7 Aug 1915.
> Court martialled 7 Oct 1915
>   "   "   8   "   "
> Condemned to death 8 Oct in the Salle des députés at 10.30
> a.m. with 7 others. (The accused numbered in all 70 of
> whom 34 were present on these two dates)
> Died at 7 a.m. on Oct 12th 1915
> E. Cavell
> with love to E. D. Cavell

The gas light in her cell burned for what was left of the night.

47

TUESDAY 12 OCTOBER: DAY

In the early hours of Tuesday morning, Sisters Elisabeth Wilkins and Beatrice Smith, and Nurses Pauline van Bockstaele and Jacqueline van Til, walked to the prison and waited outside the gates. At 5 a.m. Edith Cavell washed, folded her bed, tidied her clothes and possessions, secured her hair with a comb, again put on the clothes Elisabeth Wilkins had brought in for her trial: her blue coat and skirt, white blouse, her grey fur stole. She fixed the collar of her blouse with a gold stud, her hat with a tortoiseshell pin.

An hour later, from the adjacent cell, Louise Thuliez and Jeanne de Belleville heard her door open and close. With the pastor Paul Le Seur beside her she walked down the long prison corridor. The German guards bowed. She acknowledged them but did not speak.

Two cars with military drivers waited in the courtyard. She and Le Seur got into one. She sat between two helmeted soldiers. The car waited until Philippe Baucq and the Catholic priest Father Leyendecker came through the courtyard door. Baucq shook hands with the guards. He had been allowed a meeting with his wife the previous night on condition he did not tell her he was to be shot at dawn. He left her a letter saying he died without regrets for what he had done, that his greatest suffering was to leave her and his daughters, whom he had always loved, and would love until his last breath.

The two cars drove through the prison gate. The nurses glimpsed their matron who looked straight ahead. The cars drove through the dark streets of Brussels to the *Tir National*, the German shooting range on the edge of the city. A full company of 250 armed soldiers was there with Herr Stoeber the prosecutor, Lieutenant Behrens the German governor of St Gilles Prison and Dr Gottfried Benn, who had been present throughout the trial and had given privileged treatment to the Princess de Croÿ.

The shooting range, a large field with a steep grassy slope to catch the bullets, was muddy from the rain. In front of the slope two new white posts, vertical stakes, had been driven into the ground. To the side were two yellow coffins. Two rows of eight armed soldiers were lined up facing the slope, six paces from it. The clergymen walked with the prisoners to the stakes. Stoeber addressed the soldiers. They need have no conscience about shooting a woman, he told them; she was not a mother and her crimes were heinous.

Baucq took off his hat to the men arraigned to shoot him. '*Bonjour messieurs*,' he called. '*Devant la mort nous sommes tous des camarades.*' Stoeber silenced him and read the sentences. Behrens translated these into French.

Le Seur pressed Edith Cavell's hand and spoke of the grace of God. She asked that the Reverend Gahan reassure her mother that her soul was safe. '*Ma conscience est tranquille*,' she said. '*Je meurs pour Dieu et ma patrie.*' He walked with her to the execution post. A soldier bound her to it and bandaged her eyes. Later he told Le Seur her eyes were filled with tears. Seconds passed while Leyendecker spoke with Baucq. 'They seemed like an eternity,' Le Seur said.

An officer gave the command to shoot. Baucq shouted '*Vive la Belgique!*' There was the crack of gunfire. Edith Cavell's face streamed with blood. She jerked forward and three times her body rose up in a reflex action. One shot had gone through her forehead. There was a bullet hole as large as a fist through her heart. She remained upright at the post.

'What I saw was terrible,' Le Seur wrote. He ran forward. The soldier untied her body. Dr Benn checked she had no pulse, closed her eyes, pronounced her dead. The deed was done. Two soldiers put her in the yellow coffin then into the hastily dug grave. She was buried immediately and with no ceremony. 'The place is to remain unknown,' Benn wrote. 'She went to her death with a bearing which it is quite impossible to forget. But she acted as a man toward the Germans and deserved to be punished as a man . . . There is fear lest her death should lead to disorders . . . We must hurry, and silence and secrecy should surround her grave.'

PART SIX

48

THE REMAINS OF THE DAY AND THE FOLLOWING DAYS

Elisabeth Wilkins watched the car drive away from the gates of St Gilles to the firing range. She went to the prison office and was told to collect Edith Cavell's things in three days' time. She was now the executor of her will and acting matron. At rue de la Culture Edith Cavell's life was in place as if she had just gone out to walk the dog, except the dog was there and pining. There were her nursing books and prayer books, her walnut rocking chair, her armchair, framed photographs of family, the cushion in which were found fragments of her diary, possessions that were modest links to an unacquisitive life.

Within hours of the killings the military authorities posted *affiches* on the trees, in the boulevards, on the walls of what once had been civic buildings. When the rain stopped there was a hazy sun. Crowds huddled to read:

NOTICE
By judgement of October 9, 1915, the military tribunal has pronounced the following sentences for treason committed in time of war (for having led recruits to the enemy):
1. Philippe Baucq, architect of Brussels, to death.
2. Louise Thuliez, teacher of Lille, to death.
3. Edith Cavell, directress of a medical institution in Brussels, to death.
4. Countess Jeanne de Belleville of Montignies, to death.
5. Louis Séverin, pharmacist of Brussels, to death.

6. Herman Capiau, engineer of Wasmes, to 15 years' hard labour.

7. Madame Ada Bodart of Brussels, to 15 years' hard labour.

8. Georges Derveau, pharmacist of Pâturages, to 15 years' hard labour.

9. Princess Marie de Croÿ of Bellignies, to 10 years' hard labour.

Seventeen other accused have been sentenced to hard labour or imprisonment of from 2 to 8 years.

Eight others accused of treason in time of war have been acquitted.

The judgement rendered against Baucq and Cavell has already been executed.

Brussels October 12 1915

Government

In the prison, Louise Thuliez and Jeanne de Belleville learned of the death of Edith Cavell and Philippe Baucq when they took their morning exercise. Later that morning their relatives brought in clothes. 'We argued why let us have a change of clothes if we are to be shot?' Louise Thuliez was later to write.

Because she and Jeanne de Belleville were French, they came under the protection of Spain's Minister, the Marquis de Villalobar. Fearful for the two women's lives, he called on Brand Whitlock that morning. Whitlock told him with some complacency that the 'thirst for blood had been slaked' and there would be no more executions from that group.

Villalobar was not so sanguine. He knew the ruthlessness of Sauberzweig and that standard diplomacy would not do. He telegraphed the King of Spain, Alfonso XIII, to intercede, urged the Belgian Legation in Rome to appeal to the Pope, asked the

French Ambassador in Washington to apprise the President, Woodrow Wilson.

Brand Whitlock got up from his sickbed and spent the remainder of the day writing letters. He first sent a telegram to Walter Hines Page, the American Ambassador in London:

MR WHITLOCK, American Minister in Brussels to Mr Page.
AMERICAN LEGATION, BRUSSELS, October 12, 1915.
Your letter of September 23 and my replies of October 9 and 11. Miss Cavell sentenced yesterday and executed at 2 o'clock this morning, despite our best efforts continued until the last moment. Full report follows by mail.
WHITLOCK

He had got the 'last moment' wrong by five hours.

The Reverend Gahan that morning managed to get a telegram sent from Holland to convey the news to Edith Cavell's family. Longworth Wainwright received it at his home in Upton upon Thames on 14 October.

The president of the new Belgian School of Nurses, Monsieur Faider, called on Brand Whitlock on the morning of the 12th to appeal for the release of Edith Cavell's body so that she might be buried respectfully in a Brussels cemetery. Whitlock, who disliked the phone, passed the request on in a note to von der Lancken who called at the Legation in the afternoon. It was not possible. Her body had been interred. He had no authority to ask permission to exhume it.

Brand Whitlock then sent his account to the United States Ambassador in London, Walter Page. This was compiled from reports by his Secretary Hugh Gibson and Gaston de Leval. 'I know that you will understand without my telling you,' he wrote to Page, that we exhausted every possible effort to prevent the infliction of the death penalty, and that our failure has been felt by us as a very severe blow. I am convinced however that no step was neglected which could have had any effect. From the date we first learned of Miss Cavell's imprisonment we made frequent inquiries of the German authorities and reminded them of their promise that we should be fully informed as to developments.

They were under no misapprehension as to our interest in the matter. Although the German authorities did not inform me when the sentence had actually been passed, I learned, through an unofficial source, that judgement had been delivered and that Miss Cavell was to be executed during the night. I immediately sent Mr Gibson the Secretary of the Legation to present to Baron von der Lancken my appeal that execution of the sentence should be deferred until the Governor should consider my plea for clemency. Mr Gibson was fortunate enough to find the Spanish Minister and got him to accompany him on his visit to Baron von der Lancken. The details of the visit you will find in Mr Gibson's report to me. The other papers which are attached speak for themselves and require no comment from me.

I have, etc.

BRAND WHITLOCK

MR WHITLOCK, American Minister in Brussels, to Mr Page, AMERICAN LEGATION, BRUSSELS, October 13, 1915

It was true he had no influence over the military tribunal, which offered no explanation why Edith Cavell and Philippe Baucq were so hastily slaughtered. Sauberzweig, determined to outwit any bid for clemency, intended to avenge himself on the English and warn the citizens of Brussels not to oppose his oppression.

But efforts on Edith Cavell's behalf had not been exhaustive and only at the eleventh hour was intervention attempted.

In Brussels later that day more notices were posted by the military. One from von Bissing spoke of having uncovered and defeated a spy system, '*un espionnage*', which 'treacherously menaced the security of the German army'. Edith Cavell was now a spy and a threat to the German army. Another, from Sauberzweig, was the *ex post facto* law for which she had already been tried, condemned and shot. At the time of her killing her deeds were not a capital crime even under German military rule. There were, the Military Governor now wrote, people in hiding who belonged to an enemy army. If they declared themselves to the authorities within twenty-four hours they would be sent as prisoners of war to Germany. If not, they, 'as well as all other persons who aid them in any manner whatsoever, whether by concealing them, giving them lodging or clothing, or nourishing them, will be punished with death or with hard labour and imprisonment by virtue of the Order hereinunder': to proclaim such a ruling now, suggested that hitherto to harbour Allied soldiers was not a capital offence. Nor had it been proved that Edith Cavell's intentions were to aid the Allied army. 'My aim was not to help your enemy but to help those men who asked for my help to reach the frontier. Once across the frontier they were free,' she had told the military tribunal.

As a result of this new edict 4,000 Belgian and French soldiers presented themselves next day at the École Militaire in rue du Méridien and were sent to German prisons. This caused administrative chaos, and anger in blockaded Germany because it meant more people to feed.

Longworth Wainwright received the telegram from Stirling Gahan about Edith Cavell's death on 14 October. He wrote at once to the Foreign Secretary Sir Edward Grey:

Dear Sir,

Forgive my worrying you again so soon, I had a wire dated from Holland yesterday morning. 'Miss Edith Cavell died this morning' from Gahan chaplain, Brussels. Have you any information on what this implies?

In-house memos then winged around the Foreign Office. 'I had hoped that the Germans wouldn't go beyond imprisoning her in Germany. Their action in this matter is part and parcel of their policy of frightfulness and also I venture to think a sign of weakness,' Sir Horace Rowland, Undersecretary of State for Foreign Affairs, wrote. 'I am afraid we are powerless,' he had written about the 'Cavell Case' and his own weakness eight days before. Sir Edward Grey wired the details to Longworth Wainwright.

Deeply regret to inform you that Miss Edith Cavell has been executed by German authorities on charge of assisting escape of British soldiers. She has died as she lived devoted to service of her country.
Edward Grey

His words set the tone for a propaganda assault. He authorised a press release for the following day: 'The Foreign Office desire to state that in this country no woman convicted of assisting the King's enemies, even found guilty of espionage, has hitherto been subject to a greater penalty than a term of penal servitude.'

After the Marquis de Villalobar's intervention on behalf of Louise Thuliez and Jeanne de Belleville, the King of Spain, Alfonso XIII, asked the Kaiser for clemency to be shown them. In Rome Cardinal Bourne sent a telegram to Cardinal Hartmann, Archbishop of Cologne, requesting him to urge Wilhelm II immediately to postpone and reconsider these executions. In

America, Ambassador Jusserand asked Woodrow Wilson to intercede. A telegram was sent from the President's office to the American Minister in Berlin.

Such bold high-level intervention worked. On 20 October the Kaiser told King Alfonso he granted reprieve to the three condemned to death with Edith Cavell and Philippe Baucq. He requested a full report on the whole affair. Jeanne de Belleville and Louise Thuliez were sent to prison in Siegburg. The chemist Louis Séverin was incarcerated at Rheinbach.

The King, Kaiser, President, Foreign Secretary, Prime Minister, Governor General, Military Governor . . . These were the men who signed the papers that felled cities, sent young men, horses and dogs to die, and ordered ploughs and iron railings to be turned to armaments – or that reprieved lives and agreed peace treaties. No one had asked for their intercession on behalf of Edith Cavell.

Three days after the killing Sister Wilkins collected her matron's things from the St Gilles prison office. The governor allowed release of Edith Cavell's last letters to do with money and administrative matters but kept back the one she had written to her mother, fearing its effect on anti-German propaganda.

Sister Wilkins took the modest parcel to Mme Graux who headed the committee for the new Institute. 'I shall put the parcel as it is in my safe and this afternoon will tell the *conseil d'administration* what has been done,' Mme Graux told her.

Working with the School's accountant Monsieur Lespagnole, Sister Wilkins then drew up an inventory of Edith Cavell's possessions and packed them away. All of them fitted into a trunk and a couple of wooden boxes. Her clothes were practical though there was a silk blouse and a black lace dress. They listed it all: the blue woollen cardigan her mother knitted, which she wore when coal was scarce and she was doing her accounts. It was a 'great comfort', she had told her. 'I often wish you were here at teatime to pour the tea for me.' There were her night clothes and slippers, her bathing suit for holidays, six teaspoons, six dessert-spoons, two soup ladles, one salt cellar, a tea service for six, a box of buttons, a drawing block, a camera, a scent bottle, two brushes, a few hatpins, a cafetière and milk jug, twenty-four paintings and photographs, a clock, a satin handkerchief box, some pieces of porcelain, three wine glasses, 133 books . . .

When this work was done Sister Wilkins made arrangements to get out of Belgium. Her own safety was in question and it was now a benighted place of dark threat and harrowing memory. She had been through too much trauma, grief and fear. A new Belgian matron, Mlle de Meyer, of no interest to the Germans, was appointed in November to head the new School. The President and all members of the committee signed a letter of reference for Sister Wilkins. It spoke of her closeness to Edith Cavell, her rapport with the student nurses and patients, and how circumstances forced her to leave Belgium. She returned to England in November taking Grace Jemmett with her.

As for Jack . . . At first José looked after him and kennelled him in the garden of a house in rue de la Culture, but he howled all the time. Mlle de Meyer then took him, out of respect for Edith Cavell. She tried to keep him shut in her office but he bit the nurses and caused disturbance and the doctors wanted him put down.

Nor did life for Belgium's citizens improve. The occupying army requisitioned everything: cattle, trees, rubber, wool. Even factory machinery was shipped off to Germany. Potatoes became scarce. There were incipient riots in the markets. Impoverished people sold such possessions as they had. Whitlock wrote in his memoir that misery acted on character and made people cruel: 'the herders of the requisitioned cattle – lowing down the rue Belliard – would carelessly beat them over the muzzles with their clubs and the beasts would close their eyes and turn their heads away to escape the pain of those blows.'

What Edith Cavell had called the 'terrible dogs of war' were all unleashed. Battles at Champagne and Loos raged from September to October 1915. Five hundred thousand British soldiers and 250,000 German soldiers died or were injured.

Without a free and responsible press, rumours abounded. In one afternoon Whitlock heard that America had broken off diplomatic relations with Germany, the King of Greece had abdicated, the Crown Prince of Turkey had been put to death because he was pro-Ally, there was revolution in Bulgaria, all Englishwomen in Belgium were to be interned in a camp near Antwerp . . .

Exaggeration of Edith Cavell's activities was just another lie. 'We wait for England,' she had written to her mother in August 1914, believing 'the dear country' would swiftly send these dishonourable invaders home. A year on, and millions of men were slaughtering each other in grotesque carnage. She had helped some hundreds of men cross the border into Holland. About two hundred, she told the tribunal. It was more like fifteen hundred and some carried military information. She became drawn into a resistance network but espionage was not her motivating force. 'We sent the men to her and so did our confederates,' the Princess de Croÿ had said. Edith Cavell had asked her mother for news of some of the men, but not many letters got through. Later findings showed that at most a dozen or so of those she helped fought on.[21]

---

[21] Rowland Ryder, when researching his book *Edith Cavell* (1975), was meticulous at following up the fate of the men on her 'Hotel Register' of guests at the Institute

49

PROPAGANDA

Edith Cavell's execution made headlines in British newspapers from Monday 18 October on. *The Times, Daily Mail, Express, Evening Post, Chronicle* and *Eastern Daily Press* were avid broadcasters of patriotic propaganda. Edith Cavell and Belgium had been violated by Prussian militarism. There was speculation about what 'would befall our womanhood if the German invasion triumphed over our resistance'. Germany was the evil aggressor. Britain, its Empire of conquest forgotten, was the 'crusader for the rights of small nations, for democracy and freedom'. There were calls for those responsible to be tried as war criminals.

'Boche' and 'Hun' became shorthand for goose-stepping, helmeted, monocled sadists who killed blameless Englishwomen. On 21 October, Trafalgar Day, at a service in the Church of St Martin's in the Fields in Trafalgar Square, the Bishop of London whipped up the spirit of vengeance: 'Their foulest and latest crime was the murder in cold blood of a poor defenceless English girl – a crime dwarfing even that of the *Lusitania*. This will settle the matter once and for all about recruiting in Great Britain,' he said. 'What would Nelson have done in such a case as Miss Cavell's murder? He would not have resorted to diplomatic inquiries; he would have made inquiries with the thunder of his fleets and guns.'

Sauberzweig, Stoeber and their military tribunal had overlooked, as they enforced their understanding of justice, the law of unintended consequences. The battlefields were too hideous and deranged to record in detail, but here was a story to seduce the public. This was why each man must fight: to defend an innocent maiden, a nurse and carer. Edith Cavell's death inspired men to join up, brought America closer to joining the war and portrayed the German military as murderers of public servants. Her execution turned into a propaganda scoop for the Allies.

On 20 October Edward Grey warned Longworth Wainwright that Brand Whitlock's report of her trial and execution had been passed to the press. He hoped publication would not cause 'unnecessary pain' to her relatives. The report caused an explosion of eulogy for Edith Cavell and of vitriol for the enemy.

Mrs Cavell was drawn into the furore. Two days previously she had received a warning from the Prince de Croÿ:

17 Hobart Place
Grosvenor Gardens
London
18th Oct. 1915

Dear Mrs Cavell,
I have learned with deep sorrow the terrible news from Brussels. – It was my privilege to know and to visit your daughter often in the latter months. The great and noble work which she undertook with such admirable courage and patriotism has been deeply appreciated by all those who were associated with her; she was ever ready to come to the assistance of those who were suffering through the war. The crime for which she was convicted was Pity and Humanity which in the eyes of the Germans was a crime worthy of death.

May I beg you however to refuse to give any particulars concerning her work on behalf of the soldiers, as anything published now endangers the lives of the many others who are condemned but still unexecuted so far as we know, among whom is my own sister.

At the present moment I am writing in great haste, but I shall be very glad to give you any details in confidence concerning this most unhappy affair.

In deepest sympathy with you in your trouble which is our mutual trouble.

Believe me

Yours very sincerely

Prince Reginald de Croÿ

It was a disturbing letter for an eighty-one-year-old bereaved mother to receive, as unsettling as the one from the Countess de Borchgrave, warning her to watch out for a man with a reddish face and a flower shop in Forest Hill. It made her wonder what she might safely say to anyone, and about the extent of her daughter's undercover work.

MI5 did not want Edith Cavell's name linked to Reginald de Croÿ's, with his high-level military and diplomatic contacts. Documents released into the National Archives in London in 2002 showed how innocent they wanted her to appear: 'The British Military Authorities consider it highly undesirable that anything implicating Miss Cavell in matters of espionage should be published until the final settlement with the Germans has been made irrevocable.'

On the same day as Reginald de Croÿ's letter, Mrs Cavell also received one from Private Arthur Wood. He had survived in a turnip field after his battalion of the Cheshire Regiment was decimated at Mons. He had arrived at Edith Cavell's Nursing School in February 1915 and worked as a ward orderly until she found a guide to lead him to Holland.

'It was with deepest regret that I read of the terrible calamity that overtook your daughter,' he wrote to Mrs Cavell.

You will be surprised to receive this letter from me, a stranger, but had it not been for your daughter, I should undoubtedly have suffered the same fate. I escaped from the Germans after the battle of Mons & was in hiding in the vicinity of that town when I got into communication with your daughter.

It was your daughter who arranged for me to get to Brussels and afterwards to go from there into Holland.

I was hiding in the hospital of which your daughter was the Matron for five days and she treated me as my own Mother would have done and proved herself to be the very best friend I ever had. I am not the only English soldier that your daughter befriended, there are four more in my own Regiment besides the men of the other Regiments she helped.

I can only say she has done a great deal more for her country than most of the men who are in England at present, and although I feel the deepest sympathy for you I am sure you will be proud to have such a heroic daughter.

The letter Edith Cavell wrote the night before she died to console her mother was not passed to her. The military in Brussels said they would pass it to the American Legation if given assurance it would not be published. But they feared its propaganda effect and did not hand it over. Edith Cavell's last request had been for her mother to know her soul was safe. The letter might have been reassurance of abiding love. MI5 obtained photographs of the scene of execution and sent these to Mrs Cavell. 'I have no doubt they will prove to you a sad but precious link to Miss Cavell's memory,' an MI5 officer wrote.

In the press, accounts of Edith Cavell's execution grew lurid: she was shot as she lay in a swoon; she refused to be blindfolded; she was a young English nurse martyred by savages. Prime

Minister Asquith told the House of Commons she had faced a terrible ordeal, worse than the battlefield:

> She has taught the bravest man amongst us the supreme
> lesson of courage. Yes, and in the United Kingdom
> and throughout the Dominions of the Crown there are
> thousands of such women. A year ago we did not know
> it . . . Thank God we have living examples of all the
> qualities which have built up and sustained our Empire.
> Let us be worthy of them and endure to the end.

The objective for the government was to persuade the population to keep on fighting. 'Let Cavell be the battle cry,' the *Daily Graphic* wrote, 'let Cavell battalions be raised, pledged to avenge her.' Readers' letters to the papers were full of ways in which her memory should be avenged: German cities should be destroyed by Edith Cavell battle planes; there should be an Edith Cavell Machine Gun Regiment.

'Remember Edith Cavell' became a recruiting slogan in Britain and France on posters, leaflets and postcards that depicted her being slain. In his war diaries the novelist Rider Haggard wrote on 23 October 1915 that 'Emperor Wilhelm would have done better to lose an entire army corps than to butcher Miss Cavell.' The number of men she had helped to the Dutch border was as nothing compared to those inspired by her execution to enlist. Her death doubled recruitment in Britain from 5,000 to 10,000 a week for eight consecutive weeks – an extra 40,000 recruits. It contributed to public acceptance of military conscription which began on 2 January 1916.

The government changed its policy toward German women spies. 'It is high time we put aside all false sentimentality when it comes to dealing with cases of espionage,' Colonel Vernon Kell, director general of MI5, wrote in a confidential report that

'Who'll avenge Nurse Cavell.' Edith Cavell's photograph used for military recruitment, London 1915

October:

> The employment of women as German spies in this country is on the increase and one must consider the fact that the class of information they can acquire is very often of more value than what the ordinary male spy can obtain.
>
> We cannot afford to jeopardise the lives of our troops. We are dealing with an unscrupulous enemy who apparently do not even require evidence of espionage in order to execute a woman. I am advocating no vindictive methods but in a clear case of female espionage we should not hesitate to apply the full penalty.

'I never thought,' said Fanny Edgecombe, Edith Cavell's friend from the London Hospital, 'that all this would happen to the Edith Cavell we knew.' The propaganda and hyperbole seemed to be about someone else. 'Remember me as a nurse who tried

395

to do her duty,' Edith Cavell had asked. Her vain hope had been for peace and ordinary living to transcend the enmities of nation states.

The British government spent £120,000 a year on disseminating news via Reuters War Service. The agency wired press coverage of the story to Canada, Australia, New Zealand, South Africa, America. Headlines around the world told of Shock and Outrage. 'Intense anger and horror has swept over Great Britain,' reported the *Morning Leader* in Canada on 19 October. 'Execution of Miss Cavell Stuns the World' declared the *Cape Times* in South Africa on the 23rd. 'The Foulest Blot of All' announced the *Star* in Christchurch.

Such headlines stirred more men to offer their lives. 'Murdered by the Huns: Enlist in the 99th and Help Stop Such Atrocities', a Canadian recruitment poster read. 'She gave all: You buy Peace Bonds' was the legend on an Australian poster. At a Sydney recruitment meeting 'thousands stood bareheaded' in tribute to her memory.

In America allegiance to neutrality waned. The *New York Times* wrote, 'Every neutral nation has heard with a shock of horror the news of the execution of Miss Cavell. The World at large prays that Germany's enemies may triumph.' The *Herald* called Germany 'the moral leper of civilisation'. The *Tribune* published a cartoon showing the Kaiser gloating over the body of a woman, a smoking gun in his hand and saying 'Gott mit Uns'. There was praise for the work of Whitlock: 'Miss Cavell was shot in haste as Whitlock pleaded for her life,' the *Tribune* wrote.

Each day brought quantities of mail to Mrs Cavell, though not the letter she wanted. The Bishop of Norwich, Bertram Pollock, called on her in the last week of October. He found her bewildered: 'her little room was strewn with letters and telegrams'. A letter from Queen Alexandra's private secretary conveyed the Queen Mother's 'utmost abhorrence' at the execution and 'how deeply Her Majesty feels for you in the sad and tragic death of your daughter'. The President of the Royal British Nurses' Association wrote, 'Your daughter's heroic death is one which will always remain a lasting memorial to devotion, courage and self-sacrifice and her name will be remembered amongst those heroes who have laid down their lives for this country.' Telegrams from the exiled Belgian government and the Paris Municipal Council conveyed respect, admiration and gratitude from 'the entire population'.

It was all too severe a test for Edith's mother. She was old, her eyes were failing. She wanted her daughter's ordinary quiet presence, loving letters, holidays in West Runton, the rituals of teatime and tending the garden.

The Bishop of Durham, Handley Dunelm,[22] visited her then wrote hyperbolic letters from his palace, Auckland Castle. He promised much: everlasting life for Edith and the Reverend Cavell 'in the presence of the Lord' and a place reserved for her, the Mother.' He told her she reminded him of his own mother, 'a wonderful sheet anchor of faith'. 'I am myself the child (youngest of eight sons) of a country vicarage.' His niece and Edith had been at school together at Miss Gibson's Laurel Court in Peterborough.[23] Edith, the Bishop told Mrs Cavell, was now living 'all light and love' with their 'once suffering heartbroken Saviour'.

> Oh how she *lives* on earth in grateful memory, in Paradise in perfect bliss!! . . . in joy and felicity with Him. And HE is with you. And HIS heart knows *all about grief* and how another day he will turn it all into perfect joy.

[22] Dunelm, the Latin for Durham, was the surname taken by the city's bishops. His real name was Handley Moule
[23] Miss Gibson had offered special terms for the clergy

The Lord JESUS can and will lay His wounded hand on the aching wound of your soul and be your Peace. And ere long He will come and make an end of death.

Maybe Mrs Cavell found consolation in the Bishop's startling epistles. She told him she often found herself talking to a photograph she had of Edith, and how continually it hurt that the last letter Edith wrote to her was kept from her. God, the Bishop claimed, 'knows exactly what the pang is of the cruel keeping of those letters from you. It hurts Him! And He is preparing oh such an "overweight of joy" beyond the veil.'

Edith Cavell's moderate voice was lost in the fallout from her execution, though fighting soldiers mirrored her moderation. 'What a miserable business the Cavell agitation was,' Sergeant-Major Frederic Hillersdon Keeling wrote in a letter home:

I believe a large proportion of the men out here who think at all share my sentiments about it. I have no sympathy with people who want to execrate the whole German nation as much as possible . . . I will not hate Germans to the order of any bloody politician and the first thing I shall do after I am free will be to go to Germany and create all the ties I can with German life . . . When you are lying at rest and hear a bombardment going on you can't help thinking of the poor devils of infantry in the trenches on both sides with sympathy. You are none the worse soldier or fighter for that . . . how one dreams of the end! Of course I don't want peace to be made as things are. The job must be finished off . . . Only let it be a definite well-established peace when it does come. The Prussian monarchy must be smashed but the German people must be given a chance to live an honourable life in the world if they will dissociate themselves from the bloody system of militarism . . .

When I dream of *après la guerre* I just think of the world – this good old cheery ball of earth – as a place of exquisite beauty, adventure, joy, love and experience . . . By God! I can see the scene – before the peace, even during the armistice. The infantrymen will swarm over the parapets of the trenches on both sides and exchange every damned thing they can spare off their persons – down to their buttons and hats and bits of equipment as 'souvenirs'.

Every morning in spring in the front-line trenches I heard the larks singing soon after we stood-to about dawn. But those wretched larks made me more sad than almost anything else out here . . . Their songs are so closely associated in my mind with peaceful summer days in gardens or pleasant landscapes in Blighty. Here one knows that the larks sing at seven and the guns begin at nine or ten . . .

Have been reading Anatole France, Voltaire, and Maupassant while I have been ill . . . Voltaire is one of the great figures of all the ages – his combination of luminous sanity and passion for human rights makes him stand out even among the great. I have always ranked him far above Rousseau.

His dream of *après la guerre* was denied him. He was a writer and Cambridge scholar. He was killed on 18 August 1916, aged thirty.

Luminous sanity, a passion for human rights, the singing of larks, peaceful summer days in gardens, an end to militarism, no hatred of anyone . . . those were thoughts with which Edith Cavell concurred. Her preoccupation was not to be against the Germans but to be for the Belgians. She had always liked 'the Germans'. Her father studied in Heidelberg; she had happy memories of a family holiday there and in St Goar. It was Germans in their capacity of uniformed conquerors of the Belgians whom she despised.

50

GERMAN REACTION

Ordinary citizens in Germany were dismayed at Edith Cavell's killing and the way the German character was portrayed around the world. The *Frankfurter Zeitung* on Sunday 24 October wrote of how the military authority in Brussels 'by the device of classing as espionage deeds of widely varying nature and of twenty different categories, has been able to provide a motive for assassinating twenty times the number of people and maddening two hundred more'. The Kaiser distanced himself from the killing, ordered that no more women be shot without his sanction and after investigation recalled Sauberzweig and had him posted to the Western Front in the north of France. 'Cavell Case Causes Official's Removal' was the story in the *New York Times* for 2 November. Stoeber, the military prosecutor, was also recalled.

German officials in Brussels were humiliated. They banned the sale of the *Rotterdamsche Courant* and other Dutch papers. Von der Lancken blamed Brand Whitlock for disseminating false information. On Monday 25 October, thirteen days after Edith Cavell's execution, he summoned him to the *Politische Abteilung*. It was raining heavily. Whitlock was convalescing: 'The Baron von der Lancken, just back from his morning ride, booted, with his Iron Cross and other ribbons, the white cross of St John on his side, and a large dossier under his arm, received me with a dark, glowering face, and asked me upstairs to his little workroom where a fire was burning.'

He had highlighted passages from *The Times* and *Morning Post* with blue and red pencils. All this, he raged, was based on false information sent out by Whitlock. It made it seem that he, von der Lancken, had broken promises. It was untrue Whitlock had made frequent enquiries on Edith Cavell's behalf. He was in Brussels by courtesy of the German government. His Legation was in service to England, Germany's enemy. He had compromised American neutrality. He must publicly express regret for the press coverage and clear the German authorities from blame. His lawyer, Gaston de Leval, should be dismissed. Arrangements were under way to arrest and deport him . . .

The tirade went on. The Spanish Minister, the Marquis de Villalobar, joined them. Von der Lancken pointed to coverage in the *Graphic*. Villalobar sighed at the photograph of himself in a yachting cap at Cowes taken thirty years previously. Von der Lancken gave Whitlock pencil and paper and commanded him to make a statement, in writing, admitting falsehoods in the published account. Whitlock refused and offered to leave Belgium. 'We talked all afternoon – a terrible afternoon. I was weary and depressed – weary of the long strain, weary of negotiations in French of all accents, and I was still seedy and under the horror of that awful night.' Next day von der Lancken went to discuss the affair in Munich, the Governor General again went to Berlin and Whitlock prepared a report on the whole case for Washington.

Two days later in Brussels a new *affiche* about what had become known as 'the Cavell affair' was posted in public places:

> The United States Ambassador in London has passed papers relating to the Cavell affair to the English Government. These papers include correspondence between the United States Legation in Brussels and the German authorities in that city on the subject of the trial. The English Government immediately gave these documents to the Press and had them published by Reuters Agency.

They reported the most essential facts in an inaccurate manner. They made it appear, especially, that the German authorities had, by false promises, put off the United States Minister and kept him ignorant of the fact that the death sentence had already been pronounced and by proceeding hurriedly with the execution prevented him intervening on behalf of the accused.

Because of these published comments Sir Edward Grey considered it particularly reprehensible that the German authority did not respect its promise to keep the United States Minister informed of the progress of the trial. Such a promise was never given by the German authority which therefore could not have broken its word. The United States Minister in Brussels, in an interview with the German authority, recognised that this was the case. The Ambassador of the United States in London has been misinformed. He has been led into error by the report given by the Belgian lawyer who was legal adviser to the American Legation in Brussels. The United States Minister has now declared that the publication of these documents greatly surprised him and that he would, without delay, apprise his colleague in London and his Government of the difference between the actual facts and the story published in the report written by the Belgian lawyer.

It was calculated to set all mentioned against each other. In this it succeeded. Whitlock made no further public comment. He arranged passports and permits to get de Leval out of Belgium to Holland then England, and within a week was himself 'invited' by Washington to take a vacation in America. 'My journey has no political significance whatever,' he told journalists. *The Times*, on 9 November, reported him as 'looking tired and worn by the responsibilities and anxieties of office'.

To exonerate himself, von der Lancken also maligned Sauber-zweig to the German government. He wrote a complaining letter about him to Albert Zimmermann, the German Undersecretary of State. He said the effect of 'the Cavell case' had been as he predicted to Sauberzweig 'in our nocturnal conversation'. Sauber-zweig, he complained, even after much damaging publicity, went on making high-handed punishing decisions without consul-tation. 'His first consideration is his own self-importance even though precious interests should suffer in consequence. He does not see that no measure taken by the German authorities in Belgium can be an end in itself but must always be a means to an end.'

Zimmermann sided with Sauberzweig. On 25 October he gave an interview to the *New York Times*:

It is a pity Miss Cavell had to be executed but it was necessary. She was judged justly. The shooting of an Englishwoman for treason has caused a sensation and capital against us is being made out of the fact.

It is undoubtedly a terrible thing that the woman had to be executed; but consider what would happen to a State, particularly in war, if it let crimes aimed at the safety of its armies go unpunished because committed by women.

No criminal code in the world makes such a distinction . . . Man and woman are equal before the law and only the degree of guilt makes a difference in the sentence for the crime and its consequences.

Countless Belgian, French and English soldiers again fighting in the ranks of the Allies owe their escape to the activities of the band now found guilty whose head was the Cavell woman. Only the utmost sternness could halt such activity, carried out under the very nose of our authorities, and a Government which in such a case does not resort to the sternest measures sins against its most elementary duty toward the safety of its own army.

Were special consideration shown to women we should open the door to such activities on the part of women who are often more clever in such matters than the cleverest male spy . . .

The story was distorted each time it was told. Only by distortion could justification for State brutality be couched in moral terms. Edith Cavell transmogrified into a spy, the head of an espionage band and of a recruiting agency for soldiers, and all the more clever at her job because she was a woman.

Gottfried Benn, the doctor who sat through the military tribunal and was present at her execution, endorsed Zimmermann's view. He too claimed she was both architect and head of an espionage ring:

> Every movement of the German front was widely known within minutes, you could read it on the faces of the passers-by. Everything we did, every military event behind the front was immediately radioed to the Allies. Above all there was the activity of collecting, recruiting and organising Belgians able to carry weapons, and their transport each night by stages over the Dutch frontier to the centres of the Entente.
>
> Countless espionage trials were conducted by the German military courts every time with the same result: women had been involved. Women had thought up the plans and implemented them but women were never executed. Women were moved to Aachen and made to work in prison and at the end of the war they could count on being rewarded and treated like heroes. Every time the men were found to have been harmless and done the cooking.

The Governor General von Bissing expressed bewilderment at all the fuss: 'When thousands of innocent people have died in the war why should anyone become hysterical over the death of one guilty woman?' he asked. To his cousin he wrote on 23 October that had a pardon been granted it would have been a crime against the Fatherland.

> She ignored military law and through her efforts caused the death of many of our brave soldiers.
> Our enemies regularly cloud the real issues by calling attention to social position or sex when neither is relevant. They are happy to use a woman to work as a spy so that after her execution they can count on the sentimentality of the masses to avenge her.

After he was hurried out of Belgium, the Legation lawyer Gaston de Leval made public his blame of Edith Cavell's defence lawyer Sadi Kirschen. In interviews with the press, and lectures in Britain and the United States, he said he viewed him as negligent and in part responsible for 'the fatal ending of the tragedy'. He implied Kirschen frustrated his attempts to meet him at the time of the court martial and 'paralysed the power of action of the Legation'. In various newspapers Kirschen was then accused of treachery and deceit. A feud began between the two lawyers that went on long after the war's end.

Edith Cavell's hasty execution, within hours of sentence, was at the insistence of General von Sauberzweig out of his hatred for Britain. There was no other reason why she should have been shot and Louise Thuliez and the others spared. His authority might have been checked if von Bissing the Governor General had not been out of the country the night before the execution, if Brand Whitlock had not been ill in bed and had galvanised intervention in the preceding days, if Foreign Office ministers in London had not raised their hands in helplessness and said there was nothing they could do, if Sadi Kirschen had not angered Stoeber and his henchmen, if Thomas Braun or his father had been allowed to defend her, if she had worn her matron's uniform at her trial, if Libiez had spoken out at the tribunal, if von der Lancken had put a call through to the Kaiser. . .

The motive for her judicial murder was political not military. Sauberzweig blocked the chance of appeal by his order that her and Philippe Baucq's executions should be 'immediate'. In the summer of 1916 Herbert Hoover and Vernon Kellogg, who headed American food relief in Belgium, were in Berlin. Sauberzweig asked them to have tea with him at his hotel. They described the meeting to Brand Whitlock who wrote of it in his memoir:

> The General at once entered into a justification of his course in the case of Edith Cavell. He referred to himself, in lugubrious irony, as 'the murderer'; and to her – he was speaking German in which Mr Kellogg was thoroughly proficient – as 'die Cavell'. His explanation, advanced in justification of his conduct, was that Miss Cavell had been at the head of an extensive conspiracy to send young men to the front to kill Germans; his own son had just been the victim of a terrible wound, blinded for life by a bullet that traversed his head just behind the eyes; perhaps, argued von Sauberzweig, the boy had been shot by one of these very young men whom Miss Cavell had aided to reach the front. He said that Miss Cavell was entitled to no sympathy as a nurse since she was paid for her professional services, and that he could not have reversed or altered the judgement of the military court that had tried and sentenced her, without it reflecting on the judgement of his brother officers.

General von Sauberzweig insisted upon discussing the

case much to the embarrassment of his guests, who were of another mind about it, and he gave them the impression of a man haunted by remorse and pursued by some insatiable, irresistible impulse to discuss this subject that seemed to lie so heavily on his mind.

Slaughter continued worldwide. Despite the Kaiser's order that no more women be shot without his sanction, this did not stop the execution of Gabrielle Petit six months after Edith Cavell's death. She had nursed her boyfriend, wounded in the Battle of Antwerp, smuggled him to Holland then forwarded military intelligence to him. She was found guilty of espionage. On the day of her execution she wore a red, yellow and black rosette, refused to have her eyes bound and told her executioners, 'You will see that a Belgian woman knows how to die for her country.' At the time, her death caused no stir. After the war she was revered as a symbol of Belgian resistance. Two months after her, Louise Depache was executed for 'espionage' and helping men escape. Pauline Rameloo, Maria de Smet, Elize Grandprez and Emilie Schatteman followed in 1917.

Before Brand Whitlock took enforced leave in November 1915 a messenger from St Gilles prison delivered to the Legation Edith Cavell's annotated copy of *The Imitation of Christ* and 'a few francs and a few precious trinkets, all her poor little belongings. And yet – how vast, how noble, how rich an estate!' he wrote in his memoirs, in his not-always-helpful way of viewing things. He was away until January 1916. The 'Cavell affair', like the sinking of the *Lusitania*, contributed to America's decision to shift its neutral stance. It joined the war on 6 April 1917. Nineteen months after that the fighting ended.

51

NO MONUMENTS

In Britain she was a national hero. The Edith Cavell War Memorial Committee formed, chaired by Viscount Burnham who owned the *Daily Telegraph*. The Lord Mayor, the Bishop of London and the Chairman of London Council were on its all-male board. Asked by the committee how the family would best like Edith Cavell commemorated, Lilian Wainwright said 'no monuments' and suggested a home for retired nurses. (Edith Cavell had spoken of a plan, when her Brussels work was done, to found such a home with her sister Florence.)It was an irony that more commemorative monuments were raised to her than to any other woman caught up in the First World War.

Sir George Frampton sculpted the one commissioned for central London. The city of Westminster offered a site in St Martin's Place north-east of Trafalgar Square, close to Nelson's Column, the Lions of Victory, and national pride in the glory of conquest. Edith Cavell was to be a lone woman in this setting. Frampton, known for his statue of Peter Pan in Kensington Gardens, took no fee and called it a labour of love. He began work in 1915, though the Italian marble for his ten-foot figure of her, incorporated into a high granite column, was not available until the war's end in November 1918.

He asked Lilian Wainwright for details of Edith Cavell's uniform. She wrote to Elisabeth Wilkins who was back in Wales: 'Was it navy blue? No apron. Stiff collar and cuffs and what sort of belt? Sister Dora cap. Strings or not? If you will, do send me a full description . . . It will take a long time before you feel all right again after the horrors you have been through.'

The monument itself, in modernist mode, was of large stepped blocks of Cornish granite with at the top a solid cross – the Geneva cross of nursing, symbol of help for all – and a woman protecting a naked baby – the Mother Country protecting poor little Belgium. Beneath this FOR KING AND COUNTRY was chiselled large and then, on the four sides of the granite, HUMANITY DEVOTION FORTITUDE SACRIFICE. At the back was a lion – a British lion – 'crushing the serpent of envy, malice, spite and treachery' and above it the words FAITHFUL UNTO DEATH. The white marble figure of Edith Cavell was to face Trafalgar Square, ten feet high, manly, with HUMANITY etched over her head. Beneath her feet were engraved her hour and place of death: EDITH CAVELL DAWN BRUSSELS OCTOBER 12TH 1915.

Her words on the eve of her death – 'I realise that patriotism is not enough. I must have no hatred or bitterness towards anyone' – were initially omitted. They questioned hegemony and the integrity of war.

The family was more enthusiastic about a fund for a retirement home for nurses at Hindhead. The Bishop of Durham sent Mrs Cavell a cheque for three guineas: 'It is miserably small but about a third of my income now goes in taxes,' he told her. This fund developed into a wider charity, 'The Edith Cavell Homes of Rest for Nurses', and was in the tradition of Florence Nightingale and Eva Lückes who advocated better provision for nurses. 'We all turn to the nurse when we are ill. What shall we do for the nurse when she is ill?' its brochure read. Queen Alexandra, its patron, wrote a foreword: 'The name Florence Nightingale is for all time associated with the Crimean War. The martyred figure of Edith Cavell stands forth in this Great War for all that is symbolical of heroism. There can be no more fitting memorial to her than the proposed Edith Cavell Homes of Rest for Nurses.'

On 26 October 1915, two weeks after Edith Cavell's execution, Lord Knutsford, who as Sydney Holland had done much to transform the London Hospital when she nursed there, wrote to Lilian Wainwright from Kneesworth Hall in Royston. Queen Alexandra had sent for him that day and asked that a new nurses' block being built at the Hospital, which was to have been called the Queen Alexandra Home for Nurses, should instead be called after Edith Cavell. 'Do let her mother know this,' Knutsworth wrote. 'I think it just one of the most charming acts I have ever known.'

There was a need among people, that went beyond rank or class, to feel that decent living was again possible and that all the killing and misery were *for* something. So patriotism was ascribed to Edith Cavell, though she had warned against it as a goal with her dying words; heroism was accorded her, though what she had followed was a creed of kindness that cut through cultures; and martyrdom was assigned to her, and though she filled the criteria for it, it was visited upon her. She had not sought it or desired its glory. Her allegiance was far more to those unknown soldiers, martyrs all, who died in fields, unhelped by anyone, and whose only monument was a white cross with the inscription, 'A Soldier of the Great War Known Unto God'.

Affluent patrons subscribed to the Cavell Homes. Appeals in the *Gentlewoman* urged contributors to give as much as they could for one 'who by her martyrdom has achieved an honoured place in the history of the British nation . . . The Foundation of these Homes will provide a permanent National and Imperial Tribute to the Memory of Edith Cavell.'

By mid-1918 five Cavell Homes catered for 400 nurses a year. All were run by women and had long waiting lists. They were tranquil places. Most nurses stayed three or four weeks. The first, for seven nurses, opened at Little Wych near Bridport in June 1917. Miss Florence Way was its matron. It had a sea view and a well-stocked vegetable garden. Coombe Head in Haslemere, Surrey, followed. Both were filled by nurses recuperating from service in French field hospitals. At Raven House near Market Drayton eight nurses at a time found 'a homelike resting-place for tired workers'. Mrs Reginald Corbett, its owner, sold *pot pourri*, made from the garden's roses, at ten shillings a pound to raise funds. 'Every coin spent,' she averred, 'will keep alive the memory of the brave woman, the dream of whose life was to help nurses as should need rest by the way.'

In July 1917 in Swardeston church a stained-glass window was installed showing Edith Cavell as a uniformed nurse praying, the badge of the Red Cross on her sleeve. Her mother was principal guest at the service. Such local homage was an honour, but she was not consoled. Accolades to her daughter came daily through the door. A mountain in western Canada was named after her, another nurses' home in Brighton. 'The sacrifice and heroic work of your beloved Daughter inspired we women of Ontario to do definite work for our Flag and Country,' Alice Zelius-Laidlaw, 'Regent of the Imperial Order of Daughters of the Empire, Edith Cavell Chapter in Canada', wrote to her. But Mrs Cavell did not come to terms with this killing: the last letters undelivered, the Christian burial denied. Nor did she live to see the Armistice in November 1918. She managed in her house in Norwich for two more years after Edith's death, then was cared for by Lilian for the last months of her life at the Wainwrights' house in Henley-on-Thames. She died on 17 June 1918 and was buried in Swardeston graveyard beside her husband, in the village where she had brought up her family.

The Germans refused, while they occupied Belgium, to allow Edith Cavell any sort of burial. Until the war's end her body lay in an unmarked cemetery at the *Tir National* with forty-one others shot for 'treason'.

Fighting along the Western Front continued until November

The return of Belgium's King and Queen

1918. The Armistice at the war's end imposed a dangerous and humiliating defeat on Germany. Its terms required the abdication of Kaiser Wilhelm II; the evacuation of all occupied territory including Alsace-Lorraine, German since 1871; the military evacuation of the western bank of the Rhine and of eastern-bank bridgeheads at Mainz, Coblenz and Cologne; the surrender of their military equipment, all their submarines and much of their fleet; the annulment of various treaties that accorded conquered eastern territories to Germany; the payment of reparation for war damage; and the acceptance of the continuation of the Allied blockade. Such punishment roused the vengeance that erupted in the Second World War. Corporal Hitler, temporarily blinded by a gas attack in a trench at Ypres, called acceptance of defeat 'the greatest villainy of the century'.

The Belgian King and Queen returned to Brussels on 22 November 1918. The Princess de Croÿ was in the crowd that welcomed them. She had been imprisoned at Siegburg, with Jeanne de Belleville and Louise Thuliez, but then was moved to hospitals at Münster and Bonn and watched over by her German relatives, Duchesses and Countesses all. 'The whole boulevard was a seething mass of humanity,' she wrote of that November day:

> roofs and windows were lined with people who filled even the trees. At last we heard distant cheering which grew into a roar as it spread up to us, and a motor-car made its way through the crowd. It stopped just before us and out of it got Burgomaster Max, who was received with wild acclamation. Shortly afterwards he was followed by detachments of all the armies . . . At last a little pause, and, amidst breathless silence, a group of six on horseback came slowly through the waiting streets. Leading was our Soldier King on a white horse with the Queen by his side, both wearing simple khaki. Behind came Prince Leopold and the Duke of York, and lastly, the Count of Flanders and his sister, Princess Marie-José . . .
>
> I had stood up to get a better view, and the emotion which had seized the crowd caught me too. Suddenly what I had taken to be a pillar against which I leant began to shake, and I realised that someone was supporting me. It was a tall French General who stood there, and down whose cheeks the tears were streaming. All around I saw handkerchiefs waving and none were ashamed to give way to the deep emotion and happiness of the moment. Slowly the procession passed out of sight, going towards the Senate, where the King and the Royal Family were received by the Government.

At the Senate, three years previously, Edith Cavell had been convicted of treason. King Albert posthumously awarded her the Cross of the Order of Leopold, the Belgian government awarded her the Croix Civique, the French awarded her the Légion d'honneur.

Britain reclaimed her. An Executive Committee for the Public Funeral of Miss Edith Cavell was formed, with headed paper for correspondence. The Belgian government financed her exhumation. Her body was kept in a tin coffin in a locked room at the *Tir National* until arrangements were finalised. The British Minister in Brussels, Mr Villiers, wrote about her to Lilian Wainwright:

> The features which bear a perfectly calm expression have not suffered decomposition and were identified beyond doubt by two of the Schaerbeek Communal Authorities who knew Miss Cavell by sight.

A hair comb, a collar stud, apparently of gold, and the

Edith Cavell's funeral service, Norwich Cathedral, 14 May 1919

top of a hat pin in light tortoiseshell were found and have been preserved for presentation to you. I shall be glad to learn whether you wish that these should be cleaned or handed to you just as they are.

It seemed Edith Cavell had fulfilled a criterion of sainthood: her body had stayed incorruptible like St Teresa of Avila's in the sixteenth century. The collar stud was duly polished, the hair comb and hatpin cleaned. Florence Cavell and Lilian Wainwright and her husband went over to Brussels in May 1919 as guests of the British Legation, which now had offices there. They visited Edith Cavell's cell at St Gilles prison, which had become a venerated place, with fresh flowers placed in it each Sunday.

On 13 May, escorted by British troops sent from Cologne, her body in an oak coffin with a silver plate inscribed EDITH CAVELL – *Born Dec. 4, 1865. Died Oct. 12, 1915*, was taken on a gun carriage through the crowd-lined streets of Brussels to the Gare du Nord. Her sisters travelled with it. At the station the Reverend Gahan held a service. From Ostend the battleship *Rowena* took her coffin to the naval pier at Dover. Nurses and servicewomen led the procession to the harbour station. Church bells rang for three consecutive hours. Soldiers from the Connaught Rangers guarded her body all night.

A special train left next morning at 7.35 a.m. and arrived at Victoria station at 11.00 Nurses walked in front of the gun carriage in the procession to Westminster Abbey. There was an escort of a hundred soldiers of all ranks, there were military bands, the streets were congested with people. 'No triumphant warrior and no potentate could have received a more impressive tribute than was paid today to the mortal remains of Miss Edith Cavell as they were borne through London,' the *New York Times* wrote next day. The Dean of Westminster conducted the service. The Bishop of London described Edith Cavell as 'that brave woman who deserves a great deal from the British Empire'. The coffin was draped in the Union Jack. There was the twenty-third psalm, the Litany, the Lord's Prayer, the hymn 'Abide with Me', the sounding of the Last Post and Reveille, the playing of Chopin's Funeral March as the cortège left the Abbey.

The family had asked that she be buried in Norwich Cathedral, not Westminster Abbey. The procession passed down the south side of Parliament Square, down Bridge Street, across Victoria Embankment, down Blackfriars, Queen Victoria Street, Mansion House and Broad Street to Liverpool Street station. In it were the Lord Mayor, sheriffs, buglers, soldiers and rows and rows of nurses and women ambulance drivers. Women as citizens were more in evidence than ever. The men in the crowds that lined the pavement took off their hats as the hearse passed by.

A special train left for Norwich at 2.30 p.m. From Norwich station to the cathedral there was another procession, another gun carriage, more nurses, then a service for 'Edith Cavell, a nurse who gave her life for her countrymen', the singing of 'Now the Labourer's Task Is O'er' and 'I Know that My Redeemer Liveth', then by her graveside again 'Abide with Me', the Benediction, the Last Post. Bishop Pollock described her as 'an innocent, unselfish, devout and pretty girl . . . in the very hour of her death she has rebeckoned us to eternal things.' It was a spring evening with lilac in bloom. 'I am so glad you and I had a word with one another by the open grave . . . It was a lovely evening, wasn't it?' he wrote to Lilian Wainwright.

Edith Cavell was buried in the area called Life's Green by the south transept of the cathedral. The Cavell family asked for a plain tomb with a cross, such as was used for fallen soldiers. Her own choice might have been the churchyard at Swardeston beside her mother and father and for a simple service without fanfare or fuss.

A plethora of other monuments was then commissioned

and ceremonially unveiled. By Norwich Cathedral a sculpture by Henry Pegram showed a bronze bust of her on a stone pillar with a soldier holding up a laurel wreath. 'Edith Cavell, Nurse, Patriot and Martyr' the inscription read. In 1919 in Brussels a monument, since destroyed, showed her helping soldiers to escape. In Paris in the Jardin des Tuileries[24] the sculptor Gabriel Pech depicted a young defenceless damsel prone on the ground, shot by a German officer, but about to ascend to heaven. On 15 July 1920, outside the new Nursing School which she had worked so hard to complete, in a ceremony attended by the Queen of Belgium, the Mayor of Uccle unveiled a memorial to her and Marie Depage. It was a sculpture of two semi-naked allegorical figures, one winged, in protective stance. The School was renamed the École Edith Cavell and the street it was in, the rue de Bruxelles, was renamed rue Edith Cavell.

Nor did remembrance stop with monuments. Streets were named after her in Norwich, Brussels, London, Melbourne, Toronto, Port Louis. There were Edith Cavell hospitals in Peterborough, Auckland, Christchurch, Brisbane; schools in Vancouver, British Columbia and New Brunswick; a bridge over the Shotover River near Queenstown; a car park in Peterborough. A feature on the planet Venus was named the Cavell Corona. The French singer Édith Piaf, born two months after the execution, was named after her. There were requests for a yearly 'Cavell Day' to be commemorated throughout the British Empire.

Plaques were put up in places where she had spent any time: at Steeple Bumpstead vicarage, in Peterborough Cathedral. Framed portraits of her were hung in hospitals and public buildings, there were postcards of her, films about her: *The Woman the Germans Shot* in 1918 starring Julia Archer; *Dawn* in 1928

[24] It was destroyed by German bombs in 1940

with Sybil Thorndike;[25] *Nurse Edith Cavell* in 1939 starring Anna Neagle. There was a play, *The Martyrdom of Edith Cavell*, songs about her – 'She Was an Angel of Mercy' was one – biographies of her. At least one locomotive was named after her.

As time passed her significance became bleached. She became the monuments, street names, and hospital wards. She was a heroine, her name synonymous with courage in war.

The London statue was completed in March 1920 then draped in the English and Belgian flags. Unveiling it was a grand event, under a crimson canopy to cover the royals and dignitaries. A large crowd, including nurses from the London Hospital and a delegation from the École Edith Cavell in Brussels, watched Queen Alexandra, the Queen Mother, pull the flags away.

In 1923 the National Council of Women of Great Britain and Ireland, which campaigned for women's rights, asked for Edith Cavell's words about patriotism not being enough to be added to the monument. They said the essence of her had been omitted. They hoped her words might contribute to world peace. They were accused of being pro-German and pacifists.

The following year the first Labour government, with Ramsay MacDonald as Prime Minister, authorised the adding of PATRIOTISM IS NOT ENOUGH. I MUST HAVE NO HATRED OR BITTERNESS FOR ANYONE. The words were etched smaller than the other exhortations on the monument and looked like an afterthought. There were protests. How would it be known the words were Edith Cavell's, not the government's? Sir Lionel Earle, Permanent Undersecretary at the Office of Works, said inverted commas should be added, but this did not happen.

In 1926 in the preface to his play *Saint Joan*, Bernard Shaw commended Edith Cavell as 'another heretic' and said, 'She made it abundantly clear that she would help any fugitive or distressed

---

[25] Ramsay MacDonald feared it would have a bad effect on Anglo-German relations

person without asking whose side he was on, and acknowledging no distinction before Christ between Tommy and Jerry and Pitou the *poilu*.' He reviled the 'moral cowards' who had not from the start inscribed her true sentiment on her statue after 'a modern military Inquisition shot her out of hand'.

Virginia Woolf in her novel *The Years* in 1937 also scorned the way the State used Edith Cavell's statue as propaganda. Her two characters Eleanor and Peggy are in a taxi:

> It stopped dead under a statue: the lights shone on its cadaverous pallor.
>
> 'Always reminds me of an advertisement of sanitary towels,' said Peggy, glancing at the figure of a woman in nurse's uniform holding out her hand.
>
> Eleanor was shocked for a moment . . .
>
> 'The only fine thing that was said in the war,' she said aloud, reading the words cut on the pedestal.
>
> 'It didn't come to much,' said Peggy sharply.

Edith Cavell's soul-searching dying words belied the recruitment call of FOR KING AND COUNTRY – a sentiment that militarised her and commemorated her like a war hero. With her own words added it became a muddle of a statue. Its apex did not know what its plinth was saying.

52

ENDGAME

The 'Cavell affair' rippled on, long after the war's end. Those involved in it sought to exonerate themselves from a stain of wrongdoing, or suggestion they might have done more to save her life. Bitter accusation continued for years between Gaston de Leval and Sadi Kirschen. De Leval went on saying publicly that Kirschen had not kept him informed about what had happened in the military tribunal and had been unavailable on the night of her sentence. Kirschen countered by accusing de

Gaston de Leval (1895–1978), Belgian legal adviser to the American Legation

Leval of triggering a press campaign against him. He said he could have asked at his house and worked out how to meet him.

A month after the war's end, the two men met on Christmas Eve 1918 in the lobbies of the Palais de Justice in Brussels. Kirschen 'gave way to an act of violence' and hit de Leval. He 'assaulted him and used abusive language toward him'. Law suits followed over the next three years. Accusation and counter-accusation. Kirschen accused de Leval of slandering him, making defamatory statements about him to the press and in lectures, of allowing falsehoods to be spread and of 'imperilling the dignity of the Bar Council'. He apologised for his violence but said he had been driven to it and that de Leval presented himself as the only person to have defended Edith Cavell.

Eight appointed lawyers read evidence, listened to explanations from Kirschen, de Leval and their counsels, then gave their verdict at a Bar Council meeting in Brussels on 16 July 1921.

Kirschen's assault, they said, was reprehensible, 'contrary to the dignity of the Bar Council' and deserved 'a disciplinary penalty', but their harsher judgement was for de Leval. His official report, they said, given to the American Legation in Brussels on the day of Edith Cavell's execution, about Kirschen disappearing to the country and not keeping the Legation informed, had started off accusations in France, Britain and the United States about Maître Kirschen's professional honour. He had even been reported to be a German agent, 'betraying the sacred cause which as an Advocate, he had undertaken to defend'.

De Leval, the Council judged, made no serious attempt to meet Kirschen between 8 and 11 October 1915. Kirschen naturally felt indignant at seeing his role 'abominably misrepresented'. Nor did de Leval attempt to correct the false impression he created, rather he compounded it by saying Maître Kirschen's hands 'were stained with the blood of Miss Cavell'. He seemed dazzled by the honour of being 'the real and only defender of

Miss Cavell, and to the present day goes on maintaining M. Kirschen is in part responsible for the fatal ending of the tragedy'.

They said de Leval was the primary cause of the press accusations against Kirschen. De Leval was 'guilty of a breach of the rules of confraternity' and had 'imperilled the dignity of the Bar Council'. Kirschen's 'act of violence', though abhorrent, was 'much reduced in importance by the circumstance of the case'. They ruled that Kirschen should be censured and de Leval reprimanded. Reprimand was the higher punishment. De Leval appealed but to no avail. At a final hearing in Brussels in December 1921 the Bar Council upheld its finding and ordered both sides to share costs.

Extreme injustice led to extreme retaliation and a great deal of hatred and bitterness. Maurice Neels, the young man planted by the secret police in Philippe Baucq's cell to betray him, was hunted down by a Belgian waiter, Louis Brill. Brill followed him and frequently saw him enter the German police headquarters in the boulevard de Berlaimont at night. One night when Neels stepped from his own house into the street Brill shot him and left his body lying on the pavement. For weeks Brill eluded the spies and police, but was then caught, taken before the usual military tribunal and executed in February 1916. Yet another *affiche* was posted up:

> By judgement of February 8 and 9, 1916, the military tribunal has condemned LOUIS BRILL, waiter in a restaurant in Brussels, to the death penalty for assassination committed with firearms. The judgement has been confirmed and executed.
> Brussels, February 11 1916.

Gaston Quien, who betrayed more than twenty resistance workers, including Edith Cavell, into believing he was on their side, went to France at the war's end and was arrested as a traitor and spy. His court martial, before seven judges, began in Paris in August 1919 and lasted two weeks. The Princess de Croÿ and Louise Thuliez – both wearing their Légion d'honneur medals – gave evidence in camera; so did Ada Bodart and Elisabeth Wilkins. She wore her nurse's uniform.

The priest Father Bonsteels testified how he gave Quien a railway map, which showed the latest German modifications, because he believed his claim to be helping Allied soldiers escape. Bonsteels was subsequently arrested and sentenced to twelve years. Mme Bodart testified she had given Quien a package of annotated road maps to give to a Mme Machiel. Questioned, Quien at first denied he had looked to see what was in the package, but later said he knew it contained annotated maps. Cross-questioned, he claimed to be suffering memory loss.

Sister Wilkins, giving evidence, said it was true that when Quien arrived at the School in the guise of a fugitive Allied soldier, he had an ingrowing toenail which prevented him walking far. She did not think it was necessarily his evidence alone that indicted Edith Cavell. The house had been watched before he arrived.

Quien denied all charges. He said he might be a braggart, drunk and thief, but he was not a traitor. He was found guilty by four votes to three and sentenced to death. He appealed, and a petition for clemency signed by some of the judges was sent to the French president Raymond Poincaré. His sentence was commuted to twenty years in gaol and he was sent to Clairvaux prison in north-eastern France.

He was forty when convicted. Throughout his sentence he protested his innocence, maintained mistaken identity and wrongful imprisonment, and pleaded for retrial. Troubled with rheumatism and despised by other prisoners, he found prison life hell. While inside he inherited a lot of money which he could not use. He was released in 1937 after seventeen years. Warders said he had been a model prisoner.

At the time of his trial Pauline Randall was mentioned as having been tricked by him. It was said he plied her with drink in a café, wheedled information from her and then three days later Edith Cavell was arrested. Pauline Randall could not be traced, but the *Daily Mirror* reported a sighting of her at Clacton-on-Sea. She later went to work as a maid to a Dr Broadbent in St Albans and evidently heeded Edith Cavell's advice to say her prayers, for after attending Bible classes in St Albans she 'married' into the Salvation Army. The Army had a rule that required its officers not to marry outside it.

Antoine Depage did not remarry. After the war he was awarded the Légion d'honneur and many other accolades. He presided over the 29th Surgical Congress in France and was only the second non-French surgeon to do so. His surgical work at La Panne influenced international consensus on the treatment of the war-wounded: minimal treatment at the battlefront, rapid transport of casualties to surgical hospitals, the use of debride-ment and excision to avoid gangrene and infection.

In March 1925 he was diagnosed with an intestinal obstruc-tion. He thought he had cancer and underwent surgery with a local anaesthetic so that he could watch the operation in a mirror. The obstruction was a thrombosis which caused his death three months later. He was sixty-three.

Edith Cavell's 'dear old Jack' had a difficult war. Mlle de Meyer, matron of the new school, could not manage him and for months he stayed tethered in a kennel in a nearby garden. He howled non-stop. The Prince de Croÿ's mother, the Dowager Duchess of Croÿ, heard of his misery and offered to look after him at the Bellignies château. Nurses from the new School took him there in March 1916. They could not take him on public transport, so walked with him all the way from Brussels. A relay of nurses met him at different stages. When he arrived at the château he was stiff from months of being chained without exercise and then having to walk so far. He became very ill and maddened and bit the kennel maid and the Dowager Duchess when they tried to come near him. They were patient and persisted in helping him and he got well and, the Dowager Duchess said, 'became as good and gentle as any other dog. He was most attached and loving. But he remained dangerous to strangers.' He had the grounds of the château to explore and he behaved well with the Dowager Duchess's toy spaniels. 'He always was most good and gentle to other dogs. I had him for about seven and a half years, when he died of indigestion caused by old age. He did not suffer, having lost consciousness almost directly. I was extremely sorry to lose him.' After he died in 1923, Jack was stuffed and sent, via Norwich, to the Imperial War Museum in London where he remains on permanent display.

The Prince de Croÿ in August 1919 sailed to America on the Cunarder *Carmania* to take up the post of First Secretary at the Belgian Legation in Washington. He told the *New York Times* he would probably have shared Edith Cavell's fate if he had not been warned in time to leave the country. 'The work of reconstruction and rebuilding commerce and industry in Belgium is proceeding slowly,' he said,

> because we have not received any of the cash indemnity from Germany, and the young men of 20 and 21 years of age do not take kindly to factory life after living in the open for so long. They went into the army as boys and have never done any work before, and now that peace has come, these young men seem to prefer to wander about and smoke their pipes, but they will follow the example of their elders later and settle down, I am confident . . .

The question as to what is to be done with the seven

London Hospital nurses lay a wreath at Edith Cavell's statue in St Martin's Place, London, c. 1960

billion paper marks held by the Belgian Government is still in abeyance, and it is possible the money will be spent in trading with Germany. She was one of the largest producing countries before the war, and if the Allies decline to trade with Germany there is very little prospect of Belgium or any of the Allies receiving payment of the indemnities.

'Let only the right of conquest speak' had been the view of the Governor General Baron Moritz von Bissing. He died in Belgium in April 1917 and after a State funeral was buried in the Invalidenhof Cemetery in Berlin. Among his papers was a memorandum advising that any peace settlement should include the permanent annexation of Belgium to Germany, the exploitation of its resources and industry for German use and the disposal of King Albert and his dynasty, if necessary by death.

The military police officers Sergeant Pinkhoff and Lieutenant

Bergan were rewarded with the Iron Cross second class, for their wartime services to Germany. The Military Governor General von Sauberzweig who hastened Edith Cavell to her death did not live down his shame. Baron von der Lancken, head of the Political Section in occupied Brussels, in his memoirs wrote of her blood being on Sauberzweig's hands and that of his children. When Sauberzweig died, in April 1920, all press coverage of his death mentioned him in connection with the execution of Edith Cavell. Karl-Gustav, his one-eyed son, perhaps blinded, his father had conjectured, by one of the Allied soldiers whom Edith Cavell helped reach the Dutch border, became a Waffen-SS Colonel in the Second World War with a mandate to turn north-eastern Bosnia into an SS vassal state. Imprisoned by the British in 1946, he poisoned himself with cyanide rather than face trial in communist Yugoslavia. Dr Eduard Stoeber, the prosecutor who sent Edith Cavell, Philippe Baucq, Louis Brill and Gabrielle Petit to their deaths, was a senior military prosecutor in Hitler's regime. He died in 1960 aged eighty-eight.

In the Second World War Louise Thuliez and the Princess de Croÿ again resisted German military occupation. Louise Thuliez organised an escape network from the Auvergne district of occupied France. The Princess again sheltered fugitive soldiers at the Bellignies château. She and her chauffeur were arrested. Though beaten unconscious he refused to incriminate her and she was released through lack of evidence. 'Of course we had many of the same experiences as in the last war,' the Princess wrote in November 1946 to Elisabeth Wilkins, who was then matron of the Cottage Hospital in Chard in Somerset. 'We *had* to help our men to get away.'

Edith Cavell too would have done the same again, not in the name of heroism, but out of compassion for those who needed help and with 'sublime indifference' to the tyranny of any brutal regime.

53

REMEMBERED

'I like to look back on the days when we were young and life was fresh and beautiful and the country so desirable and sweet.'

Edith Cavell died when that life had been violated. By her words on the night of 11 October 1915, knowing she was to be shot at dawn, she rose above the squalor of war and injustice: 'Standing as I do in view of God and Eternity I know that patriotism is not enough. I must have no hatred or bitterness for anyone.'

The only medal awarded her was for her work in the Maidstone typhoid epidemic of 1897. The inscription on it, 'For loving services', applied to her life's work. She cherished her own life only in so far as she could use it to make a contribution to a better world. She liked pleasure – country walks, painting watercolours, travel, sea bathing, the company of family and friends – but pleasure was not the principle by which she lived her life. The profession of nursing, she told her probationers in her evening lectures, would lead to 'the widest social reform, the purest philanthropy, the finest humanity'. Good nurses were 'the handmaids of that science which not only assuages and heals the suffering of today, but reaches on, through ever widening circles, to the dawn of perfect manhood when disease shall be unknown, because the laws which scientists discover, and which they help to teach, shall have banished it and taught the world how to live.'

She had hurried back to Brussels when war was declared, not to find a place as a heroine or martyr, but because as a nurse she thought she would be more than ever needed. Circumstance took her to a landscape of violence and grief. She told her nurses, when enemy soldiers marched into the peaceful city of Brussels, that if any of the men were wounded they must be treated. Each was a father, husband or son. As nurses they must take no part in the quarrel. The profession of nursing knew no frontiers.

As a nurse she had seen, she said, suffering, poverty and human wretchedness in the slums of London, 'but nothing I saw there hurts me the way it does to see these proud, gay, happy people, humiliated and deprived of their men, their homes invaded by enemy soldiers that are quartered in them, their businesses ruined. I can only ask myself why oh why should these innocent people be made to suffer like this?' It was not a question she could answer, despite her belief in an interventionist God. But the lack of an answer did not blur her dream of how heaven on earth might some day be achieved. She nursed and served, not for grand redemption in the sky but to make the vicinity in which she found herself a better place. Uniformed soldiers shot her at dawn because they saw, not who she was, but what she represented to them. But they could not destroy her soul, or silence her voice, soft-spoken and clear:

The dusting should be done by ten, nurse.

Are all my things put away safely? With camphor?

Don't buy anything for me. I do very well with what I have. I should be glad to have one of your red blankets, a serviette, cup, fork, spoon and plate – not the best ones – also one or two towels and my toothbrush.

My dear old Jack! Please brush him sometimes and look after him.

There is a little child here of three or four with her mother. She looks pale and pinched for want of air.

I told you devotion would bring its own reward.

There are two sides to war – the glory and the misery. We begin to see both. We shall see the latter more clearly as time goes on.

I am but a looker-on, after all. It is not my country whose soul is desecrated and whose sacred places are laid waste. I can only feel the pity of the stranger within the gates, and admire the courage of a people enduring a long and terrible agony.

My dearest love to you, my darling Mother. I am glad to think of you all safe & I hope well, with the fleet to keep away all harm from the dear country.

I have perhaps sometimes been too strict but never knowingly unjust, and I have loved you all much more than you can know.

You have been very kind my dear and I thank you and the nurses for all you have done for me in the last ten weeks.

Tell my Mother I think my soul is safe.

I have no fear or shrinking. I have seen death so often that it is not strange or fearful to me.

Think of me as a nurse who tried to do her duty.

Please see the nurses going for their exam for the 2nd time in October *study regularly*.

Miss J. owes me (she will remember) a hundred francs. Take it to buy a clock for the entrance hall.

My love to you all. I am not afraid, but quite happy.

Your devoted Matron

Edith Cavell

NOTES AND INDEX

NOTES

Abbreviations

BL	British Library
CNL	Colindale Newspaper Library
IWM	Imperial War Museum
LH	Royal London Hospital Archive
NA	National Archive
NRO	Norfolk Record Office *www.noah.norfolk.gov.uk*
PCL	Peterborough Central Library
RMA	Ruth Moore Archive
SA	Swardeston Archive

PART ONE

I BIRTH

3 Edith Cavell was born . . . *see* marriage and burial registers for Reverend Cavell's ministry (SA). And papers of the Cavell family (NRO). And William White, *History, Gazetteer and Directory of Norfolk*, 1845. And, *Norfolk, A General History*, vol. 2, 1829

4 the front bedroom of the eighteenth-century farmhouse . . . Now called Cavell House (SA)

– even at the risk . . . Florence Nightingale, *Notes on Nursing: What it is and What it is Not*, 1859

5 the antiseptic principle . . . Joseph Lister, 'On the Antiseptic Principle in the Practice of Surgery', *Lancet* 2:353–6, 668–9 (1867)

6 Thy desire shall be . . . Genesis 3: 16

– The presence of a young female . . . Statement issued by male doctors at the Middlesex Hospital in 1863

7 The 60-foot-high tower . . . Simon Knott, *www.norfolkchurches. co.uk*

3 GROWING UP

14 life was fresh and beautiful . . . letter from Edith Cavell to her
    cousin Eddy Cavell, 11 March 1915, quoted in Helen Judson, *Edith
    Cavell*, 1941
17 I'd love to have you visit . . . ibid.
18 having deviated . . . William White, *History, Gazetteer and
    Directory of Norfolk,* 1845 poor lunatics . . . ibid. the operation for
    the *stone* . . . ibid.

4 SCHOOL

21 They are obliged to profess . . . Emily Davies in evidence to the
    1867–8 Schools Inquiry Commission. Quoted in Kathryn Hughes,
    The Victorian Governess, 1993
22 a high moral training . . . *Peterborough Advertiser*, 1884 (PCL)
24 an album of drawings . . . Claire Daunton, *Edith Cavell Her Life
    and Her Art,* 1990 (LH)

5 THE ENGLISH GOVERNESS

26 A private governess . . . Charlotte Bronte to her sister Emily, 8 June
    1839. Kathryn Hughes. And, Jane Austen, *Emma*, 1815

6 A GERMAN SUMMER

29 She went in a party . . . Diary of Alice Burne (SA)

7 THE BELGIAN GOVERNESS

36 It was an intelligent way . . . A. E. Clark-Kennedy, *Edith Cavell*,
    1965
—   A dog soon reciprocates . . . 'Nurse Cavell Dog Lover' facsimile,
    with an introduction by Rowland Jones, 1934
38 Being a governess . . . Helen Judson
41 Among articles about clauses . . . Norwich Union Insurance
    Company in-house magazine (BL)

PART TWO

8 NO HOSPITAL TRAINING

45   too old, too weak . . . Florence Nightingale, *Notes on Nursing*

46   If a patient is cold . . . ibid.

49   I have had no hospital . . . Z/1/CAVELL (LH)

9 THE FEVER NURSE

51   The infectious diseases . . . W. H. Bradley, *Notifiable Infectious Diseases,* quoted in Gwendoline Ayers, *England's First State Hospitals and the Metropolitan Asylums Board 1867–1930*, 1971

52   the sewer king . . . G. C. Cook, 'Joseph William Bazalgette', *Journal of Medical Biography*, 1999

57   known Edith Cavill . . . Z/1/CAVELL (LH)

10 THE PROBATIONER

58   the London Hospital . . . A. E. Clark-Kennedy, *The London: A Study in the Voluntary Hospital System*, 1963

61   There was only one operating theatre . . . Viscount Knutsford, *In Black and White*, 1926

64   You have chosen a profession . . . Eva Lückes, lecture to probationers, 1892. And, Eva Lückes, *General Nursing*, 1914. And Matron's annual letters to nurses, 1896–1915 N/7/1/3–23 (LH)

65   Thomas à Kempis, *The Imitation of Christ*, Edith Cavell's annotated edition, *http://onlinebooks.library.upenn.edu/webbin/book/ lookupid?key=*olbp41475

66   Be careful not to get into the habit . . . Eva Lückes, lecture to probationers, 1892 (LH)

–   for amputations . . . Eva Lückes, lecture VII (LH)

–   You have to fight . . . Eva Lückes, lecture XII (LH)

67   the elephant man, Frederick Treves, *The Elephant Man and Other Reminiscences*, 1923

–   one of the ablest . . . Frederick Treves, 'Tribute to a Great Woman', *London Hospital Gazette,* xxii, 1918

68   Edith Cavell wrote her notes . . . CI/1/1(LH)

70   If thou canst hold . . . *The Imitation of Christ*

– Edith Cavell had a self-sufficient manner . . . Eva Lückes, Register of Sisters and Nurses, N/5/4 (LH)

11 MAIDSTONE

72 Nearly half the houses . . . *Borough of Maidstone, Epidemic of Typhoid Fever, 1897* HMSO 1898 (BL)

73 through mischance . . . ibid.

12 BACK TO THE LONDON

76 the most magnificent operating . . . *The Nursing Record and Hospital World*, 22 July 1899

77 Edith Cavell had plenty . . . Eva Lückes, Register N/5 (LH)

79 Amelia Brandon was big . . . N/5 (LH). And following

13 MELLISH WARD

81 a smart sister, her nursing instincts . . . Eva Lückes, Register of Sisters and Nurses, No. 1, p. 222, N/5/4 (LH)

83 very self-opinionated . . . N/5/4 (LH)

84 struck up one of those . . . ibid.

85 Edith Cavell is not a success . . . N/4/1(LH)

14 THE INFIRMARIES

88 Gathorne Hardy Act . . . see Gwendoline Ayers, *England's First State Hospitals and the Metropolitan Asylums Board 1867–1930*

91 You will have heard . . . 2 July 1901, Matron's Correspondence, N/7(1) (LH)

92 You will I think be pleased . . . 5 November 1903, Matron's Correspondence, N/7(2) (LH)

93 I knew her . . . quoted in Helen Judson, *Edith Cavell*

94 What is she like . . . quoted in Rowland Ryder, *Edith Cavell* fresh and more suitable testimonial . . . 7 October 1904, Matron's Correspondence, N/7 (3) (LH)

95 Will you forgive me . . . Matron's Correspondence, N/7(4) (LH)

15 A HOLIDAY

97 She was very apologetic . . . N/4/1 (LH)

98   felt refreshed after . . . Matron's Correspondence, N/7(5)(LH)

–   What a great bond . . . 13 September 1906, Matron's
Correspondence, N/7(5) (LH)

99   I was asked to account . . . ibid.

–   I feel it rather . . . N/7(6) (LH)

101   Until the present . . . June 1907, N/7(7) (LH)

PART THREE

16 SETTING UP

105   Will it weary you . . . N/7(8) (LH)

109   Monsieur Depage was quite unable . . . 26 December 1907,
N/7(12) (LH)

111   three Dutch nurses . . . N/7(9) (LH). And following passing the
male catheter . . . 27 October 1907, N/7(10) (LH)

112   They go into the kitchen . . . 2 December 1907, N/7(11) (LH)

17 THE SCHOOL GOES ON

114   The contrast which they present . . . Edith Cavell, article in
Nursing Mirror and Midwives' Journal, 30 April 1907 (CNL)

116   to lie on one's bed . . . Ruth Moore, 'Nursing in Brussels'
(unpublished MS) (RMA). And 'Memories of Edith Cavell',
Nursing Mirror, 10 October 1942 (CNL)

117   I was very glad to take her . . . 7 January 1908, N/7(13) (LH)

119   Such difficulties are unavoidable . . . quoted in A. A. Hoehling,
Edith Cavell, 1958

–   not a good nurse and still less . . . 9 September 1908, N/7(14) (LH)

120   The patient is a woman . . . 24 November 1908, N/7(19) (LH)

–   A Dr Pierart asked . . . 24 October 1908, N/7(17)(LH)

–   Sister Evans – in every way devoted . . . 17 November 1908,
N/7(18) (LH)

121   Among the things that a nurse must learn . . . Armand Colard,
'Edelweiss – Les Amis de l'École Edith Cavell, Marie Depage',
Imprimerie Weissenbruch, Bruxelles, 1954. Quoted in Clark-
Kennedy, *Edith Cavell*

123   When I came in 1910 . . . Jacqueline van Til, *With Edith Cavell in
Belgium*, New York, 1922

Time', *The Nursing Mirror and Midwives' Journal*, 22 August 1914 (CNL)

157   We have just heard . . . ibid.

159   After the period . . . *Nursing Mirror*, 24 April 1915 (CNL)

160   They will only walk through . . . EC to her mother, 17 August 1914. Quoted in Clark-Kennedy, *Edith Cavell*

–   but it did not need . . . Edith Cavell, 'Brussels Under the German Rule', *Nursing Mirror,* 24 April 1915 (CNL)

161   My dearest Mother and my dear Ones . . . Edith Cavell to her mother, 19 August 1914. Quoted in Clark-Kennedy, *Edith Cavell*

–   I shall never forget . . . *With Edith Cavell in Belgium*

–   In the evening came the news . . . 'Brussels Under the German Rule' (CNL)

163   We were divided . . . ibid.

22 OCCUPATION

164   There are two sides to war . . . Edith Cavell, 'Nursing in War Time' (CNL)

166   He went to battles as an office-boy . . . Brand Whitlock, *Belgium Under the German Occupation*, 1919

–   It is the hard necessity . . . ibid.

167   give anything for an English . . . EC1(4) (IWM)

–   My darling Edith, It is almost . . . EC4(1) (IWM)

168   I hope news of the safety . . . EC2(4) (IWM)

169   I often saw . . . Ruth Moore, 'Nursing in Brussels', *Nursing Mirror*, 9 October 1975 (RMA)

173   no gaieties of any sort . . . 'Brussels Under the German Rule'(CNL)

–   You would think every day . . . Edith Cavell to her mother, EC2(8) (IWM)

23 THE LOST CHILDREN

177   Harry Beaumont was a private . . . Harry Beaumont, *Old Contemptible*, 1967

178   We had faith . . . ibid.

183   Boger had a temperature . . . statement from Mrs Millicent Battram (Sister White), 5 October 1970 (SA)

24 YORC

187 Nothing can describe . . . Princess Marie de Croÿ, *War Memories*, 1932
188 As soon as they are well . . . ibid.
192 The Countess was French . . . Louise Thuliez, *Condemned to Death*, 1934
194 Late in the afternoon . . . *Old Contemptible*

25 MY DARLING MOTHER

197 We are all well . . . EC2(5) (IWM)
198 All my thoughts . . . William J. Philpott, 'The strategic ideas of Sir John French', *Journal of Strategic Studies*, vol. 12, issue 4 December 1989
199 a bulletin of patriotic . . . Oscar E. Millard, *Uncensored: the true story of the clandestine newspaper 'La Libre Belgique'*, 1938
200 I have written to you on every . . . EC2(6) (IWM)
201 Dearest Flor . . . EC2(7) (IWM)
202 I am afraid you must . . . EC to her mother, 19 October 1914, EC2(9) (IWM)
203 I seize every opportunity . . . EC2(15) (IWM)
206 a man whose name . . . Brand Whitlock, *Belgium Under the German Occupation*, vol. I
207 She had to walk . . . 'Nursing in Brussels' (RMA)
209 My darling Mother, I take another . . . EC2(17) (IWM)

26 THE MEN WHO DIED IN SWATHES

211 The British Empire is fighting . . . Lord Kitchener, speech at the Guildhall, 9 November 1914
213 People think it is mud and wet we mind . . . Corporal James Parr, 16th London Regiment, to his family, 20 March 1916. From *War Letters of Fallen Englishmen*, ed. Laurence Housman, 1930
– Perhaps you don't know . . . Lieutenant Barnett, Leinster Regiment, 31 December 1914. *War Letters*
– As for the morals of the war . . . Captain John Crombie, Gordon Highlanders, 2 March 1917. *War Letters*

214 I have only had my boots off . . . Captain Julian Grenfell, 1st Royal
Dragoons, 24 October 1914. *War Letters*

– Oh the smell of the cows . . . Lieutenant William Grenfell, The
Rifle Brigade, 25 May 1915. *War Letters*

– Do you think that the experience . . . Lieutenant Horace Fletcher,
Royal Welch Fusiliers, early 1916. *War Letters*

216 The suffering of men at the Front . . . Captain William Mason,
Gloucestershire Regiment, autumn 1915. *War Letters*

– The road thirty yards behind us . . . Lieutenant-Colonel John
McCrae, Canadian Army Medical Service, 17 May 1915. *A Memoir
of John McCrae*, ed. Andrew Macphail

– Any faith in religion . . . Lieutenant Peter Layard, Suffolk
Regiment, March 1916. *Memoir of P. C. Layard*. Quoted in *War
Letters*

– If I live . . . Captain Thomas Kettle, Royal Dublin Fusiliers, July
1916. *War Letters*

217 It is VILE . . . Brigadier-General Philip Howele, 4th Hussars, 3
November 1914. *War Letters*

218 The wide debridement. Thomas Helling and Emmanuel Daon, 'In
Flanders Fields: the Great War, Antoine Depage and the
Resurgence of Debridement', *Annals of Surgery*, vol. 228, no. 2,
1998

27 CHRISTMAS 1914

219 Just returned to billets again . . . Captain Sir Edward Westrow
Hulse, Scots Guards, 28 December 1914. *War Letters*

224 I have a beautiful bunch of chrysanthemums . . . EC to her
mother, 22 December 1914, EC2 (16)(IWM)

– Two of them, Sergeant Jesse Tunmore . . . 'A Statement of my
Escape' (NRO)

225 I realise perhaps better than anyone . . . Cardinal Mercier;
pastorals, letters, allocutions, 1914–1917 www.archive.org/
cardinalmercier

227 What do you think of these brave people . . . EC to her mother,
EC2(16) (IWM) a huge bouquet . . . Ruth Moore, 'Memories of
Edith Cavell', *Nursing Mirror*, 10 October 1942 (RMA)

28 ORGANISATION

229   I am keeping a record . . . Edith Cavell to her mother, EC2 (4).
      And Edith Cavell's diary, EC1(1) (IWM)
230   People are wonderfully generous . . . Edith Cavell's diary, August
      1915, EC1 (IWM)

29 THE MEN SHE HELPED

240   I am writing to you to say . . . 20 January 1915, quoted in Rowland
      Ryder, *Edith Cavell*
241   acute mania . . . G. Tunmore to Mrs Cavell, 15 February 1915
      EC4(3) (IWM)
243   It is with kind permission . . . February 1915, quoted in Rowland
      Ryder
  –   Referring to it being risky . . . ibid.
247   My dear Eddy . . . 11 March 1915 (SA)
248   All is very quiet . . . EC2(18) (IWM)
250   We must foresee . . . *New York Times*, 18 April 1915
252   tell all the helpers . . . Marie de Croÿ, *War Memories*

30 WATCHED

253   There was something degrading . . . Brand Whitlock, *Belgium
      Under the German Occupation*
259   Very many happy returns . . . EC2(19) (IWM)
261   I sat in her little sitting room . . . *War Memories*

31 ARREST

266   I have had a message from Brussels . . . Ruth de Borchgrave to Mrs
      Cavell, 28 July 1915 (SA)
268   Where is your husband . . . Louise Thuliez, *Condemned to Death*
270   Pauline Randall went for a walk . . . (SA)
272   On Aug. 5th 1915 . . . Ambroise Got, *The Case of Miss Cavell*
      German documents of the trial. And '151 pages of diverse origin
      covering the trial and execution' EC10(1) (IWM)
  –   I refused to admit anything . . . Elisabeth Wilkins, unpublished
      notes (SA).
      And EC(1) (IWM). And Helen Judson, *Edith Cavell*

273 My dearest Grace . . . EC2(20) (IWM)

275 We felt as though . . . *With Edith Cavell in Belgium*

PART FIVE

32 FIRST INTERROGATION

281 No not 5,000 . . . Ambroise Got, *The Case of Miss Cavell*

282 wild and implacable . . . Brand Whitlock, *Belgium Under the German Occupation*

283 I lay particular stress . . . Got, *The Case of Miss Cavell*

286 All our suppositions . . . ibid.

–   My statements . . . . ibid.

33 BETWEEN INTERROGATIONS

289 Prisoners must obey . . . quoted in Louise Thuliez, *Condemned to Death*

291 the whole caboodle . . . quoted as interview in Rowland Ryder, *Edith Cavell*

34 THE OTHERS

295 In the circumstances . . . *Condemned to Death*

297 the scum and offscouring . . . *Belgium Under the German Occupation*

–   on a day in late August . . . *War Memories*

35 THE ESCAPE OF THE PRINCE DE CROŸ

299 A Flemish workman . . . *War Memories*

301 THE SECOND INTERROGATION

261 In this second deposition . . . *The Case of Miss Cavell.* And official German documents concerning Edith Cavell: bound volume of papers from August–December 1915 (151 pp.) EC10(1) (IWM)

303 She had blue eyes . . . *Condemned to Death*

41 SATURDAY 9 OCTOBER

346 the Imperial Military Decree . . . *Armee-Verordnungsblatt*, 2 August
1914, paras. 11–15 EC(13) (IWM)
347 From their own statements . . . EC(10) (IWM)
348 very grateful for any . . . FO 383/15 (NA)
–   Thou that rulest . . . *The Imitation of Christ*

42 SUNDAY 10 OCTOBER

350 That's only the usual . . . *Belgium Under the German Occupation*

43 MONDAY 11 OCTOBER: DAY

352 his cheeks flushed . . . G. Hostelet, 'The Story of Nurse Cavell's
Trial', *Nineteenth Century and After*, LXXXV
–   It is useless . . . *Condemned to Death*
353 We had so much . . . ibid.
354 I deem that the interests . . . EC(10) (IWM)
–   It was intolerably difficult . . . Letter from Pastor Le Seur, *Cassell's
Magazine*, no. 1970198 (1928)

44 MONDAY 11 OCTOBER: EVENING

356 I went at once . . . *Belgium Under the German Occupation*. And
FO383/15 (NA)
358 I have just heard that Miss Cavell . . . *Belgium Under the German
Occupation*. And following
359 Miss Cavell's trial . . . FO 383/15 (NA)

45 MONDAY 11 OCTOBER: NIGHT

362 What is it, gentlemen . . . *Belgium Under the German Occupation*
364 Von der Lancken was deaf . . . *Notes and Queries*, 28 March 1931
366 But it was worse to go . . . *Belgium Under the German
Occupation*

46 WHAT WAS LEFT OF THE NIGHT

367 My dear nurses, It is a very sad . . . EC2(24) (IWM) and CI/1/4
(LH)
370 If it be Thy will . . . *The Imitation of Christ*

372 like a solemn fast . . . Report by H. Stirling T. Gahan, British Chaplain in Brussels, in *Belgium Under the German Occupation*

373 Abide With Me . . . Words: Henry F. Lyte, 1847. Music: William H. Monk, 1861

– My dear Sister, Mr Gahan will give you . . . EC2(25) (IWM)

375 Arrested 5 August 1915 . . . CI/1/5 (LH)

47 TUESDAY 12 OCTOBER: DAY

378 What I saw was terrible . . . *Cassell's Magazine*, 1928

– She went to her death . . . Gottfried Benn, 'How Miss Cavell was executed: the report of an eye-witness'

PART SIX

48 THE REMAINS OF THE DAY AND THE FOLLOWING DAYS

381 By judgement of . . . *Belgium Under the German Occupation*

382 We argued why . . . *Condemned to Death*

383 Your letter of September 23 . . . *Belgium Under the German Occupation*

– I know that you will understand . . . ibid.

385 as well as all other persons . . . ibid.

386 Forgive my worrying . . . FO 383/15 (NA)

– Deeply regret to inform . . . EC5(2) (IWM)

387 I shall put the parcel . . . 17 November 1915 (SA) and CI/3(iii) (LH)

– an inventory of Edith Cavell's possessions . . . EC8(4) (IWM)

388 letter of reference . . . 25 November 1915, CI/1/3(iv) (LH)

49 PROPAGANDA

390 Their foulest and latest crime . . . October 1915, quoted in E. Protheroe, *A Noble Woman: the life story of Edith Cavell*, 1916

391 Dear Mrs Cavell, I have learned . . . EC4(5) (IWM)

392 The British Military Authorities . . . Baron to Bruce, 25 January 1919, PRO KV2/822/844 (NA)

– It was with deepest regret . . . quoted in Rowland Ryder, *Edith Cavell*

394 She has taught the bravest . . . *A Noble Woman*

– Let Cavell be the battle cry . . . quoted in Katie Pickles, *Transnational Outrage: the death and commemoration of Edith Cavell*, 2007

– In his war diaries . . . The Private Diaries of H. Rider Haggard, 1914–25

– Colonel Vernon Kell . . . (SA) and FO/383 (NA)

396 Every neutral nation . . . *Transnational Outrage*

397 utmost abhorrence . . . Rowland Grant to Mrs Cavell, 18 October 1915, EC4(6) (IWM)

– Your daughter's heroic death . . . EC4(8) (IWM)

– Telegrams from the exiled . . . EC4(7) (IWM) all light and love . . . and following. Fourteen letters from the Bishop of Durham to Mrs Cavell, 25 October 1915 to 7 October 1917, EC4(10) (IWM)

398 What a miserable business the Cavell . . . 23 December 1915. F. H. Keeling, *Letters and Recollections*, 1918

50 GERMAN REACTION

401 The Baron von der Lancken, just back . . . *Belgium Under the German Occupation*

402 The United States Ambassador . . . EC(10) (IWM)

404 His first consideration . . . Ambroise Got, *The Case of Miss Cavell*

– It is a pity . . . Charles F. Horne, ed., 'Source records of the Great War', vol. III, National Alumni, 1923

406 When thousands of innocent . . . *The Times History of the War*, vol. VI, 1916

– She ignored military law . . . quoted in A.A. Hoehling, *Edith Cavell*

407 The General at once entered . . . *Belgium Under the German Occupation*

51 NO MONUMENTS

409 Was it navy blue? . . . . 2 November 1915 (SA). And CI/1/3(v) (LH)

411 Do let her mother know . . . EC7(15) (IWM)

412 The sacrifice and heroic . . . quoted in *Transnational Outrage*

413 The Armistice at the war's end . . . see John Keegan, *The First World War*

414 The whole boulevard was a seething . . . *War Memories*

415 The features which bear . . . 19 March 1919, EC7(5) (IWM)

417 I am so glad you and I . . . Bishop of Norwich to Lilian
     Wainwright, 19 May 1919, EC(9) (IWM)

420 It stopped dead under a statue . . . Virginia Woolf, *The Years*, 1937

52 ENDGAME

422 Kirschen gave way to an act of violence . . . EC(10) (IWM)

425 but the *Daily Mirror* . . . 5 September 1919 (SA)

426 He always was most good and gentle . . . *War Memories*

 –   The work of reconstruction . . . *New York Times*, 28 August 1919

BOOKS AND ELECTRONIC SOURCES

GENERAL

Jack Batten, *Silent in an Evil Time,* 2007

Noel Boston, *The Dutiful Edith Cavell,* 14pp., 1976

Gordon Brown, *Courage: Eight Portraits,* 2007

Edith Cavell website www.edithcavell.org.uk

Jonathan Evans, *Edith Cavell,* 50pp., 2008

Elizabeth Grey, *Friend Within the Gates,* 1961

A. E. Clark-Kennedy, *Edith Cavell,* 1965

A. A. Hoehling, *Edith Cavell,* 1958

Helen Judson, *Edith Cavell,* 1941

Thomas à Kempis, *The Imitation of Christ,* Edith Cavell's annotated
     edition, http://onlinebooks.library.upenn.edu/webbin/book/
     lookupid?key=olbp41475

Katie Pickles, *Transnational Outrage: the death and commemoration of
     Edith Cavell,* 2007

E. Protheroe, *A Noble Woman: the life story of Edith Cavell,* 1916

Rowland Ryder, *Edith Cavell,* 1975

Iain Sinclair, ed., *London: City of Disappearances,* 2006

Virginia Woolf, *The Years,* 1937

www.worldwar1.com/heritage/e_cavell.htm

http://www.geuzen.org/female_icons/?p=504

EARLY YEARS

Louisa Alcott, *Little Women,* 1868

Jane Austen, *Emma,* 1815

A. D. Bayne, *Comprehensive History of Norwich,*1869

Ruth Brandon, *Other People's Daughters: the Life and Times of the
     Governess,* 2008

Owen Chadwick, *The Victorian Church,* two vols, 1970; *Victorian Miniature,* 1960

Charles Darwin, *On the Origin of Species,* 1859

Charles Dickens, *Hard Times,* 1853; *Martin Chuzzlewit,* 1842

Benjamin Disraeli, *Sybil,* 1845

Claire Daunton, *Edith Cavell: Her Life and Her Art,* 1990

Kathryn Hughes, *The Victorian Governess,* 1993

Rowland Jones, ed., 'Nurse Cavell Dog Lover' facsimile, 1934

David H. Kennet, *Norfolk Villages,* 1980

Simon Knott, www.norfolkchurches.co.uk

Norfolk, A General History, vol. 2, 1829

Liza Picard, *Victorian London: the Life of a City 1840–1870,* 2005

Mrs Humphry Ward, *Robert Elsmere,* 1880

Jerry White, *London in the Nineteenth Century,* 2007

William White, *History, Gazetteer and Directory of Norfolk,* 1845

NURSING

Brian Abel-Smith, *A History of the Nursing Profession,* 1960

Gwendoline Ayers, *England's First State Hospitals and the Metropolitan Asylums Board 1867–1930,* 1971

Charles Booth, *Life and Labour of the People in London, 1902*

Borough of Maidstone, Epidemic of Typhoid Fever, 1897, HMSO, 1898

Margaret E. Broadley, *Patients Come First: Nursing at 'The London' Between the Two World Wars,* 1980

Fleetwood Churchill, *Manual for Midwives,* 1856

A. E. Clark-Kennedy, *The London: A Study in the Voluntary Hospital System,* two vols, 1963; *London Pride: the Story of a Voluntary Hospital,* 1979

G. C. Cook, 'Joseph William Bazalgette', *Journal of Medical Biography,* 1999

Viscount Knutsford, *In Black and White,* 1926

The London Hospital Illustrated, 1990

Eva Lückes, *General Nursing,* 1914; *Hospital Sisters and their Duties,* 1893

Florence Nightingale, *Notes on Nursing: What it is and What it is Not,* 1859

Henry Sessions Soutar, *A Surgeon in Belgium,* 2006

Frederick Treves, *The Elephant Man and Other Reminiscences,* 1923

Louisa Twining, *Recollections of Workhouse Visiting,* 1880

WAR

George Adam, *Treason and Tragedy: an account of French war trials,* 1929

Harry Beaumont, *Old Contemptible,* 1967

James Cameron, *1914,* London, 1959

Princess Marie de Croÿ, *War Memories,* 1932

Martin Marix Evans, *Over the Top: Great Battles of the First World War,* 2002

Niall Ferguson, *1914: Why the World Went to War,* 1998

Martin Gilbert, *The Routledge Atlas of the First World War,* 1994

Ambroise Got, *The Case of Miss Cavell.* German documents of the trial, 1918

Robert Graves, *Goodbye to All That,* 1929

The Private Diaries of H. Rider Haggard, 1914–1925

C. Haste, *Keep the Home Fires Burning: Propaganda in the First World War,* 1977

Thomas Helling and Emmanuel Daon, 'In Flanders Fields: the Great War, Antoine Depage and the Resurgence of Debridement', *Annals of Surgery,* vol. 228, no. 2, 1998

Charles F. Horne, ed., 'Source records of the Great War', vol. III, National Alumni, 1923

Laurence Housman, ed., *War Letters of Fallen Englishmen,* 1930

F. H. Keeling, *Letters and Recollections,* 1918

John Keegan, *The First World War,* 1999; *The Face of Battle,* 1976

Ian Kershaw, *Hitler, 1889–1936: Hubris,* 1998

Albert Libiez, *L'Affaire Cavell,* 1922

Lyn Macdonald, *The Roses of No Man's Land,* 1980

Andrew Macphail, ed., *A Memoir of John McCrae,*

Cardinal Mercier; pastorals, letters, allocutions, 1914–1917, www.archive.org/cardinalmercier

Oscar E. Millard, *Uncensored: the true story of the clandestine newspaper 'La Libre Belgique'*, 1938

William J. Philpott, 'The strategic ideas of Sir John French', *Journal of Strategic Studies*, vol. 12, Issue 4, December 1989

T. Proctor, *Female Intelligence: Women and Espionage in the First World War*, 2003

Erich Maria Remarque, *All Quiet on the Western Front*, 1929

Bernard Shaw, *St Joan*, 1926

David Stevenson, *1914–1918: The History of the First World War*, 2004

Hew Strachan, *The Oxford Illustrated History of the First World War*, 1998

Louise Thuliez, *Condemned to Death*, 1934

Jacqueline van Til, *With Edith Cavell in Belgium*, New York, 1922

The Times History of the First World War

Peter Vansittart, *Voices from the Great War*, 1981

Brand Whitlock, *Belgium Under the German Occupation*, 2 vols, 1919

www.firstworldwar.com/bio/cavell.htm

ACKNOWLEDGEMENTS

All quotes are credited in 'Notes'. Source material for Edith Cavell is scattered. The main archives I have used are:

Royal London Hospital
Register of probationers no.5 LH/N/1/5
Private nursing staff register no.4 LH/N/5/4 fcf
Register of sisters and nurses no.1 LH/N/4/1
Matron's annual letters to nurses 1896–1915 LH/N/7/1/3–23
Matron's correspondence with Edith Cavell LH/N/7/7–8
Private papers of Edith Cavell PP/CAV
Memorabilia re Edith Cavell from records of the Cavell Institute (CI)

Imperial War Museum, London (IWM[EC]1–16)
Edith Cavell's diary EC1
Letters by her 1911–15 EC2
Letters to or about her 1914–17 EC4
Official correspondence about her arrest and execution EC5
Miscellaneous documents EC8
Official German documents about her EC10
Photographs EC15

The Swardeston Archive – an informal archive of letters, books, newspapers, memorabilia and photographs. See www.edithcavell.org. uk for first point of access.

Norfolk Record Office, Archive Centre and the Norfolk Regimental Museum

– access http://www.noah.norfolk.gov.uk/

Swardeston parish baptism register (PD 199/4)

Letters re Cavell memorial fund 1915–17 (PD 199/33)

Papers of the Cavell family (MC 304)

'A statement of my escape' by Sgt David Jesse Tunmore of the 1st Bn Norfolk Regiment

National Archives, Kew, London:

Georges Gaston Quien KV2/844

Correspondence concerning Edith Cavell's arrest and execution FO 372/675 and FO383/15

Cavell family census documents for 1861, 1871, 1881, 1891, 1901, 1911

Funeral arrangements and statues H045/10794/302577

In addition I have used material from the British Library, Colindale Newspaper Library, the Wellcome Library, the London Library, London Metropolitan Archives and Hackney Archives.

Picture Acknowledgements

The Art Archive: 47, 90. Corbis: 212, 215, 231. Getty Images: 175, 181. Heritage Library/Picture Norfolk: 240. Collection Peter Higginbotham: 50. Imperial War Museum: 127 (Q 32930), 159 (Q 53271), 162 (Q 88431), 288 (Q 15064A), 314 (Q 15064). Mary Evans Picture Library: 46, 52, 316. National Portrait Gallery, London: 67. Norfolk Record Office: 9. © The Royal London Hospital Archives: frontispiece, 11, 14, 15, 35, 37, 38, 39, 48, 56, 58, 59, 63, 68, 70, 77, 81, 88, 94, 108, 110, 115, 129, 136, 141, 200, 208, 250, 279, 368. Courtesy Miriam Taylor: 171. Topfoto: 395, 413 (Roger-Viollet), 415. Wellcome Library, London: 427.

ACKNOWLEDGEMENTS

My thanks and indebtedness to: Jon Riley, the best of editors. Georgina Capel, my agent for fifteen years. The Reverend Paul Burr of Swardeston, for so much help. Nick Miller and Ian Francis, archivists at Swardeston. Anny Brackx and Morwenna Jones – who read an early draft of the manuscript and made useful comments. (Anny's Belgian parents and grandparents endured German occupation during two world wars. Morwenna for years lived in Brussels in the street where Edith Cavell set up her nursing school.) Jonathan Evans, archivist at the London Hospital. The late Cecelia Doidge-Ripper who guided me to censuses, directories, county archives and parish records. Josine Meijer who did the picture research. Bill Donohoe who drew the maps. Douglas Matthews who compiled the index. Josh Ireland who steered the book through production. Terri Arthur, an American nurse, who for years has gathered information on Edith Cavell. Richard Hillier, Local Studies Librarian at Peterborough Central Library. Esther Bellamy, the Archives Assistant there. Chris Basey in Norwich. Jenny Bowman and Peter Woodward. Dr Andrew Bamji, curator of the Gillies Archives. Frédérique Hakim for her hospitality in Brussels. Patrick Pollak of patrick@rarevols.co.uk who tracked down hard-to-find books. Miriam Taylor, Ruth Moore's granddaughter, for archival material and hospitality. Naomi Narod, for more kindnesses than I can enumerate.

INDEX

267, 281; in EC's deposition 284;
arrested 297–8, 316; trial 324,
325, 330–2, 333, 334, 339, 343–4;
on ill-usage of EC in court 341;
sentenced to hard labour 348, 382;
release from Siegburg prison and
return to Brussels 413–14; testifies
against Quien 424; in resistance in
Second World War 428

Daly, Nora 84, 85
Damme, Madame van 258
Dannecker, Johann, *Ariadne on the
Panther* (sculpture) 30
Darwin, Charles, *On the Origin of
Species* 10–12
Davie, Emma 63
Davies, Emily 7, 21, 49
Dawn (film) 418
Deighton, Gertrude 63
Delaunoy, Noemie 112
Delhey, Mme Leon 168
Demonstier, Adolphe 327
Depache, Louise 408
Depage, Dr Antoine: invites EC to be
matron of Belgian Nurse Training
School 100; administration of
School 106–11, 116; conducts
operations 114; appoints EC to
St Gilles hospital 122; addresses
International Congress of Nurses,
Cologne 136; advises on design of
hospital 137; wartime duties 155,
172, 217–18, 252; plans to move
EC out of Brussels 176; identifies
wife's body 252; post-war career

and honours 425
Depage, Marie: aids husband
Antoine 111; advises on design of
hospital 137; as Sister-in-charge
of Royal Palace hospital 155, 172;
at Océan Hospital, La Panne 172;
Capiau asks to help fugitives 183;
visits USA 249–51; drowned on
Lusitania 251; monument unveiled
418
Derveau, Georges 242; forges identity
cards 191, 230; named in EC's
depositions 286, 302; trial 327,
328, 333, 338–9, 347; sentenced
348, 382
Desmet, René 299
Détry, Dr Marcel 241–2
Dewin, M. (architect) 137
Dickens, Charles: *Martin Chuzzlewit*
45; in Shoreditch 93
Dickenson, Miss (Fountains Hospital
matron) 53, 57
Dickinson, Eveline *see* McDonnell,
Eveline
Dissel, Annette van 22–3
Doman, Lance-Corporal 182, 242–3
Doren, Eugene van 199
Dorff, A. (lawyer) 326, 340–1
'Dr Finsen's Light Treatment for
Lupus' 77
Dupré, General 231
Duthilleul, Mlle 268

Earle, Sir Lionel 419
Eastern Daily Press 143, 144, 147,
149, 167

GWENDOLEN
A novel

A feminist retelling of George Eliot's *Daniel Deronda* from the point of view of its mercurial, magnetic heroine.

'Intriguing and moving'

REBECCA MEAD

Quercus

www.quercusbooks.co.uk

ALSO BY DIANA SOUHAMI

MRS KEPPEL AND HER DAUGHTER

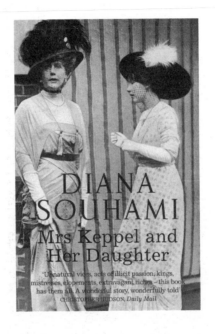

Sexual scandal, decadent royalty and heartless hypocrisy
in Edwardian England.

'Fascinating and richly textured, Souhami's style is vital,
brave and full of flair'
NEW YORK TIMES

Quercus
www.quercusbooks.co.uk

ALSO BY DIANA SOUHAMI

GRETA AND CECIL

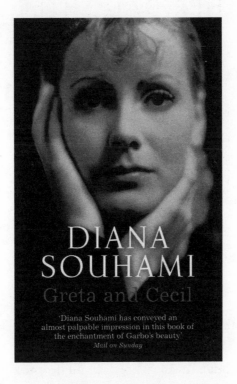

The story of the strange romance between
Greta Garbo and Cecil Beaton.

'Compelling reading'
LITERARY REVIEW

Quercus
www.quercusbooks.co.uk

ALSO BY DIANA SOUHAMI

SELKIRK'S ISLAND

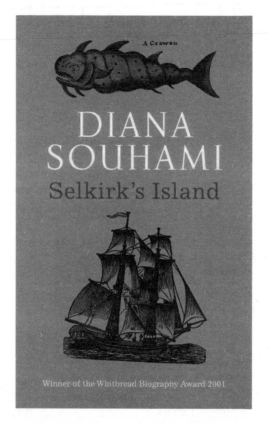

The extraordinary story of the real Robinson Crusoe.

Winner of the Whitbread Biography Award.

Quercus
www.quercusbooks.co.uk

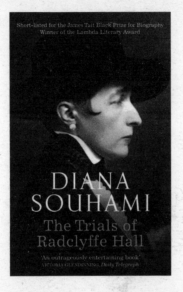

ALSO BY DIANA SOUHAMI

NATALIE AND ROMAINE

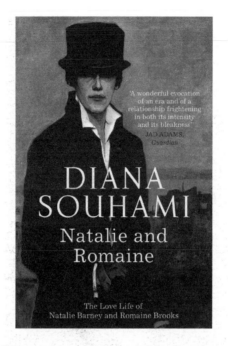

The lives and loves of two of the last century's
most dazzling wild girls.

*'Crammed with descriptions of exotic characters,
their extravagances and eccentricities, the lilies, the pearls,
the velvet-lined rooms . . .'*
SUNDAY TELEGRAPH

Quercus
www.quercusbooks.co.uk

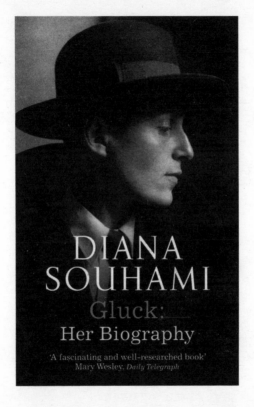

ALSO BY DIANA SOUHAMI

COCONUT CHAOS

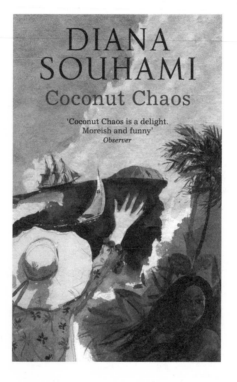

A story of mutiny on the HMS Bounty.

*'Subversive, philosophical, deliberately chaotic
and a rattling good yarn'*
INDEPENDENT

Quercus
www.quercusbooks.co.uk